Lecture Notes in Artificial Intelligence   2389

Subseries of Lecture Notes in Computer Science
Edited by J. G. Carbonell and J. Siekmann

Lecture Notes in Computer Science

Edited by G. Goos, J. Hartmanis, and J. van Leeuwen

T0223885

Springer
Berlin
Heidelberg
New York
Barcelona
Hong Kong
London
Milan
Paris
Tokyo

Elisabete Ranchhod   Nuno J. Mamede (Eds.)

Advances in Natural Language Processing

Third International Conference, PorTAL 2002
Faro, Portugal, June 23-26, 2002
Proceedings

 Springer

Series Editors

Jaime G. Carbonell,Carnegie Mellon University, Pittsburgh, PA, USA
Jörg Siekmann, University of Saarland, Saarbrücken, Germany

Volume Editors

Elisabete Ranchhod
Universidade de Lisboa e CAUTL (IST)
Av. Rovisco Pais, 1049-001 Lisboa, Portugal
E-mail:elisabet@label.ist.utl.pt

Nuno J. Mamede
Technical University of Lisbon, L2F/INESC ID Lisboa
Av. Rovisco Pais, 1049-001 Lisboa, Portugal
E-mail: nuno.mamede@acm.org

Cataloging-in-Publication Data applied for

Die Deutsche Bibliothek - CIP-Einheitsaufnahme

Advances in natural language processing : third international conference ;
proceedings / PorTAL 2002, Faro, Portugal, June 23 - 26, 2002. Elisabete
Ranchhod ; Nuno J. Mamede (ed.). - Berlin ; Heidelberg ; New York ;
Barcelona ; Hong Kong ; London ; Milan ; Paris ; Tokyo : Springer, 2002
  (Lecture notes in computer science ; Vol. 2389 : Lecture notes in
artificial intelligence)
  ISBN 3-540-43829-7

CR Subject Classification (1998): I.2.7, F.4.2-3, I.2, H.3, I.7

ISSN 0302-9743
ISBN 3-540-43829-7 Springer-Verlag Berlin Heidelberg New York

Springer-Verlag Berlin Heidelberg New York
a member of BertelsmannSpringer Science+Business Media GmbH

http://www.springer.de

© Springer-Verlag Berlin Heidelberg 2002
Printed in Germany

Typesetting: Camera-ready by author, data conversion by Boller Mediendesign
Printed on acid-free paper   SPIN 10870554   06/3142   5 4 3 2 1 0

Preface

PorTAL – Portugal for Natural Language Processing – follows two previous conferences: FracTAL, held at the Université de Franche-Comté, Besançon (France), in December 1997, and VexTAL, held at Venice International University, Cá Foscari (Italy), in November 1999. The main goals of theses conferences have been: (i) to bring together the NLP community in Europe; (ii) to strengthen the position of local NLP research in the international NLP community; (iii) to provide a friendly forum for discussion of new research and applications.

PorTAL has reconfirmed this year the goals and the high international standing of those conferences, largely due to its Program Committee, composed of renowned researchers in the field of Natural Language Processing, a third of them from Portuguese universities. This clearly contributed to the significant number of papers submitted (48) by researchers from 12 different countries.

Each paper submitted was reviewed by three reviewers, either from the Program Committee or by their commitment. All those who contributed are mentioned on the following pages. The review process led to the selection of 35 papers for oral presentation: 23 regular papers and 11 short papers. They have been published in this volume.

The conference, and this book, were structured around the eight following main topics: (i) *Pragmatics, discourse, semantics, syntax, and the lexicon*; (ii) *Interpreting and generating spoken and written language*; (iii) *Language-oriented information retrieval, question answering, summarization, and information extraction*; (iv) *Language-oriented machine learning*; (v) *Multi-lingual processing, machine translation, and translation aids*; (vi) *Natural language interfaces and dialogue systems*; (vii) *Tools and resources*; (viii) *Evaluation of systems*.

We would like to express here our thanks to all the reviewers for their quick and excellent work. We extend a special thanks to our invited speakers, Richard Sproat and Ruslan Mitkov, for their valuable contribution, which has undoubtedly increased the interest in the conference. The abstracts of their invited talks are presented at the beginning of this volume. We are indebted to a number of individuals for taking care of specific parts of the conference program: on the ground at the University of Algarve, Jorge Baptista managed the local arrangements; Cristina Mota built and maintained the PorTAL web site, which served as our principal information channel; Luísa Coheur, at L2F (INESC-ID), Paula Carvalho, and Cristina Mota, at LabEL (CAUTL), provided the indispensable administrative support.

We would like to publicly acknowledge the institutions, without whom this event would not have been possible: Centre de Recherches Lucien Tesnière, Departamento de Linguística Geral e Românica, Fundação para a Ciência e a Tecnologia, Câmara Municipal de Faro, Laboratório de Sistemas de Língua Falada, Laboratório de Engenharia da Linguagem. A special mention has to be made of the Universidade do Algarve, who generously hosted the conference.

April 2002   Elisabete Marques Ranchhod and Nuno J. Mamede

Program and Conference Co-chair

Elisabete Ranchhod Universidade de Lisboa and LabEL (CAUTL-IST)
Nuno J. Mamede, Technical University of Lisbon and L2F (INESC-ID Lisboa)

Local Chair

Jorge Baptista, Universidade do Algarve and LabEL (CAUTL-IST)

Program Committee

Alex Monaghan (Aculab plc, Ireland)
Caroline Hagège (Xerox Research Centre Europe, France)
Claire Gardent (CNRS, France)
Diamantino Freitas (University of Porto, Portugal)
Elisabete Ranchhod (University of Lisbon and LabEL, Portugal)
Éric Laporte (Université de Marne-la-Vallée, France)
Franz Gunthner (University of Munich, Germany)
Gabriel Bès (Université Blaise-Pascal, France)
Graça Nunes (Universidade de São Paulo, Brazil)
Hans Uszkoreit (Saarland University at Saarbrücken, Germany)
Inês Duarte (University of Lisbon, Portugal)
Irene Rodrigues (University of Évora, Portugal)
Isabel Trancoso (Technical University of Lisbon / L2F, Portugal)
Jacqueline Léon (CNRS et Université Paris 7, France)
João P. Neto (Technical University of Lisbon / L2F, Portugal)
Jorge Baptista (Universidade do Algarve - FCHS, Portugal)
Julia Pazj (Hungarian Academy of Sciences, Hungary)
Krzysztof Bogacki (Warsaw University, Poland)
Lauri Karttunen (Palo Alto Research Center Inc., USA)
Luís Caldas Oliveira (Technical University of Lisbon / L2F, Portugal)
M. Céu Viana (University of Lisbon / CLUL / L2F, Portugal)
Max Silberztein (IBM Watson Research Center, USA)
Nuno Mamede (Technical University of Lisbon / L2F, Portugal)
Peter Greenfield (Université de Franche-Comté, France)
Pierre-André Buvet (Université de Franche-Comté, France)
Richard Sproat (AT&T Labs Research, USA)
Rodolfo Delmonte (Universitá Cá Foscari, Italy)
Ruslan Mitkov (University of Wolverhampton, UK)
Stéphane Chaudiron (Université de Paris X, France)
Steve Abney (AT&T Labs Research, USA)
Sylviane Cardey (Université de Franche-Comté, France)
Tony B. Sardinha (Catholic University of São Paulo, Brazil)
Xavier Blanco (Univ. Autónoma de Barcelona, Spain)
Yorick Wilks (University of Sheffield, UK)

Table of Contents

Interpreting and Generating Spoken and Written Language

Language-Oriented Information Retrieval, Question Answering, Summarization, and Information Extraction

Language-Oriented Machine Learning

Multi-lingual Processing, Machine Translation, and Translation Aids

Natural Language Interfaces and Dialogue Systems

Tools and Resources

Evaluation of Systems

WordsEye: A Text-to-Scene Conversion System

Richard Sproat

AT&T Labs -- Research, Shannon Laboratory
180 Park Avenue, Room B207, P.O.Box 971
Florham Park
NJ 07932-0000
USA
rws@research.att.com
http://www.research.att.com/~rws/

Abstract. I will present WordsEye, a natural language understanding system that generates three-dimensional scenes from English descriptions of those scenes (joint work with Bob Coyne, Chris Johnson, Owen Rambow, Srinivas Bangalore).

WordsEye works by first parsing the input, using Church's (1988) part of speech tagger and a version of Michael Collins' (1999) parser. The parser output is converted into a dependency structure, and semantic rules are then applied to produce a high-level scene description. This scene description is then fed into a set of depiction rules that decide what objects to use, how to arrange them, and in the case of human figures, how to pose them depending upon the action being depicted. WordsEye also does reference resolution, which is obviously crucial for deciding whether a just-named object is in fact the same as an object previously named in the discourse.

The talk will give an overview of the current state of WordsEye, detailing the natural language processing component and the depiction component. I will show how WordsEye depicts spatial relations, actions, attributes, properties of the environment and how it does rudimentary common-sense reasoning to resolve potential conflicts in depiction. The talk will also discuss possible applications of this technology, as well as future directions for research in this area.

E.M. Ranchhod and N.J. Mamede (Eds.): PorTAL 2002, LNAI 2389, pp. 1-1, 2002.
© Springer-Verlag Berlin Heidelberg 2002

Automatic Anaphora Resolution: Limits, Impediments, and Ways Forward

Ruslan Mitkov

School of Humanities, Languages and Social Sciences,
University of Wolverhampton,
Stafford Street,
Wolverhampton,
WV1 1SB.
UK.
r.mitkov@wlv.ac.uk
http://clg.wlv.ac.uk/

Abstract. The talk will discuss both the limits of and impediments to automatic anaphora resolution and will provide suggestions as to how to overcome some of these hurdles. To start with, anaphora resolution will be introduced as a daunting NLP task requiring the employment of different sources of knowledge. As recent research focusing on robust and knowledge-poor solutions will be summarised, as well as the latest trends, it will be argued that it is the absence of sophisticated semantic and real-world knowledge that imposes limits on all current algorithms. Next, the talk will explain that the lack of reliable pre-processing tools to feed correct inputs into resolution algorithms is another impediment which imposes a limit on the success rate of automatic anaphora resolution systems. It is argued that the performance of the best anaphora resolution algorithms can drop by over 20% if fully automatic pre-processing is undertaken. Comparative results and conclusions will be presented from the evaluation of the different versions of MARS, a fully automatic anaphora resolution system based on Mitkov's knowledge-poor approach to pronoun resolution, as well as from the evaluation of other (well-known) systems developed or re-implemented by members of the Research Group in Computational Linguistics at the University of Wolverhampton. Outstanding evaluation issues will also be highlighted as a further impediment to measuring progress in anaphora resolution and a new 'evaluation workbench' will be proposed as a suitable environment for comprehensive evaluation of anaphora resolution algorithms. In addition, the issue of annotated corpora and how it is addressed at Wolverhampton will be discussed. Finally, ways forward in enhancing the performance of current algorithms will be suggested.

E.M. Ranchhod and N.J. Mamede (Eds.): PorTAL 2002, LNAI 2389, pp. 3, 2002.
© Springer-Verlag Berlin Heidelberg 2002

Feature-Based WSD: Why We Are at a Dead-End

Alessandro Cucchiarelli[1] and Paola Velardi[2]

[1] Università di Ancona, Istituto di Informatica,
Via Brecce Bianche, I-60131 Ancona, Italy
`alex@inform.unian.it`
[2] Università di Roma "La Sapienza", Dipartimento di Scienze dell'Informazione,
Via Salaria 113 I-00198 Roma, Italy
`velardi@dsi.uniroma1.it`

Abstract. The objective of this study is to shed more light on the dependence between the performance of WSD feature-based classifiers and the specific features that may be chosen to represent a word context. In this paper we show that the features commonly used to discriminate among different senses of a word (words, keywords, POS tags) are overly sparse to enable the acquisition of truly predictive rules or probabilistic models. Experimental analysis demonstrates (with some surprising result) that the acquired rules are mostly tied to surface phenomena occurring in the learning set data, and do not generalize across hyponimys of a word nor across language domains. This experiment, as conceived, has no practical application in WSD, but clearly shows the positive influence of a more semantically oriented approach to WSD. Our conclusion is that feature-based WSD is at a dead-end, as also confirmed by the recent results of Senseval 2001.

1 Introduction

The latest results of Senseval 2[1] showed little or no progress in comparison with the first Senseval contest. The best systems seem to be stack at a 70% precision and recall, at most. Though a more detailed analysis of the various systems is one of the purposes of this special issue, we believe that it is indeed necessary to investigate some of the inherent limitations of the most common approach to WSD, that is feature-based learning.

A variety of statistically based and machine learning methods have been used to learn a predictive model of word senses, using as input a feature-based representation of the context in which the word occurs. Though it begins to be acknowledged that the performance of these methods is more sensible to an appropriate selection of the features than to the adopted learning method, there are no available studies analyzing more precisely the nature of this dependence[2]. In statistical Pattern Recognition this problem is known as Feature Set

---

[1] Accessible on http://www.sle.sharp.co.uk/senseval2/
[2] A preliminary study is in Velardi and Cucchiarelli (2000)

E.M. Ranchhod and N.J. Mamede (Eds.): PorTAL 2002, LNAI 2389, pp. 5–14, 2002.

Discrimination, and several methods have been devised for appropriate feature analysis, like for example the Fisher Discriminant analysis (Fukunaga, 1990) and Boundary methods, as in Lee and Landgrebe (1993). However, these methods are applicable only to numerical features. In WSD, features are mostly symbolic, and, as shown throughout this paper, they are overly sparse. In this paper we argue that sparsity of features is the main cause of poor learning performance and eventually, this may result in a dead-end for feature based methods. In order to provide evidence to our claim, we carried out two sets of experiments, in which we study the effect of various feature combinations on performance. The first set analyzes the effect of different feature choices in a "classic" word sense disambiguation task, while the second considers the case of semantic disambiguation. The motivation of conducting these two experiments is the following:

1. The requirement of training (or even only setting ad-hoc learning parameters) for each individual ambiguous word is highly demanding for practical applications[3]. The WSD experiment has the objective to evaluate the "quality" of learning, in order to verify the possibility of generalizing - in some way - the learned sense disambiguation models. Unfortunately, this experiment shows that, for any choice of features, the learned information for a word is clearly unusable for different words, and even for the same word in a different domain.

2. It has often been observed that semantic disambiguation at a coarser level (e.g. the *location* vs. *artifact* vs. *organization* senses of *bank*) is sufficient in many applications, like Information Retrieval, Text Classification, Information Extraction. The semantic disambiguation experiment aims at verifying whether feature-based methods can be applied to the task of learning the contextual model of a semantic category, rather than that of a single word. This would reduce the training effort to a more limited amount of manual tagging. Unfortunately, even this second experiment produced a negative result, though not entirely negative. Reasonable (and useful, under the perspective of learning quality) performances have been obtained only in the case of a "canned", hardly replicable, experiment, in which we measure the effect of using increasingly coarse semantic features on performance, extracted from the SemCor semantically tagged corpus. Clearly, this result has no practical value, since it allows the disambiguation of a word given the semantic category of the surrounding words, which is unrealistic. However, the experiment demonstrates the relation between performance and feature compression, and suggests that more semantically oriented methods - i.e. methods that use some kind of coarse-grained semantic information - have a better hope of success with respect to those using syntactic and lexical features. This is also confirmed by the Senseval 2 evaluation experiment, where the best precision has been obtained by Magnini et al. (2001) with a method

---

[3] In Michalchea and Moldovan (1999), a method is presented to semi-automatically acquire training sets from the Web. Still, the amount of manual re-checking of the acquired data is far excessive if systematic WSD is to be performed on all ambiguous words of a real-world domain.

that uses WordNet domain labels as features (e.g. MEDICINE or SPORT). The recall of this method is however rather low, since domain information is available only for few words in a context.

2   Word Sense Disambiguation Experiments

2.1   Experimental Set Up

In the word sense disambiguation experiment, we used the Senseval 1 Learning and Test sets for the following words: *accident, excess, onion, shake* and *promise*. The following features have been used: P=part of speech tag, L=lemma, NE=named entity and terminological compounds (e.g. *Stratford road, world wide web*), NE_sem (e.g. NE are replaced by their semantic category, like *organization, location, street* ...). These features are extracted using the ARIOSTO linguistic processor (Basili et al. 1996). We used two windows for the context length: W= ±4 and W= ±2. Finally, we selected C4.5 and Naive Bayes as examples of inductive and probabilistic learning methods, respectively. The software packages are extracted from the *weka-3*[4] machine learning software collection.

One of the objectives of this paper is to show that the commonly used feature sets are overly sparse to allow a reliable probabilistic or rule learning. To measure feature sparseness we adopted two parameters:

1. *Feature Compression* (FC). This is defined as:

$$FC = 1 - \frac{\sum_i DVF(i)}{TVF} \ . \tag{1}$$

   where $DVF(i)$ = number of different values of feature(i) and TVF = number of values of all features in the corpus.

2. *Probability of Frequency Distribution* (PFD) of feature values. This is defined as:

$$Pr(i) = \frac{Fr(i)}{\sum_i different\ values\ of\ f^i} \ . \tag{2}$$

   where $Fr(i) = \sum_j \sum_i Fr_i(f^i = v_i)$, $Fr_i(f^i = v_i) = 1$ if $f^i = v_i$ is seen i times, otherwise $Fr_i(f^i = v_i) = 0$.

The following experiments have been performed:

Experiment 1: W=±4, features={L}
   Example:
   Sentence 1: Eighteen years ago she lost one of her six children in an <tag "532675">accident</>on Stratford Road, a tragedy which has become a pawn in the pitiless point-scoring of small-town vindictiveness.
   Extracted f-vector: <six, child, in, an, on, Stratford, Road, a, 532675>.

---

[4] http://www.cs.waikato.ac.nz/ml/weka/

Experiment 2: W=±4, features={L, P, NE}

Experiment 3: W=±2, features={L}

Experiment 4: W=±2, features={L, P, NE}
   Example of extracted f-vector from sentence 1:
   <in£preposition, an£article, on£preposition, Stratford_Road£proper_noun_ street, 532675>.

Experiment 5: W=±4, features={L, P, NE_sem}

For each experiment, we computed the error rate for the C4.5 and Naive Bayes classifier, and the baseline error as the probability of occurrence, in the Test set, of the most frequent sense in the Learning set. Finally, we used two test sets: TS1 is exactly the same used in Senseval 1, while in TS2 some sentence is removed to make the probability distribution of senses the same as in the Learning Set.

2.2   Results and Comments

Tables 1 and 2 and Fig. 1 summarize some of the outcomes. For the sake of space we report here only the data for *excess*, since the results show *invariably the same behavior* for the other words, though the absolute values of performance may vary. We observe that, for all experiments, only few feature values, for almost any choice of features, are seen more than 2-3 times in the Learning Set, and the average compression rate does not vary significantly. It is very difficult to learn anything interesting under these circumstances: it is not a matter of "not forgetting exceptions", as suggested in Daelemans et al. (1999), since almost everything is an exception, e.g. a single occurrence phenomenon! The results of TS2 demonstrate our claim of poor learning, since in TS2 the performance is very close *(excess)*, or exactly the same *(accident, promise, onion)* as that of the baseline.

Table 1. Excess, TS1

Experiment	Compr	Baseline	C4.5 Tree	Naive Bayes
1	46.7%	99.4%	70.4%	62.7%
2	46.0%	99.4%	70.4%	62.7%
3	53.8%	99.4%	70.4%	64.5%
4	53.4%	99.4%	70.4%	64.5%
5	47.5%	99.4%	70.4%	62.7%

Table 2. Excess, TS2

Experiment	Compr	Baseline	C4.5 Tree	Naive Bayes
1	44.5%	65.5%	60.0%	56.6%
2	43.9%	65.5%	60.0%	56.6%
3	54.2%	65.5%	60.0%	56.6%
4	53.6%	65.5%	60.0%	56.6%
5	45.6%	65.5%	60.0%	56.6%

Notice that similar information can be extracted - though not explicitly discussed - also from other WSD experiments in literature. For example, in Pederson (2001), Table 1 summarizes the experimental results obtained using bigram as features, on 36 Senseval 1 words, using the same *weka-3* package. In this table, among the others, the performance of a majority classifier that is the same as our baseline is computed. Only rarely the performances of the various classifiers are close to, and in some cases worst than, the majority classifier. Things get better in few specific cases, for example when the word participates in fixed expressions or "idioms", e.g. *"shake his head"*. As a matter of fact, *shake* is the only case in which there is a strong difference (100% improvement in Pedersons paper, 20% in our case, since we do not use bigrams) between the majority classifier and the "true learners" C4.5 and Bayes.

Highly repetitive patterns have a very low probability, as shown in Fig. 1, and in addition they are often uninteresting. For example, *shake* co-occurs with *"his head"* 125 times in 915 sentences. But also *"of"* co-occurs with *excess* 112 times. However, while *"head"* co-occurs only with the sense 504336 of *shake*, *"of"* co-occurs with many senses of *excess*, as shown in Tab. 3.

Table 3. Senses vs. Occurences

Sense of *excess*	Occurrences of *"excess of"*
512402	60
512403	24
512404	23
512407	4
512472	1

In a majority of cases, repetitive features are stop words, and the derived rules have poor or no power of generalization. One could assign a higher weight to "content" features (e.g. *head)*, with respect to stop words (e.g. *of)*, but as we have remarked, such content features are too rare to make any real difference.

The goal of experiment 5 was to verify whether the use of "semantic" features (e.g. replacing NEs by their semantic category NE_sem) favor the acquisition

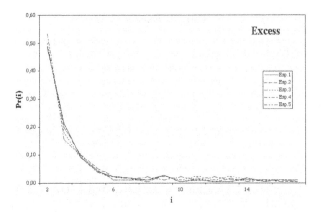

Fig. 1. Probability of Frequency Distribution for Excess.

of more interesting rules. However, NEs are too rare in the learning and test sentences to produce any significant result, as seen in Tab. 1. NE_sem produce only a 1.5 more compression, and no changes in performances (in fact, no new rules are generated).

3   Semantic Disambiguation Experiments

3.1   Experimental Set Up

The aim of this experiment is to perform semantic disambiguation, rather than word sense disambiguation. The objective is to verify the possibility to learn more general rules and/or patterns, i.e. rules that can be applied to a semantic *category*. This would significantly reduce the tagging effort, since we need a learning corpus for each category, rather than for each individual ambiguous word. A second objective is to see whether, at least in principle, more semantically oriented features reduce the sparsity of feature values.

In order to do so, we used the *SemCor* semantically tagged corpus, and we selected the following WordNet coarse grained categories: *person, location, artifact, psychological_feature*. The Learning set includes 2000 SemCor sentences for each category, plus 2000 sentences for the category *other*. The Test Set is built extracting 200 sentences for each of the five categories, not included in the Learning set.

Besides the features used in the previous experiment, we also used: CW=central word, S_0=WordNet synset, S_i=WordNet hyperonym of level i (i=1, 2, 3, 4). This means that we use the WordNet synset of a word as features, or its hyperonyms 1, 2 3 or 4 levels up in the taxonomy, as long as the word is a verb or noun. We used three windows for the context length: W=±4 W=±2 and W=0 (no context, only the central word). Finally, we selected C4.5 and Naive Bayes as examples of inductive and probabilistic learning methods, but we used also their ten-fold version (10F), available in the weka-3 packages. Table 4 summarizes 14 of over 100 experiments we performed, using almost any combination of features and window size. P now includes also NEs, since when we morphologically parse the sentences, we also extract named entities (though as shown in Sec. 2 this produces almost no advantage).

Table 4. Description of the Experiments

Experiment	Window	Features
1	± 4	L, P, CW
2	± 4	L, P
3	± 4	CW, S^0
4	± 4	S^0
5	± 2	S^0
6	± 4	CW, S^1
7	± 0	CW, S^1
8	± 4	S^1
9	± 4	S^2
10	± 4	S^3
11	± 4	S^4
12	± 2	S^3
13	± 0	CW, L
14	± 0	CW, S^0

3.2   Results and Comment

Some very interesting - and somehow odd - results emerge from Tab. 5. To summarize, experiments 1, 3 and 6 use a ± 4 window, the CW and, respectively, L, S^0 and S^1. Experiments 13, 14 and 7 use the same features as 1, 3 and 6, but no context $(W = 0)$[5]. Experiments 2, 4, and 8 are again the same as 1, 3 and 6 but use no central word CW, experiments 9, 10 and 11 use no CW and, respectively, S^2, S^3 and S^4, and finally experiments 5 and 12 are the same as 4 and 10, but use a ± 2 window.

We can observe the following:

1. When the central feature is used, the performance is considerably better than without (compare 1, 3 and 6 with 2, 4 and 8). Unfortunately, it is clear that the system classifies only on the basis of the a-priori probability of the central word (or its synset) in a given category: in fact, the performance of 1, 3 and 6 are identical to those in 13, 14 and 7, respectively! The very good performance of experiment 6 is hence completely.

---

[5] It is important to notice that, in the experiments that use synsets S^i as features, also the central word CW, when present, is replaced by its synset at the selected level.

Table 5. Summary of Experimental Results

Exp.	Compr.	Err. Base	Err. C4.5	Err. C4.5 10F	Err. Bayes	Err. Bayes 10F
1	87.28 %	80.00 %	19.70 %	19.60 %	34.60 %	32.77 %
2	87.28 %	80.00 %	59.00 %	62.90 %	59.90 %	59.43 %
3	74.00 %	80.00 %	9.70 %	10.80 %	19.50 %	19.63 %
4	74.00 %	80.00 %	80.00 %	76.30 %	66.10 %	66.10 %
5	76.89 %	80.00 %	73.80 %	75.70 %	66.70 %	67.49 %
6	82.41 %	80.00 %	4.30 %	4.20 %	13.60 %	10.83 %
7	–	80.00 %	4.30 %	4.20 %	4.30 %	4.61 %
8	82.41 %	80.00 %	71.10 %	66.50 %	52.10 %	52.08 %
9	86.57 %	80.00 %	69.80 %	53.60 %	53.40 %	34.88 %
10	91.40 %	80.00 %	58.00 %	30.80 %	48.60 %	19.15 %
11	91.42 %	80.00 %	58.30 %	28.20 %	48.00 %	19.31 %
12	92.13 %	80.00 %	72.30 %	43.70 %	54.10 %	33.74 %
13	–	80.00 %	19.90 %	19.80 %	19.90 %	20.47 %
14	–	80.00 %	9.70 %	10.80 %	9.70 %	11.59 %

2. Given the above, the only interesting experiments are 2, 4 , 5, 8, 9, 10, 11 and 12. Initially, the generalization of contexts does not produce improvements, as confirmed by the lowest values of the compression. The performance improves by gradually generalizing contexts. An intermediate grain of synsets seems to favor a better compression of the data and a better performance, as shown in Fig. 2. Here, (compare 10 and 12) a wider context does improve performance.

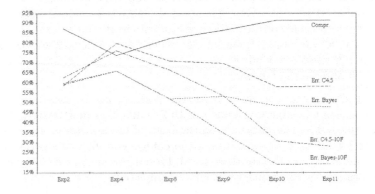

Fig. 2. Compression vs. Error.

If we now observe the rules acquired by the inductive classifier C4.5 we see that now we find rules with some generalization power.

Let us observe first "lexical" rules, i.e. those extracted in Experiment 2. In Fig.3 we find few rules with a higher predictive power.

```
Rule 587:
    fdx2 = WP
    -> class person [76.1%]

WP=Wh-pronoun

ranged/VB against/IN them/PRP the/DT Southerners/NN<PERSON> who/WP are/VB
called/JJ Bourbons/NN
```

```
Rule 191:
    fsx1 = 2%00496801
    -> class psy_feature [92.3%]

2%00496801(verb):observe, keep, maintain -- observe correctly; "keep time, keep
count, keep track of"

we/? manage/2%01721088 to/? keep/2%00496801   track/1%04485976<PSY_FEATURE> of/?
a/? Bombus/1%01282138 queen/1%01667395
```

Fig. 3. Example of extracted rules.

Rule 587 reads: "a word followed by a '*Wh-Pronoun*' (*who* in the example phrase) belongs to the class person".

When gradually generalizing the features, C4.5 generates more interesting rules, that have a very good generalization power. For example. Rule 191 reads: "if a word is preceded by a verb belonging to the synset "observe, keep, maintain" then it belongs to the class *psychological feature*". Clearly, these rules are useful only if we need to disambiguate a word with respect to another already disambiguated word, which is rarely the case. However, given two words and all their possible sense combinations, such rules could be used to express a preference.

4   What Is the Moral?

The purpose of this paper was *not* to propose a new WSD or semantic disambiguation algorithm, but rather to show the inherent limitations of feature-based approaches. Lexical features, used in the majority of cases, are overly sparse to allow any reliable form of inductive or statistical learning. In word sense disambiguation experiments, we have showed that in the overwhelming majority of cases, the learned patterns include stop words, which do not represent reliable, and general, contextual cues (as shown in the example of *"eccess of"*). Assigning a weight to "content" features (as for the *"head"* contextual cue of *shake*) would probably increase precision, but also lower the recall, since content words are found repetitively only in idiomatic or semi-idiomatic expressions, like *shake one's head*.

Semantic features, especially at an intermediate level of generality, allow for a better compression of the data, and in fact we are able to observe better performance **and** better rules, i.e. rules that generalize across words and domains. However, unambiguous semantic features are usually not available, or are too rare in context (e.g. named entity categories, unambiguous words, domain categories) in order to obtain a good recall. In summary, we believe that the feature-based WSD is at a dead-end.

Better WSD methods seems those which use semantic information extracted from other external sources, as in(Michalcea and Moldovan (2001), where the decision of a word sense is made, when possible[6], on the basis of patterns learned from WordNet glosses, SemCor and Gencor, or in Magnini et al (2001), where WordNet domain categories are used.

References

[1996] Basili, R., Pazienza M.T., Velardi P.: An Empyrical Symbolic Approach to Natural Language Processing. Artificial Intelligence (1996)

[1999] Daelemans W., Van Den Bosch A. and Zavrel J.: Forgetting Exceptions is Harmful in Language Learning. Machine Learning **34** (1999) 11–43

[1990] Fukunaga K.: Introduction to Statistical Pattern Recognition. Academic Press, NY (1990)

[1993] Lee C. and Landgrebe D.A.: Feature Extraction Based on Decision Boundaries. IEEE PAMI **15**, 4 (1993)

[2001] Magnini B., Strapparava C., Pezzulo G. and Gliozzo A.: Using Domain Information for Word Sense Disambiguation. Proc. of SenSeval 2, Toulouse, France, (2001)

[1999] R. Mihalcea and D. Moldovan: An Automatic Method for Generating Sense Tagged Corpora. Proc. of AAAI-1999, Orlando, Florida, (1999)

[2001] R. Mihalcea and D. Moldovan: Pattern Learning and Active Feature Selection for Word Sense Disambiguation. Proc. of SenSeval 2, Toulouse, France, (2001)

[2001] Pederson T.: A Decision Tree of Bigrams is an Accurate Predictor of Word Sense. Proc. of NAACL, Pittsburgh (2001)

[2000] Velardi P. and Cucchiarelli A.: Theoretical Analysis of Context-based Learning Algorithms for Word Sense Disambiguation. Proc. of ECAI-2000, Berlin (2000)

---

[6] Unfortunately Michalchea and Moldovan do not specify the contribution of the pattern matching module to performance, as compared with the instance-based learner, which they also use

Improving Feature Selection for Maximum Entropy-Based Word Sense Disambiguation*

Armando Suárez and Manuel Palomar

Departamento de Lenguajes y Sistemas Informáticos
Universidad de Alicante
Alicante, Spain
{armando, mpalomar}@dlsi.ua.es

Abstract. In this paper, an evaluation of several feature selections for word sense disambiguation is presented. The method used to classify linguistic contexts in its correct sense is based on maximum entropy probability models. In order to study their relevance for each word, several types of features have been analyzed for a few words selected from the DSO corpus. An improved definition of features in order to increase efficiency is presented as well.

1 Introduction

This paper presents the experimental results of the evaluation of several types of features in a system that implements a corpus-based method of word sense disambiguation (WSD). The method used to perform the learning over a set of sense-disambiguated examples is that of maximum entropy probability models (ME). Linguistic information is represented in the form of feature vectors, which identify the occurrence of certain attributes in contexts containing linguistic ambiguities. The context is the text surrounding an ambiguity that is relevant to the disambiguation process. The features used may be of a distinct nature: word collocations, part-of-speech labels, keywords, topic and domain information, grammatical relationships, and so on. Instead of training with the same kind of information for all words of the same part of speech, which underestimates what information is more relevant to each word, our research shows that each word is more effectively learned using a different set of features. Another important issue we take up is the size of feature vectors. We propose a new feature definition, and we demonstrate empirically that, using this new definition, results are minimally degraded while efficiency is highly improved.

At SENSEVAL-2, researchers showed the latest contributions to WSD. Some supervised systems competed in the English lexical sample tasks [1]. The John Hopkins University system combines several WSD subsystems based on different methods: decision lists [2]; transformation-based, error-driven learning [3] [4]; cosine-based vector models; decision stumps; and two feature-enhanced naive

---

* This paper has been partially supported by the Spanish Government (CICYT) under project number TIC2000-0664-C02-02.

E.M. Ranchhod and N.J. Mamede (Eds.): PorTAL 2002, LNAI 2389, pp. 15–23, 2002.
© Springer-Verlag Berlin Heidelberg 2002

Bayes systems (one trained on words, one trained on lemmas). Features include syntactic properties and grammatical relationships. The Southern Methodist University system is an instance-based learning method but also uses word-word relation patterns obtained from WordNet1.7 and Semcor, as described in [5]. The Korea University system uses a classification information model based on a discrimination score for features [6]. Those features are near surrounding words, topical contexts, and bigram contexts.

A baseline methodology for WSD is proposed in [7]. It relies on decision tree learning and naive Bayesian classifiers, using simple lexical features. This methodology includes several systems combining different classifiers based on distinct sets of features. These systems competed at SENSEVAL-2, both in the English and Spanish lexical sample tasks.

2   The Maximum Entropy Implementation

ME modeling provides a framework for integrating information for classification from many heterogeneous information sources [8]. ME probability models have been successfully applied to some NLP tasks, such as part-of-speech (POS) tagging or sentence boundary detection [9].

The WSD method used in this paper is based on conditional ME probability models. It has been implemented using a supervised learning method that consists of building word-sense classifiers using a semantically tagged corpus. Some advantages of using the ME framework are that even knowledge-poor features may be applied accurately; the ME framework thus allows a virtually unrestricted ability to represent problem-specific knowledge in the form of features.

The implementation of the ME-based WSD system used in this study was done in C++. One of its modules, the learning module, produces the classifiers for each word using a corpus that is syntactically and semantically annotated (to date, MINIPAR [10] has been used for parsing the corpus). This module has two subsystems. The first subsystem consists of two component actions: in a first step, the module processes the learning corpus in order to define the functions that will apprise the linguistic features of each context; in a second step, the module then fills in the feature vectors. The second subsystem of the learning module performs the estimation of the classification function and stores it. The system uses different parameters to characterize the contexts of particular features, and these can be distinct for each word.

Let us assume a set of contexts X and a set of classes C. The function $cl : X \rightarrow C$ chooses the class c with the highest conditional probability in the context x: $cl(x) = \arg\max_c p(c|x)$. Each feature is calculated by a function that is associated to a specific class c', and it takes the form of equation (1), where $cp(x)$ is some observable characteristic in the context[1]. The conditional probability $p(c|x)$ is defined by equation (2), where α_i is the parameter or weight

---

[1] The ME approach is not limited to binary funtions, but the optimization procedure used for the estimation of the parameters, the *Generalized Iterative Scaling* procedure, uses this feature.

of the feature i, K is the number of features defined, and $Z(x)$ is a constant to ensure that the sum of all conditional probabilities for this context is equal to 1.

$$f(x,c) = \begin{cases} 1 \text{ if } c = c' \text{ and } cp(x) = true \\ 0 \text{ otherwise} \end{cases} \tag{1}$$

$$p(c|x) = \frac{1}{Z(x)} \prod_{i=1}^{K} \alpha_i^{f_i(x,c)} \tag{2}$$

For example, let us assume these three contexts as the learning corpus in which "interest" is the word to be learned, and that all necessary syntactic information is available:

... considering the widespread >> interest 1 << in the election ...
... to the best >> interest 5 << of both governments ...
... anonymous persons expressing >> interest 1 << in the trial ...

Then, six features could be defined with the word previous to the ambiguous word and its POS-tag:

feature1: is "widespread" previous to interest#1?
feature2: is "best" previous to interest#5?
feature3: is "expressing" previous to interest#1?
feature4: is "ADJ" previous to interest#1?
feature5: is "ADJ" previous to interest#5?
feature6: is "VERB" previous to interest#1?

These functions are defined in the training phase (in the first step mentioned earlier) and depend upon the data in the corpus. They are implemented as boolean functions that are evaluated over all examples (in the second step) and fill in a feature vector (six components, for this example). Each context has its own feature vector filled in with the results of all functions. In general, for a concrete type of features (*word at position i, lemma at position i, POS-tag at position i*), a function for each possible value (*sense, value*) at position i is generated. Therefore, In the following, we refer to these kind of functions as "non-relaxed" ones.

Other types of functions can be defined, as in the example above:

feature1: is "widespread" or "expressing" previous to interest#1?
feature2: is "best" previous to interest#5?
feature3: is "ADJ" or "VERB" previous to interest#1?
feature4: is "ADJ" previous to interest#5?

These functions ("relaxed features") are based on sets of values related to concrete attributes (i.e., *words occurring in the corpus at position -1 of interest#1 contexts*). These types of features reduce the number of features to one per each sense at position i.

Section 4 illustrates that accuracy is not penalized when this feature definition is utilized. Due to the nature of the disambiguation task, the number of times that a feature generated by the first type of function is activated is very low, and feature vectors have a large number of values equal to 0. The new function drastically reduces the number of features, with a minimum of degradation in evaluation results. At the same time, new features can be incorporated into the learning process with a minimum impact on efficiency.

3   Description of Features

The set of features defined for the training of the system is described in Figure 3 and is based on the feature selection made in [11] and [12]. Each type comprises a set of "individual" features; i.e. "s features" are, in fact, one feature for each value $(word, sense, i)$ in the learning corpus, where $word$ is any word found at position $i \in \{-3, -2, -1, +1, +2, +3\}$ related to the ambiguous word, and $sense$ any possible sense. In the example of the previous section, s_{-1} (included on s features) defines 3 functions that implement 3 features; the rest of s_i features define their own functions.

- *Non-relaxed functions*
    - *0* **features**: ambiguous-word shape
    - *s* **features**: words at positions ±1, ±2, ±3
    - *p* **features**: POS-tags of words at ±1, ±2, ±3
    - *km* **features**: lemmas of nouns at any position in context, occurring at least $m\%$ times with a sense
    - *r* **features**: grammatical relation of the ambiguous word
    - *d* **features**: the word that the ambiguous word depends on
    - *m* **features**: the ambiguous word belongs to a multi-word
- *Relaxed functions*
    - *L* **features**: lemmas of content-words at ±1, ±2, ±3
    - *W* **features**: content-words at ±1, ±2, ±3
    - *S* **features**: words at ±1, ±2, ±3
    - *B* **features**: lemmas of collocations at $(-2, -1)$, $(-1, +1)$, $(+1, +2)$
    - *C* **features**: collocations at $(-2, -1)$, $(-1, +1)$, $(+1, +2)$
    - *P* **features**: POS-tags of words at ±1, ±2, ±3
    - *D* **features**: the word that the ambiguous word depends on
    - *M* **features**: the ambiguous word belongs to a multi-word

Fig. 1. List of types of features

As explained earlier, features are automatically defined and depend on the data in the training corpus. Most of these features are based on words, collocations, and part-of-speech (POS) tags in the local context. In order to evaluate the impact of relaxed functions, non-relaxed functions are also defined. A complete description of the system and some of these features can be found in [13] (with minor differences in the name of the types of features).

Using the information supplied by MINIPAR, new features were incorporated to the learning: r features refer to the grammatical relationship of the ambiguous word (*subject, object, complement*, etc.); D and d features refer to links in the dependency tree of the parsing; M and m features refer to multi-words identified by the parser ("dark ages", "interest rate", etc.).

4   Experimental Results

In this section we present the results of our evaluation. Some polysemous nouns and verbs have been selected and evaluated using the DSO sense-tagged English corpus [11]. This corpus is structured in files containing tagged examples of several nouns and verbs. Tags correspond to senses in WordNet 1.5 [14]. All examples in each file (both those from the Brown Corpus and those from the Wall Street Journal) have been processed.

Table 1 shows the best results obtained using a 10-fold cross-validation evaluation method. Several feature combinations (around 80) have been tested in order to find the best set for each selected word. The main goal was to achieve the most relevant information from the corpus for each one rather than applying the same combination of features to all words.

Table 1. 10-fold cross-validation best results on DSO files

	Senses	Examples	Features	Functions	Accur	MFS
age.N	3	491	0CsprDMk5	1587	73.8	62.3
art.N	4	393	0sprdm	1594	65.2	48.0
car.N	2	1363	s	3036	97.1	96.3
child.N	2	1057	sp	2731	90.5	81.8
church.N	3	367	0rDMCk3	228	67.9	62.0
cost.N	2	1456	0WrDM	62	90.0	89.6
head.N	7	844	sprdm	2911	80.8	41.6
interest.N	6	1479	0sprDM	4059	70.1	55.6
line.N	22	1320	0LSBCrdm	1542	54.7	22.7
work.N	6	1419	0sprdm	4784	53.2	32.9
fall.V	6	1341	LSBCrdm	503	84.9	70.1
know.V	6	1425	0rDMCk10	230	47.9	34.9
set.V	11	1246	BsprDMk5	4569	57.3	36.9
speak.V	5	510	0sp	1667	74.5	69.1
take.V	19	794	LWBCsrDMk10	3706	43.0	35.6
Averages	**7**	**1034**		**2214**	**70.1**	**56.0**
Nouns	6	1019		2253	74.3	59.3
Verbs	9	1063		2135	61.5	49.3

"Senses" is the number of distinct senses in the corpus, "Features" the feature selection with the best result, "Functions" the number of functions generated from features, and "Accur" (for "accuracy") the number of correctly classified contexts divided by the total number of contexts. Column "MFS" is the accuracy when the most-frequent-sense is selected.

In order to perform the ten tests on each word, some preprocessing of the corpus was done. For each word file in DSO, all senses were uniformly distributed in the ten folds to maintain the same sense distribution as original file in every test (each fold contains one tenth of examples of each sense, except for the tenth fold, which contains the remaining examples). Those senses that had fewer than ten examples in the original corpus file were rejected and not processed; therefore, the "Senses" column shows the number of senses effectively learned.

The data summarized in Table 1 reveal that all types of features, relaxed and non-relaxed ones, are useful. Moreover, each word has its own best-feature-selection. If such strategy of selection is assumed, for this fifteen nouns an average of 70.1% of contexts are correctly classified. This result means a gain in accuracy of 15.7% against the most-frequent-sense classification. Nouns are better classified than verbs.

0 features are very useful, both for nouns and for verbs. Nouns like "art" and "church" benefit from the use of these features because of the strong relationship between their possible shapes and their senses for the use of the plural and for capitalization (e.g. "Arts").

All best-feature-selections combine word features (W, L, s, S, B and C) depending on which is the word to evaluate. Although, s features are the most informative ones, the rest of types are selected very often (even with s features). Moreover, both relaxed and non-relaxed features are used together in almost all selections.

Part-of-speech data, p features, tend to favor more frequent senses and place less frequent senses at a disadvantage. However, in most cases, the improvement on more frequent senses success is reflected in accuracy too. Their relaxed version, P features, is never used in a best selection because the small set of possible POS labels.

D, M, d, m, and specially r features seem very useful, too, if combined with other types of attributes. Moreover, a strong relation with km features stands out.

Table 2 shows the results obtained for several selected combinations of features, in order to establish the gain in accuracy when new features are incorporated in the training. The first row (labelled as "MFS") is the base-value against which the remainder of the feature selections are measured to show the gain or loss in accuracy. The best result is obtained with the "$0sprdm$" one, a 68.8% of accuracy (14.4% more than MFS). Again, nouns obtain better results than verbs. Table 3 shows the evaluation of these last set of features on each word.

ME were also evaluated with the train and test data from SENSEVAL-2 for the Spanish lexical sample task. The results reported in this workshop for thirteen systems range from 71.2% to 51.4% for accuracy. The ME method obtained an accuracy rate of 65.03% (4th place) using $0LWsBCp$ features for all words, and 64.04% (4th place too) using $0LBk5$. In this comparison, we used the Conexor FDG parser [15]. Because this evaluation is incomplete, we intend to next test for the complete set of features in order to improve these results.

Table 2. Feature Selection Comparison of Accuracy

	All	Nouns	Verbs
MFS	**54.36**	56.88	49.32
rDM	**+6.41**	+9.80	-0.39
LB	**+7.47**	+8.25	+5.90
0rDM	**+7.76**	+11.30	+0.68
LWBC	**+7.82**	+8.63	+6.21
LWBCp	**+9.58**	+10.90	+6.92
LWBCP	**+9.71**	+11.12	+6.90
0LB	**+10.17**	+11.59	+7.33
0LWBC	**+10.18**	+11.55	+7.43
0LWBCP	**+10.91**	+12.45	+7.85
SrDM	**+11.00**	+13.13	+6.74
Wrdm	**+11.16**	+13.55	+6.36
0LWBCp	**+11.23**	+12.95	+7.78
Srdm	**+11.70**	+13.90	+7.30
0Wrdm	**+11.93**	+14.36	+7.06
0SrDM	**+11.97**	+14.23	+7.44
0Srdm	**+12.31**	+14.63	+7.66
0CrDMk3	**+12.37**	+14.04	+9.03
WCrDMk3	**+12.76**	+14.35	+9.58
sp	**+12.90**	+14.40	+9.91
LSBCrdm	**+13.14**	+14.78	+9.87
0LWBCPrDMk3	**+13.15**	+15.04	+9.38
0LSBCrdm	**+13.43**	+15.27	+9.76
0WCrDMk3	**+13.45**	+15.16	+10.04
0sp	**+13.85**	+15.66	+10.24
sprdm	**+14.39**	+16.58	+10.02
0sprdm	**+14.44**	+16.60	+10.11

Although the selection of nouns and verbs of Table 1 is the same than [12] there were some difficulties when comparing ME and boosting. The latter method was trained using only seven features because its main goal was to compare several WSD methods, but not to obtain the maximum accuracy.

5 Conclusions

In this paper, an evaluation of several types of features for supervised WSD has been presented. The study were done using an implementation of the maximum entropy probability models. The main contribution of this work is the experimental evidence that not all words are better learned with the same set of features.

For a few words selected from the DSO corpus, several combinations of features were analyzed in order to identify which were the best for each word. In addition, relaxed definitions of the functions that calculate these features were

Table 3. Results with a fixed feature selection

	0sprdm	±MFS	Functions
age.N	72.2	+10.1	1674
art.N	65.2	+18.5	1594
car.N	96.5	+1.4	3489
child.N	89.8	+8.9	3113
church.N	65.7	+4.6	1417
cost.N	89.3	+2.0	3772
head.N	80.7	+43.8	3623
interest.N	69.7	+24.6	2938
line.N	52.7	+30.8	4494
work.N	53.2	+21.5	4018
fall.V	84.3	+14.2	5804
know.V	47.4	+12.5	4711
set.V	56.0	+19.1	1922
speak.V	73.5	+4.4	3818
take.V	35.9	+0.3	4784
Averages	**68.8**	**+14.4**	**3411**
Nouns	73.5	+16.6	3013
Verbs	59.4	+10.1	4208

also presented. This is an important issue since it increases WSD efficiency and allows for the inclusion of more attributes so as to enrich the classifiers.

Future research will incorporate domain information as an additional information source for the system. *WordNet Domains* [16] is an enrichment of WordNet with subject field codes. These attributes will be incorporated into the learning of the system in the the form of features, except that domain disambiguation will be evaluated as well; that is, WordNet senses (*synsets*) will be substituted for domains labels, thereby reducing the number of possible classes into which contexts can be classified.

As we work to improve the ME method, we are also working to develop a cooperative strategy between several other methods as well, both knowledge-based and corpus-based.

References

1. SENSEVAL-2: Second international workshop on evaluating word sense disambiguation systems: system descriptions. http://www.sle.sharp.co.uk/senseval2/ (2001)
2. Yarowsky, D.: Hierarchical decision lists for word sense disambiguation. Computers and the Humanities **34** (2000)
3. Brill, E.: Transformation-based error-driven learning and natural language processing: A case study in part-of-speech tagging. Computational Linguistics **21** (1995) 543–565

4. Florian, R., Ngai, G.: Multidimensional transformation-based learning. In Daelemans, W., Zajac, R., eds.: Proceedings of CoNLL-2001, Toulouse, France (2001) 1–8
5. Mihalcea, R., Moldovan, D.: An iterative approach to word sens disambiguation. In: Proceedings of FLAIRS-2000, Orlando, FL (2000) 219–223
6. Seo, H.C., Lee, S.Z., Rim, H.C.: Classification information model. http://nlp.korea.ac.kr/ hcseo/senseval2/cim.htm (2001)
7. Pedersen, T.: A baseline methodology for word sense disambiguation. [17] 126–135
8. Manning, C.D., Schütze, H.: Foundations of Statistical Natural Language Processing. The MIT Press, Cambridge, Massachusetts (1999)
9. Ratnaparkhi, A.: Maximum Entropy Models for Natural Language Ambiguity Resolution. PhD thesis, University of Pennsylvania (1998)
10. Lin, D.: Dependency-based evaluation of minipar. In: Proceedings of the Workshop on the Evaluation of Parsing Systems, First International Conference on Language Resources and Evaluation, Granada, Spain (1998)
11. Ng, H.T., Lee, H.B.: Integrating multiple knowledge sources to disambiguate word senses: An exemplar-based approach. In Joshi, A., Palmer, M., eds.: Proceedings of the Thirty-Fourth Annual Meeting of the Association for Computational Linguistics, San Francisco, Morgan Kaufmann Publishers (1996)
12. Escudero, G., Màrquez, L., Rigau, G.: Boosting applied to word sense disambiguation. In: Proceedings of the 12th Conference on Machine Learning ECML2000, Barcelona, Spain (2000)
13. Suárez, A., Palomar, M.: Feature selection analysis for maximum entropy-based wsd. [17] 146–155
14. Miller, G.A., Beckwith, R., Fellbaum, C., Gross, D., Miller, K.J.: Five Papers on WordNet. Special Issue of the International journal of lexicography **3** (1993)
15. Tapanainen, P., Järvinen, T.: A non-projective dependency parser. In: Proceedings of the Fifth Conference on Applied Natural Language Processing. (1997) 64–71
16. Magnini, B., Strapparava, C.: Experiments in Word Domain Disambiguation for Parallel Texts. In: Proceedings of the ACL Workshop on Word Senses and Multilinguality, Hong Kong, China (2000)
17. Gelbukh, A., ed.: Proceedings of 3rd International Conference on Intelligent Text Processing and Computational Linguistics (CICLing-2002). In Gelbukh, A., ed.: Computational Linguistics and Intelligent Text Processing. Lecture Notes in Computer Science, Mexico City, Springer-Verlag (2002)

Heuristics-Based Replenishment of Collocation Databases

Igor A. Bolshakov and Alexander Gelbukh

Center of Computer Research
Nacional Polytecnical Institute
Mexico City, Mexico
{igor,gelbukh}@cic.ipn.mx

Abstract. Collocations are defined as syntactically linked and semantically plausible combinations of content words. Since collocations constitute a bulk of common texts and depend on the language, creation of collocation databases (CBDs) is important. However, manual compilation of such databases is prohibitively expensive. We present heuristics for automatic generation of new Spanish collocations based on those already present in a CBD, with the help of WordNet-like thesaurus: If a word A is semantically "similar" to a word B and a collocation $B + C$ is known, then $A + C$ presumably is a collocation of the same type given certain conditions are met.

1 Introduction

Usual texts contain numerous word combinations like Spanish (Sp.) *prestar atención* 'pay attention', *pluma fuente* 'fountain-pen', *promesa falsa* 'false promise', *partido político* 'political party', etc. We will refer to such syntactically linked and semantically plausible combinations of content words as collocations. We consider as collocations the following groups:

- idiomatic expressions like Sp. *medias tintas* 'half-measures' (literally (lit.) 'half inks') or *campo santo* 'graveyard' (lit. 'saint field'),
- expressions with standard lexical functions by Mel'čuk [5, 6, 10] like Sp. *café cargado* 'strong coffee' (lit. 'loaded coffee') or *prestar atención* 'to pay attention' (lit. 'to lend attention'), and
- free combinations like Sp. *sesión continua* 'continuous session' or *ver al joven* 'to see the lad,' that nevertheless joint only semantically combinable words.

Hence, our term *collocation* does not correspond to a mere co-occurrence of words within a short span of text [8]. It implies syntactic dependencies between the combined content words, immediate or through functional words (usually, prepositions); combined words could be linearly non-contiguous, even remote within a sentence. In this sense, the non-formal treatment of collocations in [3, 7] is just what we mean.

Since collocations usually depend on a given language and cover a bulk of texts, their knowledge is important in many areas of computational linguistics. Hence, creation of corresponding dictionaries [1] and collocation databases (CBDs) [2] is quite topical.

E.M. Ranchhod and N.J. Mamede (Eds.): PorTAL 2002, LNAI 2389, pp. 25–32, 2002.
© Springer-Verlag Berlin Heidelberg 2002

By various reasons, high completeness of collocation collections (say, for the 95% coverage of collocations in a text) seems unreachable. First of all, the efforts and the necessary amount of statistical data for collecting word co-occurrences from a large text corpus greatly exceed those for separate words. Indeed, the less probable a co-occurrence, the longer and more diversified corpus is needed to guarantee statistically significant results. Hence, for compilation of a CDB of even a moderate coverage, it is necessary to scan through (with further manual control and post-editing) a huge and highly polythematic corpus. With such aggravations, it seems reasonable to try replenishment of existing basic CDBs not only through statistical accumulation and selection but also through heuristic inference of new collocations based on their already available amount.

In this paper we propose a method of replenishment of already rather large collocation collections by means of heuristic generation of new collocations. As components of these new collocations, content words already registered in a CDB are taken, and the semantic and syntactic links between them are analyzed. The general heuristic for such kind of inference can be formulated as follows: if a word A is semantically "similar" to a word B and a collocation $B + C$ is already known then $A + C$ is presumably a collocation of the same type given certain conditions are met. Some initial ideas of such replenishment are given in [2].

Semantic similarity between words is based on the relations used in WordNet-like databases [4, 9], specifically: synonymy, hyperonymy / hyponymy (genus—species relations), meronymy / holonymy (part—whole relations), and one type of semantic derivation. Additionally, one type of semantically induced morphological categories is considered for the inference, namely, grammatical number of nouns. We also describe some counter-heuristics for filtering out wrong or dubious results of the inference.

The rules and considerations proposed below are valid for all European languages, though we consider primarily Spanish examples since our motivation was the development of a corresponding Spanish-oriented CDB.

2   General Inference Rule

Our inference rules are similar to those of formal logic. Let a content word A have semantic "similarity" of a class **S** with a word B (we denote this as A **S** B), and a collocational link of a specific dependency category **D** combine the words B and C (we denote this as B **D** C). Then the hypothesis is advanced that A and C constitute a collocation of the same category **D**:

$$(A \text{ S } B) \ \& \ (B \text{ D } C) \Rightarrow (A \text{ D } C).$$

The dependency link **D** can be of several predetermined types and of any direction, i.e., by B **D** C we mean either a syntactic dependency $B \xrightarrow{\text{D}} C$ or $B \xleftarrow{\text{D}} C$. In both parts of the formula, the direction is assumed the same.

The term *inference* is used here in a rather figurative way. Namely, the results obtained with this formula are sometimes wrong, so that we have to use counter-heuristics (filters) to minimize the number of errors.

In practice, if the inference for a given word A gives a high percentage of correct (acknowledged by a native speaker) collocations with various words C, these collocations might be stored implicitly and generated at runtime only when they are really needed. Otherwise, when the number of correct collocations generated for A by the given formula is low, the few correct ones can, after the human verification, be incorporated explicitly into the CDB, thus directly replenishing it. In any case, the errors of inferences are a good tool for perfecting the counter-heuristics.

3   Synonymy-Based Inference

Suppose that the Sp. noun *gorra* 'cap' has no collocations in a CDB, however, it forms a part of a synonymy group (synset) {*gorro, gorra, cofia, capillo, casquete, tocado*} and *gorro* 'hat' is supplied with the collocations *ponerse* 'put on' / *quitarse* 'put off' / *llevar* 'wear'... *gorro*. We can conclude that this information can be transferred to all other members of the synset that lack complete characterization, among them to the word *gorra*. Thus, from the collocation *ponerse* (*el*) *gorro* 'put on the hat' we obtain *ponerse* (*la*) *gorra* 'put on the cap'.

To formalize these considerations, we should take into account that synsets can be introduced in various ways.

Synonymy as strict equivalence ignores any semantic differences between the members of a synset. If a word μ has no collocations of a given type **D** while some Q other members of the same synset do have them, then the required collocation counterparts (the second content word of the collocation) for μ is inferred as the intersection of the Q sets of such counterparts for the other words. I.e., for any x it holds

$$\forall_{q=1}^{Q} \left(\left(\mu \; \textbf{\textit{HasSynonym}} \; s_q \right) \& \left(s_q \; \mathbf{D} \; x \right) \right) \Rightarrow \left(\mu \; \mathbf{D} \; x \right),$$

where ***HasSynonym*** is a kind of relation denoted earlier as **S**.

Synonymy with dominants supposes that there exists a dominant member within each synset expressing the common concept of the set in the most general and neutral way, like *gorro* 'hat' for the abovementioned synset. Then the inference is conducted in a different way. For any dominant, its collocations must be explicitly stored in the CDB, so that no inference is necessary for it. For a non-dominant word μ, the inference is made as follows:

- If μ belongs to only one synset {$d, s_1,... \mu, ..., s_N$} with the dominant d then any collocation valid for d is supposed to be valid for μ. I.e., for any x it holds

$$\left(\mu \; \textbf{\textit{HasDom}} \; d \right) \& \left(d \; \mathbf{D} \; x \right) \Rightarrow \left(\mu \; \mathbf{D} \; x \right),$$

  where ***HasDom*** is the relation standing for "has dominant synonym."

- If μ belongs to several synsets with different dominants D_q:

$$\left\{ d_1, s_{11}, ..., \mu, ..., s_{1N_1} \right\} \left\{ d_2, s_{21}, ..., \mu, ... s_{2N_2} \right\} ... \left\{ d_k, s_{k1}, ..., \mu, ..., s_{kN_k} \right\}$$

then those collocations are supposed valid for μ whose analogues (with d_i) are explicitly present in the CDB for all the dominants involved. This means that for any x it holds

$$\forall_{q=1}^{k} \left(\left(\mu \; \textbf{HasDom} \; d_{q} \right) \& \left(d_{q} \; \textbf{D} \; x \right) \right) \Rightarrow \left(\mu \; \textbf{D} \; x \right).$$

4   Inference Based on Hyponymy and Hyperonymy

Let the Sp. word *refresco* 'soft drink' have a vast collocation set in a CDB including collocations with verbs *echar* 'to pour' / *embotellar* 'to bottle' / *beber* 'to drink' ... *refresco*. The same information on *Pepsi* may be absent in the CDB, while *Pepsi* is registered (through **IsA** relation) as a hyponym of *refresco*. The inference assigns the information about the hyperonym to all its hyponyms that lack relevant type of collocations. Thus, it is inferred that all mentioned verbs are applicable to *Pepsi*.

Here we should bear in mind that the **IsA** relations can be structured in various ways.

Monohierarchy presupposes a unique classification hierarchy (tree) relating some content words within the CDB. Thus, a unique hyperonym corresponds to each hyponym in it, except for the uppermost node (the root of the tree) and the words not included in the hierarchy.

Suppose the relation $\textbf{IsA}^{1}$ (^{1} stands for 'one-step') gives the immediate (nearest) hyperonym h_1 for the word μ. The word h_1 is unique (if it exists) within a monohierarchy. If the collocation set for h_1 is empty, then a hyperonym h_k (of a higher level) is used, where $\textbf{IsA}^{k}$ and h_k are defined as

$$(\mu \; \textbf{IsA}^{k} \; h_k) = (\mu \; \textbf{IsA}^{1} \; h_1) \& (h_1 \; \textbf{IsA}^{1} \; h_2) \& \dots \& (h_{k-1} \; \textbf{IsA}^{1} \; h_k).$$

Inference by means of hyperonymy determines the first (i.e., with the minimal k) hyperonym h_k that has non-empty collocation set of the required type and assigns these collocations to μ. I.e., for any x it holds

$$\left(\mu \; \textbf{IsA}^{k} \; h_k \right) \& \left(h_k \; \textbf{D} \; x \right) \Rightarrow \left(\mu \; \textbf{D} \; x \right).$$

For example, if the relevant collocation set for *refresco* is empty, while for *bebida* 'a drink' is nonempty then *Pepsi* is characterized by the information borrowed from this two-step-up hyperonym.

Crosshierarchy permits content words to participate in more than one hyperonym—hyponym hierarchy based on different principles of classification. The whole structure is a directed acyclic graph; a word (except for uppermost nodes of partial hierarchies and unclassified words) can have several hyperonyms. There are various cases of replenishment in this case.

Since more then one path can go up from a word μ, we propose the following inference procedure. All k-step-up hyponyms of μ, $k = 1, 2, ...$, are searched width-first, until at least one of them has a non-empty collocation set. If there is only one non-empty set at such k-th layer, the formula given above remains valid. Otherwise the intersection of all non-empty sets is used. To represent this mathematically, we enumerate all hyponyms with non-empty collocation sets of k-th layer as $q = 1, 2, ..., Q$. Then for any x it holds

$$\forall_{q=1}^{Q} \left(\left(\mu \; \textbf{\textit{IsA}}^k \; h_{k_q} \right) \& \left(h_{k_q} \; \textbf{D} \; x \right) \right) \Rightarrow \left(\mu \; \textbf{D} \; x \right).$$

The width-first search excludes the cases when a collocation set of k-th hyperonym is taken while m-th hyperonym has non-empty set, $m < k$.

5   Inference Based on Holohymy and Meronymy

The meronymy relation (x **HasMero** y) holds when x has y as a part; holonymy (y **HasHolo** x) is the inverse relation holding when x includes y. In simple cases, both x and y are single words, e.g., Sp. (*clientela* 'clientage' **HasMero** *cliente* 'client') or (*árbol* 'tree' **HasMero** *tronco* 'trunk').

Unlike synonymy and hyperonymy, both directions of collocation transfer are possible. E.g., Sp. collocations *atender* 'to attend (to)' / *satisfacer* 'to satisfy' / *atraer* 'to attract' / *perder* 'to lose' ... *al cliente* are equally applicable to *clientela* and vice versa. The general inference rule is as follows: for any x it holds

$$(\mu \; \textbf{\textit{HasMero}} \; y) \; \& \; (y \; \textbf{D} \; x) \Rightarrow (\mu \; \textbf{D} \; x),$$
$$(\mu \; \textbf{\textit{HasHolo}} \; y) \; \& \; (y \; \textbf{D} \; x) \Rightarrow (\mu \; \textbf{D} \; x).$$

In fact, not all combinations of μ and y can be used in these formulas. The complications are implied by the fact that meronymy / holonymy can be of five different types [9]: a part proper: *dedo* 'finger' of *mano* 'hand'; a portion: *gota* 'drop' of *líquido* 'liquid'; a narrower location: *centro* 'center' of *ciudad* 'city'; a member: *jugador* 'player' of *equipo* 'team'; and a substance the whole is made of: *madera* 'wood' for *bastón* 'stick'. Not all these types are equally suitable for bi-directional inferences. The membership type seems the most facilitating, while the made-of type the least facilitating. In any case, further research is necessary to develop the filters to eliminate wrong combinations.

6   Inference Based on Semantic Derivation

Semantic derivation is the formation of new lexemes from other lexemes close in meaning. There exists at least one kind of semantic derivation in European languages that excellently suits for the inferences, namely derivation of adverbs from a corresponding adjective: Sp. *bueno* 'good' → *bien* 'well', *corto* 'short' → *cortamente* 'shortly'. The modifiers for an adjective and an adverb constituting a derivative pair are the same:

$$(\mu \; \textbf{\textit{IsDerivFrom}} \; y) \; \& \; (y \; \textbf{\textit{HasModif}} \; x) \Rightarrow (\mu \; \textbf{\textit{HasModif}} \; x).$$

E.g., Sp. (*bien* **IsDerivFrom** *bueno*) & (*bueno* **HasModif** *muy* 'very') ⇒ (*bien* **HasModif** *muy*).

7   Morphology-Based Inference

Some morphological categories are semantically induced and have explicit expression at the semantic level of text representation. The most common of these categories is grammatical number that in most languages has two values: singular and plural. Since different number values frequently imply different collocation sets, singular and plural words should be included into the CDB as separate headwords, as it has been proposed in [2]. However, if the CDB contains a collocation set of a given relation **D** for only one (supposedly more frequently used) value of number while the collocations for its counterpart are still absent in the CDB then the same set can be transferred to the word of the complementary value of number. I.e. for any x it holds

$$(\mu \; \textbf{\textit{HasComplementaryNumber}} \; y) \; \& \; (y \; \textbf{D} \; x) \Rightarrow (\mu \; \textbf{D} \; x).$$

E.g., modifiers of Sp. *información* 'information' are applicable for its more rarely used plural *informaciones*.

However, some specific modifiers frequently bring in wrong hypotheses. To filter them out, it should be taken into account that, at semantic level, singular of a noun N is usually opposed to plural through the predicates $\textbf{\textit{Single}}(N)$ vs. $\textbf{\textit{MoreThanOne}}(N)$. Hence, we can introduce a prohibitive list of words with a semantic element of singularity / uniqueness, thus combinable mainly with singular, and, vice versa, a list of words with a semantic element of collectiveness / multiplicity, thus combinable mainly with plural. For **HasModif** relation in Spanish, following are mainly plural-oriented modifiers: *muchos* 'many', *múltiples* 'multiple', *numerosos* 'numerous', *varios* 'several', *diferentes* 'different', *diversos* 'various', *distintos* 'distinct (ones)', *idénticos* 'identical', *iguales* 'equal (ones)', *desiguales* 'unequal (ones)', *de todos tipos* 'of all kinds', etc. Singular-oriented modifiers are fewer: *único* 'unique', *singular* 'single', *solitario* 'alone', *individual* 'individual', etc. The counter-heuristic (filtering) rule consists in the use of the corresponding heuristic rule only if x does not belong to the proper prohibitive list.

8   Filtering Out Wrong Hypotheses

We have already mentioned some counter-heuristics we use to filter out inference errors. Following are other filters we use.

Do not consider lexeme-specific syntactic dependencies D. The most error-prone of such dependencies is **HasValency** of verbs (= subcategorization frame). To illustrate this, consider the Spanish synset {*elegir* 'to choose, to elect', *seleccionar* 'to select', *designar* 'to assign', *optar* 'to opt', *preferir* 'to prefer', *escoger* 'to choose'}. All its members except for *optar* subcategorize for the target of selection as direct object (*elegir* / *seleccionar* / *designar* / *preferir* / *escoger algo* 'smth.'), while *optar* uses a prepositional phrase for this purpose: *optar por algo* 'to opt for smth.'. Each of them, except for *elegir* and *designar*, can introduce a prepositional complement with *entre* 'between' for options of the selection. Thus, collocations including **HasValency** relation, say, of the verb *optar* cannot be inferred correctly based on the properties of the other members of the synset.

Meanwhile, the dependencies inverse to **HasValency** can be freely used for the inferences involving nouns. Indeed, if the relation **HasValency** gives for *país* 'country' the collocations *traspasar* 'to cross' / *visitar* 'to visit' / *arruinar* 'to destroy' ... *país* then all these verbs form correct collocations with any specific country name (e.g., *Portugal*).

Ignore classifying modifiers. Some inferences for modificatory collocations also give wrong results. For example, *bayas* 'berries' as a hyperonym can have nearly any color, smell, and taste, while its hyponym *arándanos* 'blueberries' are scarcely *amarillas* 'yellow'.

Among modifiers, one rather broad class is most error-prone. Consider the wrong inference:

(*Colombia* **IsA** *país*) & (*país* **HasModif** *europeo*) ⇒ *(*Colombia* **HasModif** *europea*)

'Colombia is a country' & 'European country' ⇒ 'European Colombia'. To exclude such cases, we ignore in inferences the so-called classifying modifiers. These modifiers convert a specific noun to its hyponym, e.g., *país* 'country' → *país europeo* 'European' / *americano* 'American' / *africano* 'African'... As to other modifiers for *país*, they frequently give correct results: *agrícola* 'agricultural' / *bella* 'beautiful' / *gran* 'great' ... *Colombia*.

Unfortunately, even such filtering is rarely sufficient. E.g., the modifiers *del sur* 'Southern' or *del norte* 'Northern' change their meaning while moving from *país* to a specific country name, compare *país del norte* 'Northern country' and *Portugal del norte* 'Northern Portugal'. All such cases are to be dealt with using specific word lists.

Ignore marked words and collocations. In some printed and electronic dictionaries oriented to humans, the number of various usage marks reaches several tens. All these labels can be divided into two large groups:

- **Scope of usage**, such as *special*, *obsolete*, *vulgar*, etc., and

- **Idiomacity**, covering cases of figurative and direct interpretation (Sp. *rayo de luz* 'good idea' or 'light beam', lit. ray of light) as well as of idiomatic use only (Sp. *vara alta* 'power, high influence', lit. 'high stick').

We propose to ignore all marked items in inference, since they more frequently than not lead to wrong or dubious results. For example, Sp. *vara* 'stick' is dominant of the synset {*vara*, *varejón* 'long stick', *varal*, *garrocha*, *palo* 'thick stick'}, but we cannot correctly semantically interpret the results of the inference (*palo* **HasDom** *vara*) & (*vara* **HasModif** *alta*)$_{idiom}$ ⇒ *(*palo* **HasModif** *alto*)$_{idiom}$.

9   Conclusions

A heuristic method is developed for inferring new collocations basing on their available amount and a WordNet-like thesaurus. The main idea of the method consists in the possibility, except for some cases, to substitute a word in the existing collocation with a semantically "similar" one. We have discussed what we mean by similarity and what exceptions there are.

The types of similarity considered are synonymy, hyperonymy / holonymy, holonymy / meronymy, one kind of semantic derivation, and one semantically induced morphological category: number of nouns.

To exclude the most frequent errors, some counter-heuristics have been proposed in the form of prohibitive lists or categories of content words, lexeme-specific syntactic relations used in collocations, and the labeled dictionary items.

Using the proposed inference procedure, runtime or off-line replenishment of large collocation databases can be performed. All introduced rules are well suitable to develop a Spanish collocation DB that is now under development (ca. 10,000 collocations and semantic links). In the future, we plan to reach amounts comparable to those reported for the analogous Russian database [2]. Using of inference will facilitate this task.

References

1. Benson, M., E. Benson, and R. Ilson. *The BBI Combinatory Dictionary of English*. John Benjamin, Amsterdam / Philadelphia, 1989.

2. Bolshakov, I. A., A. Gelbukh. *A Very Large Database of Collocations and Semantic Links*. In: Mokrane Bouzeghoub et al. (eds.) *Natural Language Processing and Information Systems*. 5th International Conference on Applications NLDB-2000, Versailles, France, June 2000. Lecture Notes in Computer Science No. 1959, Springer, 2001, p. 103-114.

3. Calzolari, N., R. Bindi. *Acquisition of Lexical Information from a Large Textual Italian Corpus*. Proc. of COLING-90, Helsinki, 1990.

4. Fellbaum, Ch. (ed.) *WordNet: An Electronic Lexical Database*. MIT Press, Cambridge, London, 1998.

5. Mel'čuk, Igor. *Fraseología y diccionario en la lingüística moderna*. In: I. Uzcanga Vivar et al. (eds.) *Presencia y renovación de la lingüística francesa*. Salamanca: Ediciones Universidad, 2001, p. 267-310.

6. Mel'čuk, I., A. Zholkovsky. *The explanatory combinatorial dictionary*. In: M. Evens (ed.) *Relational models of lexicon*. Cambridge University Press. Cambridge. England, 1988, p. 41-74.

7. Satoshi Sekine et al. *Automatic Learning for Semantic Collocation*. Proc. 3rd Conf. Applied Natural Language Processing, Trento, Italy, 1992, p. 104-110.Smadja, F. *Retreiving collocations from text: Xtract*. Computational Linguistics. Vol. 19, No. 1, 1991, p. 143-177.

8. Smadja, F. *Retreiving collocations from text: Xtract*. Computational Linguistics. Vol. 19, No. 1, 1991, p. 143-177.

9. Vossen, P. (ed.). *EuroWordNet General Document*. Vers. 3 final. 2000, www.hum.uva.nl/~ewn.

10. Wanner, Leo (ed.). *Lexical Functions in Lexicography and Natural Language Processing*. Studies in Language Companion Series, ser.31. John Benjamin, Amsterdam/ Philadelphia, 1996.

On the Analysis of Locative Phrases with Graphs and Lexicon-Grammar: The Classifier/Proper Noun Pairing

Matthieu Constant

University of Marne-la-Vallée, 5 bld Descartes, Champs-sur-Marne,
77 454 Marne-la-Vallée Cedex 2, France
mconstant@iv-mlv.fr

Abstract. This paper analyses French locative prepositional phrases containing a location proper name *Npr* (e.g. *Méditerranée*) and its associated classifier *Nc* (e.g. *mer*). The (*Nc, Npr*) pairs are formally described with the aid of elementary sentences. We study their syntactic properties within adverbial support verb constructions and encode them in a Lexicon-Grammar Matrix. From this matrix, we build grammars in the form of graphs and evaluate their application to a journalistic corpus.

1 Introduction

The analysis of adverbials is an important issue in Natural Language Processing (NLP) due to the fact that adverbials can be inserted anywhere in sentences and thus make sentence analysis more difficult. The adverbials we are concerned with are of the form *Prep NP* (cf. Table 1), and more precisely with French locative *PP*s containing a location proper name *Npr* (e.g. *Paris*) and its associated classifier *Nc* (e.g. *ville*), where intuitively *Npr* names a place which belongs to a category *Nc*. Our study is domain-independent but is limited to *PP*s of the internal form:

Loc (Det1 + E) Nc [de (Det + E) + E] Npr (= Loc X')
= : *dans la (ville de Paris+ mer Méditerranée)*

They can be part of constructions of the form *N0 Vsup Loc N1*, e.g.

L'annonce de sa promotion a eu lieu dans le village de Nay

Where *Vsup* =: *avoir lieu* (*to take place*), *Npr* =: *Nay* and *Nc* =: *village*.

Our objective is to complete the lists of frozen and semi-frozen adverbials accumulated in the framework of the lexicon-grammar theory [7,9]. Those adverbials are encoded in electronic compound dictionaries (used in the linguistic platform INTEX [16,17]) and in Lexicon-Grammar Matrices (LGMs). Some complex adverbials (e.g. time adverbials [1,11]) have been described with Finite State Transducers (FSTs): they can be seen as an extension of electronic dictionaries [10]. These linguistic re-

E.M. Ranchhod and N.J. Mamede (Eds.): PorTAL 2002, LNAI 2389, pp. 33-42, 2002.

sources should be of great use in concrete applications such as information retrieval [4], phrase translation [5] and phrase segmentation for summarization [2,18].

In this paper, we not only automatically relate an *Npr* to its appropriate classifier (or semantic class) as many studies have already made [3,14,19], but we also provide, for each classifier *Nc* of a given list, a limited distribution of locative prepositions *Loc* that enter in the adverbial elementary sentence *N0 Vsup Loc X'*. This provides a solid basis for disambiguating *PP*s, e.g. distinguishing between arguments of predicates and adverbials. In the example below, as *à la ville de Paris* cannot be an adverbial (cf. section 3), it is necessarily an argument of the predicate *subvention* that enters in the elementary structure *N0 donner Det subvention à N1*.

Le gouvernement a donné une subvention à la dernière minute à la ville de Paris
(At the last minute, the government gave a subvention to the city of Paris)

First, we shall briefly study the construction *N0 Vsup Loc X'* from a linguistic point of view. Then, on the basis of this study, we shall describe how to build locative grammars with LGMs and graphs. Finally, we apply these grammars to journalistic corpora and evaluate the results.

Table 1. Notations

S	Sentence
NP	Noun Phrase
PP	Prepositional Phrase
Vsup	Support verb
Ni	*i*th nominal argument of a predicate (where *i* is an integer)
Prep	Preposition
Loc	Locative Preposition
Det, Det1	Determiners
E	Empty element
UN	The singular indefinite determiners *un* or *une* (a or an)
LE	*le, la* (the)
POSS	Possessive determiner

2   A Brief Linguistic Study

This linguistic study is limited to a few properties to clarify the paper. *Nc* and *Npr* can be related to each other in the sentence:

> *(1) (E + Det) Npr être (UN + des) Nc*
> := *Paris est une ville* (Paris is a city)
>   *La Méditerranée est une mer*

Det is a definite determiner whose form only depends on *Npr* [12]. It is strictly limited to the set {*le, la, les*}. The sentence (1) can be reduced into three nominal constructions:

Det1 Nc Npr := *la mer Méditerranée* (the Mediterranean sea)
Det1 Nc de Npr := *la ville de Paris* (the city of Paris)
Det1 Nc de Det Npr := *les îles des Canaries* (the Canaries Islands)

2.1 Syntactic Properties of (*Nc, Npr*) Pairs in Noun Phrases

Det1 is LE or POSS. Note that *'un'* is strictly forbidden when the NP does not contain a modifier located at the end of it:

Une ville de Paris, embellie pour les fêtes

Det1 can also be in the plural for some (*Nc, Npr*) like (*île,Canaries*) because *Canaries* are islands [6]. *Det1* is also in the plural when several *Npr* with the same *Nc* are coordinated such as:

Les villes de Paris et (de+E) Lyon = la ville de Paris et la ville de Lyon

A given pair (*Nc, Npr*) does not always enter into all the constructions. Acceptability essentially depends on *Npr*:

L'île (de+E) Malte
L'île (*E+de la+*de) Martinique
Les îles (E+de les+*de) Canaries

Modifiers can also be inserted between the constituents. The markers *M1*, *M2* and *M3* show where modifiers can be placed into the *NP*s:

Det M1 Nc M2 de (E + Det) Npr M3
Det M1 Nc Npr M3

Moreover, some (*Nc, Npr*) only occur in the nominal forms; that is, they do not occur in the elementary sentence (1). They can be seen as compounds. Modifiers marked *M2* are forbidden in this case:

*Le Nord est une mer
La mer (E+ ?*déchainée) du Nord me fascine (where *du = de le*)

2.2 Syntactic Properties of (*Nc, Npr*) Pairs in the Construction *N0 Vsup Loc N1*

Now, we examine the form *N0 Vsup Loc X'*. We study the distribution of its constituents. Let *Vsup* be *être* (to be). Let *Loc* be *dans, à, en* and *E*, very frequent locative prepositions in French. Our study is then reduced to:

(2) N0 être (dans + à + en + E) (Det1+E) Nc de (Det+E) Npr
(3) N0 être (dans + à + en + E) (Det1+E) Nc Npr

The sequence *Loc (Det1+E)* is limited to the set *{dans Det1, à det1, en, E}*, but each *Nc* has its own properties. Precise information on pairs cannot be encoded without at least an exhaustive study of all classifiers *Nc*, as illustrated in the following examples:

> *Max est (*E + *en + dans la + *à la) ville de Paris*
> *Max est (*E + en + dans la + *à la) mer (Méditerranée + du Nord)*
> *Max est (E + *en + dans la + ?à la) rue (de la Paix + Censier)*
> *Max est (E + *en +*dans le + à le) métro République*

We notice that preposition distribution is different for constructions (2) and (3):

> *Max est (*E + en + dans la + *à la) région Ile-de-France*
> *Max est (*E + *en + dans la + *à la) région de l'Ile-de-France*

The constructions with the prepositions *E* and *en* do not accept modifiers M1 (2.1):

> *Belle rue de Rivoli, les passants se marchent les uns sur les autres.*
> *En magnifique mer Méditerranée, la marée est peu marquée*

We notice that the adjective *plein* can be inserted in these cases; but it is part of the compound preposition *en plein*:

> *Max est égaré en pleine mer Méditerranée*

3   Construction of Locative Grammars

3.1 NNPR Matrix Description

It has been shown in Section 2 that syntactic properties of *NP*s essentially depend on *Npr* (2.1) and on *Nc* for the prepositional distribution (2.2). A systematic study of *Npr* is necessary to encode the *NP*s precisely, which is time consuming due to number of *Npr*. In this section, our objective is to encode the syntactic properties of the form *N0 Vsup Loc X'*, which essentially depend on the classifiers (but not only [6]). To this end, we established a list of about one hundred *N*s. We encoded the properties of each element of the list into a Lexicon-Grammar Matrix (LGM) as in [8]. Each column corresponds to one property; that is, for example, to one *PP* form. Each row contains one lexical entry (one *Nc* in our case). At the intersection of a row and a column, a plus sign indicates that the corresponding *Nc* enters into the corresponding property, a minus sign, that it does not; and finally, a string indicates lexical information. Lexicon entries are displayed in rows and syntactic properties in columns. We show a sample of the LGM in Table 2.

Table 2. Lexicon-Grammar Matrix *PNNpr* where P1 =: *en Nc Npr*; P2= : *en Nc de (E+Det) Npr* ; P3 =: *dans LE Nc Npr* ; P4 =: *dans LE Nc de (E+Det) Npr* ; P5 =: *à LE Nc Npr ;* P6 =: *à LE Nc de (E+Det) Npr* ; P7 =: *Nc Npr* ; P8 =: *Nc de (E+Det) Npr*

		(N0+Que S) avoir lieu Loc N1							
N	N plural	Loc N1							
		P1	P2	P3	P4	P5	P6	P7	P8
fleuve	-	-	-	+	+	-	-	-	-
Gare	-	+	+	+	+	+	+	+	+
Gave	-	-	-	-	+	-	-	-	-
ghetto	-	-	-	-	+	-	-	-	-
glacier	-	-	-	+	+	+	+	-	-
Golfe	-	-	-	+	+	-	-	-	-
Île	+	-	-	+	+	+	+	-	-

3.2 Reference Grammars

LGM is a simple and clear representation. Nevertheless, it cannot be directly applied to texts. By transforming the LGM into Finite State Graphs (FSG), the linguistic information encoded in the LGM can be applied. In this sub-section, we describe the process of transforming an LGM into an FSG. A simple way of doing this is to build a reference graph [13,15]. From this graph that represents the set of all possible forms, a graph will be created for each lexical entry. A transition @*i* (where *i* is an integer) is seen as a variable that refers to the *i*th column (or property) of the matrix. For each lexical entry (or each row), a new graph is automatically constructed from the reference graph by:

-   removing the transition @*i* when the intersection of the *i*th column and the current row is '-'
-   replacing @*i* by <E> (the empty element) when '+'
-   replacing @i by the content of the intersection of the *i*th column and the current row, by default

The reference graph shown in Graph 1 (Fig. 1) represents a grammar that describes the forms *Loc N1* (presented above). Grey boxes represents sub-graphs. The graph **LE** describes the set {*le, la, l'*}; **Det**, the set {*le, la, les, l'*}; **POSS**, the possessive determiners like *mon, ma, ton, ta*, etc.; **Npr** describes the proper noun by the means of the tag <PRE> that stands for a word beginning with an uppercase letter. It recognises simple forms like *Paris* and complex ones like *Pyrénées-Atlantiques* and *La Havane*. <@1.N:p> stands for the plural form of the classifier symbolised by @1 (first column of the matrix): *Nc* for noun and *p* for plural. From Graph 1 (Fig. 1), we obtain Graph 2 (Fig. 2) for the lexical entry *mer*. All forbidden paths are automatically removed according to the LGM codification.

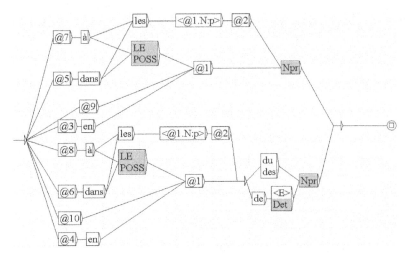

Fig. 1. Reference graph

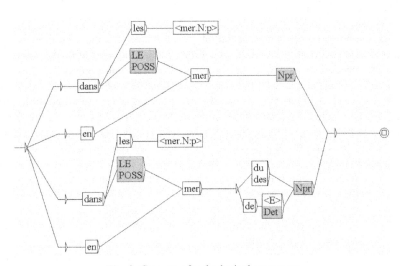

Fig. 2. Grammar for the lexical entry *mer*

4 Application of Locative Grammars: Some Experiments

4.1 Description of the Experiment

We apply locative grammars to a corpus. Our corpus consists of one year of the electronic version of the French newspaper *Le Monde* (year 1993). It comprises about ten million words. It is of great interest because of the quality of the writing and the large variety of themes that are treated. We undertook three experiments. The first one consists in applying a basic grammar that describes the forms *Loc X'* without modifiers and with a small set of simple prepositions (Section 3). In the second experiment, we enlarge the set of prepositions with around three hundred compound locative prepositions. We manually included those prepositions into a graph (called **Loc**), after extracting them from the lists provided in [9] (e.g. *aux alentours de, en amont de*). We assume that these new prepositions have the same behaviour as the preposition *dans*. That means that if a construction allows the preposition *dans*, all the compounds are allowed. Finally, we add modifiers in our grammar by inserting a graph **Modif** at positions *M1* and *M2* as described in Section 2. **Modif** represents a general modifier of the form (<ADV>+<E>) <A>, where <ADV> stands for an adverb and <A> for an adjective.

4.2 Results of Experiments

The number of occurrences automatically found in our corpus for experiments 1, 2 and 3 are respectively *1,977*, *2,026* and *2,190*. We first observe that the *PP*s described are very rare: maximum 2,190 utterances in a 10-million word text. The classifier nouns occur 35,000 times on their own; that means that 6% of them are part of *PP*s recognized. Furthermore, we observe that 90% of the forms are base forms; that is, without modifiers and with a simple preposition (*dans, à, en* or *E*). Thus, the description of the modifiers and the compound locative prepositions is useful for only 10% of the forms. We provide below a selection of the concordances obtained:

~ *.{S} Un peu plus tard, arrêt à la gare Saint-Lazare, que la patrouille parcourt en t*
~ *aires se compliquent aussi dans le déjà difficile département des Alpes-Maritimes.*
~ *ue Saddam, situé à une quarantaine de kilomètres à le nord de la ville de Mossoul*
~ *enseigne des Bonnes Choses, rue Falguière, où le cassoulet mijotait de éternité.{S}*
~ *ire et bancaire à le Trésor, rue de Bercy à Paris, qui vont avoir à émettre environ*
~ *ordement de marchandises dans le port de Rotterdam, le plus important du monde,*
~ *détruite par la guerre.{S} " Dans le village de Jocoaitique, qui se relève peu à peu*
~ *Yaoundé, ont été reconduits dans la province anglophone du Nord-Ouest.{S}*
~ *oirs ont été tués par balles dans le ghetto noir de Tokoza, à l'est de Johannesbourg*
~ *a foule de un policier noir, dans la cité de Evaton, la veille du Jour de l'an.{S} L*
~ *00 soldats français déployés dans la région de Hoddour.{S} M. Mellick a fait cette*
~ *piégée, mercredi 10 février, en plein centre du port pétrolier de Barrancabermeja,*
~ [A] *son " bouchon " de la rue Vavin : " Là cuit un cassoulet de Castelnaudary.{S}*
~ [B] *eu plus tard dans une rue de Naplouse, en Cisjordanie occupée. {S} Ancien co*
~ [C] *usée de la SEITA, 12, rue Surcouf, 75007 Paris ;{S} tél.{S} : 45-66-60-17.{S}*
~ [D] *mois après la mise en route de Gabcikovo, la catastrophe annoncée ne a pas e*
~ [E] *-vous, c' était le 3 avril, dans le quartier sud de Manchester, à St Peter's Squar*
~ [G] *succède à un socialiste dans le plus petit canton de l'Hérault : Maurice Requi*
~ [H] *grand compagnon de route de Dave Holland et de Portal, présente un nouveau*

4.3 Problems Encountered

In this section, we briefly list some issues and ways to resolve them. The main problem encountered is noise: 434 utterances out of 2190 should not be recognized (i.e. around 20% of noise), which is not negligible. There are several reasons for this. The first is the use of the empty preposition and the ambiguity of the empty element. Many *Loc X'* where *Nc* accepts this preposition belong to a larger *NP*, as in [A] (in the concordances of 4.2). The application of a grammar representing an *NP* described in 2.1 with the longest match rule removes a large part of the noise. Therefore, [A] is now recognised as a NP (*la rue Vavin*). Using this method, we remove 382 utterances. Thus, we significantly reduce noise to 50 utterances i.e. about 2.3%. Errors like [B] should be removable through the application of a grammar of a general *NP*. Although [C] is well parsed, it could be part of a longer unit, a mail address (*12, rue Surcouf, 75007 Paris*). Note that this case appears 712 times in our corpus (28% of the total occurrences). Another problem comes from the use of modifiers in our grammars: *sud* in [E] (*Manchester* is not a *quartier*). The presence of superlatives creates noise such as in [G]: a way of removing it is to construct special superlative grammars. The generality of *Npr* is another issue. For example, a sequence like *la ville de Pagnol* (that is translated by *Pagnol's city*) is recognised: *Pagnol* is the name of a personality and not the name of a city. This problem can be solved by the use of dictionaries of proper nouns. In [G], the classifier *route* is part of the French compound *compagnon de route* (fellow traveller). The application of compound dictionaries should remove the wrong parsing.

5 Conclusion and Perspectives

This paper briefly studies the behaviour of the pair (*Nc*, *Npr*) within *NP*s and *PP*s. From the theory, we encode general syntactic rules into an LGM and then in the form of graphs. We then apply some of these grammars to a journalistic corpus. This method appears to be of great interest for Natural Language Processing even if, at first, it creates considerable noise (4.3). Furthermore, the linguistic study produces precise syntactic information on the sequences of the form *Loc X'*. It is also a source of semantic information, by associating an *Nc* to an unknown *Npr*. Moreover, we project to build dictionaries of locative *Npr* containing syntactic information or to complete existing ones.

6 References

1.   Baptista, J.: Manhã, Tarde, Noite: analysis of temporal adverbs using local grammars. Seminarios de Linguistica 3, Faro, Universidade do Algarve (1999) 5–31

2.   Boguraev, B., Neff, M.: Discourse Segmentation in aid of documentation summarization. In: Proceedings of Hawaii International Conference on System Sciences (HICSS-33), Minitrack on Digital Documents Understanding. Maui, Hawaii (2000)

3. Cucchiarelli, A., Luzi, D., Velardi, P.: Semantic tagging of unknown proper nouns. Natural Language Engineering, Vol. 5:2. Cambridge University Press (1999) 171–185

4. Domingues, C.: Etude d'outils informatiques et linguistiques pour l'aide à la recherche d'information dans un corpus documentaire. Thèse de doctorat en informatique, Université de Marne-la-Vallée (2001)

5. Fairon, C., Senellart, J.: Classes d'expressions bilingues gérées par des transducteurs finis, dates et titres de personnalité (anglais-français). Linguistique contrastive et traduction, Approches empiriques. Louvain-la-Neuve (1999)

6. Garrigues, M.: Prepositions and the names of countries and islands: a local grammar for the automatic analysis of texts. Language Research, Vol. 31:2. Seoul, Language Research Institute, Seoul National University (1995) 309–334

7. Gross, M.: Grammaire transformationnelle du français. Vol. 3, Syntaxe de l'adverbe. Paris, ASSTRIL, Université Paris 7 (1986)

8. Gross, M., Constructing Lexicon-Grammars. In: Atkins, B.T.S., Zampolli, A. (eds.): Computational Approaches to the Lexicon. Oxford University Press, Oxford (1994) 213–263

9. Gross, M.: Les formes *être Prép X* du français. Lingvisticae Investigationes, Vol. XX:2. John Benjamins, Amsterdam Philadelphia (1996) 217–270

10. Gross, M.: The Construction of Local Grammars. In: E. Roche and Y. Schabes (Eds.): Finite State Language Processing. The MIT Press, Cambridge, Mass. (1997) 329–352

11. Maurel, D.: Adverbes de date: étude préliminaire à leur traitement automatique. Lingvisticae Investigationes, Vol. XIV:1. John Benjamins, Amsterdam Philadelphia (1990) 31–63

12. Maurel D., Piton, O.: Un dictionnaire de noms propres pour *INTEX* : les noms propres géographiques. In : Fairon, C. (ed.): Analyse lexicale et syntaxique : le système INTEX. Lingvisticae Investigationes, Vol. XXII. John Benjamins, Amsterdam Philadelphia (1998) 279–289.

13. Roche, E.: Analyse syntaxique transformationnelle du français par transducteurs et lexique-grammaire. Thèse de doctorat, Paris, Université Paris 7 (1993)

14. Senellart, J.: Locating noun phrases with finite state transducers. In: Proceedings of the 17th International Conference on Computational Linguistics (COLING98). Montreal (1998) 1212–1219

15. Senellart, J.: Reconnaissance automatique des entrées du lexique-grammaire des expressions figées. Travaux de linguistique. Bruxelles (1999)

16. Silberztein, M.: Dictionnaires électroniques et analyse automatique de textes : Le système INTEX. Masson, Paris (1993)

17. Silberztein, M.: INTEX: a corpus processing system. In: Proceedings of the 15th International Conference on Computational Linguistics (COLING94). Kyoto, Japan (1994) 579–582

18. Silberztein, M.: INTEX at IBM. In: Dister, A. (Ed.): Actes des Troisièmes Journées INTEX. Revue Informatique et Statistique dans les Sciences humaines. Liège (2000) 319–332

19. Wakao, T., Gaizauskas, R., Wilks, Y.: Evaluation of an algorithm for the recognition and classification of proper names. In: Proceedings of the 16th International Conference on Computational Linguistics (COLING96), Copenhagen (1996) 418–423

The Role of Pause Occurrence and Pause Duration in the Signaling of Narrative Structure

Miguel Oliveira

Instituto de Linguística Teórica e Computacional (ILTEC)
Lisboa, 1550-109, Portugal
mjo@iltec.pt
http://www.iltec.pt

Abstract. This paper addresses the prosodic feature of pause and its distribution in spontaneous narrative in relation to the role it plays in signaling narrative structure. Pause duration and pause occurrence were taken as variables for the present analysis. The results indicate that both variables consistently mark narrative section boundaries, suggesting thus that pause is a very important structuring device in oral narratives.

1. Introduction

Pauses are primarily considered to be "periods of silence in the speech of a person" ([27]: 221). Obviously, not all "periods of silence" are pauses and not only "periods of silence" characterize a pause. In order for a "period of silence" to be considered a pause, it must occur between vocalizations. In other words, silent gaps that occur in speech as a result of taciturnity or reticence, for example, are not considered pauses. Additionally, other phenomena that do not necessarily correspond to the definition of pause presented above are sometimes considered to be so in the literature, such as filled pauses (vocal hesitations: "uh," "er," etc.), repeats, false starts, syllabic or vocalic prolongations, discourse markers, etc. ([27]: 221).

Pauses perform multiple functions. Their occurrence is determined by several factors such as anxiety, emphasis, interruption, intersubjectivity, availability, breathing, syntactic complexity, etc. ([27]: 221). However, what necessitates pause is of little interest in this study. Rather, pauses are mainly regarded as a linguistic cue for narrative segmentation.

It is generally accepted that among all the prosodic features available to the speaker for signaling structure in a text, pause is one of the most efficient ([5], [31], [2]). It is expected that at some points in the telling of a story, boundaries are more likely to occur than at other points. Such boundaries are often realized as a period of silence of varying length, in conjunction with other acoustic cues.

In this paper it is hypothesized that the segmentation of narrative into sections is systematically evidenced in speech by means of pause occurrence and length — speakers systematically signal the end of a narrative section by producing a pause of long duration. Pauses of shorter duration are, on the other hand, regarded as a cue for

E.M. Ranchhod and N.J. Mamede (Eds.): PorTAL 2002, LNAI 2389, pp. 43-51, 2002.
© Springer-Verlag Berlin Heidelberg 2002

non-finality — speakers would use them to indicate that the following information has some sort of semantic connection with the previous one.

2. Methods

The material used in the present study derives from a larger investigation on the role of prosodic features in the organization of spontaneous narratives ([26]). A total of 17 narratives told in the course of a "spontaneous interview" ([35]) were chosen for this analysis. In order to avoid the so-called "risk of circularity", a series of methodoligical procedures, which included the involvement of five experts in intonation and two experts in discourse analysis, were taken (see [26] for a detailed discussion on these procedures). A specific model of narrative analysis, the Labovian Evaluative Model ([19]), was used for the purpose of the analysis.

This study is restricted to silent pauses, defined by [13: 203] as "a period of vocal inactivity of a certain duration embedded in the stream of speech." It does not include the occurrence of filled pauses or any other phenomena that include vocalization since they have a very limited incidence in speech ([13], [2]) and are not primarily used as a means of signaling boundaries in discourse ([2], [34]).

There is very little agreement among researchers concerning the cut-off point for defining a silent pause. The range varies greatly, going from as long as 3 seconds ([33]) to as short as 80 milliseconds ([21]). The most common cut-off point, however, is up to 250 ms after the precedent of Goldman-Eisler ([8], [9], [10], [11]). According to [10], the consequences of adopting a minimum cut-off point well above 250 ms are numerous, since 71.5% of all pauses occur in the duration interval between 250 ms and 1 sec (see also [4] for a similar claim). She also points out that the consequences of adopting no minimum cut-off point are serious as well, since short periods of silence — which cannot be considered as psychologically functional pauses — are required for articulation. Following the tradition initiated by Goldman-Eisler ([8], [9], [10], [11]), the present study adopts a cut-off point of 250 ms. for the definition of pause.

3. Pause Occurrence as a Narrative Boundary Predictor

Table 1 below displays the number of absolute occurrences of pauses at narrative boundaries, at boundaries that do not correspond to narrative boundaries and of pauses found elsewhere in the narratives.

Table 1. Distribution of pauses: total number of occurrences (percentages in parenthesis) at narrative boundaries, non-narrative boundaries and elsewhere, broken down for narratives and total values over narratives

Narratives	Narrative Boundary	Non-narrative Boundary	Elsewhere	Total
01	4 (36)	6 (55)	1 (9)	11
02	3 (23)	8 (62)	2 (15)	13
03	3 (13)	17 (74)	3 (13)	23
04	5 (29)	11 (65)	1 (6)	17
05	0 (0)	19 (66)	10 (34)	29
06	5 (15)	25 (74)	4 (11)	34
07	2 (11)	10 (53)	7 (36)	19
08	4 (27)	11 (73)	0 (0)	15
09	3 (20)	11 (73)	1 (7)	15
10	8 (18)	31 (67)	7 (15)	46
11	3 (17)	12 (67)	3 (16)	18
12	3 (22)	8 (57)	3 (21)	14
13	6 (27)	13 (59)	3 (14)	22
14	8 (33)	16 (67)	0 (0)	24
15	2 (20)	7 (70)	1 (10)	10
16	4 (45)	3 (33)	2 (22)	9
17	5 (26)	8 (42)	6 (32)	19
Total	68 (20)	216 (64)	54 (16)	338

The values in the above table should be considered with caution. Apparently, they suggest that pauses occur more often at non-narrative boundaries than at any other location (216 versus 122 pauses). This is true, if one takes into consideration the absolute numbers only. It is also true, however, that the number of boundaries that do not correspond to narrative boundaries in the data is much greater (510 versus 117). In other words, only 19% of all intonation boundaries in the narratives correspond to narrative boundaries. Therefore, the absolute numbers in Table 1 do not say much about the distribution of pauses in the data as a function of the type of boundary where they occur.

In order to determine whether the type of boundary determines the occurrence of pause in narrative discourse, the distribution of pauses at narrative and non-narrative boundaries must be considered as a function of the actual number of each type of boundary. The proportion of occurrence and non-occurrence of pauses in narrative and non-narrative boundaries can be found in the pareto chart below (Figure 1):

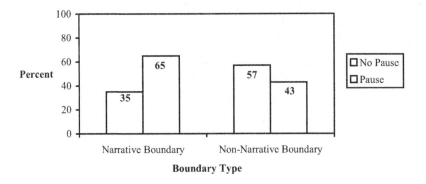

Fig. 1. Distribution of pauses at narrative and
non-narrative boundaries (pareto chart)

It is clear now that a pattern in terms of occurrence of pause in relation to type of boundary does exist in the present data. In 65% of the time that a boundary corresponds to the end/beginning of a narrative section, a pause will occur. If the boundary is not a narrative boundary, this number drops to 43%. This difference is statistically significant (χ^2=16.722, df=609, p<0.0001). Therefore, it's not always the case that an intonation unit boundary will determine the occurrence of a pause, as the literature proposes (Gee & Grosjean 1984; Rosenfield 1987). The occurrence of pause in discourse seems to be correlated with a higher-level segmentation.

Table 2 below gives the total number of narrative boundaries and occurrence of pauses in all seventeen narratives, giving a more detailed look at the distribution of pauses as a function of the type of boundary in the data:

Table 2. Total number of narrative boundaries and occurrence of pauses, broken down by narrative, and percentage values over narratives

Narratives	Boundaries	Pauses	%
01	4	4	100
02	4	3	75
03	4	3	75
04	7	5	71
05	6	0	0
06	8	5	63
07	4	2	50
08	4	4	100
09	6	3	50
10	10	8	80
11	6	3	50
12	6	3	50
13	8	6	75
14	8	8	100

Narratives	Boundaries	Pauses	%
15	3	2	67
16	8	3	37
17	7	5	71
Total	103	67	65

Three narratives in the data (01, 08 and 14) are characterized by the presence of a pause at *all narrative boundaries*, as Table 2 above reveals. However, exceptions are also present. Narrative 05, for example, contains no pauses at narrative boundaries at all. Notwithstanding, what seems to be pertinent here is that with the exception of narratives 05 and 16, all the other narratives present a minimum of 50% of pause occurrence in the narrative boundary condition.

These results indicate that pause occurrence is a reliable indicator of narrative boundary. The next step is to investigate whether pause duration also plays a role in the identifying of such boundary.

4. Pause Duration as a Narrative Boundary Signal

A number of studies confirm the general hypothesis concerning pause duration as an indicator of boundaries between larger discourse units: the longer a pause is, the greater the chances that the place where it occurs coincides with a major discursive break (see, for example, [5], [6], [12], [16], [17], [18], [20], [22], [28], [29], [31], among others). However, none of these authors attempt to relate *narrative structure* to pausal phenomena using an independent framework of narrative analysis.

Table 3 brings the mean values of duration for each narrative, as a function of the location where they occur.

Table 3. Mean pause duration (standard deviation in parenthesis) at narrative boundaries, non-narrative boundaries and elsewhere, broken down for narratives and total values over narratives. The duration values are expressed in seconds

Narratives	Narrative Boundary	Non-narrative Boundary	Elsewhere	Average
01	1.32 (0.89)	0.77 (0.33)	0.43 (N/A)	0.94 (0.63)
02	0.49 (0.18)	0.72 (0.27)	0.68 (0.18)	0.66 (0.25)
03	0.79 (0.24)	0.79 (0.30)	0.65 (0.27)	0.77 (0.28)
04	1.12 (0.44)	0.72 (0.38)	0.40 (N/A)	0.82 (0.43)
05	N/A	0.76 (0.43)	0.88 (0.24)	0.80 (0.37)
06	1.57 (0.49)	0.95 (0.68)	0.54 (0.29)	0.99 (0.67)
07	0.98 (0.99)	0.67 (0.24)	0.62 (0.33)	0.68 (0.27)
08	0.81 (0.44)	0.74 (0.30)	N/A	0.76 (0.33)
09	0.97 (0.55)	0.85 (0.44)	0.62 (N/A)	0.86 (0.44)
10	0.63 (0.11)	0.63 (0.32)	0.43 (0.15)	0.60 (0.28)
11	0.35 (0.11)	0.57 (0.28)	0.36 (0.05)	0.50 (0.25)

Narratives	Narrative Boundary	Non-narrative Boundary	Elsewhere	Average
12	0.86 (0.21)	0.62 (0.26)	0.92 (0.47)	0.74 (0.31)
13	1.32 (0.57)	1.07 (0.78)	1.20 (0.68)	1.15 (0.70)
14	0.58 (0.33)	0.55 (0.33)	N/A	0.56 (0.32)
15	0.87 (0.86)	0.47 (0.20)	0.59 (N/A)	0.56 (0.37)
16	1.00 (0.37)	0.55 (0.03)	0.51 (0.03)	0.74 (0.34)
17	0.92 (0.48)	0.77 (0.32)	0.73 (0.25)	0.79 (0.34)
Average	0.92 (0.51)	0.74 (0.44)	0.68 (0.33)	0.76 (0.44)

The mean duration of pauses occurring at narrative boundaries (0.92 s) differs significantly from those occurring at non-narrative boundaries (0.74 s). T-test result ($t=-2.821$, $df=282$, $p<0.01$) confirms this finding by showing a significant correlation between narrative boundary and longer pause duration.

Again, a considerable amount of variation within narratives can be seen. Narratives 02, 03, 05, 10 and 11 do not follow the general pattern. The mean duration of pauses at narrative and non-narrative boundaries are the same for narratives 03 and 10, while narratives 02 and 11 have a mean pause duration longer at non-narrative boundaries than at narrative boundaries. As discussed above, narrative 05 does not present any pauses at all at narrative boundaries. This is of course an exception.

Interestingly, narrative 05 is also inconsistent with the others in that it displays a high mean duration of pauses at *non-boundary* sites. Only narrative 12 shares this property. It should be pointed out, however, that while narrative 05 presents a large number of pauses at locations that do not correspond to any type of boundary (a total of 10 out of 29), narrative 12 has only a few (a total of 03 out of 14). Nonetheless, two of these pauses are also the longest in the whole narrative.

Analyses of variance were carried out with "pause duration" as a dependent variable and "narrative" and "participant" as fixed factors. Results show significant effects for both "narrative" (F $(16,283)=3.04$, $p<0.0001$) and "participant" (F $(7,283)=6.2866$, $p<0.001$). Post-hoc tests (Tukey-Kramer multiple comparisons) for "narrative" show that narrative 13 differs significantly from narratives 10, 14, 15 and 11 and that narrative 06 also differ from the same ones except for 15. Note that both narratives (13 and 06) were produced by the same participant (08). As for the variable "participant," Tukey-Kramer tests reveal that participant 08 differs significantly from participants 5, 7, 4, 3 and 2, while participant 1 differs significantly from participant 3 only. Table 2.6 below brings the actual mean duration of pause for each participant, along with standard deviations.

Table 4. Mean pause duration and the corresponding standard deviation for each participant. Values are expressed in seconds

Narrative	01	02	03	04	05	06	07	08
Mean duration	0.85	0.61	0.60	0.63	0.77	0.76	0.80	1.06
Sd	0.41	0.32	0.30	0.32	0.33	0.43	0.25	0.68

Participant 8 (narratives 01, 06 and 13) not only has the longest average pause duration, but also the largest standard deviation. Some of the pauses that are employed in the narratives produced by participant 8 were, in relation to the others, exceptionally long, contributing to the large standard deviation displayed in Table 4. Long pauses constitute, most of the time, what [7] calls "semantic" pauses.

What is important to highlight is that both pause occurrence and pause duration prove to be significant predictors of narrative boundary. Narrative boundaries are characterized by the presence of a pause of longer duration, while non-narrative boundaries do not require the presence of a pause. When they occur, they tend to be shorter than those at narrative boundaries.

5. Conclusion

It was hypothesized here, on the basis of the Labovian model of narrative analysis, that pausing reflects narrative structure — longer pauses are more likely to occur at the end of a narrative section than elsewhere in a narrative. The analyses confirmed the hypotheses. It was demonstrated that pausing is a strong indicator of narrative boundary: at the end of a narrative section, storytellers often produce a pause of longer duration to indicate that a given 'chunk of information' is completed and that a new 'chunk' is about to begin. This is in accordance with the findings in both psycholinguistic research (see [1], [2], [10], [23], [32], among others) and computational linguistic research (see [12], [149, [15], [22], [24], [25], [30], among others). Longer pauses are extremely important in the production of speech for two reasons. First, they give the speaker time to adequately formulate the next group of information. Second, they are very significant in speech perception, because they help the audience to cognitively digest the input.

References

1. Butterworth, B.: Evidence from pause in speech. In B. Butterworth. Language Production: Speech and Talk. Academic Press, London (1980) 155-176.
2. Brotherton, P.: Speaking and not speaking; Process for translating ideas into speech. In A. Siegman & S. Feldestein. Of Time and Speech. Lawrence Erlbaum, Hillsdale, N. J. (1979) 178-209.
3. Collier, R., Piyper, J. R. d. & Sanderman, A: Perceived prosodic boundaries and their phonetic correlates. Proceeding of the ARPA Workshop on Human Language Technology. Morgan Kaufman Publishers, Plainsboro, New Jersey, USA (1993).
4. Dalton, P. & Hardcastle, W. J.: Disorders of Fluency an Their Effects on Communication. London (1977).
5. Gee, J. P. & Grosjean, F.: Empirical evidence for narrative structure. Cognitive Science 8 (1984) 59-85.
6. Gee, J. P. & Kegl, J. A.: Narrative/story structure, pausing and ASL. Discourse Processes 9 (1983) 391-422.
7. Glukhov, A. A.: Statistical analysis of speech pauses for Romance and Germanic languages. Soviet Physics. Acoustics 21 (1975) 71-72.

8. Goldman-Eisler, F.: Speech analysis and mental processes. Language and Speech 1 (1958) 59-75.
9. Goldman-Eisler, F.: The rate of changes in the rate of articulation. Language and Speech 4 (1961) 171-174.
10. Goldman-Eisler, F.: Psycholinguistics: experiments in spontaneous speech. Academic Press, London, New York (1968).
11. Goldman-Eisler, F. Pauses, clauses, sentences. Language and Speech 15 (1972) 103-113.
12. Grosz, B. & Hirschberg, J.: Some intonational characteristics of discourse structure. Proceeding of the International Conference on Spoken Language Processing, Banff (1992).
13. Hieke, A. E., Kowal, S. & O'Connell, D. C.: The trouble with "articulatory pauses". Language and Speech 26 (1983) 203-214.
14. Hirschberg, J. & Grosz, B.: Intonation features of local and global discourse structure. Proceeding of the DARPA Workshop on Spoken Language Systems, Arden House (1992).
15. Hirschberg, J., Nakatani, C. H. & Grosz, B. J.: Conveying discourse structure through intonation variation. Proceeding of the ESCA Workshop on Spoken Dialogue Systems: Theories and Applications. ESCA, Visgo, Denmark (1995).
16. Kowal, S. & O'Connell, D. C.: Some temporal aspects of stories told while or after watching a film. Bulletin of the Psychonomic Society 25(5) (1987) 364-366.
17. Kowal, S., O'Connell, D. C. & Sabin, E. J.: Development of temporal patterning and vocal hesitation in spontaneous narratives. Journal of Psycholinguistic Research 4 (1975) 195-207.
18. Kowal, S., Wiese, S. & O'Connell, D.: The use of time in storytelling. Language and Speech 26(4) (1983) 377-392.
19. Labov, W.: The transformation of experience in narrative syntax. Language in the inner City. University of Pennsylvania Press, Philadelphia (1972) 354-98.
20. Levin, H., Schaffer, C. & Snow, C.: The Prosodic and Paralinguistic Features of Reading and Telling Stories. Language and Speech 25(1) (1982) 43-54.
21. Levin, H., Silverman, I. & Ford, B.: Hesitations in children's speech during explanation and description. Journal of Verbal Learning and Verbal Behavior 6 (1965) 560-564.
22. Litman, D. J. & Passonneau, R. J.: Empirical evidence for intention-based discourse segmentation. Proceeding of the ACL Workshop on Intentionality and Structure in Discourse Relations (1993).
23. Maclay, H. & Osgood, C. E.: Hesitation phenomena in spontaneous English speech. Word 15 (1959) 19.
24. Nakatani, C.: Accenting on pronouns and proper names in spontaneous narratives. Proceeding of the ESCA Workshop on Prosody, Lund, Sweden (1993).
25. Nakatani, C. H. & Hirschberg, J.: Discourse structure in spoken language: Studies on speech corpora. Proceeding of the AAAI Symposium Series: Empirical Methods in Discourse Interpretation and Generation (1995).
26. Oliveira, M.: Prosodic Features in Spontaneous Narratives. Ph.D. Thesis, Simon Fraser University (2000).
27. O'Connell, D. C. & Kowal, S.: Pausology. In W. A. Sedelow & S. Y. Sedelow. Computers in Language Research 2. Mouton Publishers, Berlin, New York, Amsterdam (1983) 221-301.
28. Pakosz, M. & Flashner, V.: Prosodic features and narrative strategies. Papers and studies in contrastive linguistics 24 (1988) 33-46.
29. Passonneau, R. J. & Litman, D. J. : Intention-based segmentation: Human reliability and correlation with linguistic cues. Proceeding of the 31st Annual Meeting of the Association for Computational Linguistics (ACL-93), Columbus, Ohio (1993).
30. Passonneau, R. J. & Litman, D. J.: Discourse Segmentation by Human and Automated Means. Computational Linguistics 23(1) (1997) 103-139.
31. Rosenfield, B.: Pauses in Oral and written Narratives. Boston University, Boston (1987).

32. Siegman, A. & Feldestein, S. (eds.): Of Time and Speech. Lawrence Erlbaum, Hillsdale, N. J. (1979).
33. Siegman, A. W. & Pope, B.: Ambiguity and verbal fluency in the TAT. Journal of Consulting Psychology 30 (1966) 239-245.
34. Stenström, A.-B.: Pauses in monologue and dialogue. In E. Svartvik. The London-Lund Corpus of Spoken English. Description and Research. Lund University Press, Lund (1990) 211-252.
35. Wolfson, N.: Speech events and natural speech. Language in Society 5 (1976) 189-209.

A Grammar-Based System to Solve Temporal Expressions in Spanish Texts*

Patricio Martínez-Barco, Estela Saquete, and Rafael Muñoz

Departamento de Lenguajes y Sistemas Informáticos
Universidad de Alicante
Carretera de San Vicente del Raspeig - Alicante - Spain
Tel. +34965903653 Fax.+34965909326
patricio@dlsi.ua.es, Estela.Saquete@ua.es, rafael@dlsi.ua.es

Abstract. This paper shows a system for the recognition of temporal expressions in Spanish and the resolution of their temporal reference. The system is based on a temporal expression (TE) grammar and an inference engine for the identification and recognition of temporal expressions, and for the resolution respectively. The inference engine includes the necessary information to perform the date operation based on the recognized expressions. For further information treatment, the output is proposed by means of XML tags in order to add standard information of the absolute dates obtained.

1 Introduction

Several studies about temporal expressions (TE) have been developed in the last years. Basically, the core of these methods is the use of a temporal model that is able to interpret different formats for date and time expressions. One of the most relevant studies was developed in [3, 7]. This model is based on the application of empirical methods using the focus theory proposed in [2].

In this paper a proposal of a temporal model based on grammar for the recognition of TEs in Spanish is presented, as well as an approximation to the resolution of the anaphoric relations introduced by them, as is explained in [6]. The domain is restricted to articles published at online newspapers. In a text of that kind of domain there are dates with typical representations like, for example: 23/01/2000 o *23 de enero del 2000* (23rd of January of 2000), but we can find references to dates named previously too, for example: *dos días antes* (two days before), *la semana anterior* (the previous week), etc. This kind of anaphoric relation should be solved and mapped to dates with a standard format for a more efficient analysis of the text. For that, we use a grammar for the recognition of TEs with its correspondent temporal parser, and a inference engine where we keep the rules that permits to map these expressions in a standard format that we have chosen: dd/mm/yyyy. Once the kind of reference and the interpretation

---

* This paper has been supported by the Spanish Government (MCYT) under grant TIC2000-0664-C02-01/02.

E.M. Ranchhod and N.J. Mamede (Eds.): PorTAL 2002, LNAI 2389, pp. 53–61, 2002.

of the expression is solved, it is very easy to tag the text with the XML tags we have defined. Successful results have been obtained after the evaluation of this proposal.

2   Recognition of Temporal Expressions and Its Temporal Reference

In Figure 1 the graphic representation of the system proposed for the recognition of TEs and for the resolution of its references is shown, according to the temporal model proposed. The texts are tagged with lexical and morphological information and this information is the input to the temporal parser. This temporal parser is implemented using an ascending technique (chart parser) and it is based on the grammar we show below. Once the parser recognizes the TEs in the text, these are introduced into the resolution unit, which will update the value of the reference according to the date it is referring and generate the XML tags for each expression. We can find anaphoric and not anaphoric TEs. The grammar in Tables 1 and 2 is used to discriminate between anaphoric and not anaphoric expressions.

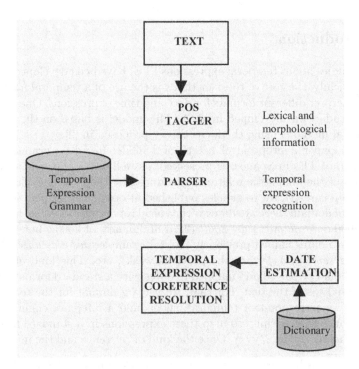

Fig. 1. Graphic representation of the system proposed

The parser uses a grammar based on two different kinds of rules. On one hand there are rules for the date and time recognition (non-anaphoric expressions 12/06/1975) and on the other hand there are rules for the temporal reference recognition (anaphoric TEs that need the location of another complete TE to be understood "two days before"). The grammar proposed recognize the large amount of date and time formats. In Table 1 a sample of some of the rules that have been defined in our system for the date recognition can be observed[1].

```
fecha→ dd+'/'+mm+'/'+(yy)yy                              (12/06/1975)
                                                        (06/12/1975)
fecha→ dd+'-'+mes+'-'+(yy)yy                         (12-junio-1975)
                                                      (12-Jun.-1975)
fecha→ dd+'de'+mm+'de'+(yy)yy                  (12 de junio de 1975)
                                             (12th of June of 1975)
fecha→ ('El')+diasemana+dd+'de'+mes+'de'+(yy)yy
                                    (El domingo 12 de junio de 1975)
                                     (Sunday, 12th of June of 1975)
fecha→ mes+'de'+yy(yy)                             (Febrero de 1975)
                                                 (February of 1975)
fecha→ dd+'de'+mes+'de'+(yy)yy+'a las'+hora
                              (12 de junio de 1975 a las 6 y media)
                              (12th of June of 1975 at half past six)
dd→ ['01'||'02'||'03'||...||'31']
dia→ ['uno'||'dos'||...||'treinta y uno']      [one||two||...||thirty one]
mm→ ['01'||'02'||'03'||...||'12']
mes→ ['enero'||'febrero'||'marzo'||'abril'||'mayo'||'junio'||'julio'
      ||'agosto'||'septiembre'||'octubre'||'noviembre'||'diciembre']
                        (January||February||March||April||May||June||July
                      ||August||September||October||November||December)
a→ ['1'||'2'||'3'||...||'9'||'0']
diasemana→ ['lunes'||'martes'||'miércoles'||'jueves'||'viernes'
                                          ||'sábado'||'domingo']
          (Monday||Tuesday||Wednesday||Thursday||Friday||Saturday||Sunday)
hora→ hh+':'+mm+(':'+ss)                                      (time)
hora→ (hh+('y'||'menos')+'cuarto'||hh+'y media'||...)
                            (a quarter past||to)||a half past||...)
```

Table 1. Sample of rules for the dates recognition

There are two types of temporal references that should be treated: the time adverbs (i.e. yesterday, tomorrow) and the nominal phrases that are referring to

---

[1] The nomenclature in which the rules are above-mentioned is the one used in the data dictionaries of the information systems. Words between brackets are optional, words between square brackets, [ ] mean that only one of them appear in the rule and words between keys, { } will be repeated one or more times in the rule.

temporal relationships (i.e. the day after, the day before). In Table 2 we show some of the rules used for the detection of every kind of reference.

Time Adverbs	referencia→ 'ayer' *(yesterday)* referencia→ 'mañana' *(tomorrow)* referencia→ 'anteayer' *(the day before yesterday)* referencia→ 'anoche' *(last night)*

Temporal Nominal Phrases	referencia→ 'el próximo'+['día'‖'mes'‖'año']
	                                       (the next day‖month‖year)
	referencia→ 'un'+['día'‖'mes'‖'año']+'después'
	                                     (a day‖month‖year later)
	referencia→ num+['días'‖'meses'‖'años']+'después'
	                               (num days‖months‖years later)
	referencia→ 'un'+['día'‖'mes'‖'año']+'antes'
	                                     (a day‖month‖year before)
	referencia→ num+['días'‖'meses'‖'años']+'antes'
	                               (num days‖months‖years before)
	referencia→ 'dentro'+'de'+'un'+['día'‖'mes'‖'año']
	                                 (within a day‖month‖year)
	referencia→ 'dentro'+'de'+num+['días'‖'meses'‖'años']
	                             (within num days‖months‖years)
	referencia→ 'el pasado'+['día'‖'mes'‖'año']
	                                   (the last day‖month‖year)
	referencia→ 'el'+['día'‖'mes'‖'año']+'siguiente'
	                                   (the next day‖month‖year)
	referencia→ 'los'+num+['días'‖'meses'‖'años']+'siguientes'
	                             (the num next days‖months‖years)
	referencia→ 'el'+['día'‖'mes'‖'año']+'pasado'
	                                   (the last day‖month‖year)
	referencia→ 'los'+num+['días'‖'meses'‖'años']+'pasados'
	                             (the last num days‖months‖years)
	num→ ['dos'‖'tres'‖'cuatro'‖'cinco'‖...]
	                                     (two‖three‖four‖five‖...)

Table 2. Sample of rules for the reference recognition

3   Anaphoric Relation Resolution Based on a Temporal Model

For the anaphoric relation resolution we use a inference engine that interpretes every reference named before. In some cases the references are estimated using the newspaper's date (FechaP). Others refer to a date named before in the text that is being analysed (FechaA). For these cases, a temporal model that allows to know over what date the dictionary operations are going to be done, is defined.

This model is based on the two rules below and it is only applicable to these dates that are not FechaP, since for FechaP there is nothing to resolve:

1. By default, the newspaper's date is used as a base referent (TE) if it exits, if not, the system date is used.
2. In case of finding a non-anaphoric TE, it is stored as FechaA. This value is updated everytime that a non-anaphoric TE appears in the text.

Moreover, some functions will be used, like Day(date), Month(date), and Year(date) that provides the day, the month and the year respectively. DayI and DayF represent the first and the last day of the month.

The operation "+1" used in some entries of the dictionary is able to interpret the dates to give a correct date. That is, if the function Mes(date) returns 12 and the operation "+1" is applied over that value, the return value will be 01 and one year will be increased. In Table 3 some of the entries of the dictionary used in the inference engine are shown.

REFERENCE	DICCIONARY ENTRY
'ayer' *(yesterday)*	Day(FechaP)-1/Month(FechaP)/Year(FechaP)
'anteayer' *(the day before yesterday)*	Day(FechaP)-2/Month(FechaP)/Year(FechaP)
'anoche' *(last night)*	Day(FechaP)-1/Month(FechaP)/Year(FechaP) [09:00-05:00]
'el próximo día' *(the next day)*	Day(FechaP)+1/Month(FechaP)/Year(FechaP)
'un mes después' *(a month later)*	[DayI/Month(FechaA)+1/Year(FechaA)-- DayF/Month(FechaA)+1/Year(FechaA)]
num+'años después' *(num years later)*	[01/01/Year(FechaA)+num -- 31/12/Year(FechaA)+num]
'un día antes' *(a day before)*	Day(FechaA)-1/Month(FechaA)/Year(FechaA)
'dentro de un año' *(within a year)*	[01/01/Year(FechaA)+1 -- 31/12/Year(FechaA)+1]
'dentro de'+num+'días' *(within num days)*	Day(FechaA)+num/Month(FechaA)/Year(FechaA)
'el mes siguiente' *(the next month)*	[DayI/Month(FechaA)+1/Year(FechaA) -- DayF/Month(FechaA)+1/Year(FechaA)]
'los'+num+'meses pasados' *(the num last months)*	[DayI/Month(FechaA)-num/Year(FechaA) -- DayF/Month(FechaA)-1/Year(FechaA)]

Table 3. Sample of some of the entries of the dictionary

Moreover, the inference engine has the relationship between numeric and string expressions of days and months, that is, one have the value 1 and July is 07.

4   Tagging of Temporal Expressions

Several proposals for the annotation of TEs have been arisen in the last few years [8] [4] since some research institutions have started to work on different aspects of temporal information. However there is not a consensus on what and how temporal information should be identified in text. In this section, a set of XML tags is defined in order to standardize anaphoric and non-anaphoric TEs. Our proposal is driven by a dual motivation: a) to reflect the results of our temporal-reference resolution system and b) to standardize the date-time format in Internet texts. In Table 4, a sample of this tagging is shown. These tags show the following structure:

```
<DATE_TIME(_REF) TYPE="value" VALDATE1="value" VALTIME1="value"
VALDATE2="value" VALTIME2="value" >expression</DATE_TIME>
```

Where DATE_TIME is the name of the tag for non-anaphoric TEs, and VAL-DATE# and VALTIME# store the range of dates and times obtained from the inference engine. Moreover, VALDATE2 and VALTIME2 is used to establish ranges. Also, VALTIME1 could be omitted if only a date is specified. VAL-DATE2, VALTIME1 and VALTIME2 are optional args.

After that, an structured document is obtained. The use of XML allows us to take advantage of the XML schema in which the tag language is defined. This schema let an application know if the XML file is valid and well-formed. The schema defines the different kind of elements, attributes and entities that are allowed, and can express some limitations to combine them. Moreover, it uses the same syntax the schemata can be extended. Once the XML file has been generated, a parser of our XML needs to be defined to make the information useful.

The unit that makes the estimation of the dates will accede to the right entry in the inference engine in each case and it will apply the function specified obtaining a date in the format dd/mm/yyyy or a range of dates. So, at that point the anaphoric relation will have been resolved.

Next, two examples where the tagging has been performed are shown:

(a) La oficina de Congresos de la Universidad ha propuesto 5 congresos
    para <DATE_TIME_REF VALDATE1="01/01/2000" VALDATE2="31/12/2000">
    este año </DATE_TIME_REF>, sin embargo, el crecimiento para
    <DATE_TIME_REF VALDATE1="01/01/2001" VALDATE2="31/12/2001"> el próximo
    año</DATE_TIME_REF> será superior a los 15. Por otro lado, el Director
    de la oficina ofrece <DATE_TIME_REF VALDATE1="26/04/2000" > mañana
    </DATE_TIME_REF> una conferencia.

ABSOLUTE TAGS (non-anaphoric TEs)

`<DATE_TIME VALDATE1="12/06/2001">`
  `12 de junio de 2001`
`</DATE_TIME>`

`<DATE_TIME VALDATE1="12/06/2001" VALTIME1="20:30">`
  `12 de junio de 2001 a las ocho y media de la tarde`
`</DATE_TIME>`

`<DATE_TIME VALDATE1="12/06/2001" VALTIME1="20:00"`
              `VALDATE2="12/06/2001" VALTIME2="21:00" >`
  `12 de junio de 2001 entre las ocho y las nueve de la tarde`
`</DATE_TIME>`

REFERENCE TAGS (anaphoric TEs)

`<DATE_TIME_REF VALDATE1="11/06/2002">`
  `ayer`
`</DATE_TIME_REF>`

`<DATE_TIME_REF VALDATE1="01/01/2002" VALDATE2="31/12/2007">`
  `los 5 años siguientes`
`</DATE_TIME_REF>`

Table 4. Sample of the tags generated

(*The University Conference Office has proposed 5 conferences for [this year], how-ever, the increase for [the next year] will be over 15. On the other hand, the Office Manager offers [tomorrow] a lecture*)
Assumed that the newspaper's date is 25/04/2000, the system returns a period of time [01/01/2001-31/12/2001] for the reference *el próximo año* (the next year) and 26/04/2000 for the reference *mañana* (tomorrow).

(b) `El <DATE_TIME VALDATE1="25/01/1999">25 de enero de 1999</DATE_TIME>,`
`la Oficina de Congresos de la Universidad de Alicante propuso dos`
`congresos que fueron cancelados <DATE_TIME_REF VALDATE1="27/01/1999">`
`dos días después </DATE_TIME_REF>`
(*The 25th of January of 1999, the University Conference Office of Alicante pro-posed two conferences that were cancelled two days later*)
In this case there is a date in the text before the reference. This date will be detected as 25/01/1999, so that the reference *dos días después* (two days later) will be translated as 27/01/1999.

5 System Evaluation

In the system above, two different units have been implemented. On one hand a parser has been implemented in LPA Prolog, because this language based on logic programming provides simple tools for the grammar construction making the implementation of parsers easier. However, Visual Basic was the program-ming language used for the implementation of the temporal anaphoric relation resolution unit because it includes a large amount of tools for handling dates and defining date operations. The definition of an appropriate interface has allowed the interconnection between the two units. Finally, the evaluation of the system has been done with a sample extracted from 16 articles. These articles belong to the digital edition on the Internet of two Spanish newspapers describing international news.

The total number of TE(237) in the corpus was manually verified; from these, the system was able to identify 204, but it only tagged 195 accurately. Thus, the recall was 82,28 % and the precision 95,55 %.

Although the obtained results are highly successful, we have detected some fails that have been deeply analyzed. As it can be observed by the results, our system could be improved in some aspects. Below, a study of the problems detected and their possible improvements is shown:

- The unit that resolve the temporal references is not able to resolve undetermined temporal references like: *hace unos cuantos días* (some days before) accurately. A human could give an approximate interpretation of its reference, but never a specific date o range of dates. We probably take a decision here using semantic information. For example, if the sentence is "some days before", the system will suppose that is less time than a week, because we usually use the word "week" referring to seven days.
- In the newspaper's articles, sometimes there are expressions like *el sábado hubo cinco accidentes en la N-III* (Saturday there were five accidents in the N-III road). To resolve this kind of references we should need context information of the sentence where the reference is. That information could be the time of the sentence's verb. If the verb is a past verb, that indicates us that we have to solve a reference like *el sábado pasado* (last Saturday), whereas if it is a future verb it refers to *el sábado próximo* (the next Saturday). Because of our system does not use semantic or context information we assume this kind of reference is referring to the last day, not the next, because the news usually tells us facts occurred previously.
- It is possible we have expressions that make reference to an event or a fact and, despite they are not TEs themselves, they have implicit the date o period of time when it occurred. For example: *ganó el mundial y al día siguiente se lesionó* (he won the World Champion and the next day he hurt himself). In that case, *el mundial* has implicit the date when it was celebrated, and this date will be need to resolve *el día siguiente*.

6   Conclusions

In this paper a system for TEs recognition and their reference resolution has been presented, based on a temporal model proposed. The system has two different units: the parser based on a TE grammar, which allows to identify these kind of expressions and a anaphoric relation resolution unit which is based in a inference engine and make a transformation of the expressions to dates, resolving their reference in this way. The evaluation of the system shows successful results of precision and recall for our proposal.

For future works, it is pretended to extend the system with the temporal references that are not treated in this paper. Moreover, the study of the verbal forms in the sentences where the references are found will improve the system efficiency solving some kind of expressions as proposed in [5].

References

[1] *ACL Workshop On Temporal And Spatial Information Processing*, Toulouse (France), 2001.

[2] B. Grosz and C. Sidner. Attentions, intentions and the structure of discourse. *Computational Linguistics*, 12:175–204, March 1986.

[3] R. Guillén, D. Farwell, and J. Wiebe. Handling temporal relations in scheduling dialogues for an mt system. Technical report, Computing Research Laboratory, New Mexico State University. Las Cruces, New Mexico., 1995.

[4] G. Kameyama and F. Arosio. The Annotation of Temporal Information in Natural Language Sentences. In *Proceedings of the ACL Workshop On Temporal And Spatial Information Processing* [1].

[5] H. Kamp and U. Reyle. *From Discourse to Logic.* Kluwer Academic Publisher, Dordrecht, The Netherlands, 1993.

[6] E. Saquete and P. Martínez-Barco. Grammar Specification for the Recognition of Temporal Expressions. In *Proceedings of the Machine Translation and multilingual applications in the new millennium, MT2000*, pages 21.1–21.7, Exeter, UK, 2000.

[7] J.M. Wiebe, T.P. O'Hara, T. Ohrstrom-Sandgren, and K.J. McKeever. An Empirical Approach to Temporal Reference Resolution. *Journal of Artificial Intelligence Research*, 9:247–293, 1998.

[8] G. Wilson, B. Sundheim, and L. Ferro. A Multilingual Approach to Annotating and Extracting Temporal Information. In *Proceedings of the ACL Workshop On Temporal And Spatial Information Processing* [1].

Semantic Information in Anaphora Resolution

R. Muñoz, M. Saiz-Noeda, and A. Montoyo

Grupo de investigación del Procesamiento del Lenguaje y Sistemas de Información.
Departamento de Lenguajes y Sistemas Informáticos. Universidad de Alicante. Spain
{rafael,max,montoyo}@dsli.ua.es

Abstract. Building a NLP system requires the adding of linguistic phenomena resolution. One of the most relevant tasks regarding to these phenomena is the coreference resolution. Coreference is defined as a semantic phenomenon and, therefore, apart from the morphological and syntactic information that is highly useful, adding semantic sources improves the capabilities of such a NLP system. In this paper, a complete NLP system is proposed. This system counts on a WSD module that provide semantic information needed for the coreference resolution. This coreference resolution will deal with both pronouns and definite descriptions (DD), two of the most important parts of the anaphora resolution research area. The WSD module is a variant of the Specification Marks Method [7] where for each word in a text a domain label is selected instead of a sense label.

1 Introduction

Coreference resolution consists of establishing a relation between an anaphoric expression and an antecedent. Different kinds of anaphoric expressions can be located in the text, such as pronouns, DDs, etc. Moreover, different information sources are needed in order to guarantee an adequate resolution. The majority of the anaphora resolvers, extensively cited at the literature, only use morphological and syntactic information [3, 6, 10]. In this paper, we focus on the resolution of pronouns and DDs using morphological, syntactic and semantic information.

The need of semantic information adds a new problem to be solved, Word Sense Disambiguation (WSD), which is one of the most important task for any natural language processing system. Therefore, we propose a way to deal with this problem starting with the hypothesis that many sense distinctions are not relevant for anaphora resolution [14, 5]. Moreover, we want to investigate how the polysemy reduction caused by domain clustering can help to improve the anaphora resolution. In this paper we propose to use a variant of the Specification Marks Method [7] where for each word in a text a domain label is selected instead of a sense label.

2 Preprocessing and Resources

In this section we describe the tools and resources employed in developing a new method, based on semantic information, to anaphora resolution in unrestricted

E.M. Ranchhod and N.J. Mamede (Eds.): PorTAL 2002, LNAI 2389, pp. 63–70, 2002.

Spanish texts. The Spanish text goes through a preprocessing stage. The first step in preprocessing consists of using a part-of-speech (POS) tagger to automatically assign morphological information (POS tags). Next, it also performs a surface syntactic parsing using dependency links that show the head-modifier relations between words. This kind of information is used for extracting NPs constituent parts, and these NPs are the input for a Word Sense Disambiguation module. This module returns all the head nouns with a domain sense assigned from all the head nouns that appear in the context of a sentence. Figure 1 shows WSD process and the resources used by this module:

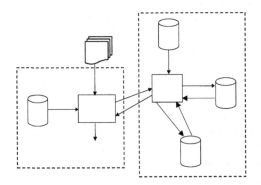

Fig. 1. *Process and resources used by WSD module*

- Spanish WordNet is a generic database with 30,000 senses. The Spanish WordNet will be linked through the English WordNet 1.5, so each English synonym will be associated with its equivalent in Spanish.
- WordNet 1.5 mapped to WordNet 1.6 is a complete mapping of the nominal, verbal, adjetival and adverbial parts of WordNet 1.5 onto WordNet 1.6 [1]
- WordNet Domain [4] is an extension of WordNet 1.6 where synsets are clustered by means of domain labels.

3   Domain Specification Marks Method

The WSD method used in this paper consists of a variant of the Specification Marks Method, which we named Domain Specification Marks Method (DSMM), where for each head noun in a text a domain label is selected instead of a sense label. The Specification Marks Method (SMM) is applied for the automatic resolution of lexical ambiguity of groups of words, whose different possible senses are related. The disambiguation is resolved with the use of the Spanish WordNet lexical knowledge base. This method requires the knowledge of how many of the words are grouped around a Specification Mark, which is similar to a semantic class in the WordNet taxonomy. The word sense in the subhierarchy that contains the greatest number of words for the corresponding Specification Mark will be chosen for the sense disambiguation of a noun in a given group of words. It has been shown in [8] that the SMM works successfully with groups of words that are semantically related. Therefore, a relevant consequence of the application of this method with domain labels is the reduction of the word polysemy (i.e. the number of domains for a word is generally lower than the number of senses for the word). That is, domain labels (i.e. Health, Sport, etc) provide a way to establish semantic relations among word senses, grouping them into clusters. Detailed explanation of the Specification Marks Method can be found in [7]. Next, we describe the steps to obtain the domain label of WordNet Domain from the word sense obtained by SMM:

1. Starting from the Spanish word sense already disambiguated by the SMM, we should obtain the corresponding synset in WordNet 1.5. For this task, the Spanish WordNet has been used to disambiguate the Spanish word sense. It allows us to calculate the intersections among the Spanish synsets and the English synsets version 1.5. For example, the output of the SMM applied to the word "planta → *plant*" is the Spanish Synset "Planta#2". As the two WordNets are linked (i.e. they share synset offsets), therefore the intersection determines the synset of WordNet 1.5, which is "Plant#2".

2. WordNet 1.5 is mapped with the WordNet 1.6, therefore the synsets obtained in step 1 are searched in this resource. Then, the synset 1.6 corresponding to the previous synset 1.5 is obtained. For example, the synset 1.5 "plant#2" is mapped to the synset 1.6 "Plant#2".

3. Finally, the synset 1.6 obtained in step 2 is searched for in the WordNet Domain, where the synsets have been annotated with one or more domain labels. For example, the synset 1.6 "00008864" belonging to the sense "plant#2" is searched for in the WordNet Domain giving the label "botany".

4 Anaphora Resolution

Anaphora is one of the most frequent linguistic phenomena used that should be solved in order to establish the coherence in a text. Different kinds of anaphoric expressions can be found in the text, such as pronouns, DDs and adjectives. Each type of anaphoric expression needs a specific way of resolution due to their different features. Pronouns and DDs are the most usual grammatical expressions used to refer to a person, and object, an event, etc. All NPs used to describe the same specific concept, the same entity of real world, will be related or closed in some way.

We illustrate in figure 2 the proposed architecture for resolving the anaphora. The following section shows both method to solve pronouns and DD using the previously described domain labels.

4.1 Pronoun Resolution

Pronominal anaphora, unlike others, requires a special treatment from the semantical point of view. In general, pronouns do not provide semantic information

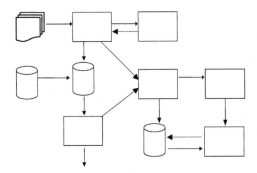

Fig. 2. *Architecture for resolving the anaphora*

at all. This fact forces the use of the semantic information provided by the verb accompanied by the anaphor. Through the verb, it is possible to establish connections between the pronoun and its possible antecedent due to the antecedent must be semantically compatible with the verb of the anaphor which refers to and in its same syntactic role. According to this, the application of semantic knowledge in pronoun resolution requires not only morphological and syntactic analysis but also semantic features related to candidate NPs and verbs. Traditional approaches based on limited knowledge have used morphological agreement and syntactic restrictions in order to reject incompatible candidates. Furthermore, some approaches have included also the semantic information defining compatibility relations between nouns (subjects and complements) and verbs through collocation patterns manually stated in order to be applied in the resolution process.

The automatic obtention of this patterns from the corpus would allow the application of the pronoun resolution method in any domain. In this way, the pronoun resolution module included in this system will deal with personal, demonstrative, reflexive and omitted pronouns. Next section will show the detailed aspects of this pronoun resolution algorithm.

Algorithm for Pronoun Resolution The algorithm go through different steps:

- Pronoun identification: the text has been previously morphologically tagged and syntactically parsed. This syntactic parsing includes also information about syntactic roles of the NPs and pronouns. In this step, the pronoun is detected through its morphological label. This step also includes a set of rules for the identification of omitted pronouns.
- Candidate list construction: depending on the type of pronoun, the algorithm selects the *solution searching space*, that is, the minimum portion of text where the correct antecedent should be found. According to this, the reflexive pronouns will find the solution in the same clause, while personal and demostrative pronouns will find it no more than two sentences before. All the

NPs contained in this solution searching space are added to the candidate list with all their morpho-syntactic information.

- Semantic pattern set building: while processing the corpus, all the noun in a subject, direct object or indirect object role are included with their corresponding verbs into a set of semantic patterns. Patterns are formed not only by the textual word but by the semantic domain concepts obtained from the WSD module.
- Constraint application: morphological agreement, and syntactic restrictions are applied in order to reject incompatible candidates. Classical morpho-syntactic rules are enriched with semantic information provided from Spanish WordNet regarding to *anymacy* or *group* features. The application of these enrichment is detailed in next section.
- Preference application: morphological, syntactic, structural, statistical and semantic information contributes their own features to a weighting system to decide the candidate most probable to be the correct antecedent. Next two sections will explain the semantic constraint and preference rules.

Semantic Constraints Semantic constraints, as mentioned above, are applied to morphological agreement in order to avoid the rejection of potentially correct candidates. This occurs in group names where their referent pronoun can be singular or plural (i.e. in Spanish, just as in English, although the NP 'the police' is singular, it is possible to refer to it with the pronouns 'it' or 'they', singular and plural respectively). Furthermore, semantic constraints are also useful for reject candidates that agree morphologically but that has incompatible features from the syntactical-semantic point of view. Therefore, third-person masculine and feminine personal pronoun in a subject role cannot refer to a noun-phrase without animate feature. In other languages such as English, as commented above, some pronouns provide semantic characteristics such as '+person' (he/she) or '-person' (it). The method proposed in [11] takes advantage of these features to considerably improve the anaphora resolution success rate. The semantical or ontological features used in this constraints are extracted from the set of concepts contained in the Top Ontology of EuroWordNet [13].

Semantic Preferences If the candidate list contains more than one NPs after the constraint application, the preferences will decide the most probable one to be the correct antecedent. Apart from structural preferences (the nearer or the more repeated the candidate is, the more probable it is the antecedent), morphological preferences (candidates with the same number as the anaphor are preferred) and syntactic preferences (the candidates with the same syntactic role as the anaphor are preferred) there are a group of preferences that are extracted from semantic features of nouns and verbs:

- NPs that are not of time, direction, quantity or abstract are preferred. The study of the corpus reveal that this kind of nouns are not the solution of the pronoun in almost 100% of the times. This semantic features are also extracted from the Top Ontology of EuroWordNet'.

- NPs semantically more compatible with the verb of the pronoun are preferred. For this preference, the set of learned semantic patterns is used. The semantic pattern set contains the verb and the NP in its own syntactic role (subject, direct or indirect complement). For the NP in the pattern, there is available its domain label and its ontological features according to the EuroWordNet Top Ontology. Both are possible thanks to the WSD module enriched with the DSMM. This way, the compatibility is provided in two levels: 1) It will be considered more compatible the candidate that are represented by the ontological concept most relevant (in terms of frequency) in the semantic pattern set with the syntactic role and the verb of the pronoun. 2) Furthermore, it will be considered more compatible the candidate that shares domain label with the verb of the pronoun. For determining this compatibility, the WSD module studies the nouns contained in the gloss of the verb and deduces its domain label.

All these semantic sources contribute their own weight to the pronoun resolution module for the selection of the antecedent.

4.2   Definite Description Resolution

As in pronoun resolution, DD treatment requieres the use of several information sources, among which semantic information plays an important role. For DD treatment, the semantic information is used to identify some non-anaphoric definite description, to build the list of candidates and choose the adequate antecedent from the candidate list. As in pronoun resolution, the verb of the sentence helps to choose the antecedent for a specific kind of DD: thematic role. According to [9], different kinds of DDs can be found in the text. Thematic role is a DD which antecedent is related to the verb of the sentence (the seller, to sell). Solving this kind of DD, the verb of the sentence contained the antecedent plays an important role. In order to establish this relation a lexical resource as EuroWordNet is used (involved agent and role agent relationships). Traditional approaches based on knowledge, extensively cited in the literature as [12, 2], use morphologic and syntactic information. Although Vieira and Poesio's algorithm also uses semantic information extracted from WordNet, the evaluation carried out was manually made and the scores achieved were not so successful.

DD treatment presents different features to take in account to develop an effective resolution algorithm. Three factors kept in mind in DD resolution: accessibility space, non-anaphoric identification and resolution of anaphoric DDs. Our algorithm uses three different information sourcea (morphological, syntactic and semantic) to solve the three main problems of DD resolution. The accessibility space for pronouns is only a limited number of sentences. However, the accessibility space for DDs is greater. For this reason, the number of potential candidates can be very high for very large texts. So, if the coreference algorithm compares the DD with all candidates and the number of them is high then the algorithm becomes slow. Unlike other authors that reduce the number of previous sentences to be considered as the anaphoric accessibility space, our algorithm proposes the use of domain labels to group the NPs. This grouping is used to identify some non-anaphoric DDs (remaining non-anaphoric DDs will be classified by coreference algorithm) and to build the list of candidates for each DD. A DD looks for their antecedent along the previous NPs with the same domain label. This fact makes possible the use of a full anaphoric space made up of all previous sentences with the reduction of comparisons. The coreference algorithm provides an antecedent of a DD or if no candidate is found classifies it as non-anaphoric. The coreference algorithm is a system based on weighted heuristics. These heuristics treat the relation between heads and modifiers of both NPs (candidate and DD). Moreover, DDs can establish different kinds of relations with their antecedent. A definite description can refer to the full antecedent (identity coreference) or a part of the antecedent (part-of, set-member, set-subset). Our algorithm resolves the identity and part-of coreferences. If no candidate is selected as antecedent then the DD is re-classified as non-anaphoric. If more than one candidate is proposed then the closest candidate is selected.

Algorithm for DD Resolution DD algorithm go through different steps:

- DD identification: the algorithm goes through the text (previously tagged with POS, syntactic and semantic information) extracting all NPs. Once the NP is found, its type (definite or indefinite) is identified according to the first constituent of NP.
- NPs grouping: the head of a NP contains the domain label provided by the module of Domain Specification Marks Method. This domain label is used to cluster all NPs (definite and indefinite). As the parser also tags the pronouns as NPs, the antecedent resolution of the pronoun module is also used.
- Identification of non-anaphoric DDs: previous step also helps to identify some non-anaphoric definite descriptions. If the noun phase (DD) processed cannot be grouped with previous NPs (if it is the first with a specific domain label) then the DD is classified as non-anaphoric.
- Candidate list construction: the list of candidates for DD is made up of all previous NPs with the same domain label.
- Antecedent selection: a set of heuristics using morphological and semantic information are applied in order to choose the more adequate antecedent from the list of candidates. These heuristics treat the relation between head nouns and between modifiers of anaphoric expression and candidates.

5   Experimental Work

The experimental work carried out was focused on two different task: word sense disambiguation and anaphora resolution. Regarding to WSD task, SMM has been applied for the automatic resolution of lexical ambiguity of groups of words giving success rates of 70%. With reference to anaphora resolution, semantic information adding has allowed the raising of the success rates and the treatment of other types of DD, such as bridging reference. In average, success rate for anaphora resolution has been improved from 76% to the 85% [10, 11, 9].

6 Conclusions

We have presented an anaphora resolution algorithm based on semantic information to solve pronouns and DD. In addition to classical semantic information provided by the word sense number in WordNet, domain labels are used to cluster NPs. This clustering helps us to reduce the number of candidates. Experimental work shows that the use of WSD based on this domain labels improves the values of anaphora resolution task.

References

[1] J. Daudé, L. Padró, and G. Rigau. A Complete WN1.5 to WN1.6 Mapping. In *Proceedings of the NAACL Workshop WordNet and Other Lexical Resources: Applications, Extensions and Customisations.*, pages 83–88, 2001.

[2] M. Kameyama. Recognizing Referential Links: An Information Extraction Perspective. In Mitkov, R. and Boguraev, B., editor, *Proceedings of ACL/EACL*, pages 46–53, 1997.

[3] S. Lappin and H.J. Leass. An algorithm for pronominal anaphora resolution. *Computational Linguistics*, 20(4):535–561, 1994.

[4] B. Magnini and G. Cavaglia. Integrating subject field codes into WordNet. In *Proceedings of the LREC-2000*, 2000.

[5] B. Magnini and C. Strapparava. Experiments in Word Domain Disambiguation for Parallel Texts. In *Proceedings of the ACL Workshop on Word Senses and Multilinguality*, 2000.

[6] R. Mitkov. Robust pronoun resolution with limited knowledge. In ACL, editor, *Proceedings of the COLING-ACL'98*, pages 869–875, Montreal, Canada, 1998.

[7] A. Montoyo and M. Palomar. Word Sense Disambiguation with Specification Marks in Unrestricted Texts. In *Proceedings of the DEXA-2000*, pages 103–107. IEEE Computer Society, September 2000.

[8] A. Montoyo, M. Palomar, and G. Rigau. WordNet Enrichment with Classification Systems. In *Proceedings of the NAACL Workshop WordNet and Other Lexical Resources: Applications, Extensions and Customisations.*, pages 101–106, 2001.

[9] R. Muñoz, M. Palomar, and A. Ferrández. Processing of Spanish Definite Descriptions. In O. Cairo et al., editor, *Proceeding of MICAI*, volume 1793 of *LNAI*, pages 526–537, 2000.

[10] M. Palomar, A. Ferrández, L. Moreno, P. Martínez-Barco, J. Peral, M. Saiz-Noeda, and R. Muñoz. An Algorithm for Anaphora Resolution in Spanish Texts. *Computational Linguistics*, 27(4):545–567, 2001.

[11] M. Saiz-Noeda, J. Peral, and A. Suárez. Semantic Compatibility Techniques for Anaphora Resolution. In *Proceedings of ACIDCA'2000*, Tunisia, 2000.

[12] R. Vieira and M. Poesio. An Empiricall Based System for Processing Definite Descriptions. *Computational Linguistics*, 26(4):539–593, 2000.

[13] P. Vossen, L. Bloksma, H. Rodriguez, S. Climent, N. Calzolari, A. Roventini, F. Bertagna, A. Alonge, and W. Peters. The EuroWordNet Base Concepts and Top Ontology. Technical report, University of Amsterdam, EuroWordNet, LE2-4003 TR-11, 1998.

[14] Y. Wilks and M. Stevenson. Word sense disambiguation using optimised combination of knowledge sources. In *Proceedings of COLING-ACL'98*, 1998.

A Type of Transitive Inalienable Possession Construction in Korean

Gohsran Chung

Gaspard Monge Institute, University of Marne-la-Vallée
77454 Marne-la-Vallée, France
gchung@univ-mlv.fr

Abstract. In this paper, we present an analysis of sentences containing a Korean transitive verb that has a human subject and a direct object NP whose structure is N_a-gen N_b, where N_b denotes a body-part or an object-part. Theses sentences constitute one of the inalienable possession constructions and are related by an operation of restructuring to double accusative sentences. Three factors (i.e., inalienability between the elements of NP, their separability and metonymic relation) allow us to extract, from all superficially identical verbs, a semantically and syntactically homogenous class : we call it corporal-contact verbs.

1 Introduction

In the framework of Lexicon-Grammar [3], we aim to analyze a type of Korean transitive construction which has the following paraphrases, called operation of restructuring[1] :

(1)   *doli-ga   ([ina-ûi   son]-ûl   +[ina-lûl]   [son-ûl])   gûlg-nûn-da*
        Doli-ntf ([Ina-gen *hand*]-acc + [*Ina*-acc] [*hand*-acc]) scratch-pre-StDec
        « Doli scratches (the hand of Ina + Ina by the hand) »

We observe this restructuring and attempt to formulate the conditions that trigger it. We also define a class of Korean transitive verbs directly related to these properties : we call them corporal-contact verbs (Vcc). Guillet & Leclère [4] analyze similar French verbal constructions that make use of the appropriate substantives (containing N_{bp} or N_{op}) entering into the restructuring. Charles Fillmore [2] compares the "surface-contact" verbs group *(hit, slap, strike)* to "change-of-state" verbs group *(break, beat, shatter)* ; the former is an excellent English example equivalent to our so-called corporal-contact verbs (Vcc).

---

[1] Abbreviations: ntf (nominative); gen (genitive); acc (accusative); p. (all other postpositions followed by the equivalent prepositions); pre (present tense); pas (past tense); sfd (determinative suffix); StDec (terminal suffix of declarative mode); Comp (complementizer).

E.M. Ranchhod and N.J. Mamede (Eds.): PorTAL 2002, LNAI 2389, pp. 71-74, 2002.
© Springer-Verlag Berlin Heidelberg 2002

2 Delimitation of Data and Distributional Properties

Compare the following sentences having the same distribution, viz., a human subject and a direct object NP of type N_{hum}-gen N_{bp} :

(2)   *doli-ga* [*ina-ûi   son*]-*ûl   (bithû + johaha)-n-da*
        Doli-ntf [*Ina*-gen *hand*]-acc *(wring + like)*-pre-StDec
        « *Doli (wrings + likes) the hands Ina* »

In spite of their surface similarity, there is, however, an important difference. The verbs like *johaha- (like)* admit a sentential direct object :

(3)   *doli-ga* [*ina-ga   ûmsik-ûl   mandû-nûn gôt*]-*ûl   johaha-n-da*
        Doli-ntf [*Ina*-ntf *cuisine*-acc *make*-sfd Comp]-acc *like*-pre-StDec
        « *Doli likes that Ina cooks* »

while verbs like *bithû(l)- (wring)* can't take a similar type in this position. Such verbs denote a corporal-contact effected by a human and, moreover, can have another type of direct object, N_{-hum}-gen N_{op} :

(4)   *doli-ga* [*yônphil-ûi   k'ût*]-*ûl   bithû-n-da*
        Doli-ntf [*pencil*-gen   *tip*]-acc *wring*-pre-StDec
        « *Doli wrings the tip of the pencil* »

Hence the data analyzed in this paper are restricted to those verbs taking two kinds of direct object (N_{hum}-gen N_{bp} or N_{-hum}-gen N_{op}) and, at the same time, refusing a sentential direct object.

3 Restructuring Operation and Its Conditions

Criteria discussed in the preceding section allow us to choose about 600 Korean verbs out of about 8000. Many of them, but not all, activate the operation of restructuring which consists in splitting the NP into two independent elements. It leads to a double accusative sentence which contains two identical N-acc sequences as analyzed in sentences (1). This restructuring is applied to all constructions of Vcc, but isn't exclusive for this type of construction. Numerous transitive verbs permit also this restructuring. Nevertheless, three factors directly related to the restructuring in the constructions of Vcc have an important role to identify this class and to reduce, among 600 verbs, to those which constitute our final lexicon.

3.1 Condition of Inalienability

In constructions of Vcc there is a relation of inalienable possession between the possessor (N_{hum} or N_{-hum}) and the possessed (N_{bp} or N_{op}). This relation is a crucial factor that triggers the restructuring. An NP which has an *alienable* relation cannot trigger it:

(5)   *doli-ga* (*[ina-ûi   gabang]-lûl* + *[ina-lûl] [gabang-ûl]*) *munjilû-n-da*
        Doli-ntf (*[Ina*-gen *bag]*-acc   + *[Ina*-acc] [*bag*-acc]) *rub*-pre-StDec
        « *Doli rubs (the bag of Ina* + **Ina by the bag) »*

3.2 Condition of Separability

Following verb has exactly the same distribution as the Vcc and confirms the inalienability condition. But the elements of the NP are not separable and don't give rise to restructuring :

(6)   *doli-ga   ([byông-ûi judungi]-lûl + *([byông-ûl] [judungi-lûl])   k'ät'ûly-ôt-da*
       *Doli-*ntf *([bottle-*gen *mouth]-*acc+*([bottle-*acc][*mouth-*acc])*break-*pas-StDec
       « *Doli broke (the mouth of the vase + *the vase by the mouth)* »

Therefore another condition, called the "separability," intervenes. In short, for restructuring to apply, the two elements of NP have to be separable. Two transformations can reinforce the separability: passivization introducing a double nominative construction and extraction of the separated elements in the cleft sentence [4] (p.102-103).

3.3 Conditions of Metonymic Relation

The third condition is a metonymic relation between the two elements of NP. This relation permits to delete the N_{bp} and the deletion doesn't change the meaning of the sentence :

(7)   *doli-ga   ([chingu-ûi   môli]-ûl + chingu-lûl)   t'äly-ôt-da*
       *Doli-*ntf *([friend-*gen *head]-*acc + *friend-*acc) *strike-*pas-StDéc
       « *Doli struck (the head of his friend + his friend)* »

We include in our lexicon verbs which permit the insertion or deletion of the N_{bp}.
    For some verbs, the deletion of N_{bp} gives rise to change the meaning of verb :

(8)   *doli-ga   ([ina-ûi   son]-ûl   + ina-lûl)   t'adokgôlyo-t-da*
       *Doli-*ntf *([Ina-*gen *hand]-*acc + *Ina-*acc) *tap/console-*pas-StDéc
       « *Doli (tapped the hand of Ina + consoled Ina)* »

In this case the Korean verb *t'adokgôlida* has a double entry : concrete meaning *(tap)* entering into our lexicon and abstract meaning *(console)* which permits to insert a sentential direct object : for example *yonggi-lûl gajilago (to having the courage)*.
    The last type of verbs to analyze is verbs like *immatchumhada (kiss)*. This verb takes in direct object position a superficial NP of type N_{hum}-gen N_{bp} or a human substantive (having a metonymic relation with its N_{bp}) as like as *t'älida (strike)* in (7) :

(9)   *doli-ga   ([ina-ûi   p'yam]-e   + ina-(ege+ wa))   immatchumhä-t-da*
       *Doli-*ntf *([Ina-*gen *cheeks]-*p.at + *Ina-*(p.at + p.with)) *kiss-*pas-StDec
       « *Doli kissed (at the cheeks of Ina + (at + with) Ina)* »

However, the direct object is combined with the postposition *-e/ege* or *-wa*, but not with the accusative postposition *-ûl/lûl* with which the Vcc combine normally. So we exclude this type of verbs from our lexicon. Note that the substantives like *môli (head)* and *p'yam (cheeks)* in (7, 9) are appropriate substantives in the sense of Guillet & Leclère [4] (p.119) and Harris [5] (p.113-115).

4   Conclusion

In conclusion, the restructuring and its directly related factors yield to the final list. Among 600 verbs having the distribution of direct object NP, N_{hum}-gen N_{bp} or N_{-hum}-gen N_{op}, about 320 enter into the class termed corporal-contact verbs. This class is defined in the following ways. Semantically, they characterize the action drawing a corporal-contact of a human with another human or with an object like : *anda (embrace), k'ojipda (pinch), balbda (tread on), chada (kick at), galgäda (spank), jolûda (strangle)* etc. Syntactically, they are defined by the following set of structures :

(A) $\quad$ N_{hum}-ntf [N_a-gen N_b]-acc V $\quad$ « (N_{hum})$_0$ V (N_b of N_a)$_1$ » ($N_b = N_{bp} + N_{op}$)

(B)[Rest] = N_{hum}-ntf [N_a-acc] [N_b-acc] V $\quad$ « (N_{hum})$_0$ V N_a by N_b »

(C)[N_{bp} z.] = N_{hum}-ntf (N_{hum})$_a$-acc V $\quad$ « (N_{hum})$_0$ V (N_{hum})$_a$ »

(D) $\quad$ *N_{hum}-ntf (P-comp)-acc V $\quad$ « (N_{hum})$_0$ V (that S + to Inf)$_1$ »

(E) $\quad$ *N_{hum}-ntf N_{hum}-p.wa V $\quad$ « (N_{hum})$_0$ V with (N_{hum})$_1$ »

(F) $\quad$ *N_{hum}-ntf [N_a-gen N_b]-p.e V $\quad$ « (N_{hum})$_0$ V at (N_b of N_a) »

(G) $\quad$ *N_{hum}-ntf N_{hum}-acc (P-comp + E) V $\quad$ « (N_{hum})$_0$ V (N_{hum})$_1$ ((that S + to Inf)$_2$ + E) »

This analysis permits to establish a specific lexicon of Korean transitive verbs concerning a type of inalienable possession construction directly related to a double accusative sentence. The double accusative sentence is often discussed in the framework of Korean generative grammar [1][6][7][8][9][10], but they normally focus on the syntactic status of the first accusative sequence comparing with another type of double accusative sentence. Contrary to theses approaches, we have developed the relationship between sentences related by the variation of genitive and accusative postpositions.

References

1. Cho, D.-I.: Multiple accusative constructions and verb movement. In : MIT Working Papers in Linguistics 16 (1992) 11-25.
2. Fillmore, Ch.: The Grammar of Hitting and Breaking. In : Roderick A. Jacobs & Peter S. Rosenbaum (eds.): Readings in English Transformational Grammar, Ginn and Company (1970) 120-133.
3. Gross, M.: Méthode en syntaxe. Hermann, Paris (1975).
4. Guillet, A., Leclère, Ch.: Restructuration du groupe nominal. In: Langages 63, Larousse, Paris (1981) 99-126.
5. Harris, Z.: Notes du cours de syntaxe. In : M. Gross (trad.): Le Seuil, Paris (1976).
6. Kang, M.-Y.: Possessor Raising in Korean. In: S. Kuno et al. (eds.): Harvard Studies in Korean Linguistics II, Harvard University (1987) 80-88.
7. Kim, K.-H.: (The grammar of the phrasal structure and the double object constructions in Korean (Korean version)). In: Munbôp Yôngu 5 (1984) 87-127.
8. Kim, Y.-H.: (Exploration of the Korean Syntax (Korean version)). Thap, Seoul (1988).
9. Sung, G.-S.: (About the phenomena of double occurrences of the subject and the object in Korean (Korean version)). In: Munbôp Yôngu 1 (1974) 209-235.
10. Yi, G.-H.: (Study of the Korean case postposition -ûl/lûl (Korean version)). Thap, Seoul (1988)

The Treatment of Numbers in Polish by Graphs

Krzysztof Bogacki

Warsaw University
Kbogacki1@poczta.onet.pl

Abstract. We describe Polish numerals in terms of finite state automata represented by graphs. As compared to French and English, the Polish system is more complicated due to the existence of a seven-case noun declension. It is shown how different numerals select specific cases of their nominal complement in a nominal phrase of the form Numeral+Noun and how the syntactic position of some cardinals in compound structures governs the choice of the appropriate case of the nominal regime.

The expression of the numbers constitutes in Polish a domain which can be easily described by means of final state automata similar to those which we find in INTEX. Numbers appear in many contexts: as simple words or in compounds, as single words or in phrases in which they govern other nouns. In what follows, we present a local grammar which covers Polish cardinal numerals.

The Polish system differs in several points from the French, English, American, Spanish, Italian or German ones. Therefore its description could not be a pure and simple adaptation of French or of English.. In English, the numerals can be described by a series of graphs which are linked together. The point of departure is constituted by DnumTxt1_9.grf and DnumTxt10_19.grf which respectively give a list of cardinals ranging from 1 to 9 and another one of the forms between 10 and 19. The graph Dnum20_99.grf adds the lexical items of tens (from 20 to 90) and along with DnumTxt1_9.grf generates/recognizes structures such as *twenty-two, thirty-three, seventy-seven* etc. The numbers up to 999999 are described by the graph DnumTxt10^3_10^6-1.grf which combines all of them illustrating the principle of interweaving. It is easy to describe the phrases of the type Numeral+Noun bearing in mind that the selection of the appropriate form of the noun is governed by the numeral and that the choice one has involves two values: singular or plural. In Polish the situation is more complicated and the number of grammatical values to take in consideration is higher.

In Polish, the description of numbers calls for thirty graphs (instead of 7 for French and English). Its specificity depends of three factors:

E.M. Ranchhod and N.J. Mamede (Eds.): PorTAL 2002, LNAI 2389, pp. 75-78, 2002.
© Springer-Verlag Berlin Heidelberg 2002

- a complex government of the nominal regime which we explaine in detail below;
- the fact that the form of the number noun is conditionned by its position inside the compound number;
- numbers superior to 1000 use the word *tysiąc* 'one thousand' which has nominal and not numeral morphology.

The main factor of complication comes from the existence of a seven-case declension. Unlike in West Indo-European languages, it is not possible to predict the correct form of the nominal regime on the basis of the fact that the numeral in the phrase is superior to 1 or equal to 1. Indeed, the choice of the nominal form is governed by three rules below:

- the regime is in the nominative case singular after the numeral *jeden* 'one' when it is the only numeral employed in the NP (*jeden koń* 'one horse'). If, however, *jeden* ends a compound numeral, the regime is in the genitive case plural, cf. *dwadzieścia jeden koni* ' twenty one horses ';
- the regime appears in the nominative case plural after the numeral of the class: *dwa* 'two', *trzy* 'three', *cztery* 'four', cf. *(dwa+trzy+cztery) konie* '(two+three+four) horses', *dwadzieścia dwa konie* '22 horses', *trzydzieści trzy konie* '33 horses', *czterdzieści cztery konie* '44 horses';
- the regime is in the genitive case plural after a simple numeral superior to 4 or after a compound ending by *jeden* or by a numeral superior to 4 (*pięć koni* '5 horses', *sto koni* '100 horses', *dwadzieścia jeden koni* '21 horses', *dwadzieścia pięć koni* '25 horses').

Such a behavior imposes the subdivision of the numerals into three classes: *jeden* on one hand, *dwa, trzy, cztery* on the other and, finally, *pięć* and above. It is crucial here to distinguish also between uses of *jeden* as a part of a compound numeral and as a single word. In the third place, let us mention the heterogeneity of the numerals which, from 1000 up, use nouns (*tysiąc* '1000', *milion* '10^6' etc.) next to pure numerals. Indeed, *tysiąc* follows the paradigm of male inanimate nouns. On the other hand, *tysiąc* imposes its syntax on the nominal regime if it follows it immediately: it requires a genitive plural. This rule is however cancelled when *tysiąc* is followed by one of the following numerals: *jeden, dwa, trzy, cztery*.

Things being what they are, the system of Polish numerals is described as follows. Those ranging from 1 to 999999 are represented by means of several graphs. All of them take into account two types of uses: without nominal regime and with a nominal regime in the appropriate case. For the cardinals of this series, we are going to proceed in two stages, the threshold being established by 1000. First of all, we create four graphs for numerals going from 1 to 9: two graphs for *jeden* as it is employed as a single numeral (jeden.grf) or ends a compounnd cardinal (*jeden koń* 'a horse' vs. *dwadzieścia jeden koni* '21 horses' – jedenF.grf), a graph for the cardinals from 2 to 4 (*dwa+trzy+cztery konie* '2+3+4 horses' – 2_4.grf) and a graph for the cardinals between 5 and 9 (*pięć+sześć+siedem+osiem+dziewięć koni* '5+6+7+8+9 horses'- 5_9.grf). Cf:

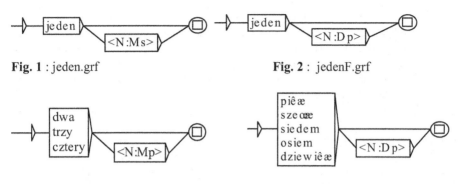

Fig. 1 : jeden.grf   **Fig. 2** : jedenF.grf

Fig. 3. 2_4.grf   **Fig. 4.** 5_9.grf

The graph 10_19.grf covers the cardinals from 10 to 19.The graph 1_99.grf, built from elements above, corresponds to the cardinals going from 1 to 99. The extension up to 999 would call for a graph into which we would introduce a constituent taking care of the names of hundreds. Combined with the graph 1_99.grf, it makes possible the recognition of the cardinals from 1 up to 999. The graph 1_99F differs from 1_99.grf by the fact that it does not contain jeden.grf as a sub-graph, replaced by jedenF.grf. Indeed, we exclude *(sto+dwieście+trzysta+...) jeden koń* for the benefit of *(sto+dwieście+trzysta+...) jeden koni* '(101+201+301+...) horses'. JedenF.grf is thus called in the top of 1_999.grf and included in 20_99.grf.

The graph 1_Mln-1.grf adds the names of hundreds of thousands and takes into account cardinal numerals inferior to 1000.

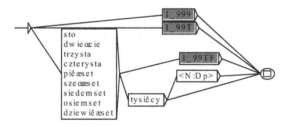

Fig. 5. 1_Mln-1.grf

Here are the auxiliary graphs contained in it:
- 1_99T.grf which covers the zone extending from 1000 to 99999,
- its variant, 1_99TF.grf, intended for the final position of the cardinal numeral: *dziewięćdziesiąt jeden tysięcy koni* '91.000 horses' vs. *dziewięćdziesiąt jeden tysięcy cztery konie* '91.004 horses' vs. *dziewięćdziesiąt jeden tysięcy pięć koni* '91.005 horses',
- two graphs describing the behavior of *jeden* followed by *tysiąc*: jedenT.grf for the final position and jedenTF.grf inside a cardinal numeral: *tysiąc dwa konie* '1002 horses' vs *tysiąc koni* '1000 horses',

- one graph (2_4T.grf) covering the zone extending from 2000 to 4999 and the other one (5_9T.grf) suitable for the zone from 5000 to 9999,
- the graphs 10-19T.grf managing the cardinal numerals from 10000 to 19999 and 20_90T.grf for numerals going from 20000 to 90999,
- the graph 1_999F.grf obtained from 1_999.grf by replacement of the sub-graph 1_99.grf by 1_99F.grf which is necessary to prevent *tysiąc jeden koń '1001 horse'.

Except for the constituent which precedes the word tysięcy 'one thousand' (genitive plural), the graphs 5_9.grf and 10-19T.grf are identical and could be merged if we stopped our description of the numerals at 19999. Forms like 22.000 (dwadzieścia dwa tysiące), 25.000 (dwadzieścia pięć tysięcy) require however two different graphs which must exclude the combination of the names of tens with those of thousands equal and higher than 10 up to 19: *dwadzieścia jedenaście tysięcy *'twenty and eleven thousand'. On the other hand, we are forced to propose two different graphs for the zone extending from 2000 as the initial numerals in 2_4T.grf and in 5_9T.grf assign different cases to their regime.

The noun tysiąc '1000' in the series of T-graphs, depends on the preceding numeral which imposes it an appropriate case. It substitutes itself for the regime coming immediately after the cardinal of a lower rank. In its turn, the complement to tysiąc can be a noun, always in the plural genitive (tysiąc krów 'one thousand cows'), or a numeral with its nominal complement in the appropriate case (tysiąc pięć metrów '1005 meters', tysiąc dwa metry '1002 meters') imbricated in 1_Mln-1.grf.

The graph 1_Mln-1.grf generates/recognizes the numbers from 1 until 999999 which is sufficient, for example, for the elaboration of the system of the expression of the most common dates. The extension of the system beyond 999999 appeals to the same mechanism. It is made by the annexation of new elements ordered hierarchically: milion '10^6', miliard, '10^9', bilion, '10^12', trylion, '10^15', etc. All of them work as nouns and open a position to their regime. In its own graph, every element of this series substitutes the graph immediately lower to the place of the knot < N>.

Conclusion

Even if we eliminate, as we made it here, the structures and the forms considered as regional, archaic, rare, or incorrect (i. e..* tysiąc i jeden), the Polish numerals present a degree of complication superior to that of the corresponding forms in French and in English. The comparison of our graphs with those elaborated for the West European languages accounts for the complexity of the system of numeration due to the existence, in Polish, of the nominal declension and of a specific syntax of dwa 'two', trzy 'three' and cztery 'four'.

From Syntax to Semantics: Taking Advantages of 5P

Luísa Coheur[1] and Nuno Mamede[2]

[1] (L²F(INESC-ID)/GRIL)
[2] (L²F(INESC-ID)/IST)
Spoken Language Systems Lab, R. Alves Redol, 9, 1000-029 Lisbon, Portugal
{luisa.coheur,nuno.mamede}@inesc-id.pt

Abstract. This paper states how to profit from 5P's arrows formalism to go from a text with its surface structure to a chosen semantic representation. We emphasize on this formalism flexibility both to connect models and to define sets of conditions (over that connections) that will trigger semantic functions.

1 Introduction

5P ([4], [3]) is a paradigm which goals are much the same than the ones of other linguistics approaches for the study and processing of Natural Language (NL). However, these same goals are reached in particular ways. This paper states how to take advantage of 5P's arrows formalism to go from syntax to semantics. We start by presenting the 5P ingredients. Then, we explain how we use the arrows formalism to connect models and to define sets of conditions (over that connections) to which semantic functions are associated. Finally, we present an example of application having First Order Logic (FOL) and Discourse Representation Structures (DRS) as representation targets.
We would like to make clear that we make our own interpretation/use of this paradigm, which does not necessarily reflect that of 5P.

2 Some 5P Ingredients

Nuclear phrases are very close to Abney's chunks [1] (see [6] for a detailed explanation of how to identify nuclear phrases and a comparison with chunks and other similar structures). In the linguistic descriptions made within 5P, nuclear phrases play an important role, as they have (among others) the useful characteristic of not having internal recursivity if coordination is excluded [5].
5P offers a formalism allowing to describe sequences verifying a set of properties ([3]). These sequences – nuclear or non nuclear phrases, etc. – are called models. In order to connect models, 5P offers the arrows properties, that we following present within our own interpretation/extention (see [3] for details over the ori-/ginal formalism).
A basic arrow property expresses a link between two syntactic elements (the source and the target) within a model (the current model). As an example, if we

E.M. Ranchhod and N.J. Mamede (Eds.): PorTAL 2002, LNAI 2389, pp. 79–82, 2002.

have a nominal nuclear phrase (nn), and an adjectival nuclear phrase (an) inside a nominal phrase (n) and, moreover, an relates with nn, we say that an arrows nn in n and we write an $\rightarrow_n$ nn, being: a) an the source; b)nn the target; c)n the current model. In order to add more expressiveness to this formalism, it can be extended with restrictions over the:

- current model (ex: an $\rightarrow_n$ nn [restrictions over n])
- source or target[1] (ex: an(restrictions over an)$\rightarrow_n$nn(restrictions over nn))
- upper model (ex: an $\rightarrow_n$ nn ↑[restrictions over the model above n])

Each restriction set is divided in 2 sets, separated by a slash (/): a set of restrictions to satisfy and a set of restrictions that can not be verified.
These restrictions can be of one of the following types (adj is for adjective, pn for prepositional nuclear phrase, det for determiner and vn to verbal nuclear phrase):

- existence: x (ex: an(adj/) $\rightarrow_n$ nn [/pn] (adj exists in an. pn doesn't in n));
- nuclear: °x (ex: det $\rightarrow_{nn}$ adj [°adj/] (adj exists in nn and is the nucleus));
- linear: x $<^*$ y if x precedes y (x < y, if x immediately precedes y)(ex: an $\rightarrow_n$ nn [nn $<^*$ an/] (both nn and an exists in n. nn precedes an));
- arrowing: x $\rightarrow$ y (ex: an $\rightarrow_n$ nn [pn→nn/](pn, nn exist in n. pn arrows nn)).

3   Connecting Models

Consider the classic example *Saw the man in the house with a telescope*. As Allen says in [2], there are five interpretations arising from the different attachments. By retrieving nuclear phrases, we obtain:

   $(saw)_{vn}$ $(the\ man)_{nn}$ $(in\ the\ house)_{pn}$ $(with\ a\ telescope)_{pn}$

By using the following arrows properties[2]:

   nn $\rightarrow_s$ vn, pn $\rightarrow_s$ vn | nn, pn' $\rightarrow_s$ pn [pn $<_s$ pn']

the 5 hypotheses are obtained, without having to duplicate the basic syntactic structures (in all nn $\rightarrow_s$ vn):

   H_1:pn $\rightarrow_s$ vn, pn' $\rightarrow_s$ vn, H_2:pn $\rightarrow_s$ vn, pn' $\rightarrow$ pn, H_3:pn $\rightarrow_s$ nn, pn' $\rightarrow_s$ vn, H_4:pn $\rightarrow_s$ nn, pn' $\rightarrow_s$ nn, H_5:pn $\rightarrow_s$ nn, pn' $\rightarrow_s$ pn

However, with these arrows, a sixth interpretation, corresponding to a false ambiguity[3], becomes possible: pn $\rightarrow_s$ vn, pn $\rightarrow_s$ nn. By adding restrictions over the arrows, this solution would be avoided. Alternatively, accepting that no arrows crossing is allowed, this sixth hypothesis is no longer possible.

4   From Syntax to Semantics

Associating semantic functions to syntactic rules is a classic procedure in NL processing. It was started by Montague, being [8] a good illustration of this

---

[1] If they are models, and not categories.
[2] The vertical slash denotes "or", and we use pn' to distinguish the pn on the left (pn) from the one on the right (pn').
[3] Someone (in the house) saw a man who had a telescope.

method. Nowadays, it is still used in most prominent theories. However, and as pointed in [4], there are no syntactic rules in 5P, in the sense of conventional grammar rules, *i.e.*, representing part of a tree structure. From this, we can say that 5P does not allow the association of semantic rules with syntactic rules, for the simple reason that it has no syntactic rules. So, the question is, over which structures will semantic functions operate? The answer is very simple: over the arrows properties[4]. As an example, if a arrows b in c defines a syntactic context, a semantic function f can be associated with it[5], and we note it by:

a $\rightarrow_c$ b: f_c(b, a)

Notice that a syntactic context can be defined over a set of arrows:

a_1,..., a_n $\rightarrow_c$ b: f_c(b, a_1, ..., a_n)

Due to the extended arrows formalism, the conditions that trigger semantic functions can be very precise. As an example in Portuguese, consider the an *algum*. *algum* means *some*, but if this an appears after the nn, it means *none*[6]. We express this with:

algum$\rightarrow_{an}$*algum*[nn<an/]: f_{an}(*algum*)[7] and *algum*$\rightarrow_{an}$*algum*: g_{an}(*algum*)

The next example shows how this formalism allows dispensing with labels. Consider the sentence (*Jones*)$_{nn}$ (*owns*)$_{vn}$ (*Ulysses*)$_{nn}$ from [7]. If we decide that our surface structure only has nuclear phrases, we obtain the two nn at the same level. Nevertheless, the first nn is the subject, and the second the object[8], and we want to be able to distinguish them, as this will have obvious influence in the semantic results. So, if we use the following arrows, we are able to associate with each one the appropriate semantic function:

nn$\rightarrow_{svn}$[nn<vn]: g_s(vn,nn)(subject), and nn$\rightarrow_{svn}$[vn<nn]:h_s(vn,nn)(object)

That is, without having to add extra labels, the subject and the object are identified by their own syntactic properties.

5   Semantic Functions

We now show how to go from a text in which the nuclear phrases were identified, to a semantic representation (either in FOL or DRS).

Continuing with the example from the previous section, consider that the semantic associated with the nn *Jones* is Jones(z) and with the vn *owns* is owns(x, y). These will help us to illustrate the following functions:

- θ(A) returns the semantics associated with A (ex: θ(*Jones*) = Jones(z));
- ABS$_i$(A) returns the ith variable associated with θ(A)(ex: ABS$_1$(vn) = x, ABS$_2$(vn) = y and ABS$_1$(nn) = z);
- [X/Y]S replaces Y by X in S (ex: [ABS$_1$(vn)/ABS$_1$(nn)]θ(nn) = [x/z]Jones(z) = Jones(x));

---

[4] In 5P, they say that a set of arrows originates a graph, which is the input to semantic functions [3].

[5] We say that the syntactic condition a $\rightarrow_c$ b triggers the semantic function f_c(b, a).

[6] (*algum*)$_{an}$(*rapaz*)$_{nn}$ means *some boy*, and (*rapaz*)$_{nn}$ (*algum*)$_{an}$ means *no boy*.

[7] If a $\rightarrow_b$ a, instead of f_b(a, a) we note the associated semantic function as f_b(a).

[8] Note that we are not considering the passive voice.

- ADD($\{x_1, ..., x_m\}$, j, S) adds $\theta(x_1), ..., \theta(x_m)$ to S (which can be a formula, a DRS, etc.), in position j (undetermined (_) or with a precise meaning) (ex: being given the drs = $(\{x, y\}, \{\})^9$, then ADD($\{\theta(vn)\}$, 2, drs) = ($\{x, y\}$, $\{\text{owns}(x, y)\}$)).

Consider the following three syntactic contexts/semantic functions pairs:

nn$\rightarrow_s$vn [nn<vn]: g_s(vn, nn), nn$\rightarrow_s$vn [vn<nn]: h_s(vn, nn), vn$\rightarrow_s$vn: f_s(vn).

Take FOL as the representation language. If $F = \emptyset$, by defining the functions as:

$(1) f_s(vn) = \text{ADD}(\{\theta(vn)\}, \_, F)$

$(2) g_s(vn, nn) = \text{ADD}(\{[\text{ABS}_1(vn)/\text{ABS}_1(nn)]\theta(nn)\}, \_, F)$

$(3) h_s(vn, nn) = \text{ADD}([\text{ABS}_2(vn)/\text{ABS}_1 (nn)]\theta(nn), \_, F)$

we obtain: $F =_{(1)} \{\text{owns}(x, y)\} =_{(2)} \{\text{Jones}(x), \text{owns}(x, y)\} =_{(3)} \{\text{Jones}(x), \text{owns}(x, y), \text{Ulysses}(y)\}^{10}$.

Take now DRS's. If drs = $(\{\}, \{\})$, 1 denotes the set of reference markers, 2 the conditions set, and the functions are defined as:

$(1) f_s(vn) = \text{ADD}(\{\text{ABS}_1(vn), \text{ABS}_2(vn)\}, 1, \text{ADD}(\theta(vn), 2, drs))$

$(2) g_s(vn, nn) = \text{ADD}([\text{ABS}_1(vn)/\text{ABS}_1(nn)]\theta(nn), 2, drs)$

$(3) h_s(vn, nn) = \text{ADD}([\text{ABS}_2(vn)/\text{ABS}_1(nn)]\theta(nn), 2, drs)$

we obtain: drs $=_{(1)}$ ($\{x, y\}$, $\{\text{owns}(x, y)\}$) $=_{(2)}$ ($\{x, y\}$, $\{\text{Jones}(x), \text{owns}(x, y)\}$)$=_{(3)}$ ($\{x, y\}$, $\{\text{Jones}(x), \text{owns}(x, y), \text{Ulysses}(y)\}$)

6   Conclusions and Further Work

We showed how to profit from 5P arrows formalism, which, enriched with restrictions, is used both to connect models and to precise syntactic triggers to the semantic analysis. As future work, we will continue to explore this formalism's potentialities.

References

[1] Steven Abney. *Parsing by Chunks*. Kluwer Academic Publishers, 1991.
[2] James Allen. *Natural Language Understanding (second edition)*. The Benjamin Cummings Publishing Company, Inc, 1995.
[3] G. Bès and C. Hagège. Properties in 5p (soon in the GRIL pages). November, 2001.
[4] Gabriel G. Bès. La phrase verbal noyau en français. In *in Recherches sur le français parlé, 15*. Université de Provence, France, 1999.
[5] C. Hagège and G. Bès. Delimitação das construções relativas e completivas na análise de superfície de textos. In *PROPOR'99*, pages 93–104, Portugal, 1999.
[6] Caroline Hagège. *Analyse Syntatic Automatique du Portugais*. PhD thesis, Université Blaise Pascal, Clermont-Ferrand, France, 2000.
[7] H. Kamp and U. Reyle. *From Discourse to logic*. Kluwer Academic Publishers, 93.
[8] Richard Montague. The proper treatment of quantification in ordinary english. In R.H. Thomason, editor, *Formal Philosophy. Selected papers of Richard Montague*, pages 247–270. Yale University Press, New Haven, 1974.

---

[9] In the canonical set-theoretical notation.

[10] *i.e.*, Jones(x) $\land$ owns(x, y) $\land$ Ulysses(y).

Processing Discontinuity

Marcel Cori

Université Paris X and CNRS MoDyCo,
200 av. de la République, 92000 Nanterre, France,
`mcori@u-paris10.fr`

Abstract. We present a natural language parsing method which takes care of one case of discontinuity: the case of disjunct constituents. The method is based on Espinal's three-dimensional structures. A formal definition of these structures is given. The parsing is processed with an augmented CKY algorithm.

1 Introduction

Discontinuous constituency, or discontinuity, is an old well-known problem for syntactic models and for Natural language parsing.

Discontinuous trees were introduced for representing discontinuity. They have received several formalizations, for McCawley (1982) to Bunt (1996), but these formalizations lack to give convenient grammars able to generate the appropriate discontinuous structures.

According to a different point of view, Espinal (1991), after a linguistic analysis of *disjunct constitutents*, proposed a "three-dimensional" representation, made of different trees belonging to distinct planes. Three-dimensional structures, however, have not been really formalized.

In this paper, we describe a parsing method based on Espinal's tridimensional structures. We think that this method should apply, with some modifications, to other formalisms. A bottom-up approach being more natural, the parsing algorithm has been defined as an augmentation of the classical CKY algorithm (Hays, 1962, inter alia).

This algorithm is a first step for processing discontinuity in the framework of Polychrome tree grammars (Cori & Marandin, 1994). In this framework discontinuity is represented without discontinuous structures.

2 The Problem

2.1 The Linguistic Data

We will say that there is discontinuity when the sequence of words constituting a phrase is split into two parts by one or several other phrases:

(1)   a. *He waked your friend up.*

     b. *John talked, of course, about politics.*

     c. *Jean a vraisemblablement oublié de faire son devoir.*

     d. *Pierre a, le pauvre, perdu son emploi.*

E.M. Ranchhod and N.J. Mamede (Eds.): PorTAL 2002, LNAI 2389, pp. 83–86, 2002.

e. *Pierre a, le pauvre, Marie en a pleuré, perdu son emploi.*

f. *Pierre a, Marie la pauvre en a pleuré, perdu son emploi.*

Among these examples, (1.a) can be distinguished, since the constituent *waked up* necessarily needs the constituent *your friend*. In all other cases we preserve a well-formed sentence even if removing the *disjunct constituent* (henceforth DC). We will call *interpolation* the phenomenon. The (split) structure in which the DC occurs will be the *host structure*, and the position where the DC is inserted an *interpolation site (IS)*.

Notice that there are special cases of interpolation without discontinuity:

(2)   a. *Pierre est intelligent, je trouve.*

      b. *Le pauvre, Pierre a perdu son emploi.*

Interpolation and discontinuity are therefore two distinct phenomena, which only partially overlap. In the following, we focus on DCs, and we assume that some other cases of discontinuity would be treated with the same formal and algorithmic tools.

2.2   Characterizing Interpolation

The following facts characterize interpolation (see Espinal, 1991):

- (A) DCs belong to any maximal category: NP, S, S', AP, AdvP, PP.

- (B) The only portion of sentence structure immune to interpolation in French is between the article and the head noun in NP, the clitic pronoun and the verb in VP, the case preposition (*à*, *de*) and NP in PP.

(3)   a. * *Il vraisemblablement a oublié de faire son devoir*

      b. * *Le, Marie le trouve très énervant, chercheur a fait son exposé*

- (C) DCs are not involved in grammatical relations with the other constituents of their host phrases.

- (D) Interpolation is submitted to occupability constraints.

- (E) Several distinct constituents may occur in a same IS (example 1.e).

2.3   Formal Tools for Representing Discontinuity

The most frequent works to represent DCs have been devised to represent discontinuous constituency in general. Hence the construction of *discontinuous trees*: these structures, first introduced by McCawley (1982), differ from the classical trees used as phrase markers by the fact that Nontangling condition and Exclusivity condition (Wall, 1972) do not hold.

Another thesis (Espinal, 1991) is that host structure and DCs are unrelated syntactic structures. They belong to different planes which intersect at "the line where structural precedence relations among terminal nodes are specified". The resulting structure is a *three-dimensional structure* (henceforth *TDS*), made of several distinct trees, in which the set of all leaves constitutes a totally ordered set. The roots of these trees are labeled by every maximal category. Two DCs, or a DC and a host structure cannot overlap. We shall consider that a DC may be the host structure of another DC, and so on, in order to be able to handle a sentence like (1.f). We give in fig. 1 a structure for the VP and its DC of example (1.d).

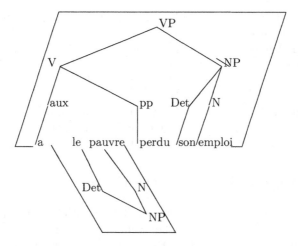

Fig. 1. A three-dimensional structure

3 A Formalization of TDSs

3.1 Definition of a TDS

A TDS is defined as being a quadruple $A = \langle X, L, D, P \rangle$ where X is the set of nodes, L is the labelling function, $D \subseteq X \times X$ is a partial order, the dominance relation, $P \subseteq X \times X$ is a strict partial order, the precedence relation, and such that the four following conditions are satisfied:

(i) $\forall x, y \in X \ (\langle x, y \rangle \in P \ \lor \ \langle y, x \rangle \in P) \Rightarrow (\langle x, y \rangle \notin D \ \land \ \langle y, x \rangle \notin D)$

(ii) $\forall x, y \in l(A) \ \ x \neq y \Rightarrow (\langle x, y \rangle \in P \ \lor \ \langle y, x \rangle \in P)$

(iii) $\forall x, y \in X \ \ \langle x, y \rangle \in P \ \Leftrightarrow \ (\forall u \in l(x) \ \forall v \in l(y) \ \langle u, v \rangle \in P)$

(iv) For all $x, y \in X$ such that $\langle x, y \rangle \notin D$ and $\langle y, x \rangle \notin D$ and $\langle x, y \rangle \notin P$ and $\langle y, x \rangle \notin P$, one in the two following conditions is satisfied:

(iv.1) $\forall z \in l(x) \ \forall u, v \in l(y) \ (\langle z, u \rangle \in P \land \langle z, v \rangle \in P) \lor (\langle u, z \rangle \in P \land \langle v, z \rangle \in P)$

(iv.2) $\forall z \in l(y) \ \forall u, v \in l(x) \ (\langle z, u \rangle \in P \land \langle z, v \rangle \in P) \lor (\langle u, z \rangle \in P \land \langle v, z \rangle \in P)$

where $l(A)$ is the set of the leaves of the tree, and $l(x)$ the set of leaves dominated by a node x.

3.2 Properties

Property 1: Non-tangling condition holds.

Property 2: Single-mother condition holds.

Property 3: There is a total order over the daughters of a given node.

The definition of tree admissibility is based on the latter property.

3.3 Grammars and Admissibility

A grammar is given by $G = \langle Cat, Cat_M, \mathcal{R}, \mathcal{R}_I \rangle$, where Cat is the set of categories, Cat_M is the subset of Cat made of maximal categories, $\mathcal{R}$ contains rules such as $\alpha \rightarrow \beta\gamma$ with $\alpha, \beta, \gamma \in Cat$ (the grammar is supposed to be in Chomsky normal form) and $\mathcal{R}_I$ is a subset of $\mathcal{R}$.

Definition: A node x (representing a phrase) in a TDS A is a *host node* iff there are two nodes $z_1, z_2 \in l(x)$ such that:

(i) $\exists w \in l(A) - l(x)$ $\langle z_1, w \rangle \in P$ and $\langle w, z_2 \rangle \in P$

(ii) $\forall y$ $z_1, z_2 \in l(y) \Rightarrow \langle y, x \rangle \in D$

Definition: A TDS is admissible from the grammar iff (1) each of its local subtrees is licensed by one of the rules of $\mathcal{R}$, and (2) this rule is in $\mathcal{R}_I$ when the root of the corresponding local subtree is a host node.

4   An Augmented CKY Algorithm

We assume that in the input data of the algorithm is a sequence of m sets of categories: $S_1^1, \ldots, S_1^m$. The algorithm builds sets of phrases S_n^j, where n indicates the number of words in the phrase and j the position in the sentence of the last word of the phrase.

The augmentation is performed by taking a *fifo* list, the list of sets which are *candidates* to contain a DC. So, in the list are recorded ordered pairs $\langle n, j \rangle$. The list is intialized with the pair $\langle 0, 0 \rangle$ (case without DC), and with all pairs $\langle 1, j \rangle$ for the sets S_1^j containing a maximal category (for instance an adverb).

For each DC candidate, a parsing of the sentence is attempted. Three cases are then distinguished for building the phrase sets: (1) the phrases which are before the DC, (2) the phrases which are after the DC, and (3) the phrases which are hosts of the DC. In case (3), it is necessary to verify that the host structure is a phrase corresponding to a rule of $\mathcal{R}_I$.

Pairs are added to the fifo list at some steps of the iteration, in (2) for the case of several constituents in a same IS and in (3) for the case of DCs contained inside another DC.

References

1. Bunt H.C. (1996). Formal tools for modelling and processing discontinuous constituency. In H.C. Bunt & A. van Horck Eds. *Discontinuous Constituency*, p. 63-85. Berlin: De Gruyter.
2. Cori M. & Marandin J.-M. (1994). Polychrome tree grammars (PTGs): a formal presentation. In C. Martin-Vide, Ed., *Current issues in Mathematical Linguistics*, p. 141-149, Amsterdam : North-Holland.
3. Espinal M.T. (1991). The representation of disjunct constituents. *Language* **67-4**, 726-762.
4. Hays D.G. (1962). Automatic language-data processing. In H. Borko, Ed., *Computer Applications in the Behavorial Sciences*, p. 394-421, Englewood Cliffs, New Jersey: Prentice Hall.
5. McCawley J. (1982). Parentheticals and Discontinuous Constituent Structure. *Linguistic Inquiry*, **13**, 91-106.
6. Wall R. (1972). *Introduction to Mathematical Linguistics*. Englewood Cliffs: Prentice-Hall.

Resolution of Demonstrative Anaphoric References in Portuguese Written Texts

Victor Sant'Anna, Vera L.S. de Lima

Av. Ipiranga, 6681 Prédio 30, bloco 4,
90619-9000, Porto Alegre, Brazil
{victorms, vera}@inf.pucrs.br

Abstract. This paper presents a proposal for resolving demonstrative anaphoric references on the basis of written Portuguese text corpus. Our study examined the possibility for applying a selection of merely heuristic and syntactical rules into a computational model aimed at the resolutions anaphoric references. Our proposal has been experimented and evaluated: its resolution capacity revealed more than 90% precision with 80% and better recall.

1 Introduction

The purpose of this work is to report our studies focusing a proposal for identifying and resolving the demonstrative anaphoric references based on written Portuguese texts.

In order to investigate a computational model fitting the resolution of demonstrative anaphoric references in Portuguese written texts, we examined the possibility for applying the selection of merely heuristic and syntactical rules.

Our research did not assess certain groups of words that is commonly classified as demonstratives in some grammar books. According to Castilho [1], the inclusion of *tal* (such), *semelhante* (such), *mesmo* (self) and *próprio* (self) into the category of demonstratives is quite questionable in Portuguese grammatical tradition.

Castilho also claims that several Portuguese linguists (e.g. Rodrigues, Câmara Jr., Raposo and Pontes) have even defended the idea that demonstratives and definite articles (determiners) should be scheduled into the same grammatical category. For our proposal, Castilho's work will allow us to treat the demonstrative phrases as *definite descriptions*.

2 The Corpus, the Pronouns, and the Categorization

Our work was processed on two corpora composed by 13 texts that were selected from a scientific magazine reporting Brazilian national researches.[1] The first corpus, a training corpus, totalized an amount of eight texts (12121 words), in which exercises

---

[1] *Ciência Hoje* Magazine - published by SBPC

E.M. Ranchhod and N.J. Mamede (Eds.): PorTAL 2002, LNAI 2389, pp. 87-90, 2002.

and adjusts on rules and algorithms were performed. The second one, a test corpus, comprehended five texts (14145 words), in which we evaluated the applicability of the adopted rules and algorithms for demonstrative anaphors resolution.

In the training corpus, while searching for appropriate strategies for demonstratives resolution, we noticed that the nominal demonstratives could be subdivided into two major groups:

- *Determiners or Adnominal Demonstratives (AdnDems)*: the ones playing as determiners in noun phrases, which will form, together with the head noun, a *pronominal phrase*. Their most important characteristic is to allow a semantic treatment in resolution. This *pronominal phrase* behaves just like the *definite descriptions*. WE will treat only the *AdnDems* classified as *anaphoric same-head*.

- *Inflective Nominal Demonstratives (InflDems)*: the same demonstratives of the previous group, assuming, however, a pronominal function, i.e., the demonstratives play the role of a head noun.

Table 1. Demonstratives treated in the corpora

	AdnDems - only same-head Este, esse, aquela (this, that, that) and gender & number inflections	*InflDems* Este, esse, aquela, o (this, that, that, it) and gender & number inflections	Total
Training corpus	23	21	44
Test corpus	30	37	67

3   Anaphoric References Resolution for Group AdnDems

Considering the occurrence of demonstrative noun phrases of type *same-head*, we used Poesio and Vieira's approach [2], where there is no need of semantic data for resolution:

1. sub-segmentation filter: excerpts from texts which are delimited by parenthesis or dash (explanatory appositive) are not to be considered for resolving the anaphoric terms external to these excerpts;
2. „heuristic" segmentation: elimination of the candidates that appear in the sentences preceding the current or the previous ones;
3. referential distance restriction: only the last twenty candidates will be selected;
4. identity restriction: the head of the candidates should be the same of the anaphoric term;
5. co-referential classification: the most recent of the reminiscent candidates will be selected;

We noticed that the cases without the support of this algorithm could demand the introduction of semantic data. For a possible alteration in this algorithm, it might be introduced data related to the „standard form" (e.g.: singular masculine form or radical) of both anaphoric term and the candidate to referrer.

4   Anaphoric References Resolution for Group *InflDems*

Proposed Algorithm:

1. restriction between comparatives: in cases where the pronouns *este* (this) and *esse* (that) appear accompanied by the pronoun *aquele* (those) in the same sentence, and preceded by a clause or sentence in which the candidates are divided into two groups that are distinguished from each other by the terms *tanto... quanto...* (as... as...), *entre... ou ...* (between... or...), *entre... e...* (between... and...), just one of these groups of candidates to resolution will be considered. The pronouns *este* (this) and *esse* (that) have, as candidates, the noun phrases of the group in a shorter referential distance, and the pronoun *aquele* (those) has, as a candidate, the noun phrases of the group in a longer referential distance.

2. recency restriction: candidates are noun phrases belonging to the *complex noun phrase* immediately before to the anaphoric term. The *complex noun phrase* is a noun phrase containing other noun phrases, that are usually connected either by the preposition *de* (of) or by the conjunctions *e* (and) and *ou* (or).

3. gender and number restriction: candidates are eliminated due to gender and number restriction;

4. ranking position: candidates that are preceded by definite article with gender and number appearing to be the same of the anaphoric term receive different values and are best classified.

No attempt concerning the option for reminiscent candidate is done after the application of the rules mentioned above. We observed that, in the training corpus, the introduction of semantic data might be necessary for that disambiguation. Some criteria for referential distance on a complex noun phrase, demand further investigations.

5   Conclusion

The purpose of this work was to propose a computational model suitable to the resolution of nominal demonstrative anaphoric references on a portuguese written texts corpus.

Our study investigated the possibility for applying a selection of purely heuristic and syntactical rules in the resolution of nominal demonstrative pronouns.

Demonstratives were scheduled in two generical classes (namely: *adnominal demonstratives* and *inflective nominal demonstratives*). Each of these classes presented particular features, suggesting differentiated strategies for resolution.

By performing the steps described in the previous sections, we obtained initially a rate of 88,64% recall for resolving demonstrative anaphoric references, in the training corpus. This result, which computes the cases where the program detected the impossibility for resolution as being an error, had an index of 82,09% recall, in the test corpus.

The precision rate computes only the cases where the program decides for anaphoric resolution. A precision rate of 100% was reached in the training corpus, and of 93,22% in the test corpus.

Table 2. Results

	AdnDems - same-head	*InflDems*	Total
Recall training cor- pus	23/23 (100%)	16/21 (76.19%)	39/44 (86.64%)
Precision Training cor- pus	23/23 (100%)	16/16 (100%)	39/39 (100%)
Recall Test corpus	29/30 (96.67%)	26/37 (70.27%)	55/67 (82.09%)
Precision Test corpus	29/30 (96.67%)	26/29 (89.66%)	55/59 (93.22%)

These results point towards the possibility for utilizing, in most of cases, purely syntactical features in anaphoric references resolution (with no use of semantic information). The set of rules and strategies we employed in our research presents, in our opinion, a high precision in the demonstrative anaphoric references resolution.

References

1. Castilho, A.: Mostrativos. In: „Gramática do português falado", UNICAMP, Campinas (1990) V.3.
2. Poesio, M., Vieira, R.: *A Corpus-Based Investigation of Definite Description Use.* Computational Linguistics, Computational Linguistics, (1998) 24/2, pp. 183—216
3. Baldwin, F.: CogNIAC: High Precision Coreference with Limited Knowledge and Linguistic Resources. In: „Workshop on Operational Factors In Practical, Robust, Anaphora Resolution for Unrestricted Texts", R. Mitkov & B. Boguraev, ed., Madrid, Spain (1997)
4. Mitkov, R., STYS, M.: *Robust reference resolution with limited knowledge.* In: „The International Conference on Computational Linguistics" (1998)
5. Byron, D., Allen, J.: *Applying Genetic Algorithms to Pronoun Resolution.* In: „National Conference on Artificial Intelligence" (1999)
8. Passonneau, R., Litman, D.: Empirical Analysis of Three Dimensions of Spoken Discourse: Segmentation, Coherence and Linguistic Devices. In: „Computational and Conversational Discourse : Burning Issues - An Interdisciplinary Account". E. Hovy & D. Scott, ed., Springer-Verlag, Berlin (1996)

Large Vocabulary Continuous Speech Recognition Using Weighted Finite-State Transducers

Diamantino Caseiro and Isabel Trancoso

INESC-ID/IST, Rua Alves Redol 9, Lisbon, Portugal
{dcaseiro,Isabel.Trancoso}@l2f.inesc-id.pt

Abstract. Weighted finite-state transducers are an unifying formalism for the implementation and integration of the various knowledge sources and structures typical of a large vocabulary continuous speech recognition system.
In this work we show how those knowledge sources can be converted to this formalism, and how they can be integrated in an optimized network, using our finite-state library and tools.
Experiments performed using our system showed the importance of the optimization of the integrated network, and allowed us to obtain very significant improvements in the speed of the recognizer.

1 Introduction

A finite-state transducer (FST) is a computational model similar to a finite-state automaton, but with an extra label associated with each edge. That *output* label, allows the FST to model *relations* and mappings between languages, while retaining some of the excellent computational properties of finite-state automata. FSTs have been widely used in natural language processing, but their use in automatic speech recognition (ASR) is still not widespread, although there has been a growing interess in the community, specially following the pioneering work on the use of weighted finite-state transducers (WFSTs) developed at AT&T Labs.

In the WFST approach, the recognition problem is reduced to building an *integrated network* using WFST composition of all the components in the system, and then searching for the best path in the network.

Different systems use different components, but a typical system can include $S \circ A \circ C \circ P \circ L \circ G$, where S represents the acoustic speech signal, A the acoustic models, C the context-dependency transducer, P represents phonological rules, L the lexicon and G the language model.

In [1], the compositions included the levels from the acoustic model to the language model, resulting in a *phone_id-to-word* WFST ($C \circ L \circ G$). A phone recognizer, constrained with the network, was used to decode the utterance. Later, in [2], the composition was extended to the level of the distribution ($A \circ C \circ L \circ G$). As the resulting network N was very large and contained many long

E.M. Ranchhod and N.J. Mamede (Eds.): PorTAL 2002, LNAI 2389, pp. 91–99, 2002.

linear paths[1], it was factorized into two transducers $N = H \circ F$, where H replaces each linear path with a unique identification code, and F is similar to N but with each linear path replaced with an edge labeled with the linear path code. The recognition was performed using the previous recognizer and the F network. The linear paths were directly supported as "phones" in the phone recognizer. During the composition of the various components, the operations of determinization and minimization were used to reduce the size of the intermediate transducers. The size of the resulting transducer was not much larger than the language model (in [2] it was respectively 2.1 and 2.5 times bigger for bigram and trigram language models) and allowed the efficient use of cross word acoustic models (the use of cross word triphones only increased the size of the transducer in 2.5%).

The Spoken Language Systems Group of the Massachusetts Institute of Technology (MIT) has been also developing a similar approach, in their Jupiter conversational system. One of the main characteristics of their work [3] is the use of phonological rules (represented by a WFST P) in the recognition cascade $C \circ P \circ L \circ G$.

In the next section we describe how to model the components of a state-of-the-art large vocabulary continuous speech recognizer (LVCSR) as weighted finite-state transducers. In section 3, we present our finite-state speech recognition system, and in section 4, some recognition experiments. Finally, in section 5, we summarize the main conclusions.

2   Representation of Speech Recognition Components as WFSTs

2.1   Acoustic Models

Acoustic models implemented as hidden Markov models (HMMs) can be compiled to WFSTs with a similar topology. The input label of each edge is a symbol representing the distribution of the destination state of the HMM. Its weight is the transition probability and the output label is epsilon, except for the edges leaving the initial state that output a symbol representing the model. Every path that traverses the transducer must output one, and only one, symbol. The transducer A containing all the models can be built using the concatenative closure of the union of the individual models A_i $A = (A_1 \cup A_2 \cup \ldots \cup A_n)^*$.

2.2   Context Dependency

In a context independent system, each acoustic model described in the previous section can represent a specific phone. But most state-of-the-art recognition systems are context dependent. That is, the acoustic model used to represent a phone is selected depending on the particular context of the phone (for example, in triphone systems each phone has different models for each combination of

---

[1] A linear path is a path where its states, other than the first and the last, have at most one incoming and one outgoing transition.

previous and next phones). Context dependent systems thus allow much more detailed modeling.

The transformation from context independent to context dependent can be modeled by interposing a transducer C between the acoustic models and the lexicon, that will implement the context dependent to independent relation[2][1].

To build the transducer C we build its inverse by connecting the edges as show on table 1 for each triphone[3] $a - b + c$, right biphone $b + c$, left biphone $a - b$ and uniphone b[4]. Those edges connect states that represent particular contexts.

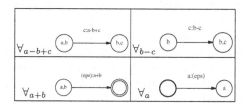

Table 1. Construction of the inverse context dependency transducer.

2.3   Pronunciation Lexicon

We may regard a pronunciation as a transducer from phone sequences into a word. In most systems, the pronunciation of a word is modeled as a sequence of phones.

The pronunciation can be modeled as the trivial linear transducer with one edge for each phone in the sequence. Each edge has as input label the corresponding phone (or model), and has unitary weight. One of the edges in the sequence may have the pronunciation probability and must have the word as output; all other edges should have epsilon output. The transducer L corresponding to the complete lexicon is the concatenative closure of the union of the individual pronunciation transducers. In LVCSR systems, the lexicon L is commonly organized as a tree [4]. We can transform the linear transducer to a tree form by sharing prefixes, or we can transform if to an even more general form, using the generic weighted transducer determinization algorithm [5].

2.4   Language Models

There is a long tradition of using finite-state acceptors to model sentences in speech recognition. They are used in limited domains and in dialog systems to specify the acceptable sentences. In large vocabulary applications they are used

---

[2] That is, a transduction from the models that represent context dependent units to the lexicon that is represented in terms of context independent phones.

[3] $a - b + c$ should be read as the version of b that has a on the left and c on the right.

[4] We name a context independent unit *uniphone* when used in a system that also contains context dependent units.

to constrain the search in latter passes of multiple pass systems. Such lattice or finite-state language models can be trivially converted to WFSTs. However, the main language model methodology in LVCSR consists of local stochastic grammars specified as word n-grams.

One simple way to convert an n-gram language model to an automaton G, consists of creating a state for each possible context, and placing weighted edges between contexts labeled with the word and weighted with the n-gram probability. This exact conversion requires a number of edges proportional to the number of all possible n-grams and not only to the number of n-grams observed in the training text. Hence, this conversion is only possible for small vocabulary and low order language models.

The alternative is to resort to finite-state approximations. One approximation consists of creating a state for each context existing in the model. This state is the origin of all the edges that model n-gram probabilities with that context in the language model. Back-offs to lower order contexts are implemented as an epsilon edge from the higher order context to the lower. This is an approximation, because there may be multiple paths in the resulting automaton for the same n-gram with different probability values. From the point of view of the recognition, this can be a problem because, if the back-off path probability is higher than the explicit probability, the former will be erroneously preferred. In practice, the approximation works very well, being widely used. In figure 1 we show an example of a finite-state approximation to a trigram back-off language model with a vocabulary of two words a and b. Each state is labeled with the context it represents (the empty context is shown as $*$, the probability weights as P and the back-off weights as B).

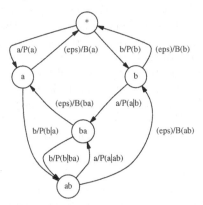

Fig. 1. Finite-state approximation to a trigram language model.

2.5   Optimization of the Integrated Network

One of the advantages of the WFST approach is that the integrated network resulting from the composition of the various component WFSTs can be optimized. The optimization is performed by combining 4 main operations:

Epsilon removal can be performed in some of the WFSTs. But it has to be done with care, as its use can blow up the size of the transducer (it should not be done on the approximated n-gram language model, for example).

Determinization is very important, as it reduces the redundancy of the integrated network, allowing prefix sharing.

Pushing redistributes the weights of the network without changing its topology. Pushing the weights towards the initial state has a very positive effect on the search. It can be seen as implementing a generalization of language model "look-ahead". Pushing is performed as part of the weighted minimization algorithm.

Minimization can be performed after determinization and returns the minimal deterministic equivalent transducer. Its main effect is the reduction of the memory required to use the network.

Determinization, pushing and minimization should be performed on the integrated network, but these operations can also be applied at various stages during the composition of the components WFSTs in order to reduce the size of the intermediate results.

Composition of the Lexicon with the Language Model The integration of the speech recognition components using WFST composition, although conceptually simple, is a difficult task because of the size of the transducers involved. In particular, the determinization of the composition of the lexicon with the language model requires very large amounts of memory due to the very large size of the language model WFST.

In the AT&T approach, the lexicon transducer is linear [5] and it is disambiguated by adding dummy symbols to the end of the pronunciations. The lexicon can be ambiguous due to homophone words, or due to the pronunciation of some words being a prefix of other words. It is very important to disambiguate the lexicon, otherwise the determinization algorithm might not terminate. Another important aspect is that the output label should be the produced by the first edge of the pronunciation (to avoid the generation of non-coaccessible states[6] during composition). The linear lexicon is then composed with the language model, and the resulting transducer is determinized using the general weighted transducer determinization algorithm. This final determinization step requires an order of magnitude more memory than the size of the resulting transducer[7].

To address the problem of the memory required to build and optimize the integrated network, we developed a specialized algorithm for the composition of the lexicon with the language model [6]. That algorithm performs composition, determinization and pushing in one step, allowing an "on-the-fly" implementation [7]. It is also very memory efficient, requiring approximately the same

---

[5] Meaning that no part of the pronunciations is shared.

[6] Non-coaccessible states have no path to a final state.

[7] The main reason is that the determinization algorithm for weighted transducers is similar to the classic subset construction algorithm and needs to store a *set* of original states for each state of the result WFST.

memory as the resulting transducer. It can approximate the minimization step, yielding a transducer only 2-5% larger than the minimal one. The algorithm is based on the fact that the composition of deterministic (sequential) transducers is also deterministic[8]. The usual composition algorithm cannot be used to exploit this result, as it would generate impractical amounts of non-coaccessible states. Our algorithm avoids the generation of those states by using look-ahead information on the lexicon transducer.

3   Finite-State Recognition System

3.1   Finite-State Library

In order to build a speech recognition system we started by implementing an object-oriented library to manipulate finite-state machines. The design of the library closely followed the one presented in [9]. The library allows the representation of finite-state machines and their manipulation. Most finite-state operations are represented as sub-classes of an abstract finite-state machine, and have "on-the-fly" or "lazy" implementations, so that very complex expressions can be represented and used, without the need for very large intermediate results.

The library was designed from the start to be used in speech processing and allows the efficient use of very large automata with up to tens of millions of states. It also includes specialized modules for manipulating acoustic models, lexicon models, language models, acoustic vectors and other data used in speech processing. One particularity is the use of specialized classes that have the interface of finite-state machines, but that are implemented using the Turing-machine power of a computer language. For example, the context-dependency transducer shown in section 2.2 requires a number of states that is the square of the size of the alphabet, making it impractical for some frequent tasks with many thousands of symbols in the alphabet[8]. The library includes a WFST class that implements this transducer using very little memory.

3.2   Command Line Tools

The library was used to develop command line tools to convert automatic speech recognition components in standard file formats to WFSTs. Other tools implement WFST operations such as: composition, determinization, label pushing, weight pushing, our algorithm for the composition of the lexicon with the language model, etc

3.3   Decoder

The speech recognizer or decoder is based on a time-synchronous token-passing implementation of the Viterbi algorithm. Its main characteristic is that it has

---

[8] For example, to build segment pairs in speech corpora for use in concatenative speech-synthesis.

very little knowledge of the structure of the search space. As it is specified as a *distributions-to-words* WFST, previously build using the finite-state command line tools. The decoder can accept either Gaussian-mixture distributions or scaled likelihoods obtained from the output of a neural network (hybrid mode). It can be used to find the best hypothesis or it can generate a lattice or word graph.

One version of the decoder accepts as input the acoustic A, lexicon L and language model G WFSTs, and performs the composition and optimization of $A \circ L \circ G$ dynamically "on-the-fly", using our algorithm. The overhead of building the network "on-the-fly" is only about 20% in the latest implementation.

4   Recognition Experiments

In this section we describe some recognition experiments performed to evaluate the WFST approach. All the experiments were based on the BD-PÚBLICO corpus[10] (a European Portuguese corpus equivalent in size and purpose to WSJ0). The experiments were performed using a standard 600MHz pentium III PC, with 1GB of RAM.

We used a European Portuguese lexicon with 27k words and trigram back-off language models, trained from 46 million words from the online edition of the PÚBLICO newspaper, corresponding to the years from 1995 to 1998. The lexicon and language models were converted to WFSTs.

The acoustic model topology consisted of a sequence of states with no self-loops to enforce the minimal duration of the model, and one final state with a self-loop. The acoustic models were encoded into a single acoustic model WFST.

The acoustic observation distributions were modeled using a combination of the output of various neural networks[11].

In order to analyze the effects of the various finite-state optimizations on the integrated network, we plotted the variation of the word error rate (WER) and recognition time when using different pruning factors.

In figure 2, we show the performance obtained when using three integrated composition networks with various degrees of optimization. The first one was determinized $(det(A \circ L \circ G))$; the second one was determinized and pushed $(push\ det(A \circ L \circ G))$; the third one used a minimal language model $(push\ det(A \circ L \circ (min\ push\ det(G))))$; and finally we used a minimal integrated network $(min\ push\ det(A \circ L \circ G))$;

We see that, as expected, the network optimizations did not change the asymptotic WER. But they led to a dramatic improvement of the speed of the recognition system.

5   Conclusions

In this paper, we presented finite-state methods that allow the various knowledge sources and structures of a large vocabulary continuous speech recognition

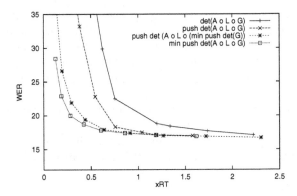

Fig. 2. Effect of various optimizations of the integrated network.

system to be implemented in the unifying formalism of WFSTs. In particular, we described our finite-state library and how it was used to implement a toolbox that allows the conversion of standard speech recognition components to WF-STs. Our recognition experiments verified the importance of the optimization of the integrated network, almost reaching the asymptotic accuracy in real time.

6   Acknowledgements

The present work is part of Diamantino Caseiro's PhD thesis, initially sponsored by a FCT scholarship (PRAXIS XXI/BD/15836/98). This work was also partially funded by IST-HLT European program project ALERT. INESC-ID Lisboa had support from the POSI program of the 'Quadro Comunitario de Apoio III'.

References

[1] M. Mohri, M. Riley, D. Hindle, A. Ljolje, and F. Pereira. Full expansion of context-dependent networks in large vocabulary speech recognition. In *Proc. ICASSP '98*, Seattle, USA, May 1998.

[2] M. Mohri and M. Riley. Integrated context-dependent networks in very large vocabulary speech recognition. In *Proc. Eurospeech '99*, Budapest, Hungary, September 1999.

[3] J. Glass, T. Hazen, and I. Hetherington. Real-time telephone-based speech recognition in the jupiter domain. In *Proc. ICASSP '2001*, Utah, USA, May 2001.

[4] R. Haeb-Umbach and H. Ney. Improvements in beam search for 10000-word continuous-speech recognition. In *IEEE Transactions on Speech and Audio Processing*, April 1994.

[5] M. Mohri, F. Pereira, and M. Riley. Weighted automata in text and speech processing. In *ECAI 96 Workshop*, August 1996.

[6] D. Caseiro and I. Trancoso. On integrating the lexicon with the language model. In *Proc. Eurospeech '2001*, September 2001.

[7] D. Caseiro and I. Trancoso. Transducer composition for "on-the-fly" lexicon and language model integration. In *ASRU 2001 Workshop*, December 2001.

[8] M. Mohri. Finite-state transducers in language and speech processing. *Computational Linguistics*, 23(2):269–311, June 1997.

[9] M. Mohri, F.Pereira, and M. Riley. A rational design for a weighted finite-state transducer library. In *Automata Implementation. Second International Workshop on Implementing Automata, WIA '97*. Springer Verlag, 1998. Lecture Notes in Computer Science 1436.

[10] J. Neto, C. Martins, H. Meinedo, and L. Almeida. The design of a large vocabulary speech corpus for portuguese. In *Proc. Eurospeech '97*, September 1997.

[11] H. Meinedo and J. Neto. Combination of acoustic models in continuous speech recognition hybrid systems. In *Proc. ICSLP '2000*, Beijing, China, October 2000.

Building Language Models for Continuous Speech Recognition Systems

Nuno Souto, Hugo Meinedo, João P. Neto

L^{2}F - Spoken Language Systems Laboratory, INESC ID Lisboa / IST
R. Alves Redol, 9, 1000-029 Lisboa, Portugal
http://l2f.inesc-id.pt/

Abstract. This paper describes the work developed in the creation of language models for a continuous speech recognition system for the Portuguese language. First we discuss the process we use to create and update a text corpus based on newspaper editions collected from the Web from which we were able to generate N-gram language models. We also present the procedure we use to improve those models for a Broadcast News (BN) recognition task by interpolating them with a BN transcriptions based language model. Finally the paper details a method used to generate morpheme-based language models.

1. Introduction

In a continuous speech recognition system it is necessary to introduce linguistic restrictions through the use of a language model in the recognition system. Every language model we have been using are N-gram statistical models. These models use the previous N-1 words as its sole information source for predicting the current word, requiring large amounts of training data to obtain valid N-gram statistics. To obtain these large amounts of text, we have been collecting Portuguese newspaper editions available on the web during the last years.

The kind of texts that should be used to training a language model depends on the tasks where the model is going to be used. For example, if we want to create a language model to be used in a medical reports recognition task, it should be built using large amounts of medical reports or any other medicine related texts. If we want to create a more generic language model we should use more generic texts like newspaper texts. These generic models can also be used to generate task-adapted models when large amounts of related texts are not available, by interpolating a generic language model with a smaller model generated from specific text.

Section 2 gives a brief explanation on how a language model is used in a speech recognition system. Section 3 presents the process we use to create and update a large text corpus based on newspaper editions collected from the Web, from which we generate N-gram language models. Section 4 describes the use of interpolation as a technique to improve a language model for a specific task. In section 5 a method for generating morpheme-based language models is introduced. In Section 6 the results of some experiments using the language models described in the previous sections are shown. Section 7 presents some conclusions and further work to be done.

E.M. Ranchhod and N.J. Mamede (Eds.): PorTAL 2002, LNAI 2389, pp. 101-110, 2002.
© Springer-Verlag Berlin Heidelberg 2002

2. The Use of Language Models in a Speech Recognition System

In general, the acoustic component of speech recognition systems produces a sequence of phonemes or phonetic segments that can be a set of hypotheses, which correspond to text recognized by the system. During the recognition, the sequence of symbols generated by the acoustic component is compared with the set of words present in the lexicon as to produce the optimal sequence of words that will compose the system's final output. It is important to introduce rules during this stage that can describe linguistic restrictions present in the language and can allow the reduction of the number of possible valid phoneme sequences. This is accomplished through the use of a language model in the system. A language model comprises two main components: the vocabulary which is a set of words that can be recognized by the system and the grammar which is a set of rules that regulate the way the words of the vocabulary can be arranged into groups and form sentences. The grammar can be made of formal linguistic rules or can be a stochastic model. The linguistic models introduce strong restrictions in allowable sequences of words but can become computational demanding when incorporating in a speech recognition system. They also have the problem of not allowing the appearance of grammatically incorrect sentences that are often present in spontaneous speech. This makes the stochastic models based on probabilities for sequences of words more attractive for use in speech recognition systems due to their robustness and simplicity. To create this kind of models it is required to use large amounts of training data as to obtain valid statistics that allow the construction of robust stochastic language models.

3. N-gram Language Model Creation

Presently the language models we are using in our speech recognition system have been created using text corpus obtained from the online newspaper editions collected daily from the web. The main reason for this is the facility offered by the Web for collecting the large amounts of texts required for building N-gram language models. The texts collected are newspaper texts since these are very general and closely related with the task where we presently develop our speech recognition system, which is a Broadcast News (BN) recognition task. Nevertheless they are mainly composed of written language, which does not reveal the spontaneous nature frequently present in spoken language.

Our previous language models were based on a text corpus built solely from "Público" newspaper editions available on the web and had about 46 million words. During the last years we have started collecting other Portuguese newspapers from the web, which allowed us to start building considerably larger text corpus. Recently a new corpus named CETEMPúblico [1] containing extracts from the "Público" newspaper editions from 1991 to 1998, with a total of 180 million words, was made available. This corpus was added to our own corpus, but as they both partially overlapped, special care was taken as to avoid inserting twice the same newspaper editions.

To create a language model we need to have the text corpus in a simplified SGML format. In this format, there can be only one sentence per line and each sentence is delimited by the tags <s> e </s>. The collected web pages are written in HTML format and so they must be converted to SGML format using several tools. First all the HTML formatting tags are removed as well as all the text that does not belong to the newspaper articles. Whenever possible, a tag with the topic is added to the beginning of the article to keep them identified by subject. Repeated or very similar articles existing in the same newspaper edition or also existing in the edition from the previous day are removed. This first processing stage allows us to obtain the newspaper edition's articles in clean text and is executed automatically every day as soon as a newspaper is collected. Then it is necessary to convert the texts so that every number, date, money amount, time, ordinal number, web address and some abbreviations are written in full. All the text is converted to small caps, separated in one sentence per line, all the punctuation is removed or written in full and the delimiter tags are added. These stages are performed only when we want to create or update a text corpus, which we usually do every six months. In Table 1 we present some statistics of the latest updates to our newspaper based corpus.

Table 1. Number of words and sentences in the newspaper based corpus in the last updates.

	texts_2000	texts_2001a	texts_2001
total_words	335.7M	384.1M	434.4M
total_sentences	17.4M	20.7M	24.0M

With the text corpus built in this format it is possible to generate language models using either the CMU-Cambridge SLM Toolkit [2] or the SRI Language Modeling Toolkit. We have been using CMU-Cambridge Toolkit more often because of some memory problems we are having with SRI Toolkit.

Before we can start building language models we must create the vocabulary. Currently we are limiting our vocabulary size to 64k words. This vocabulary was first created using 56k different words selected from the text corpus according to their weighted class frequencies of occurrence. Different weights were used for each class of words. All new words, from a total of 12,812 different words, present in the transcripts of the training data of our BN database were added to the vocabulary giving a total of 57,564 words. The margin to the 64k is being kept to incorporate new words of the still unfinished training data transcripts.

From the vocabulary we were able to build the pronunciation lexicon. To obtain the pronunciations we used different lexica available in our lab. For the words not present in those lexica (mostly proper names, foreign names and some verbal forms) we used an automatic grapheme-phone system to generate corresponding pronunciations. Our present lexicon has a total of 65,895 different pronunciations. The lexicon has more pronunciations than the total number of words present in the vocabulary because many of the words have more than one pronunciation.

When a language model is created it is necessary to have some way of testing its quality. The most important method for doing this is to use the model in the application it was designed for and watch its impact in the overall performance. In the case of a language model designed for a speech recognition system, the best way of testing its quality is to just evaluate the word error rate (WER) obtained when the model is used in the system. However this method is not very efficient, as it needs a lot of computer processing for reliably measuring the WER, being very time consuming. So alternative methods must be used instead. Perplexity is often used as a measure of the quality of a language model as it tests the capability of a model for predicting an unseen text which is a text not used in the model training. Perplexity of a model relative to a text with n words is defined as [3]:

$$\mathbf{PP{=}2^{LP}} \quad \text{where } LP = \left(\frac{1}{n}\right)\log P'\left(w_1...w_n\right) \tag{1}$$

P' is the probability estimation of the sequence of n words given by the language model. Perplexity can be seen as the average size of the word set over which a word recognized by the system is chosen, and so the lower its value the better. It is a measure that depends on the model and on the text used for the test, and so to compare different models one should use the same texts. Perplexity does not take into account acoustic similarity between words, which means that lower perplexity values may not result in lower WER during recognition.

Even with large amounts of texts there are always sequences with N words that are not observed in the training texts but whose occurrence should be allowed. To enable this, some of the probabilistic mass of the observed events must be discounted and distributed as backoff values to the observed N-grams of order lower than N. The probability of occurrence of an unobserved N-gram is determined through a recursive method that uses the probabilities and backoff values of N-grams with order lower than N. There are various methods for the discounting redistribution of probabilistic mass, like linear discounting, absolute discounting, Good Touring discounting, etc.

In Table 2 we present the perplexity values obtained with several different language models computed on the transcriptions from the evaluation set of our BN database. These are backoff 4-grams models using absolute discounting, extracted from the newspaper text corpus during its latest updates: end of 2000, first semester of 2001 (2001a) and end of 2001. Some of the models were created with cutoff values of 2, 2, and 2 respectively for the 2-grams, 3-grams and 4-grams while others were created with cutoff values of 2, 3, and 4. A cutoff value means that only n-grams with a frequency of occurrence greater than the cutoff will be used in the model. It is clear that with small increments in the cutoff values we can create smaller models with just a little loss on the perplexity.

Table 2. Perplexity obtained with several newspaper based language models on the evaluation set transcriptions of the BN database.

Model	Evaluation	Dimension (.gz)
n4.2_2_2.2000	149.7	226 Mb
n4.2_2_2.2001a	145.9	255.6 Mb
n4.2_3_4.2001a	149.8	162.9 Mb
n4.2_2_2.2001	143.9	274 Mb
n4.2_3_4.2001	148.0	174 Mb

4. Language Model Interpolation

A language model generated from newspaper texts becomes too much adapted to the type of language used in those texts and when it is used in a continuous speech recognition system applied to a BN task it will not perform as good as one would expect because the sentences spoken in BN are not exactly like the sentences written in the newspaper. If we created a language model from BN manual transcriptions it would probably be more adequate for this kind of speech recognition task but we do not have enough BN transcriptions to generate a satisfactory language model. However we can adapt the language model to the BN task by interpolating a model created from the newspaper texts with a model created from BN transcriptions.

Linear interpolation is a way of combining n different information sources,

$$P_{\text{int erpolated}}(w \mid h) = \sum_{i=1}^{n} \gamma_i P_i(w \mid h) \tag{2}$$

where $0 < \gamma_i \leq 1$ and $\sum_{i=1}^{n} \gamma_i = 1$.

The optimal interpolation weights are computed with regard to the BN transcriptions of the evaluation set, which means the resulting model will have the minimum perplexity possible for the evaluation set using a mixture of those two models [3]. These weights are not guaranteed to be optimal regarding the rest of the data where the model is going to be used but as long as the evaluation set is large enough and representative, the weights will be nearly optimal for the rest of the data.

We use the "interpolate" program of the CMU Cambridge toolkit to calculate the optimal weights using the Expectation Maximization algorithm (EM). To execute the interpolation for creating a new model we use the SRI-LM toolkit, which allows us to mix language models and specify the weights, we wish to use for each.

The interpolated models we have created are obtained mixing the newspaper based model from previous section with a backoff 3-gram model using absolute discounting based on the BN training set transcriptions.

In Table 3 we present the perplexities obtained from the interpolated models between the BN transcriptions and the n4.2_3_4.2001a and n4.2_3_4.2001 models together with the optimal weights applied to the interpolation. The perplexity values shown were computed over the transcriptions from the evaluation set and also over a small text set based on newspaper texts from the second semester of 2001, which could not be used to test the perplexity of the complete 2001 based models since those texts were used in their creation and would cause a very low perplexity value.

From the table it is clear that even using a very small model based in BN transcriptions we can obtain some improvement in the perplexity of the interpolated model.

Table 3. Perplexity obtained with interpolated language models and their components on the evaluation set transcriptions of the BN database and on a small newspaper text set.

Model	$\gamma_{Newspaper}$	$\gamma_{BNtranscriptions}$	Evaluation	Newspaper
BNtranscriptions_corpus.n3.0_0	-	-	551.6	1080.9
n4.2_3_4.2001a	-	-	149.8	138.3
interpolated_2_3_4.2001a	0.825	0.175	140.3	141
n4.2_3_4.2001	-	-	148.0	-
interpolated_2_3_4.2001	0.829	0.171	139.5	-

5. Morpheme-Based Language Model

One of the main problems with speech recognition systems are the words that can be spoken during a speech recognition task but do not exist within the system's vocabulary. These are called out of vocabulary words (OOV's). The easiest solution would be to just extend the size of the vocabulary to push the OOV's rate beyond a reasonable limit but this is not very efficient, especially for highly inflectional languages like Portuguese, French and German. The problem in this kind of languages is the great vocabulary expansion caused by the large number of different words derived from basic words. Many words have different forms for singular and plural and may also change with the gender. This implies that we need to have vocabularies with much larger dimensions to obtain coverage similar to English. To get an idea on the differences between English and a highly inflectional languages like Portuguese, we compare the number of different forms of the verb "to sing" in Portuguese ("cantar") and English in the Simple Present, in Table 4.

Table 4. Comparison of the forms of the verb "to sing" in the Simple Present, between Portuguese and English.

Portuguese	Canto, Cantas, Canta, Cantamos, Cantais, Cantam
English	Sing, Sings

As we can see, while in English there are only two different forms (sing, sings), in Portuguese there are six forms. Moreover, in Portuguese many verbs have the simple conjugation forms (Ex:"moveu"/ moved) but also pronominal conjugation forms (Ex: "moveu-a" / moved her), which can have a great number of different forms and may depend on the gender.

We have been working and developing a possible solution, which we already started discussing in [4,5], consisting on a decomposition method based on a partial morphological analysis of the words. On our previous studies, we classified morphologically all the words present in our previous newspaper "Público" based database and realized that about 35% of the words were verbal inflections. Actually the verb is the most variable word class in the Portuguese language being the inflectional derivation the main mechanism for generating the different forms of a verb. In the inflectional derivation, words are formed through the combination of a root with a prefix, a suffix or both. This took us to conclude that a morphological decomposition of the regular verbs on their roots and suffixes would allow us to achieve a significant reduction on the vocabulary dimension.

Using specific tools and a hand made list containing all the possible regular verbs suffixes (813 different suffixes) we decompose the vocabulary and also words in the entire text corpus used to generate the usual word-based language models. This results in a whole new decomposed text corpus from which we can create morpheme-based language models. During this process a list, containing all of the words decomposed and respective roots and suffixes, is generated. To avoid ambiguity during the reconstruction of the words, the decomposition should only be performed when the root and suffix do not exist both as words. For example the word "como" ("eat") can not be decomposed because it would result in a sequence of existing words "com o" ("with the").

The decomposition must also be performed at the phonetic level, which means the lexicon must also be decomposed using a specific designed tool. This tool searches the original lexicon for the words that are supposed to be decomposed and then, for each word, tries to identify the phonemes of the word that belong to the root and those that belong to the suffix, using a set of pronunciation rules. The resulting lexicon keeps all the different pronunciations found for each root and suffix.

For the decomposition method to work, we need to have a post-processing step that joins back the morphemes, using the list with the decomposed words, so that we only have complete words at the system's output. To avoid incoherence during recognition some restrictions must be introduced in the language model. To avoid the occurrence of a word or an incorrect suffix after a root that is not also a word we force all the n-grams ending with it to have zero for its backoff value. We also force the unigrams probabilities to be zero for all the suffixes that are not also words. This avoids the occurrence of a suffix after a word or an incorrect radical.

The method just described to create morpheme-based language models has an interesting aspect. Any word capable of being decomposed in a root and a suffix both existing in the new decomposed vocabulary, can be recognized by the system even if the complete word didn't exist in the original vocabulary, as long as it was observed in the training text corpus. This happens because the morpheme-based language model can capture those decomposed words in the text corpus through the 2-grams, 3-grams, etc., containing their roots and suffixes and the rebuilding information is stored in the list of the decomposed words that is used in post-processing stage. In this way, although we are reducing the vocabulary dimension used in the recognition system, the total vocabulary admitted by the system is being expanded. Just to get an idea, our last decomposition produced a list of 114,432 decomposed words which is a much larger number than the total number of words in our original vocabulary (57,765 words). This capability for expanding the vocabulary could be further exploited to allow the recognition of words composed of a root and a suffix existing in the new decomposed vocabulary even if those words were not observed in the training texts.

6. Speech Recognition Experiments

To make the speech recognition experiments we used our baseline recognizer AUDIMUS [6], which was originally developed with a corpus of read newspaper text. It is a hybrid system that combines the temporal modeling capabilities of Hidden Markov Models (HMMs) with the pattern discriminative classification capabilities of multiplayer perceptrons (MLPs) [7]. In this hybrid HMM/MLP system a Markov process is used to model the basic temporal nature of the speech signal. Three MLPs, each associated with a different feature extraction process, are used for the acoustic modeling of AUDIMUS. A MLP estimates context-independent posterior phone probabilities given the acoustic data at each frame. The phone probabilities generated at the output of the MLPs classifiers are combined using an appropriate algorithm [6]. All MLPs use the same phone set constituted by 38 phones for the Portuguese Language plus the silence. The combination algorithm merges together the probabilities associated with the same phone. It was this system that served as baseline for the development of the BN system. To develop this system we have been collecting and building a Portuguese BN database comprising two main corpus [8]. The first corpus is comprised of approximately 80 hours to be used as training and test sets for the speech recognition systems. The second with more than 150 hours is aimed for the development of automatic topic detection algorithms. The collection of both corpus is completed. The first corpus was automatically transcribed using our baseline speech recognition system AUDIMUS and was manually corrected and annotated. We are currently using only 22 and half hours for the training of the system. For the system's evaluation we are using part of the development test set with a net duration of approximately 3 hours.

In Table 5 we present the word error rate (WER) obtained when using some of the language models created within the speech recognition system used to recognize the evaluation data of the BN database. From the results we can see that as expected the interpolated models achieved the lowest WER values. This confirms the previsions we made based on the best perplexity values obtained with these models in the BN evaluation transcriptions.

Table 5. WER obtained with the speech recognition system in a BN recognition task using different language models. F0 refers to sentences of prepared speech, with low background noise and good quality speech signal. All F refers to all possible focus conditions (including F0) [8].

Model	F0	All F
n4.2_2_2.2001a	17.2%	32.9%
n4.2_3_4.2001a	16.9%	32.9%
BNtranscriptions_corpus.n3.0_0	34.3%	49.2%
interpolated_2_3_4.2001a	16.3%	32.8%
interpolated_2_3_4.2001	16.3%	32.6%

In Table 6 it is presented the WER obtained with a morpheme based language model used in the recognition of the evaluation data of the BN database. It is also presented the same results obtained with a similar word-based language model. These results were obtained with a different trained and aligned acoustic model. We can see that a small degradation resulted when using the morpheme based language model.

Table 6. WER obtained with a morpheme based language model used in the recognition of the evaluation data of the BN database.

Model	F0	All F
n4.2_2_2.2001a	17.2%	32.9%
n4.dec.2_2_2.2001a	20.3%	36.8%

7. Conclusions

This paper reported our work on developing language models for a continuous speech recognition system for the Portuguese language. We started by showing the method we have been using to create and update a text corpus with large dimensions using collected newspaper editions from the Web. This text corpus is used to generate N-gram language models. It was shown that through interpolation it is possible to improve a newspaper texts based language model using a small BN manual transcriptions based model, decreasing the WER of a speech recognition system applied to a BN recognition task. This proved to be a very effective method for creating language models more adapted to specific tasks when there are not enough amounts of related texts available. In the future, the availability of more training data on our BN database will result on the upgrade of the transcriptions based language model improving even further the interpolated model.

We presented a method for vocabulary decomposition based on morphological analysis of words. This method allowed us to reduce the vocabulary dimension with a small degradation in the WER obtained. We believe that in the future a more sophisticated morpheme-based language model can be implemented.

8. Acknowledgments

This work was partially funded by IST-HLT European program project ALERT and by FCT project POSI/33846/PLP/2000. Two of the authors, Nuno Souto and Hugo Meinedo, were supported by scholarships in the scope of the FCT project POSI/33846/PLP/2000. INESC ID Lisboa had support from the POSI Program of the "Quadro Comunitário de Apoio III".

References

1. Paulo Rocha and Diana Santos, "CETEMPúblico: Um corpus de grandes dimensões de linguagem jornalística portuguesa", in Proceedings PROPOR'2000, Brasil, 2000 (Portuguese text) [http://cgi.portugues.mct.pt/cetempublico/].

2. P. Clarkson and R. Rosenfeld, "Statistical Language Modeling Using the CMU-Cambridge Toolkit", in Proceedings of EUROSPEECH 97, Rhodes, Greece, 1997.
3. Ronald Rosenfeld, "Adaptive Statistical Language Modeling: A Maximum Entropy Approach", PhD Thesis, School of Computer Science, Carnegie Mellon University, Pittsburgh, 1994.
4. Ciro Martins, "Modelos de Linguagem no Reconhecimento de Fala Contínua", Tese de Mestrado, Instituto Superior Técnico, Universidade Técnica de Lisboa, Lisboa, 1998 (Portuguese text).
5. Ciro Martins, João P. Neto, Luís B. Almeida, "Using Partial Morphological Analysis in Language Modeling Estimation for Large Vocabulary Portuguese Speech Recognition", in Proceedings of Eurospeech 1999, Budapest, Hungary, 1999.
6. H. Meinedo and J. Neto, "Combination of acoustic models in continuous speech recognition hybrid systems", in Proceedings ICSLP 2000, Beijing, China, 2000.
7. H. Bourlard and N. Morgan, *Connectionist Speech Recognition - A Hybrid Approach*, Kluwer Academic Press, 1994
8. H. Meinedo, N. Souto and J. Neto, "Broadcast News speech recognition for the Portuguese language", in Proceedings ASRU, Italy, 2001.

Relevant Information Extraction Driven with Rhetorical Schemas to Summarize Scientific Papers

Mariem Ellouze and Abdelmajid Ben Hamadou

Laboratoire LARIS, Faculté des Sciences Economiques et de Gestion de Sfax
B.P. 1088- 3018 Sfax - Tunisie
Mariem.Ellouze@Planet.tn,
Abdelmajid.Benhamadou@fsegs.rnu.tn

Abstract. Automatic summaries are often subject to several criticisms (e.g., lack of cohesion and coherence). In this paper, we propose an approach that uses coherent *Summary-Schemas* (templates) conceived from the rhetorical structure of scientific papers including their abstracts. The Summary-Schemas embed rhetorical roles specified by signatures (sets of positional, structural, linguistic and thematic features) that guide the search for appropriate sentences in the source text.

1 Introduction

Automatic summarization systems based on passages (sentences) extraction process (e.g. [2], …) are liable to generate incoherent „abstract", i.e., abstracts where the thread of ideas does not reflect conventional rhetorical structures and the textual substance presents "holes" due to, for example, unresolved anaphors. However, such systems are more promising than the Knowledge-Based abstract generation ones (e.g. [5], …) since they escape the domain dependency constraint.

To overcome the above inefficiencies and produce well formed summaries for scientific papers, we have proposed in [3] the use of Summary-Schemas: coherent configurations formed by rhetorical roles derived from high level rhetorical structures of scientific papers. Our idea of instantiating linguistic material for the summary by using schemas joins others present in the literature (e.g. [7], [8]).

In this paper, we present a new classification of our Summary-Schemas and propose the specification of signatures for the rhetorical schema roles. The signatures are used to look for appropriate textual segments in the source text.

2 Information Relevance in a Summary of a Scientific Paper

The corpus which we analyzed consists of scientific papers and their authors' abstracts, written in French and collected from proceedings of conferences and scientific journals. The examined papers cover various domains : data processing, agriculture, medicine, etc. Our analysis of the authors' abstracts and the full texts has mainly given

E.M. Ranchhod and N.J. Mamede (Eds.): PorTAL 2002, LNAI 2389, pp. 111-114, 2002.
© Springer-Verlag Berlin Heidelberg 2002

rise to the following three observations : 1) the abstract generally states the purpose or topic of the paper, background motivation for the research, used methods and techniques, experimental results and evaluation of the presented work; 2) the content of the abstract can express the structure of the paper; and 3) independently of the domain, certain phrasal patterns are widely used to indicate the topic, background, methods, results, etc.

3   Rhetorical Schemas for Summaries of Scientific Papers

According to our corpus study, we have identified three basic rhetorical configurations for summaries, that we call *Meta-Schemas*: *Problem-Solution, Document Plan* and *Problem-Solution + Document-Plan*. The *Document-Plan* structure encapsulates rhetorical roles that give an overview on the contents of the sections in the text. The *Problem-Solution* structure can be extended with other rhetorical roles, e.g., *Situation, Purpose, Results, Evaluation* and *Future Work*.

The Meta-Schemas encapsulate the above rhetorical roles in *slots,* each of which can embed various rhetorical sub-roles. For example, in the slot *Situation*, we can find information such as *Basic information (Background), Previous work, ...* In the slot *Solution*, we can find information such as *Proposed Solution, Description of the solution, Advantage of the solution.* The resulting hierarchy of information allows us to derive several schemas from a given Meta-Schema. Figure1 illustrates schemas derived from the Meta-Schema *Problem – Solution*.

Previous Work		Previous Work		Problem
Problem		Problem		Proposed Solution
Solution		Aim		Advantages of Solution
		Proposed Solution		Evaluation
		Described Solution		Future Work

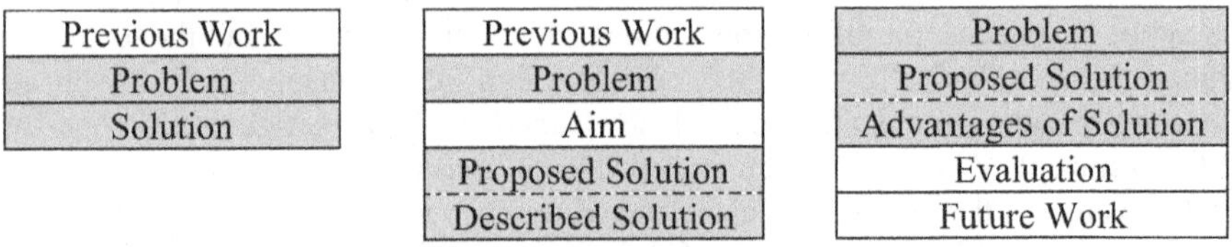

Fig. 1. Examples of schemas derived from the Meta-Schema *Problem-Solution*.

4   Modeling Slots of Schemas with Signatures

To model rhetorical roles of slots in a Summary-Schema, it is necessary to look for textual regularities and generic structures that reflect the same semantics within the various textual segments. We proceeded, on one hand, in the alignment of the sentences of authors' summaries with sentences of the source text (similar to [6] and [8]). On the other hand, we studied all the sentences conveying the above defined rhetorical roles in the source text.

The regularities are perceived through surface markers used to establish, for each slot, a set of *signatures* that translate the slot rhetorical roles. Table 1 shows a signature of the *Previous Work* Slot.

Table 1. Signature of the *Previous Work* slot.

Marker	Surface realizations
Location :	At the beginning of the text
Proper Name :	{X, Y, Riguet, ...}
Bibliographic Reference:	{[X 1998], Y (1990), ...}
Tenses of the main verb:	{Past, present}
Anteriority :	{à l'origine, ...}
Other Persons/Other Work :	{aux travaux de, ...}
Nominal Thematic Group :	{Yes possibly}

5   Implementation of Embedded-Knowledge in Summary-Schemas

The search of co-occurrences of markers in textual segments is driven both by patterns (containing linguistic expressions) and constraints. The linguistic knowledge, patterns and constraints are implemented using the *Contextual Exploration Model* proposed in [1]. This model is based on the concepts of tasks, markers, classes and rules. Linguistic markers with identical semantics are grouped into classes that are divided indicators and indices. This linguistic knowledge is associated with the Summary-Schema task. To this task, we associate a set of rules assigning rhetorical roles to textual segments of the source text. A rule is triggered by an indicator and a co-occurrence of indices that reflect a given pattern. It is executed if certain constraints are satisfied. The set of rules is written with a formal language and then translated into Java classes. The knowledge model associated with the schemas is stored in a relational data base.

6   The Summary Generation Process

Given the above knowledge embedded in our summary-schemas, the summary generation process operates in four steps. In the first step, the source text is pre-treated in order to determine the text structural units (titles, paragraphs, sentences, etc.) and identify the thematic nominal groups of titles and the proper nouns.

In the second step, the user selects a Meta-Schema filling the information of interest. The Meta-Schema *Document-Plan* offers an indicative brief characterization for specialists. The Meta-Schemas *Problem-Solution* and *Problem-Solution+Document-Plan* give many informative extended representations for novices. The Meta-Schema *Problem-Solution* can also offer a targeted representation for users having particular interests (e.g., Results).

Once the user selects a Meta-schema, he dynamically establishes a desired schema that conveys some rhetorical roles. For example, he can add to the generic structure of the *Problem–Solution* Meta-Schema the rhetorical roles *Previous Work, Results*, and *Future Work*. This alternative is supervised by the system to maintain coherence. Only a Summary-Schema having the following rhetorical structure „*Previous Work, Problem to be solved, Proposed Solution, Results, Future Work*" is accepted.

In the third step, the generation process starts looking for the appropriate text segments. To optimize the search for textual fragments semantically representing the rhetorical roles of the chosen schema, the generation process considers first the structural and positional features. For example, to look for the textual segments representing *Previous work*, the search process is confined to the early paragraphs of the section „Introduction" (and possibly in the section which follows „Introduction").

After finding the appropriate textual segments, the generation process injects them in the suited slots of the schema established by the user and generates a „first draft" of the „summary". This „summary" can sometimes be unreadable (presence of anaphors, connectors, etc.). To increase the readability, we proposed in [4] operations for the addition and suppression of informative units.

7 Conclusion

In this paper, we have presented an approach that uses Summary-Schemas to instantiate suited and coherent summaries for scientific papers. Currently, we are examining techniques that ensure the cohesion of the generated summaries. In addition, we will be examining how to extend our summary-schemas in order to recognize scientific paper types, e.g., implementation, overview, synthesis.

References

1. Ben Hazez, S., Desclés, J.P., Minel, J.L., Modèle d'exploration contextuelle pour l'analyse sémantique des textes, In TALN, France (2001)
2. Berri, J., Cartier, E., Desclés, J. P., Jackiewicz, A., Minel, J. L., SAPHIR, un système automatique de filtrage de textes, In TALN ' 96, Marseille, France, (May 1996)
3. Ellouze, M., Ben Hamadou, A., Utilisation de schémas de résumés en vue d'améliorer la qualité des extraits et des résumés automatiques, In RIFRA'98, Sfax, Tunisie, (1998).
4. Ellouze, M., Ben Hamadou, A., Enhancing readability in automatic summaries by using schemas, In TSD'99, Pilsen, Czech, (September 1999)
5. Hahn, U., Concept-Oriented Summarising in the Text Condensation System TOPIC, In Intelligent Summarizing Text for Communications, Hannover, Germany, (11-13 /12/1993)
6. Kupiec, J., Pedersen, J., Chen, F., A trainable document summarizer, In SIGIR ' 95, Seattle WA, the USA (1995)
7. Paice, C.D., Constructing literature abstracts by computers: Techniques and prospects, In Information Processing and Management, Vol. 31, N°5, (1990)
8. Teufel, S., Moens, M., Sentence extraction and Rhetorical Classification for Flexible Abstracts. In AAAI Spring Symposium on Intelligent Text Summarization, Stanford, (1998)

Mapping an Automated Survey Coding Task into a Probabilistic Text Categorization Framework*

Daniela Giorgetti[1], Irina Prodanof[1], and Fabrizio Sebastiani[2]

[1] Istituto di Linguistica Computazionale del CNR di Pisa, Italia.
{daniela.giorgetti, irina.prodanof}@ilc.cnr.it
[2] Istituto di Elaborazione dell'Informazione del CNR di Pisa, Italia.
fabrizio@iei.pi.cnr.it

Abstract This paper describes how to apply a probabilistic Text Categorization method to a different and new domain where documents are answers to open end questionnaires and codes viewed as categories consist of a hierarchical model. A reduced size training set may be used taking advantage of the hierarchical organization of categories. The system developed in this framework aims at helping psychologists in the evaluation of open end surveys inquiring about job candidates' competencies.

1 Introduction

Text Categorization (TC for short) aims at the classification of a text document under one or more predefined categories deciding where the document belongs to, relying just on its content. TC is usually applied to automatic indexing for boolean Information Retrieval (IR for short), document organization, document filtering, word sense disambiguation, categorization of Web pages into hierarchical catalogues, but to our knowledge there are very few attempts at using it for more unusual tasks such as automatic essay grading [4]. Our TC approach to survey coding is part of the JobNet project, which is developing a temporary job agency on the Web, where job applications and job offers have to be matched with efficient and effective criteria. Job candidates connect to the Web site, and after the registration they have to fill in some forms with their personal data, education titles, skills and so on. Besides these standard forms there is a final survey form with open end questions which inquire the candidate's competencies as defined in a psychological behaviorist model. As the psychologists' coding of these surveys is both costly and time consuming we are exploring ways to reduce their amount of work through an automatic evaluation of free form texts.

---

* Research supported by the Sintesi company (Perugia, Italia), which funds the JobNet project.

E.M. Ranchhod and N.J. Mamede (Eds.): PorTAL 2002, LNAI 2389, pp. 115–124, 2002.

Synopsis. In Section 2 we describe more in detail the automatic survey coding task, stressing its originality with respect to "traditional" TC and IR tasks. In Section 3 we overview the approaches previously used for text coding, focussing on their drawbacks w.r.t. our task. In Section 4 we give an idea of the underlying model of the hierarchical code categories in JobNet, in Section 5 we introduce a probabilistic approach to TC augmented with a statistical technique which takes advantage of the hierarchical structure of categories, in Section 6 we show how to adapt and instantiate the improved probabilistic TC approach to our case, and in Section 7 we draw our conclusions.

2   Automated Survey Coding

Hand coding of open end surveys is a classical problem from the social sciences, but up to now there are very few attempts at automating the task, though the Internet world wide diffusion has made it possible to collect huge quantities of such text data from e.g. market surveys and exploratory interviews. In the literature we have found just a few papers which deal with the automatic coding issue, by Perrin [8] by Pratt and Mays [9], by Raud and Fallig [10], and by Viechnicki [14], and none of them applies a TC solution to the problem. Supervised coding of an answer means to find its meaningful part and attach to it a code label from a predefined set of code labels. Reformulating the aim of the process in terms of TC we can say that supervised coding for each answer (or part of it) looks for the category it belongs to (in our case we may also have answers that do not belong to any of the predefined categories) as defined by a predetermined set of categories.

2.1   Automated Survey Coding Vs. Information Retrieval

Automatic Survey Coding (ASC for short) shares some aspects of IR since they both operate on unstructured text documents, but there are differences in the data as well as in the nature of the task [14], the main being:

- the length of documents, which is usually much shorter in ASC (6.86 terms on average as stated in [14] versus 50 terms on average as stated in [2]).
- the style of language, which is usually more informal and close to spoken language in ASC, while typical IR documents have a more formal and fixed structure, as they usually come from the academics, news, and technical fields.
- homogeneity of answers depends heavily on the formulation of the questions (queries in IR terms).
- the nature of the task is different as in IR we look for documents relevant to a certain query, while in ASC we have to systematically evaluate all the answers and assign them, if appropriate, to one or more of the predetermined categories.

2.2   Automated Survey Coding Vs. Text Categorization

Although we redefine our coding problem as a TC problem we have to point out that ASC has its own peculiarity both in the data (e.g. style and homogeneity of language) and the nature of the task. Moreover, the examples, i.e. the training set, are usually already available in TC (e.g. classified ads), while in ASC building a training set may mean to code the whole set of questionnaires, thus eliminating the necessity of an automatic coder (classifier in TC terms).

2.3   Automated Survey Coding Vs. Text Clustering

ASC differs from Text Clustering as in the latter the clustering is a bottom up process, where we start from data and group them according to some similarity criteria without any predefined categories (*qualitative content analysis* in social science terms), whilst the former applies a top down class-driven process as data is assigned to a predefined category set (*quantitative content analysis* in social science terms).

3   Other Approaches to Automated Survey Coding

Text coding, and more in general text content analysis in social sciences, is a long-standing issue, and several software systems have been developed to aid solving this task [1]. Most of these software systems either facilitate the users to hand-code their data and view them in various ways or perform automatic coding relying mostly on word based dictionaries. In the automatic coding case, text fragments are assigned to a specific category if they contain words matching those in the dictionary relevant to the category. One of the disadvantages of this approach is that dictionaries have to be created *before* the coding process begins, and thus it does not rely on the data being analyzed. As this approach is word based it also needs some explicit mechanism to disambiguate word meanings. There exist different variations of the dictionary approach; for instance in one of the two methods described in [14] words defining categories are mutually related through Boolean operators, thus allowing a better characterization of categories. Rule based coding systems are another kind of approach to automatic text coding. Rules can be derived automatically or by hand trying to capture and organize the coders' knowledge of the domain. One such system is described in [8], and relies on the ability of inferring coding rules from pre-coded samples of text. The rule based approach relies on pattern matching, and can be more sophisticated than the dictionary based approach, which relies just on word matching in its basic version, but it still doesn't make use of any form of learning to predict the likelihood of patterns in text. A third approach, which uses neural networks to code answers to open end questions is proposed in [10], but it is stressed that the method works well in the case of supervised learning, only if the distribution of the various input patterns is stable and predictable.

4   Hierarchical Code Categories in JobNet

JobNet domain consists of a set of questionnaires filled in via Web pages by temporary job seekers. Answers are open end but their length is limited to 2 or 3 sentences each. The aim of the questionnaire is to discover the best profiles for a given job offer, through the interpretation and coding of its answers in terms of a competence model. Competencies in JobNet derive from a theoretical model developed in the 70s by the Harvard psychologist David McClelland[1], but such model has become operative and widely used only in the 90s (e.g. adopted by Alcatel). The basic idea is to identify what differentiate outstanding job performers from the average ones. The notion of competence is orthogonal to the notion of technical skill and it is defined by L. Spencer and S. Spencer [12, 13], as "an underlying characteristic of an individual that is casually related to criterion-referenced effective and/or superior performance in a job or situation". One of the most important tools to identify competencies is the Behavioral Event Interview (BEI), where the job candidate has to give an example of a situation or task which led her to take a certain course of action. For the selection in JobNet, a new focused BEI interview protocol has been developed, represented by a written survey, where specific competencies are being investigated. For example, to inquiry about achievement competencies, questions are of the kind: "What did you do to reach your goal", in a context where the candidate is describing a difficult situation she faced. Competence models developed by the Hay Group [3] and adapted by the JobNet psychologists are scaled, i.e., not only is it important to identify the presence of a competence but also the grade of its presence, because that is what makes the difference between outstanding candidates and the others. The developed model is described by a scaled competence dictionary organized in hierarchical competence groups, where the four main clusters are:

- Realization competencies
- Relational competencies
- Cognitive competencies
- Crisis management competencies

Each of these groups includes from 4 to 7 competencies, for example, the cognitive competencies group includes Analytical Reasoning (AR), Conceptual Thinking (CONC), Information Seeking (INF), Synthetical Thinking (ST). Each of these competencies includes from 3 to 8 behavior indicators, i.e., typical behaviors that reveal different grades of competence in a certain task.

5   Bayesian TC Improved by Shrinkage Applied to Hierarchical Categories

The problem of TC is usually dealt with using not only Machine Learning tehniques, but also techniques from fields such as Information Retrieval, Data

---

[1] McClelland (1917-1998) also founded the McBer company for human resources management that today is part of the Hay Group.

Mining applied to unstructured text (also called Text Mining), and Natural Language Processing. Here we briefly recall which are the fundamental steps for the automatic categorization of a document (see [11] for a thorough introduction to the field):

- the generation of a *text representation* automatically interpretable by a classifier, which may have three substeps: pre-processing, indexing, and term reduction
- the application of a method for building a classifier by induction from a set of pre-categorized documents, called *training set*
- the evaluation of the quality of the classifier obtained experimentally from a set of pre-categorized documents disjoint from the set used for training, called *test set*.

5.1   Bayesian TC

We describe more in detail the probabilistic bayesian approach [7] to TC (adopting the notation in [6]), as it has been shown to be very effective in many cases, and we have decided to start our experimentation in JobNet in such a framework. A probabilistic classifier given a document d and a category c returns a normalized real number in $[0, 1]$ representing its grade of certainty that document d belongs to category c. In probabilistic approaches textual data is assumed to be generated by an unknown parametric mixture model (parameterized by θ), whose parameters are estimated by means of a collection of labeled training examples. Categorization of a previously unseen document is then achieved using Bayes rule to estimate the category that is most likely to have generated the new document.

$$P(d_i|\theta) = \sum_{j=1}^{|C|} P(c_j|\theta)P(d_i|c_j;\theta) \tag{1}$$

In a multinomial model a document d_i is seen as an ordered sequence of word events (as many as the length of d_i) drawn from the same vocabulary V [5]. Under the Naive Bayes assumption that each word event in a document is independent of the word's context and position in it given its class, the document may be represented by the usual *bag of words* vector and the classification task then coincides with the choice of the category that maximizes the probability of generating the words appearing in the document. Moreover we assume that the length of the document $|d_i|$ is independent of the category. Though these hypotheses are violated by real data (e.g. the probability of seeing in this paper the word *categorization* after the word *text* is greater than with other preceding words) Naive Bayes classifiers have been shown to behave very well in many TC applications. The probability of generating a document d_i given its category c_j and the model θ is:

$$P(d_i|c_j;\theta) = P(|d_i|) \prod_{k=1}^{|d_i|} P(w_{d_{ik}}|c_j;\theta) \tag{2}$$

where $w_{d_{ik}}$ denotes the word in position k of document d_i, the subscript d_{ik} indicates an index into the vocabulary, and $|d_i|$ denotes document d_i length. The category prior probability $P(c_j|\theta)$ may be estimated by:

$$P(c_j|\theta) = \frac{\sum_{i=1}^{|D|} P(c_j|d_i)}{|D|} \tag{3}$$

Given these estimates of the parameters computed from the training documents, classification can be performed by calculating the posterior probability of each category given the words observed in the test document, and selecting the category with the highest probability.

$$P(c_j|d_i;\hat\theta) = \frac{P(c_j|\hat\theta)P(d_i|c_j;\hat\theta)}{P(d_i|\hat\theta)} = \frac{P(c_j|\hat\theta)\prod_{k=1}^{|d_i|} P(w_{d_{ik}}|c_j;\hat\theta)}{\sum_{r=1}^{|C|} P(c_r|\hat\theta)\prod_{k=1}^{|d_i|} P(w_{d_{ik}}|c_r;\hat\theta)} \tag{4}$$

The first equality is obtained by Bayes rule, while in the second we substitute Equations 1 and 2 for $P(d_i|\hat\theta)$ and $P(d_i|c_j;\hat\theta)$. The probability of word w_t given class c_j is expressed by the *maximum likelihood* (ML) estimate:

$$P(w_t|c_j;\hat\theta) = \frac{1 + \sum_{i=1}^{|D|} N(w_t,d_i)P(c_j|d_i)}{|V| + \sum_{s=1}^{|V|} \sum_{i=1}^{|D|} N(w_s,d_i)P(c_j|d_i)} \tag{5}$$

where $N(w_t,d_i)$ denotes the frequency of word w_t in document d_i. To avoid having probability 0 for previously unseen words, Laplace smoothing is used (1 at the numerator and $|V|$ at the denominator).

5.2   Shrinkage for Hierarchical Categories

Shrinkage is a statistical technique first adopted in a TC context by McCallum et al. [6] to improve the estimation of the probabilistic model parameters when classes are organized hierarchically. Although they use this technique with a Naive Bayes classifier, shrinkage can be used with all parametric classifiers, i.e., classifiers whose model parameters are estimated from a training set. The leaves of the hierarchy often have few scattered training data, while their ancestors comprise more data but less specific than data in the leaves (as their data come from all of their descendants). The idea is to trade specifity for robustness estimating the probability in a node through a linear interpolation of all the ML probabilities along the path from the root to the node in exam. The improved estimate of the probability of word w_t given category c_j is expressed by:

$$P(w_t|c_j;\breve\theta_j) = \lambda_j^1 \hat\theta_{jt}^1 + \lambda_j^2 \hat\theta_{jt}^2 + \ldots + \lambda_j^k \hat\theta_{jt}^k = \sum_{r=0}^{k+1} \lambda_j^r \hat\theta_{jt}^r \tag{6}$$

where k is the depth in the tree of category c_j, $\hat\theta_{jt}^0 = \hat\theta_{jt}$, $\hat\theta_{jt}^r$ estimates are obtained according to (5), and λ_j^r are the interpolation weights, with $\sum_{r=0}^{k+1} \lambda_j^r =$

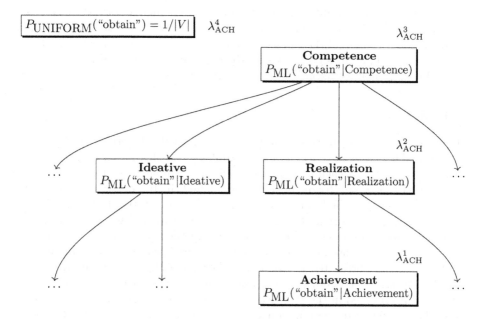

Fig. 1. Shrinkage for a better estimate of the probability of word *"obtain"* given the *"Achievement"* category consists of the linear interpolation of the ML estimates from the leaf to the root, with the addition of a uniform probability

1. Note that (6) assumes the existence of a "virtual" parent $\pi^{k+1}(c_j)$ of the root characterized by the uniform estimate, i.e. such that $\hat{\theta}_{jt}^{k+1} = \frac{1}{|\mathcal{V}|}$ for all $w_t \in \mathcal{V}$; this is done in order to smooth the parameters for those terms that are rare also in the root category (i.e. in the entire training set), and eliminates the need for Laplace smoothing. The λ_j^r weights are determined by applying a variant of the *expectation maximization* (EM) algorithm on a validation set.

6   The JobNet Approach

The key aspect of the automatic coding method in JobNet is the capability of coding properly linguistic patterns which may be very different in the terms they use, but entailing the same competence. Sentences which do not share any keyword may be assigned to the very same competence category, and it is not clear a priori whether the statistic distribution of words may be related to the semantics of coding.

The JobNet questionnaire requires the description of a real or imaginary situation in first person singular and with sentences describing precisely dialogues, thoughts, and emotions (not generic phrases like e.g. "Yes, that's right") the candidate had *during* the situation she's describing. We believe that a hierarchical approach to the automatic coding is better than a flat one in our case, as there are not many training data available, and manual coding is a costly activity. In the JobNet hierarchy internal nodes are trivial, i.e., they just contain training data from all of their descendants, and therefore they may be viewed as a generalization, a gross grain view of the categories below. In Fig. 1 we sketch how shrinkage may be applied to our hierarchy of competencies.

6.1   Scenario

In our competence hierarchical model we have 22 leaf categories plus 4 internal nodes, and hence we have to build a probabilistic classifier for each of them (i.e., a unigram model for each node in terms of statistical language modelling). Our training instances are (fragments of) answers, and the target concepts classifiers have to learn are of the kind "answer denoting an orientation to leadership" or "answer denoting an orientation to teamwork" (we leave out for the moment the internal grades). In order to apply a Bayesian method we have to define how to represent the text, and how to calculate the required prior estimates. In our first setting, text is represented by the bag of words paradigm, where each distinct word in the text represents a feature whose value is given by the number of times the word is observed in the text. No stemming is applied but we can use a stop word list to eliminate the function words. Let us assume a 400 manually coded answers uniformly distributed over the 4 main clusters. For example, consider the 100 documents in the Realization cluster having the distribution in Fig. 2.

Let us instantiate the Naive Bayes Equation to estimate the category of a given answer by simplifying Eq. 4 to:

$$C_{\mathcal{NB}} = argmax_{c_j \in \mathcal{C}} P(c_j|\hat{\theta}) \prod_{k=1}^{|d_i|} P(w_{d_{ik}}|c_j; \hat{\theta}) \qquad (7)$$

$\mathcal{C}_{\mathcal{NB}}$ is the category which maximizes the probability of observing the words occurring in d_i under the hypothesis of mutual independence of the attributes. To estimate the prior probability $P(c_j|\hat{\theta})$ we use the percentages obtained by the training data, dividing the number of instances belonging to category c_j by the total number of instances. For instance, $P(\text{"Accuracy"}) = .05$.

$P(w_{d_{ik}}|c_j; \hat{\theta})$ in a leaf node is given by Eq. 6, where the $\hat{\theta}_{jt}^r$ estimates are obtained by the combination of the ML probabilities along the path to the node. For each ancestor, data from its child in the path under exam are subtracted in order to avoid counting them twice. Note that we don't need Laplace smoothing as we use a pseudo-root with uniform probability (Eq. 5), i.e., $P(w_{d_{ik}} = 1/|V|)$. To estimate the ML probability $P(w_{d_{ik}}|c_j; \hat{\theta})$ we have $|d_i| * |V| * |C|$ combinations, where $|d_i|$ is the document length, $|V|$ is the dictionary size (about 100.000 entries in the Italian dictionary, much reduced in the dictionary obtained from the training data), and $|C|$ is the number of categories. The number of combinations is reduced to $|V| * |C|$ by assuming that $P(a_l = w_{d_{ik}}|c_j; \hat{\theta}) = P(a_m = w_{d_{ik}}|c_j; \hat{\theta}) \forall j, k, l, m$, i.e., the probability of a word occurrence given its category is independent of its position in the observed text.

	positive samples	negative samples	percentage
Achievement	40	360	10
Initiative	10	390	2.5
Accuracy	20	380	5
Directivity	30	370	7.5

Fig. 2. Distribution of samples for the *"Realization"* cluster.

7   Conclusion and Future Work

The main contribution of this paper is the description of a new approach to an
Automated Survey Coding task by means of Text Categorization probabilistic
techniques. Preliminary experiments indicate that this approach performs better
than previous approaches, though we need to compare more results on homogeneous datasets, as the nature of input data may affect the final results. An
open issue regards the feature selection; we start as a baseline from a bag of
words text representation, but we believe that alternative approaches to feature
selection (e.g. n-grams or patterns) might be much more effective in our case.
Though we describe here a probabilistic TC approach, other TC methods should
be investigated as well.

References

[1] Melina Alexa and Cornelia Zuell. Text analysis software: Commonalities, differ-
    ences and limitations: The results of a review. *Quality & Quantity*, (34):299–321,
    2000.
[2] Susan T. Dumais, John Platt, David Heckerman, and Mehran Sahami. Inductive
    learning algorithms and representations for text categorization. In Georges Gar-
    darin, James C. French, Niki Pissinou, Kia Makki, and Luc Bouganim, editors,
    *Proceedings of CIKM-98, 7th ACM International Conference on Information and
    Knowledge Management*, pages 148–155, Bethesda, US, 1998. ACM Press, New
    York, US.
[3] Hay Group. Web site: http://www.haygroup.com. Last visited on April 8, 2002.
[4] Leah S. Larkey. Automatic essay grading using text categorization techniques.
    In W. Bruce Croft, Alistair Moffat, Cornelis J. van Rijsbergen, Ross Wilkin-
    son, and Justin Zobel, editors, *Proceedings of SIGIR-98, 21st ACM International
    Conference on Research and Development in Information Retrieval*, pages 90–95,
    Melbourne, AU, 1998. ACM Press, New York, US.
[5] Andrew K. McCallum and Kamal Nigam. A comparison of event models for
    Naive Bayes text classification. In *Proceedings of AAAI/ICML-98 Workshop on
    Learning for Text Categorization*, pages 41–48, Madison, US, 1998. AAAI Press.
[6] Andrew K. McCallum, Ronald Rosenfeld, Tom M. Mitchell, and Andrew Y. Ng.
    Improving text classification by shrinkage in a hierarchy of classes. In Jude W.
    Shavlik, editor, *Proceedings of ICML-98, 15th International Conference on Ma-
    chine Learning*, pages 359–367, Madison, US, 1998. Morgan Kaufmann Publishers,
    San Francisco, US.

[7] Tom M. Mitchell. *Machine Learning*. McGraw Hill, New York, US, 1997.

[8] Andrew J. Perrin. The CodeRead system: Using natural language processing to automate coding of qualitative data. *Social Science Computer Review*, 19(2):213–220, 2001.

[9] Daniel J. Pratt and William Mays. Automatic coding of transcript data for a survey of recent college graduates. In *Proceedings of the section on Survey Methods of the American Statistical Association Annual Meeting*, pages 796–801, 1989.

[10] Raymond Raud and Michael Fallig. Automating the coding process with neural networks, 1995.

[11] Fabrizio Sebastiani. Machine learning in automated text categorization. *ACM Computing Surveys*, 34(1):1–47, 2002.

[12] Lyle M. Spencer and Signe M. Spencer. *Competence at Work: models for Superior Performance*. John Wiley & Sons, New York, US, 1993.

[13] Lyle M. Spencer and Signe M. Spencer. *Competenza nel Lavoro - Modelli per una Performance Superiore*. Franco Angeli, 1995.

[14] Peter Viechnicki. A performance evaluation of automatic survey classifiers. In Vasant Honavar and Giora Slutzki, editors, *Proceedings of ICGI-98, 4th International Colloquium on Grammatical Inference*, pages 244–256, Ames, US, 1998. Springer Verlag, Heidelberg, DE. Published in the "Lecture Notes in Computer Science" series, number 1433.

Combining Multiclass Maximum Entropy Text Classifiers with Neural Network Voting

Philipp Koehn[1,2]

[1] Whizbang! Labs, Provo, UT 84604, USA
[2] Information Sciences Institute, USC, Marina del Rey, CA 90292, USA
koehn@isi.edu

Abstract. We improve a high-accuracy maximum entropy classifier by combining an ensemble of classifiers with neural network voting. In our experiments we demonstrate significantly superior performance both over a single classifier as well as over the use of the traditional weighted-sum voting approach. Specifically, we apply this to a maximum entropy classifier on a large scale multi-class text categorization task: the online job directory Flipdog[1] with over half a million jobs in 65 categories.

1 Ensemble Learning

For classification problems, supervised learning methods train a classifier on a set of labeled training examples which fall into several classes. The classifier can then be used to predict the class of a new instance. Each instance is represented by a set of features, which have to be carefully chosen.

For example: The task may be to classify job descriptions into several categories such as Chemical Engineering or Hospitality/Recreation (see Figure 1). In this case, the words in the description can be used as features. The classifier tries to learn which words (or combination of words) predict the category of the job description.

This type of problem has been called **Text Categorization**. An excellent overview of this field is presented by Sebastiani [12]. This problem has previously been addressed with Maximum Entropy Classification [9]. In this paper we will point out a weakness of this method and show how to overcome it by using an ensemble of maximum entropy classifiers trained on different feature sets.

A recent thread in machine learning research concerns itself with **Ensemble Learning**: instead of training a single classifier, a set (or ensemble) of classifiers is used. The classifiers are trained on different sets of training examples, most often using the same learning algorithm. Subsequently, the classifiers are combined by voting.

This seemingly simple idea has been applied to a variety of problems and learning methods. Consistently, superior results are obtained opposed to using just one classifier trained on all the training examples.

---

[1] Available online at http://www.flipdog.com/. Job descriptions are collected from company web sites.

E.M. Ranchhod and N.J. Mamede (Eds.): PorTAL 2002, LNAI 2389, pp. 125–131, 2002.

> **Slot Technician**
> Graduate of mechanical program and one to two years
> electronics experience preferred. Applies electrical the-
> ory and related knowledge to test and modify electrical
> gaming machinery and equipment. Requires frequent
> standing, walking, reaching, stooping and crouching;
> excellent hand-eye coordination and fine motor hand
> and wrist movements. Good close, color and peripheral
> vision required. Must be capable of lifting/carrying
> weights of up to 100 pounds. Moderate to loud noise
> level conditions.

Category: Hospitality / Recreation

Fig. 1. Example of an job description, as used in the experiments of this paper.

Some general strategies in this approach have emerged: In **Bagging** [2], subsets of the training data are constructed by randomly selecting training examples. For each of the subsets a classifier is trained. The classifiers are combined
by averaging the predictions of the single classifiers.

Boosting [5] iteratively defines new training sets and trains a classifier on
these. This classifier is typically called a **Weak Learner** – we will also use this
terminology in this paper, even though the maximum entropy learner we use is
clearly not a weak learning algorithm. First, the weak learner is trained on the
entire training set. Then, an instance weight is assigned to each training example,
which is higher for examples that have been misclassified, although they are part
of the training set. A second weak learner is trained on this weighted training
set. The weighting of the training set and the training of a new weak learner is
done for a number of rounds. Ultimately, a final classifier is formed by combining
the weak learners. Boosting has been used with many learning algorithms acting
as a weak learner, ranging from simple feature detectors [13] to decision trees
[11].

In addition to bagging and boosting, there has also been research on combining a more heterogeneous set of weak learners. Different training algorithms
may be combined – see the learning scheme by Goldman and Zhou [6], or work
by Zhang et al. [15] as well as Larkey and Croft [7]. Herein, we propose to combine classifiers trained by the same algorithm – maximum entropy – but using
a different feature set for each classifier.

The formula for **Voting** – combining the results of classifiers – usually takes
the form of a weighted sum (or weighted linear combination):

$$confid(class) = \sum_i weight_i * confid_i(class) \tag{1}$$

Each weak learner i provides a confidence value $confid_i(class)$ for its prediction of a certain class. For each class, these confidence values are weighted

by a factor $weight_i$ and combined to an overall confidence value $confid(class)$. Finally, the class with the highest combined confidence is the predicted class of the combined classifier.

2   Neural Network Voting

Our approach views voting as a separate classification task: the correct class is to be determined by a number of input values, namely the confidence values from each weak learner for each class. Wolpert [14] introduces this view on combining classifiers, calling it **Stacked Generalization**.

Many different machine learning methods could be used for combining weak learners. Domingos [3] proposes Bayesian averaging, where the weights for the weighted sum is computed based on the probability of a weak learner given an example with its class assignment. Pennock et al. [10] provide a theoretical treatment of this issue, arguing for weighted sum voting. Zhang et al. [15] use a neural network to combine a statistical model, a memory-based learner and a neural network for protein secondary structure prediction. An overview to the issues in combining classifiers is presented by Alpaydın [1].

We chose neural network back-propagation as the learning algorithm for this task, due to its ability to work well with real-numbered values and its ability to cope with a large number of inputs without need for model simplifications.

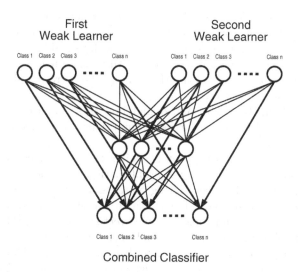

Fig. 2. The architecture of the neural network that combines the classification results of the weak learners.

Figure 2 shows the network architecture. We use a standard multi-layered network with a simple addition. The confidence values for each class and weak learner are used as input nodes. The output layer provides confidence values for each class. The input layer is fully connected with a hidden layer, which in turn is fully connected with the output layer. In addition to this, each output node receives incoming connections from the input nodes of the corresponding class. This addition results in increased accuracy of 1.0%.

Training in this framework requires splitting the labeled data into three sets:

- a **Primary Training Set** is used for training the weak learners.
- a **Secondary Training Set** is classified by each weak learner, providing the training data for neural network voting.
- a **Testing Set** is used for evaluating neural network voting on the weak learners.

The split of the training set into a primary and secondary training set is motivated by the following: The maximum entropy classifiers already reach almost perfect performance on the training sets. If we would train the neural network on these classification decisions for the same training examples, it would not likely learn anything useful. By using a previously unseen secondary training set, the neural network will have a better chance to learn when to trust which classifier, since they disagree more often.

3   Maximum Entropy Classification

We use a maximum entropy classifier as the weak learner for our text classification problem. A good introduction to maximum entropy classification is presented by Manning and Schütze [8]. Generally speaking, maximum entropy learning ensures the expected frequency with which a feature occurs in a class, as seen in the training data, to be the same as the corresponding probability in the model of the training data.

While observing the constraints of matching these empirical expectations, the classification model makes no further assumptions. In other words, it maintains maximum entropy.

Maximum entropy classification is similar to Naive Bayes. However, it overcomes some effects of Naive Bayes' problematic independence assumption[2]. To illustrate this point: Two correlating features in Naive Bayes learning would falsely contribute with doubled strength to classification decisions. Maximum entropy, on the other hand, ensures the correct frequency of both features in the model by distributing probability mass between them.

The classifier applied herein is described in detail by Nigam et al. [9]. We use as features words, bigrams, and trigrams occurring in the document and in the title. We also tried to introduce syntactic features such as subject-object relationships, but we found no improvement.

---

[2] This independence assumption may not be very harmful [4]

4   Experiments

We will now describe our experiments which show the performance gains of neural network voting. Using 130,000 training examples, we classify job descriptions in 65 categories. We have to deal with mislabeled examples and borderline cases that lie between categories. Based on a small-scale analysis to assess inter-annotator agreement, we estimate that the best performance a classifier (human or machine) could achieve is roughly in the mid-80 percent accuracy range.

For the given task, the maximum entropy classifier already achieves very high accuracy. It performs superior to Naive Bayes, error correcting output codes layered over binary boosted decision trees, sequential covering rule learner and other algorithms[3]. The performance of the classifier is 72.3% accuracy on a 30,000 example testing set. The 95% confidence interval for statistical significance is 72.3±0.5%.

An error analysis revealed that about half of the errors derive from mislabeled testing data or borderline cases. However, there is also a large number of examples where the title of the job description gives a clear indication of the job's category, while confusing words in the text of the description mislead the classifier. Apparently the classifier was not able to give sufficient weight to the job title.

Clearly, there is a much larger number of words in the text than in the title. Still, the inability to pick the title words as important features, even when they are marked up as such, is a surprising weakness of the maximum entropy classifier.

One idea would be to use boosting to address the discovered weakness. However, the classifier performs over 99 percent accurate on the training data. Since boosting increases the weight of mislabeled examples, and there are hardly any, not much can be expected from re-weighting the examples.

Instead, we train new classifiers on different feature sets. The most obvious, of course, is to train a classifier just on the job title. We are then faced with the issue of combining the original classifier with the classifier trained just on the title words. This is where we apply our neural network voting strategy, as described in Section 2.

For neural network voting, we split the original training set into a primary training set (115,000 training examples) and a secondary training set (15,000 training examples). Training of the neural network uses the secondary testing set, as described in Section 2.

Figure 3 shows the learning curve of the neural network algorithm over time. While the accuracy for the secondary training set is increasing consistently, the accuracy for the testing set increases initially, but then decreases slightly when over-fitting sets in.

We compare neural network voting with the use of a weighted sum for combining classifier. When using a weighted sum, we determined the weights by

---

[3] According to private communication with Dallan Quass and Andrew McCallum

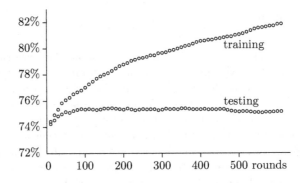

Fig. 3. Learning curve for neural network voting – both for the secondary training set and the testing set.

hand through experimentation. We tried a variety of weight setting and found a large range of settings with very similar results on the testing set.

The results of our experiments on combining different types of classifiers are summarized in Figure 4. By adding a second classifier trained on titles alone using a weighted sum, we improve accuracy over the original classifier by 0.8%. Using neural network voting instead results in a 3.6% accuracy boost.

Classifiers	Voting Method	Accuracy
title	-	61.5%
original	-	72.3%
original + title	weighted sum	73.0%
original + title	neural network voting	75.9%

Fig. 4. Overview of Results: Single classifiers vs. combination of classifiers with neural network voting, weighted sum of confidence values.

5   Conclusions

The results of our experiments are twofold: Firstly, we discovered a weakness of maximum entropy learning for text classification and showed how to overcome it with an ensemble learning method. Secondly, we showed that the use of neural network voting is superior to the traditional use of a weighted sum for this type of model combination.

Acknowledgment

I would like to thank everybody at Whizbang! Labs for creating a great environment that enabled this research.

References

[1] Ethem Alpaydın. Techniques for combining multiple learners. In *Proceedings of Engineering of Intelligent Systems*, volume 2, pages 6–12, 1998.

[2] Leo Breiman. Bagging predictors. *Machine Learning*, 24:123–140, 1996.

[3] Pedro Domingos. Bayesian averaging of classifiers and the overfitting problem. In *Proceedings of the 17th International Conference on Machine Learning*, pages 223–230, 2000.

[4] Pedro Domingos and Michael Pazzani. Beyond independence: Conditions for the optimality of the simple bayesian classifier. In *Proceedings of the 13th International Conference on Machine Learning*, pages 105–112, 1996.

[5] Yoav Freund and Robert E. Schapire. Experiments with a new boosting algorithm. In *Proceedings of the 13th International Conference on Machine Learning*, pages 148–156, 1996.

[6] Sally Goldman and Yah Zhou. Enhancing supervised learning with unlabeled data. In *Proceedings of the 17th International Conference on Machine Learning*, pages 327–334, 2000.

[7] Leah S. Larkey and W. Bruce Croft. Combining classifiers in text categorization. In *Proceedings of 19th Annual International Conference on Research and Development in Information Retrieval (SIGIR 96)*, pages 289–297, 1996.

[8] Christopher Manning and Hinrich Schütze. *Foundations of Statistical Natural Language Processing*. MIT Press, 1999.

[9] Kamal Nigam, John Lafferty, and Andrew McCallum. Using maximum entropy for text classification. In *IJCAI Workshop on Information Filtering*, 1999.

[10] David M. Pennock, Pedrito Maynard-Reid, C. Lee Giles, and Eric Horvitz. A normative examination of ensemble learning algorithms. In *Proceedings of the 17th International Conference on Machine Learning*, pages 735–742, 2000.

[11] J. R. Quinlan. Boosting first-order learning. In *Proceedings of the 7th International Workshop on Algorithmic Learning Theory*, pages 143–155, 1996.

[12] Fabrizio Sebastiani. Machine learning in automated text categorisation. Technical Report IEI-B4-31-1999, Istituto di Elaborazione dell'Informazione, Consiglio Nazionale delle Ricerche, Pisa, IT, 1999. Submitted for publication to *ACM Computing Surveys*.

[13] Robert E. Shapire and Yoram Singer. Boostexter: A system for multiclass multi-label text categorization. Technical report, AT&T Labs – Research, 1998.

[14] David H. Wolpert. Stacked generalization. *Neural Network*, 5:241–259, 1992.

[15] X. Zhang, J. P. Mesirov, and D. L. Waltz. Hybrid system for protein secondary structure prediction. *Journal of Molecular Biology*, 225:1049–1063, 1992.

Compound Temporal Adverbs
in Portuguese and in Spanish*

Jorge Baptista[1], Dolors Català Guitart[2]

[1] Universidade do Algarve – FCHS, Campus de Gambelas, P – 8000 Faro, Portugal
jbaptis@ualg.pt
http://w3.ualg.pt/~jbaptis
[2] Universitat Autònoma de Barcelona - Departament de Filología Francesa i
Romànica, edifici B, E - 08193 Belaterra, Barcelona, Spain
dolors.catala@uab.es
http://seneca.uab.es/filfrirom

Abstract. This paper reports on an ongoing research on temporal adverbs and
deals with the problem of processing a family of Portuguese and Spanish compound temporal adverbs, in a contrastive approach, aiming at building finite
state transducers to translate them from one language into the other. Because of
the large number of combinations involved and their complexity, it is not easy
to list them in full. However, their modularity and relative independence from
the surrounding sentence make them especially apt for a formal description using a finite state approach.

1 Introduction

Time-related nouns (*Ntmp*) Pt: *manhã, tarde, noite/* Sp: *mañana, tarde, noche*
'*morning, afternoon, evening/ night*', here abbreviated as *MTN*, often appear in texts
as part of complex temporal adverbs [1], [6], [7]. Those circumstantial adverbs of
time are prepositional phrases basically formed by the combination of a preposition, a
determinant, a *Ntmp* and eventually by a modifier. A detailed study of the sequences
in which they appear shows they enter many combinations with other *Ntmp* and time-
related adverbs forming complex temporal adverbs. Most of them are semantically
transparent but syntactically frozen.

2 Simple Combinations: *Prep Det Ntmp*

We start with the simplest adverbs, formed by a preposition, a determiner and the
Ntmp =: *MTN*. Concerning preposition, we have considered those expressing a *basic*
temporal localization (Pt: *a, de, em, por/* Sp: *a, de, en, por*), *duration* (Pt: *durante, ao
longo de/* Sp: *durante, a lo largo de*), *beginning* (Pt: *a partir de, desde/* Sp: *a partir*

* This research was partly supported by FCT (Project POSI/PLP/34729/99) and EU
(Socrates).

E.M. Ranchhod and N.J. Mamede (Eds.): PorTAL 2002, LNAI 2389, pp. 133-136, 2002.

de, desde), *end* (Pt: *até a*/ Sp: *hacia, hasta*) and also those indicating *approximate* indications (Pt: *perto de, por volta de*/ Sp: *sobre*) [1].

In some cases, there is a complete lexical correspondence between both languages, as can be seen in the following pairs: Pt: *O João fez isso de* (*manhã* + *tarde* + *noite*)/ Sp: *Juan ha hecho eso de* (*mañana* + *tarde* + *noche*) 'John did this in the morning, afternoon, evening/ at night' [2]. In both languages these *Ntmp* can combine with the indefinite article, but then the adverbs do not express temporal localization, but rather the duration of the process: Pt: *O João fez isso numa* (*manhã* + *tarde* + *noite*)/ Sp: *Juan ha hecho eso en una* (*mañana* + *tarde* + *noche*) 'John did this in one morning, afternoon, evening/ night'. Also, both Portuguese and Spanish do not allow combinations of these three *Ntmp* with *Prep* =: *em*/*en* with the definite article *la* unless they are followed by a modifier: Pt: *O João fez isso na* (*manhã* + *tarde* + *noite*) (*E + *de domingo*) / Sp: *Juan ha hecho eso en la* (*mañana* + *tarde* + *noche*) (*E + *de domingo*) 'John did this in the morning/ afternoon/evening/ at night of Sunday.

However, soon many differences appear. With *Prep* =: *a* [3], Portuguese admits only two *Ntmp*, while Spanish has none of these forms: Pt: *O João fez isso à* (*manhã + *tarde* + *noite*)/ Sp: *Juan ha hecho eso a la* (*mañana + *tarde + *noche) 'John did this at the morning/ afternoon/ evening/ at night'.

In both languages, there are three basic demonstratives Pt: *esta, essa, aquela*/ Sp: *esta, esa, aquella*. There is no adverb with *Prep* =: *a* or *de* with these determiners in either languages. In Spanish the demonstratives can combine with *Prep* =: *en*, and this *Prep* can also be reduced before them. However, in Portuguese several restrictions can be observed: *Prep*=: *em* is not allowed before demonstrative *esta* while *essa and aquela* are obligatorily introduced by *em*.

This kind of restriction can vary depending on the preposition introducing the adverb, the *Ntmp* itself and the determiner of the *Ntmp*. Therefore, a very detailed description of such combinations is necessary in order to build finite state transducers able to make adequate translations between the two languages.

3 Complex Combinations

The basic adverbs mentioned above can further accept several modifiers, involving other *Ntmp*, for example:

(i) the *days of the week*: Pt: *O João fez isso na manhã de sexta-feira*/ Sp: *Juan hizo eso en la mañana del viernes* 'John did this on the morning of Friday';

(ii) *dates* (day - month – year, either isolated or in combination): Pt: *O João fez isso na manhã de 14 de Abril de 2002*/ Sp: *Juan hizo eso en la mañana del 14 abril de 2002* 'John did this on the morning of April 14, 2002'; and

(iii) a limited set of time adverbs, e.g. Pt: *ontem, hoje* and *amanhã*/ Sp: *ayer, hoy* and

---

[1] For clarity of presentation, examples in this paper will be taken mostly from the set of basic time-location adverbs.

[2] The English literal translation of the examples is only meant to show the syntactic phenomena and its acceptability is irrelevant for the purpose of this paper.

[3] In Portuguese some *Prep* are contracted with the articles; in Spanish this morphological contraction usually does not occur, e.g. Pt: *na* (= *em* + *a*) *manhã de ontem*/ Sp: *en la mañana de ayer* 'yesterday morning'.

mañana): Pt: *O João fez isso durante a manhã de ontem*/ Sp: *Juan hizo eso durante la mañana de ayer* 'John did this during the morning of yesterday';

These temporal elements can also be combined in (sometimes long) appositive sequences: Pt: *O João fez isso na sexta-feira, dia 14 de Abril de 2002 pela manhã*/ Sp: *Juan hizo eso el viernes, día 14 abril de 2002 por la mañana* 'John did this on friday, April 14, 2002 by the morning'.

The *Ntmps* =: *MTN* can also appear as modifiers of time adverbs built around the *Ntmp* =: *hora* 'hour': Pt: *O João fez isso às duas* (E + *horas*) *da* (*manhã* + *tarde* + *noite*)/ Sp: *Juan hizo eso a las dos* (E + *horas*) *de la* (*mañana* + *tarde* + *noche*) 'John did this at two o'clock of the morning/ afternoon/ night'. Cultural differences between the two languages give rise to different sets of values that can be associated with each *de MTN* modifier. For instance, Spanish speakers would accept: Sp: *Juan hizo eso a las ocho* (E + *horas*) *de la* (*tarde* + *noche*) 'John did this at eight o'clock of the afternoon/ night', but Portuguese speakers would rather use: Pt: *O João fez isso às oito* (E + *horas*) *da* (*tarde + *noite*) 'John did this at eight o'clock of the night'.

4 Finite State Transducers

Temporal adverbs such as those briefly described above [4] constitute a set of linguistic expressions particularly well suited for representation by means of finite state transducers (noted FST) [5], both for their modularity and for their relative independence from the sentence in which they appear. The method of representing them in FST has proved both efficient and adequate [1], [6], [7]. Our purpose here, however, is not only to build a set of lexical FST to be used in recognition of adverbs in a text, but also to use them as a starting point to build FST that could provide appropriate translation for each adverb, having Portuguese and Spanish both as source and target languages [6]. To do this, two separate sets of FST were built, one for each source and target language-pair (i.e. language-pairs *pt > sp* and *sp > pt*), using *INTEX* [7] linguistic development environment both to create the FST and to apply them to corpora [8].

---

[4] There are even more complex combinations designating time intervals, composed of adverbs expressing beginning and end, e.g.: Pt: *O João trabalhou das 8* (E + *horas*) *da noite de ontem até às 6* (E + *horas*) *da manhã de hoje*/ Sp: *Juan ha trabajado de las ocho* (E + *horas*) *de la noche de ayer hasta las 6* (E + *horas*) *de la mañana de hoy* 'John worked from 8 o'clock of the evening of yesterday until 6 o'clock of the morning of today', but these were not taken in consideration in this paper.

[5] See [4], [5], [10], [11], [12], [13] for an overview of the use of FST in linguistic description.

[6] In our FST, both the *input* and the *output* are inflected forms of the source language and target language, respectively. Therefore, already available linguistic resources for Portuguese [3], [8], [9] and Spanish [2] were not used at this stage. For certain adverbs that include free elements, such as the adjective *fria* (cold) in the otherwise compound adverb *numa* (E + *fria*) *manhã de Inverno* 'in a cold winter morning' it will be necessary to use them.

[7] See [12], [13] for a detailed description of *INTEX*.

[8] The Portuguese corpus consists of the first fragment of the *CETEMPúblico*, taken from the daily newspaper *Público* (http://cgi.portugues.mct.pt/cetempublico, 2002-04-02). It forms a text file of 58,790 KB, with 9,632,423 words. The Spanish corpus is somehow similar in content, but a little smaller. It is composed of texts from the CD edition of the newspaper *El Mundo* of 1995 and consists of a text file of 40,497 KB, with 6,540,493 words.

Up to now, a large variety of combinations have been described for both language-pairs. It is difficult to report precise figures because local grammars for expressions involving numerical values, i.e. *hour* and *dates*, generate an overwhelming number of combinations. If we disregard those grammars, the Portuguese FST of compound adverbs represents over 8,500 different combinations, and the Spanish FST over 9,300.

5 Final Remarks

Considering the family of time-adverbs here described for the purpose of translation, the differences between the two languages are mainly syntactic. The forms of the source language have to be mapped onto the target language with extreme detail. For the most part, an equivalent, if somehow slightly different, form exists. Several elements that compose these complex adverbs present some modularity, and are often used in different combinations, which make them particularly apt for a finite state approach.

References

1. Baptista, J: Manhã, tarde, noite. Analysis of temporal adverbs using local grammars. Seminários de Linguística 3 (1999) 5–31
2. Blanco, X.: Les dictionnaires électroniques de l'espagnol (DELASs et DELACs). 17ème Colloque Lexiques et Grammaires Comparés (Guernesey, October 4-7, 1998)
3. Eleutério, S., Ranchhod, E., Freire, H. Baptista, J.: A System of Electronic Dictionaries of Portuguese. Lingvisticae Investigationes 19-1 (1995) 57–82
4. Gross, M.: The Construction of Local Grammars. In Schabes,Y. Roche, E. (eds.): Finite State Language Processing. MIT Press/Bradford. Cambridge/ London (1997) 329–354
5. Gross, M.: Construção de gramáticas locais e autómatos finitos. In Ranchhod, (org.) 2001: Tratamento das Línguas por Computador. Uma Introdução à Linguística Computacional e suas Aplicações. Caminho, Lisboa (2001) 91–131
6. Maurel, D.: Adverbes de date: étude préliminaire à leur traitement automatique. Lingvisticae Investigationes 14–1(1990) 31–63
7. Maurel, D.: Reconnaissance automatique d'un groupe nominal prépositionnel. Exemple des adverbes de date. Lexique 11 (1992) 147–161
8. Ranchhod, E.: O uso de dicionários e de autómatos finitos na representação lexical das línguas naturais. In Ranchhod, E. (org.): Tratamento das Línguas por Computador. Uma Introdução à Linguística Computacional e suas Aplicações. Caminho, Lisboa (2001) 13–48.
9. Ranchhod, E., Mota, C., Baptista, J.: A Computational Lexicon of Portuguese for Automatic Text Parsing. SIGLEX'99: Standardizing Lexical Ressources. 37th Annual Meeting of the ACL. College Park, Mariland, USA. (1997) 74–81
10. Ranchhod, E. (org.): Tratamento das Línguas por Computador. Uma introdução à Linguística Computacional e suas Aplicações. Caminho, Lisboa (2001)
11. Schabes, Y., Roche, E. (eds.): Finite State Language Processing. MIT Press/Bradford. Cambridge/ London (1997)
12. Silberztein, M.: Dictionnaires électroniques et analyse automatique de textes. Le système INTEX. Masson, Paris (1997)
13. Silberztein, M.: INTEX Manual. ASSTRIL, Paris (2000). http://www.bestweb.net/~intex/ downloads/ Manual.pdf (2002-04-02)

Description of a Multilingual Database of Proper Names

Thierry Grass[1], Denis Maurel[2], Odile Piton[3]

[1]Groupe de recherché Langues et représentation (Université de Tours)
Laboratoire de Linguistique Informatique (CNRS, UMR 7546)
grass@univ-tours.fr
[2]LI (Laboratoire d'Informatique de l'Université de Tours)
maurel@univ-tours.fr
[3]CERMSEM(Université Paris 1)
piton@univ-paris1.fr

Abstract. This paper deals with a classification of proper names which has been chosen as a structure for an electronic multilingual dictionary. This dictionary is not only a list of word, but also a relational data base: we present the relations between proper names that justify this choice.

1   Introduction

Project PROLEX: started in 1994, launched by Denis Maurel, based at the University of Tours (France), it aims at an automatic processing of proper names [5]. This project associates both linguists and computer scientists. It began with the creation of a database of toponyms containing more than 70000 entries of toponyms and their derivatives. This project was extended to all proper names with Nathalie Friburger's research on anthroponyms [2]. Thierry Grass, working on translation of proper names, continued the extension of the database, adding more than 15000 entries translated into German [3].

Method of classification: There is a two level hierarchy corresponding to primary semantic features like *human*, *location*, *concrete* or *event* for the first level and to conceptual homogeneous lexical fields for the second level in a relation of hyponymy of a generic term. The first level is that of hypertypes, the second that of types. We also define relations between proper names. So, we build a relational database and not only a list of word.

Hypertypes: From the five hypertypes defined by Bauer [1:53-59]: *anthroponyms* (personal names), *toponyms* (place names), *ergonyms* (object and work names), *praxonyms* (event names), *phenonyms* (names of phenomena), only four were retained, making a common hypertype for events and phenomena names that are called *pragmonyms*. These four hypertypes constitute the first level. The interest of the first level is to enter minimal information about a proper name. Mainly, it is possible to recognize the hypertype from the context, without any special research in an encyclopedia. Otherwise, some automatic procedures have been already developed to add new proper names.

Types: On a second level, over 30 types were defined, for the organization of a structured bilingual relational database of proper names and using, in addition to

E.M. Ranchhod and N.J. Mamede (Eds.): PorTAL 2002, LNAI 2389, pp. 137-140, 2002.
© Springer-Verlag Berlin Heidelberg 2002

Bauer's classification, those of Koß [4:422-444], for economical proper names, and Zabeeh [7:53]. It was always necessary to arbitrate between contingencies which are too strong if the types are too numerous. These types are determined by homogeneous characteristics and a quite homogeneous syntactical behavior.

The types are linked to the hypertypes by a relation. Each proper name is associated to only one type, otherwise, we consider them as homonyms and we duplicate their entries, i.e. *Loire* as an hydronym and *Loire* as a subdivision of France (*département*) administered by a prefect.

This classification is useful for both human and machine translation: a typology means also a part of a definition and gives an information that allows the translator to associate essential conceptual features to a proper name. The types lead also to general translation instructions [3].

Translation: Proper names can consist in a monolexical (*Athènes*) or polylexical unit (*Banque des règlements internationaux*). The entire proper name can be translated (Leonardo da Vinci's work *La Joconde* will be translated into German by *Mona Lisa*) or only a part of it. There is no regularity inside a particular type: some proper nouns like the football team *Manchester United* won't be translated in French or German whereas *Ajax Amsterdam* will be syntactically adapted in *l'Ajax d'Amsterdam* in French and stay as it is in German. There is only one table for each language with links to the translation in another language. There are four different main cases for translation from French into German:

1. the proper name remains as it is (*Paris*),
2. there is a translation or a transcription (*Strasbourg = Strassburg*),
3. there are two different constructions with a partial translation (*Université de Tours = Universität Tours*),
4. there is one polylexical unit corresponding to one monolexical unit (*Lac de Constance = Bodensee*).

A code is assigned for gender, number and determination for each language, both criteria vary from language to language.

2   Typology

Anthroponyms: This hypertype corresponds to human individual or collective:

(1) Family name (*Saint-Exupéry*). Some family names appear in combinations with a middle name (*George W. Bush*) or are preceded by a civility (*Mme Aubry*), a title (*Maître Robert Badinter*) or followed by some typical words (*Sammy Davis junior*). Some pseudonyms are pen-names (*Richard Bachman* for *Stephen King*). We rejected the idea of making one particular type for pseudonyms and nicknames because there is mostly no indication in a text that shows that a family name is a pseudonym.

(2) First names (*Charles*) appear mostly in combination with a family name.

(3) Celebrities names have in common that they consist of family names which are used without first names. The criterion is the lack of a civility (*Mr, Me, Dr*) or an introductory (*président*) in relation with a family name in a text.

(4) Dynasties or people names (*Mérovingiens, Francs*).

(5) Divinity, mythical or fictive personal names (*Zeus, Hercule, Merlin*).

(6) Firms names (*Nestlé, General Electric, BASF*).

(7) Associations or political parties (*Parti démocrate-chrétien*).

(8) Artistic ensembles or sporting clubs names include football teams (*Manchester United*) as well as rock groups (*The Smashing Pumpkins*).

(9) Public or private institution names content items such as universities (*université de Dublin*), hospitals (*hôpital Beth Israel*), institutions (*Cour suprême*) etc.

(10) Names of international and non governmental organizations (*Unesco*).

(11) Names of inhabitants of a country, a town or a region (*New Yorkais*).

Toponyms: This other classical hypertype corresponds to the location. Bauer [1:55-57] defined types as micro- and macrotoponyms which have been replaced in the database, because they are too vague:

(12) Country name (*Portugal*).

(13) Region name means a subdivision of a country (*Algarve*). Islands (*Maui*) belong to this type if they are not an independent state (*Bahamas*).

(14) Town and village names (*Faro*).

(15) Name of a group of countries (*Union européenne*).

(16) Quarter, road and street names (*Bronx, RN 7, Cinquième avenue*).

(17) Building names include names for parks and gardens, monuments, bridges, theatres, etc. (*Jardin du Luxembourg, Tour Eiffel*).

(18) Hydronyms are water areas, river or stream names (*océan Atlantique, Seine*).

(19) Geonyms (from old Greek γη meaning *earth*) are natural geographical sites (*Forêt amazonienne, Mont-Blanc*), defined as natural forms of landscape, elements of physical geography like mountains, glaciers, caves, plains or forests.

(20) Celestial objects names (which are defined by a place and not as a phenomenon as by Bauer) include planets and asteroids, galaxies, etc. (*Jupiter*).

(21) Fictive or mythical places names (*Atlantide, Océan circumterrestre*).

(22) Public or private institutions names which are also collective humans.

Ergonyms, from old Greek έργον (*work, power*): Proper names that designate something concrete or abstract produced by an human being:

(23) Brand name or trade mark (*Mercedes, Microsoft Word*).

(24) Firm name which are also considered as collective humans (*Aventis*).

(25) Work name for books, films, theorems, etc. (*L'Odyssée*).

(26) Fictive or mythical object name (*Excalibur*).

(27) Vessels names (*Titanic*).

(28) Decorations (Légion d'honneur)

Pragmonyms, from old Greek πραγμα (*facts, events*):

(29) Meteorological event name (*cyclone Mitch*).

(30) Historical or political event name (*Révolution française*).

(31) Sporting or cultural event name (*Jeux Olympiques*).

(32) Feast name with a cyclic character (*Pâques*).

3   Relations within the Database

Expansion: The dissociation of the tables by language also concerns the typical left or right expansions of proper names that are mostly translated. Some expansions are a part of the proper name, i.e. *SA* (*société anonyme*), and cannot be translated (*Groupe Peugeot SA = Peugeot SA Gruppe*).

Synonymy: Contrary to what seems to a commonly accepted idea, a lot of proper names do have synonyms, i.e. almost all countries have a short and a long form *France* and *République française* [6]. Acronyms can be also considered as synonyms and we created a special relation for them.

Polysemy: There are difficulties in associating a single type to a proper name, *Coca Cola* is a company as well as a trade mark. Two strategies are possible to treat polysemical proper names: either to associate a single type to a proper name with different entries for the same form, or to associate all possible types to a single form, which can be source of confusion.

Meronymy: The tables of meronyms list proper names that are themselves specified by another proper name in a relation of inclusion.

4   Conclusion and Future Prospects

There are two requirements: on the one hand, the types must be sufficiently discriminative so that it is possible for a non specialist to assign one type to each proper name which is found; on the other hand, the types must be sufficiently precise to constitute the beginning of a definition.

The efficiency of the method has been verified in the complete edition of the French newspaper *Le Monde* dated January 15, 1999: After having applied the *Intex* dictionaries of common words, all remaining words have been manually treated.

References

1. Bauer, G. (²1998), Namenkunde des Deutschen, Berlin, Germ. Lehrbuchsammlung Band 21.
2. Friburger N., Maurel D. (2001), Elaboration d'une cascade de transducteurs pour l'extraction de motifs : l'exemple des noms de personnes, Huitième conférence annuelle sur le traitement automatique des langues naturelles (TALN 2001) (Actes p. 183-192), Tours, 2-5 juillet.
3. Grass T. (2000), Typologie et traductibilité des noms propres de l'allemand vers le français, TAL, 41-3, 643-669.
4. Koß G. (1999), Was ist 'Ökonymie'?, Beiträge zur Namensforschung, 34-4, Heidelberg, Universitätsverlag C. Winter, 373-444.
5. Maurel D., Belleil C., Eggert E., Piton O. (1996), Le projet PROLEX, séminaire Représentations et Outils pour les Bases Lexicales, Morphologie Robuste de l'action Lexique du GDR-PRC CHM, (Actes p. 164-175), Grenoble, 13-14 novembre.
6. Piton O., Maurel D. (1997), Le traitement informatique de la géographie politique internationale, Colloque FRACTAL 97, Besançon, 10-12 décembre, in Bulag, 321-328.
7. Zabeeh, F. (1968), What's in a Name? - An Inquiry into the Semantics and Pragmatics of Proper Names, Den Haag, Martinus Nijhoff.

A Project of Speech Input and Output in an E-commerce Application

Diamantino Freitas[1], António Moura[2], Daniela Braga[3], Helder Ferreira[1],
João Paulo Teixeira[2], Maria João Barros[2], Paulo Gouveia[2], Vagner Latsch[1]

[1]Faculdade de Engenharia da Universidade do Porto,
`{dfreitas, hfilipe, vagner}@fe.up.pt`
[2]Instituto Politécnico de Bragança
`{joaopt, moura, mjbarros, pgouveia}@ipb.pt`
[3]Escola Superior de Educação – Instituto Politécnico do Porto
`dbraga@ese.ipp.pt`

Abstract. The present paper describes the work done during the last year in the development of European Portuguese (EP) speech recognition and synthesis channels for an Internet e-commerce application. The objective of this work was to develop the appropriate speech input and output, to enable the user to more comfortably use an e-commerce web site issuing commands and options under guidance of a menu system. The speech interface operation guidelines are briefly described in their principles and resulting specifications for the speech channels, namely, menu structure and operation dynamics, and in the following, the system software approach and the speech recognition and synthesis modules are presented. A discussion is done about some project trade-offs and results obtained so far. Future perspectives of the on-going work are also presented.

1 Introduction

Use of e-commerce applications on the Internet is steadily growing and motivates for advances in user interfacing that provide additional comfort and ease of use. It is a type of application in which, depending on the target area of e-commerce, vocabularies can be moderately short to allow the introduction of small speech recognition engines. In the present work the food supply area of e-commerce was the target and the work presented in this paper is co-ordinated with the general interface design, under the responsibility of a project partner.

The products categories in this field of business are structured by the IFLS standard[1] that provides a tree-type of organization with 3 levels. Some of the most typical problems arise from the presence of foreign words in product names, causing increased difficulty in speech synthesis, from the dynamics of the interface, in response to users commands, and from the acoustical noise and room conditions, the latter causing problems at voice pick-up for speech recognition. In the present approach a listen-and-select mechanism was adopted by the interface design partner employing

---

[1] Institut Français pour le développement des Liens et Services Industrie-Commerce.

E.M. Ranchhod and N.J. Mamede (Eds.): PorTAL 2002, LNAI 2389, pp. 141-150, 2002.

speech prompts issued by the system whenever a user action is required or information is conveyed to the user. The adoption of a menu driven interface with natural numbering of items from lists, allowed the use of an isolated word recognition approach. The rather low-count in the global vocabulary for speech recognition together with a small perplexity at each menu, consisting mainly of the menu keywords together with integer numbers and operational commands, indicated a moderate difficulty for the recognition task in this aspect.

In the speech output channel, the present application posed a number of relevant problems, specially in the aspects connected to naturalness of output speech. Following the conclusions of the work of *COST 258*[2], the areas of quality at segmental and supra-segmental levels were addressed. At the segmental level, the diphone concatenation concept was adopted and two signal generation techniques were implemented. Firstly, a formant-based generator was produced in the direct sequence of existing know-how. Due to the limitations in signal quality typical of the formant-based approach, a second signal generator was started in the project and finalized by its end, this one based on time concatenation of original speech diphones, using a specially developed technique based on RELP-OLA[3] synthesis and a second diphone database, developed for the purpose, in the scope of a larger EP database development described elsewhere [1]. Not less important for synthetic speech naturalness are the supra-segmental level aspects. Text analysis and pre-processing for phonetic conversion and the generation of adequate prosodic contours for the speech signal, mainly in the f0 and segmental durations domains, were considered. For both processes, an *XML*-based[4] part-of-speech tagger (LAB205ML) was developed in order to supply contextual and structural information to each subsequent module in the speech synthesizer chain. The prosodic programming required a substantial number of studies including production of specific speech and linguistic databases. The main phrase categories used in the e-commerce system interface were identified and the corresponding prosodic patterns extracted, stylized and programmed.

Another general problem was the software interface with the operating system of the PC terminal under *Windows*. The *Microsoft SAPI 4.0*[5] system was adopted and a reasonably good compatibility with the browser software was achieved, together with a stable management of the input and output speech processes. An object-oriented programming approach was used along the work enabling the complex interpenetration of text information down to the signal generation level, for use when necessary.

2   The Voice Interface Operation

The communication of the speech channels with the multimedia system of the PC and the browser application is achieved through the *SAPI 4.0* that implements a set of

---

[2] COST 258 – Naturalness of Synthetic Speech (http://www.unil.ch/imm/docs/LAIP/COST_258/cost258.htm)
[3] Residual Excited Linear Prediction – OverLap and Add.
[4] Extensible Mark-up Language.
[5] SAPI – Speech Application Program Interface.

components and interfaces for communication with text-to-speech (*TTS*) and speech recognition (*SR*) systems [2][3].

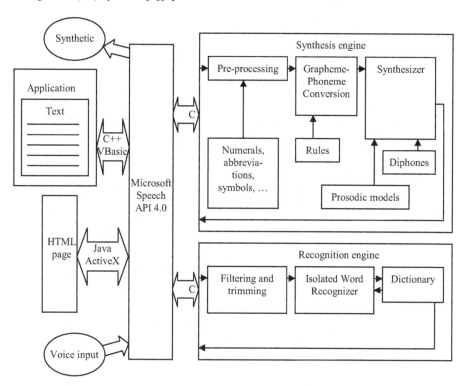

Fig. 1. General architecture of a SAPI compatible application.

Figure 1 illustrates the architecture of a generic application that employs *TTS* conversion and isolated word recognition (*IWR*).

The diagram can be interpreted at two levels: the speech channels level and the application level. The application with voice menu navigation uses both speech channels. These channels implement in a direct or indirect way the functions that the application requires at each phase. The central issue is to implement the channels software in a way compatible with most applications. The *SAPI* is placed between the application and system levels. The *TTS* e *SR* systems are called *engines* in the *API* and are installed in the operating system. Through the *SAPI* the (or each) application queries the available engines and chooses the preferred voice/language for *TTS* or the preferred *SR*. The implemented components belong to several complexity levels and it is up to the application to select the best at each moment. The lower the component level the more direct is the access to the engines.

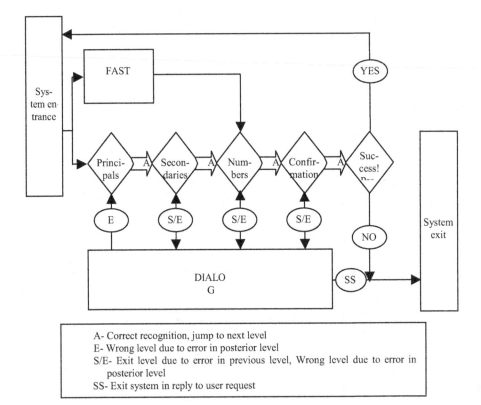

Fig. 2. The IFLS hierarchy and its interface

The 3 *API*s of lower level are: DirectTextToSpeech, DirectSpeechRecognition and Audio Object. All are based in COM[6] object programming [4]. In the first 2 APIs it is up to the engines to implement the interfaces and the objects. In the case of the Audio Object both the interfaces and objects are implemented already and ready to be used by the engines.

Common characteristics in both *TTS* e *SR* engines are their *dll*[7] shape that implements objects and interfaces. The first object needed is the *enumerator* that supplies the application information about a specific engine. After selection of an engine the *engine* object is created. Each object possesses its own characteristics of *TTS* or *SR* operation.

---

[6] COM - Component Object Model.
[7] dll - Dynamic link library.

2.1 IFLS Structure and Menu Voice Interface

In order to clarify the requirements of the voice interface tasks, the IFLS-based system recognition structure is briefly presented. It is divided into levels, organised in a hierarchic way, with sequential access between levels, as can be seen in Figure 2.

3 The Speech Recognition Module

This section reports the development of the speech recognition module for isolated words of a restrict vocabulary including natural numbers. It's a speaker dependent system, which uses speaker adaptation techniques.

3.1 Architecture

The system is based on a discrete hidden Markov model approach. It is composed of the following parts: pre-processor (filtering and endpoint detection), features extraction, codebooks generation, array quantization, models training, adaptation and word recognizer. The recognizer internal architecture is presented in Figure 3 below. Development of all modules was done in C programming language.

3.2 Recording of Speech Data Base

A one speaker database was recorded at 16 ksamples/sec, 16 bits, mono. The entire database was recorded with the same type of microphone in quiet conditions, with the microphone positioned at about 15 cms from the mouth, slightly below and to the side. Some trial recordings were done with different positions for testing and selection purposes. The recordings were done in 6 sessions, three at night and three during the day, distributed along a period of two months.

The database consists of a phonetically rich 15 minutes speech recording, suitable for the codebook generation, and an average of 100 sound samples (70 for training and 30 for testing) of each word to recognize in the system (natural numbers and vocabulary words). In order to achieve the best possible scores in word recognition, the database quality was an important point that was considered.

3.3 The Recognition System

Pre-processing: In order to remove low frequency noise (and DC baseline), all sound input signals need to be pre-processed. A 4th-order, IIR band-pass filter was introduced for the band 100Hz-7,8KHz. To eliminate silence segments before and after utterances, an endpoint detector algorithm was developed.

Features extraction: Energy, delta-energy, mel-cepstral, delta-mel-cepstral and delta-delta-mel-cepstral coefficients were extracted, making a total of 38 coefficients. Codebook generation: The system codebook, with 128 elements, is calculated from the total of the 15 minutes phonetically rich recorded speech, after the features extraction. Array quantization: The sound signal was divided into 20 ms frames, 50% overlapping, and each frame was quantized on the calculated codebook. When the utterances are quantized the system can process the next stage.

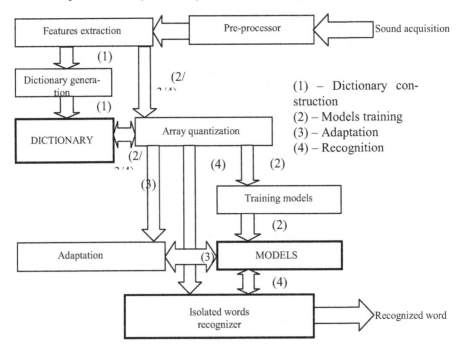

Fig.3. The Recognition System Architecture

Models Training: The training algorithm implemented is based on discrete hidden Markov models with 3 states per syllable. Adaptation: The adaptation algorithm implemented to adapt the recognizer to another user is also based on discrete hidden Markov models and the average duration of each word. Words Recognizer: The homogeneous and first order hidden Markov models were trained using the Baum-Welsch algorithm and also uses an estimate of the average duration of the word. The selection of the recognized word is done using a maximum likelihood estimator – MLE over the quantized signal and duration data.

Besides the *engine* object, the recognition engine requires a *grammar* object. The engine contains the filtering and signal cut algorithms. The grammar object itself performs the recognition.

The recognition system works with a fair precision presenting some sensitivity to ambient noise, what is to be expected in the actual technology. Use of a close-talk microphone, refinement of the algorithms and models with a larger database will lead to a higher robustness of the system.

4   The Speech Synthesis System

4.1   Text Pre-processing

The text-to-speech system presented in Figure 4 below receives the text to be synthesized through the *SAPI* and creates an internal object whose structure comprehends a full range of text characteristics and parsing information, from initial text down to the phone level. This structure is then filled-up by the subsequent processes. The text is afterwards passed through a pre-processing phase where mainly numerals, abbreviations and other symbols are converted into a readable full-length text form. The first step for conversion is to detect the category of the expression (number, abbreviation, etc). This module is still under development. Meanwhile a basic set of categories is automatically detected (integer numerals for instance), the more sophisticated categories still require mark-up. Manual mark-up is possible in the scope of the present application although not advisable as a method. The next step is the conversion itself that is already fully developed, and comprehends most of the possible categories of expressions. In this stage the text is already split into smaller units, paragraphs or phrases, and buffered to speed up the process.

4.2   Linguistic Analysis

A morph-syntactic analysis of the pre-processed text is done, in order to prepare an adequate prosodic manipulation [5]. For this purpose a rule-based grammar was created, and is presently in the programming phase, in PROLOG, on top of a morphologic analyzer from PRIBERAM. It provides a text parsing function into phrasal groups, with some morphologic disambiguation (a preliminary version). As they become increasingly available in the on-going development work of this project, the results of the morph-syntactic analysis, are used for the selection of the prosodic pattern [6] of intonation from a set of models that were determined in specific studies for the present application. Proposed prosodic categories in the model library include declarative, interrogative and imperative modes with a comprehensive range of relevant sub-modes. This development is described in more depth elsewhere [7].
The results of the, above referred, conversion and analysis, allow mark-up of the text using a mark-up language, called Lab205ML, created specially for this purpose. This language comprehends prosodic mark-up of phrasal groups. The use of mark-up is interesting for transmission of parsing and text structure information between successive modules of the TTS system. It also allows forced selection of text conversion modalities or prosodic patterns when needed.
This can be interesting in the present type of applications where the texts to be read by the system are limited in type, in structure and in communication modality.

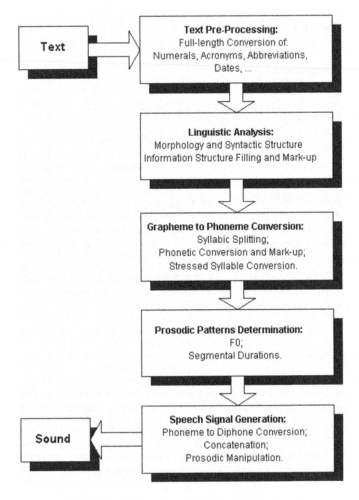

Fig.4. The Text-to-Speech System Architecture

For this purpose a mark-up development system was created to assist manual or semi-automatic text mark-up to be used by the contents editor.

4.3 Text Conversion, Prosodic Pattern Selection, and Signal Generation

Each phrase will subsequently pass through the operation of grapheme-phoneme conversion (phonetic transcription). This conversion maps the set of characters into one set of symbols that represent the sound units (phonemes).

The implemented algorithm converts a sequence of graphical ASCII[8] characters, into SAMPA[9] phonetic characters. For example, the phrase: "Uma frase declarativa."

---

[8] ASCII- American National Standard Code for Information Interchange.

is converted into: /_um6fraz@d@kl6r6tiv6_/. The conversion algorithm, that also performs syllabic division, stressed syllable detection, and some co-articulation transformations, inserts marks of beginning of phrase, word and syllable and marks of stressed syllable, into the converted text sequence. The mark of stressed syllable, for instance, will be used later in the prosodic processing phase for time placement of word accent.

The sequence of phonemes with prosodic information, indicates which diphones to concatenate for database search and collection and the results passed to the signal-processing phase by means of the selected time units concatenation synthesizer. This unit is selectable between 2 types: a 4-formant with improved L-F model excitation source [8] and improved mouth radiation filter, and one RELP-OLA concatenation device with original speech diphones. The synthesizer in any case is prepared for processing the speech signal according to the prosodic f0 and duration patterns prepared from the linguistic analysis. For the intonation (f0) pattern, the Fujisaki model [9] was used for manipulation. For segmental durations a statistical model was built using artificial neural networks. The speech signal then obtained is buffered and delivered to the operating system sound sub-system.

5   Present Status of Results, Conclusions, and Future Perspectives

The set of speech channels has been integrated with the Internet application of e-commerce to produce a prototype whose functionality has been proved. The prototype is presently under tests and final adjustments to enter the phase of user tests. In the speech recognition channel the speaker dependent approach produces some recognition errors with other speakers and the adaptation scheme must be used. A much larger database is presently under preparation to circumvent this limitation together with evolution of the adaptation scheme. A next version of the recognizer will be based on a semi-continuous HMM approach for improved resolution.

The speech synthesis channel is presently capable of reading the text materials of the application and most of the general texts as well. Some improvements in the text pre-processing are being done at the levels of automatic classification of expressions for full-length conversion (special numerals, etc) and phonetic conversion (treatment of rules exceptions).

The morph-syntactic analysis device is being continuously improved with programming and tuning of rules (and exceptions). For the moment the automatic operation of the prosodic module is only capable of identifying some types of phrasal groups and defaults to the basic ones. The prosodic behavior of the synthesizer is therefore still not fully natural. Extrapolating from the near past the impact of improvements on naturalness it can be concluded that naturalness will still increase very much with the conclusion of the mentioned developments.

Regarding segmental quality the two signal generators behave differently. The formant based version is capable of a good phonetic realization due to the diphone approach and the improved source, but lacks naturalness at the spectral level due to the

---

[9] SAMPA- Speech Assessment Methods Phonetic Alphabet.

limitations of the employed model. The RELP-OLA synthesizer produces a better segmental quality, but prosodic manipulation is more difficult. Users opinions favour the RELP-OLA device for segmental quality, but formal tests need to be performed in near to real situations for solid conclusions to be taken. At the signal level, objective tests are under way using a spectral distance approach.

A formal evaluation of the errors at the different text processing phases is currently under way. The method used is based on large manually tagged texts, different from the ones used for development, that are used as references for calculation of error rates.

6 Acknowledgements

The authors wish to acknowledge and thank: AdI (Agência de Inovação - MCT) for the support granted to the project where this work is inscribed. COST 258 – Naturalness of Synthetic Speech, for the great scientific impact in the present work. PRIBERAM, for licensing their morphological analyzer for EP (http://www.priberam.pt).

7 References

1. "Phonetic Events from the Labeling of the European Portuguese Database for Speech Synthesis, FEUP/IPB-DB", J. P. Teixeira, D. Freitas, D. Braga, M. J. Barros, V. Latsch, Proceedings of "EUROSPEECH 2001", Aalborg, Denmark, September 2001.
2. Microsoft Speech API 4.0. http://www.microsoft.com/iit/onlinedocs.
3. Developing a text-to-Speech Engine. http://www.microsoft.com/iit/onlinedocs.
4. Dr. GUI on Components, COM and ATL. http://msdn.Microsoft.com/library.
5. "Estudio de Técnicas de Processado Lingüístico y Acústico para Sistemas de Conversión Texto-Voz en Español basados en Conactenación de Unidades", Lopez, Eduardo, Doctoral Thesis, Universidad Politécnica de Madrid, (1993).
6. Cruz-Ferreira, Madalena; "Intonation in European Portuguese", in Hirst, D.; Di-Cristo, A.; Intonational Systems, Cambridge University Press, (1998).
7. "Correlation between Phonetic factors and linguistic events regarding a prosodic pattern of European Portuguese: a practical proposal", D. Freitas, D. Braga, M. J. Barros, V.Latsch, J. P. Teixeira, Proceedings of "ICSP2001 – International Conference on Speech Processing", Seoul, August 2001.
8. Childers, Donald G. "Speech processing an synthesis toolboxes," John Wiley &Sons, inc. (1999).
9. Fujisaki, Y. et al.; Computing Prosody, Spring New York, USA, ISBN 0-387-94804-X, (1997), ch. 3, pp. 27-40.

Ambiguity Reports for Flexible Dialog Management

Kerstin Bücher[1], Michael Knorr[1], and Bernd Ludwig[2]

[1] Computer Science Institute (Inf 8)
[2] Computer Science Institute (Inf 5),
University of Erlangen-Nuremberg, Haberstr. 2, 91058 Erlangen, Germany

Abstract. The ability to react flexibly on misunderstandings between user and system is an important factor for the acceptance of spoken dialog systems. This paper addresses the issue of grounding utterances in task-oriented human-computer dialogs. It focuses on the aspect of handling ambiguities while parsing output from a speech recognizer: The parser detects the origin and the type of ambiguities which are reported to the dialog manager as comments to the list of readings for the user's utterance. This way, disambiguation is delegated to the dialog manager and accomplished either by exploiting the application situation or by initiating clarification dialogs that are suitable for the dialog situation.

1 Introduction

One of the main reasons for failed human-computer interactions is the system's difficulty to integrate new utterances in the dialog context. There are two dimensions of integration to be considered: The relation between the phrases within an utterance and the utterance's meaning within the dialog context.

Usually, implementations of dialog managers rely blindly on the results computed by speech recognizer and parser. In human-human dialogs, however, the participants often reassure themselves whether they are understanding the speaker, i.e. whether they are integrating phrases in utterances and utterances in context in the expected way. Rethinking the possible system-internal interaction has lead us to an approach that combines closely the processes of parsing an utterance and its integration in a dialog, thereby improving the cooperation between the parser and the dialog manager: We reorganize the classical chart parsing approach by splitting parsing into two phases; first, segmenting an utterance into chunks and, second, relating these to each other in terms of dependencies determined by syntactic, semantic, and pragmatic constraints. Discourse Representation Structures (see [9]) are composed and rated. When the parser discovers an ambiguity it creates an ambiguity report for the dialog manager which might be able to disambiguate the utterance using the dialog context. If the dialog manager fails to select a single discourse representation structure (DRS) in order to integrate the parsed utterance in the dialog context, it uses the content of the ambiguity report to initiate a clarification dialog, acting flexibly depending on the situation [1].

---

[1] The research presented in this paper has been carried out and tested in the framework of the EMBASSI project (Grant N*: 01IL9904F8) providing multi-modal assistance for controlling audio and video equipment.

In section 2 we explain the parsing process, in section 3 and section 4 we present the implementation of the parser; finally, section 5 shows how the parsing results are integrated in the dialog situation.

2   Two-Phase Parsing

Building a grammar for the parsing of spoken German has two challenges: First, the parser has to be able to process utterances that are ungrammatical or incomplete, since this is typical for spontaneous speech, and due to recognition errors. Second, German is a language with a fairly free word order, also allowing for discontinuous constituents. Therefore, the grammar cannot rely only on linear sequence as its main concept. We try to overcome these problems by designing a two-phase parsing process.

The first phase works with a grammar that employs phrase structure rules to build chunks (similar to [1]) consisting of a head element and its complement, i.e. a possible filler of a free position in the head's (X-Bar-) structure. A chunk may also consist only of its head. The combination of two elements is constrained by their feature structure, and by linear order requirements: Only elements that are adjacent to each other and that occur in a fixed order can be connected to form a chunk.

Let's consider an example. The utterance "Den Krimi um acht anschauen" ("Record the detective story at eight") is analyzed as a sequence of three chunks: the DP "den Krimi" built by conjoining the determiner "den" (the syntactic head) and the NP "Krimi", the PP "um acht", and the VP "anschauen".

Chunks are not only syntactically correct units but are semantically well-formed, too. In the lexicon, each element has in its entry information about its morphological features and its semantics, represented as a DRS. When combining two elements, the parser checks the compatibility of the morphological features and merges their DRSs resulting in a chunk-DRS. This way, each chunk gets an interpretation. In case of an ill-formed input, the utterance can be at least partially interpreted. To find an interpretation of the entire utterance the relation between the chunk(-interpretations) has to be examined. This is put off to the second phase.

Note that in the first phase only those elements are combined that occur in a fixed order: While "den Krimi" is well-formed, the reverse order "Krimi den" is not. In contrast, the chunks themselves are not restricted to a certain position within the sentence: Either sequence, "Um acht den Krimi anschauen" and "Den Krimi um acht anschauen", is grammatical. The first parsing step also ignores the fact that the PP "um acht" may be attached to either the DP "den Krimi" or the VP modifying the start-time of the recording action. These issues again are subject to the parsing process in phase two.

The second phase relies on a kind of dependency grammar that for each chunk of phase 1 gives a list of possible syntactic functions the chunk may have. The options are constrained by the morphological features of the chunk, e.g. an NP chunk can function as subject only if its case feature has nominative as its value. Then, the valencies [2] of

---

[2] The term *valency* here is used in a broader sense: it includes not only obligatory elements but all semantically and pragmatically suitable modifications and their syntactic representations, e.g. attributes for nouns or adverbials for verbs. The suitability of the modification is determined by the application ontology.

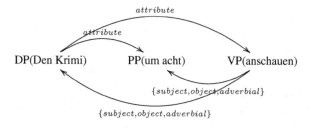

Fig. 1. Dependencies for "Den Krimi um acht anschauen"

each chunk are filled by combining it with other chunks, e.g. building a VP from a verb and its direct object. Again, these combinations are gated by syntactic and semantic constraints. Informations about the valencies of a specific chunk are stored in its case frame which is selected by its semantic head: In the case of the DP "den Krimi" it is not the syntactic head DET but the content word "Krimi" whose case frame is to be used. Ambiguity arises when a chunk is a possible filler of more than one valency of one or more other chunks.

How this kind of parsing ambiguities are handled is the topic of the remainder of the paper. The result of parsing phase 2, however, gives at least one interpretation of the whole utterance. A characteristic property of this second phase is that we control the chunk-combination process at four linguistic levels: Each combination is checked for its morphologic, syntactic, semantic, and pragmatic correctness.

3   Implementation of the Parser

As explained before, the second phase of the parser uses dependency grammar to find relations between chunks building an agenda of possible dependencies that are checked for syntactic and semantic viability. It then traverses the dependency tree to built readings for the utterance. Finally the most probable interpretations are selected.

3.1   Checking the Dependencies

In the first part, the parser constructs an agenda which contains all possible dependencies between all chunks. For each chunk that has a case frame the parser takes all dependencies for its syntactic category from the dependency file. If, for example, the chunk is a VP, the parser finds the dependencies `subject`, `(direct) object` and `adverbial`. For all other chunks that do not overlap with this chunk it creates an agenda element for each dependency. Figure 1 shows the eight dependencies put on the agenda for the example.

For each dependency the syntactic check tests, if the dependent chunk category is suitable to satisfy the valency and if the constraints on the features of dependent and regent are met In our example, the PP could be an attribute to the DP or an adverbial to the VP and the DP is the direct object of the VP. For the semantic check the parser goes through all syntactically suitable slots of the regent's case frame and checks whether

---

for each chunk C in G **do**
  for each s in filled-slots(C) **do**
    $D :=$ slot-filler(s)
    for each r_1 in readings(D) **do**
      new $:= \emptyset$
      for each r_2 in readings(C) **do**
        if $\neg$overlaps(r_1, r_2) **then**
          $r_3 :=$ merge(r_1, r_2)
          $h_1 :=$ head(r_1); $h_2 =$ head(r_2)

$$r_3 := r_3 + \left[\frac{h_1 \; h_2)}{\text{role}(s)(h_2, h_1)} \right]$$

          new $:=$ new $\cup \{r_3\}$
        endif
      endfor
      readings(C) $:=$ readings(C) $\cup$ new
    endfor
  endfor
endfor

Table 1. Algorithm for assembling interpretations

the dependent chunk meets the semantic and pragmatic requirements of a slot. If more than one slot matches an ambiguity report is generated (see section 4). In the example, all remaining dependencies pass the semantic test.

3.2   Assembling Interpretations and Selecting the Best

When the parser has checked all possible dependencies, it traverses the dependency graph G in a bottom-up fashion to build the possible interpretations of the utterance. For each chunk C, a set of readings (readings(C) – a set of DRSs) is determined that covers all possible meanings of the chunk and its subordinate chunks according to the found dependencies. The parser traverses every reading r_1 of every chunk D filling a slot of C and constructs new readings r_3 by combining r_1 with every reading r_2 of C. A new DRS r_3 is built by merging the DRSs of both readings and connecting their head discourse referents with the role found in the case frame. The combination of the DRSs fails when the parts of the utterance described by the readings overlap or the slot for the subordinate chunk is already filled. When all chunks are parsed, each chunk contains a set of readings: "den Krimi", for example, has a reading on its own and for its combination with the PP. Finally the parser selects the readings for further processing by checking all DRSs. It deletes readings that are subsumed by a higher scored reading. The remaining DRSs are passed to the dialog manager. The score of a chart edge or reading is calculated from a number of specific scores:

- An acoustic score obtained from the speech recognizer
- The length of the utterance part spanned by the reading
- The dialog context. When the dialog manager asks a question, it sends the expected answers to the parser. Readings containing one of them are scored higher.
- Each valency has an associated score, which is higher for essential slots than for facultative ones.
- When two chunks with the same syntactic and semantic structure follow each other, we assume that the second is a repair of the first and rate it higher.

If it is not possible to construct a reading that spans the whole utterance, the best fragments will be handed to the dialog manager.

$$S_1 = \begin{array}{|l|} \hline \text{w, } \Delta_1 \\ \hline \text{AvEvent(w)} \\ \text{has-genre(w, "Krimi")} \\ \text{Genre("Krimi")} \\ \text{has-timeinterval(w, } \Delta_1) \\ \hline \end{array} \quad S_2 = \begin{array}{|l|} \hline \text{x, y} \\ \hline \text{TimeInterval(x)} \\ \text{has-starttime(x, y)} \\ \text{Clocktime(y)} \\ \text{has-hour(y, 8)} \\ \hline \end{array} \quad S_3 = \begin{array}{|l|} \hline \text{z, } \Delta_2, \Delta_3 \\ \hline \text{Play(z)} \\ \text{has-avevent(z, } \Delta_2) \\ \text{has-timeinterval(z, } \Delta_3) \\ \hline \end{array}$$

$$P_1 = \begin{bmatrix} \Delta_0 \to S_3 \\ \Delta_1 \to S_2 \\ \Delta_2 \to S_1 \end{bmatrix} \quad P_2 = \begin{bmatrix} \Delta_0 \to S_3 \\ \Delta_2 \to S_1 \\ \Delta_3 \to S_2 \end{bmatrix}$$

$$\begin{array}{|l|} \hline \text{z, w, x, y} \\ \hline \text{Play(z) has-avevent(z, w)} \\ \text{AvEvent(w) has-genre(w, "Krimi") Genre("Krimi")} \\ \text{has-timeinterval(w,x)} \\ \text{TimeInterval(x) has-starttime(x,y) Clocktime(y) has-hour(y, 8)} \\ \hline \end{array}$$

Fig. 2. DRS pool, plugging functions and unpacked DRS for "Den Krimi um acht anschauen". The concept `Play` represents viewing actions, `AvEvent` films (on TV or from video).

3.3 Packed DRS

To build the semantic representations for the different readings of the input the chunk representations are combined to larger representations. In the case of ambiguities, we can not simply throw away a representation once it is used in a larger one, since it still may be needed to build a different reading. Thus, we get many representations built from the same basic parts. Therefore, we decided that instead of actually constructing the DRSs we just create "building plans". Additionally, we keep a pool of DRS segments. These segments have disjunctive nodes (denoted Δ_n) at which other segments (denoted S_n) can be plugged in. Apart from that, the disjunctive nodes are used like discourse referents. At the end of the parse, the DRS for the best interpretations are created from the segments according to plugging functions (the "building plans", denoted P_n). This process starts with looking up the root segment under the root node Δ_0. Then the disjunctive nodes of the root segment are filled with other segments according to the plugging function. If no value is defined for a disjunctive node, the condition in which it appears is removed. This is repeated for each segment plugged in, until every disjunctive node is either filled or removed.

Figure 2 shows the slightly simplified DRS pool for the example "Den Krimi um acht anschauen", containing a DRS segment for each of the three chunks. In the center, it shows the plugging functions for the two best interpretations. P_1 describes the reading in which the film starts at eight, P_2 the reading in which viewing starts at eight. Unpacking the DRS described by P_1 starts with the root node Δ_0, which is filled with segment S_3. This segment has two disjunctive nodes, Δ_2 and Δ_3. Δ_3 is not filled in P_1. Hence, the condition has-timeinterval(z, Δ_3) is removed. Δ_2 is filled by segment S_1. This means, both segments are merged and Δ_2 is replaced by w. In the same way Δ_1 is filled by S_2. The unpacked DRS is shown in the right of figure 2. During parsing a number of plugging functions are constructed which only cover a part of the utterance.

In the example all segments are used in the plugging functions. This is not always the case. If a lexical ambiguity exists, there will usually be a segment for each reading of the ambiguous word, while only one of these readings can be used in a plugging function.[3]

4   Ambiguity Reports

In many systems the parsing results, i.e. a list of scored readings, is simply passed to the dialog manager, which is left to its own devices to figure out the differences between the readings. In our framework, however, the parser informs the dialog manager about the ambiguities causing these differences. If it can not resolve the ambiguity itself, by using dialog context or user preferences, it can at least use this information to ask the user a well directed clarification question. Therefore, the parser marks all ambiguities when they arise, so they can be traced through the parse. It also creates an ambiguity report, which is sent to the dialog manager, if the ambiguity can not be resolved during parsing. This ambiguity report contains a DRS that describes the type of the ambiguity and its variants. The readings that follow from using a variant are specified with the affects-reading condition. The meaning in which the variants differ is recorded under has-content. Depending on the point were it arises, an ambiguity is classified as lexical, pragmatic, attachment ambiguity or filler ambiguity. Whenever entries with different concepts for a word are retrieved from the lexicon the parser classifies this as *lexical ambiguity*. A common example of lexical ambiguities in our domain are names of songs that double as band names. "Fiddler's Green" for example is an Irish folk song but is also the name of an Irish speed folk group. Occasionally, words can be used in different pragmatic contexts leading to *pragmatic ambiguity*, an example would be the sentence "I love detective stories". In the domain model the word "love" can be mapped to different concepts: GiveFavouriteAvEventLocation selects the user's favorite TV station, and GiveFavouriteGenre the favorite genre.

The example "Den Krimi um acht anschauen" features an *attachment ambiguity*. If "um acht" is dependent of "Krimi" the utterance refers to a TV program starting at eight. If it is dependent of "anschauen" the utterance could also refer to a detective story recorded on video[4]. The parser realizes this when it finds two valid dependencies with "um acht" as dependent. At this point it generates the ambiguity report shown in figure 4. The DRSs of the possible attachment points are stored in has-content. Additionally, the role has-pp is used to store the pragmatic extension of the phrase that caused the ambiguity.

---

[3] Superficially, our approach is quite similar to Johan Bos' unplugged DRS [6]. However, there are important differences: In our unpacking algorithm conditions are removed when their disjunctive nodes are not filled; in other underspecified representations [10] all disjunctive nodes have to be filled, so this situation can not arise. Usually all segments are required to be used in every plugging function. This restriction allows other representations to use simple constraints to specify the possible pluggings, while we currently use lists of plugging functions. We hope to find a set of constraints suitable for defining our plugging functions in the future.

[4] One could argue that the PP should be shared between DP and VP as it is done in underspecified representations. However, if a parser contains several ambiguities the attachment decision made here can influence later decisions of the parser. Additionally it means moving the burden of disambiguation to other components.

```
has-AvEventLocation: String       the name of the TV station
has-Title:           String       the program's title
has-TimeInterval:    TimeInterval duration and starting time
has-source:          String       Tuner, VCR, or MPEG stream
```

Fig. 3. Definition of `AvEvent`

Repairs often lead to *filler ambiguities*. In the example, "I want to watch the thriller at eight, not at nine", two chunks compete for the `has-starttime` slot of "thriller". Therefore the parser creates an ambiguity report recording the prospective fillers as variants and additionally the chunk for which they compete as anchor. In this case the eight o'clock reading gets higher scores, so the ambiguity can be resolved.

5   Modeling Rational Dialogs

This section discusses the incorporation of ambiguity reports in the structure of a dialog. In the EMBASSI application, pragmatic information about TV programs is stored in a data structure called `AvEvent` defined as in figure 3. Information about such `AvEvents` is stored in DRSs as the one in figure 4. On an `AvEvent`, several methods can be applied:

– `Record`: Stores an `AvEvent` on a video cassette. with the help of an VCR.
– `Play`: Displays an `AvEvent` on a TV. Different sources are possible: a tuner for currently transmitted programs, a VCR for stored programs, and a MPEG stream decoder which can process data stream from the internet.
– `GiveInformation`: Shows information about `AvEvents`.

In a dialog that is typical for the scenario, the user and the system negotiate about `AvEvents` and the actions to be performed on them. It is the system's task to get enough information from the user to relief her/him from the burden to know how to use the audio/video devices. In [3,7,8] it is argued that dialog as a form of rational interaction is a means of cooperatively executing tasks for joint purposes. Allwood [2] adds that any dialog consists of successive communicative contributions. They are actions in a multi-layered plan of interaction fulfilling certain communicative functions. The effect of such actions is an update of the current belief structures ([4]) of the dialog participants. So, dialog interpretation gets linked with cognitive modeling [5].

The approach to dialog analysis presented here strictly separates the dialog situation as the current state of the interaction from the application situation as the current state of application pragmatics: Utterances evoke actions in the application situation, thereby changing the application's state. In the dialogue below, utterance **User**$_1$ and **User**$_2$ tell the system to select `AvEvents` from the TV program according to preferences for the current user. The joint purpose of both utterance is reached by giving the responses in **System**$_2$ and **System**$_4$. **User**$_5$ and **System**$_6$ formulate and achieve another joint purpose that can be reached by retrieving appropriate information about `AvEvents`. However, **User**$_7$ asks for executing the `Play` method on a `AvEvent` instead of `GiveInformation`. The response in **System**$_{10}$ informs the user about the successful execution.

During "negotiating" about pragmatic tasks in this way, new speech acts are motivated to keep the interaction going until the joint purpose has been reached. Only if one of its readings can be integrated in the plan for the current joint purpose, an utterance can have such an effect. As mentioned in section 4, there are situations in which output from the parser is ambiguous for the dialog manager and the content of its belief structure does not suffice for disambiguation. In such a case, updating the dialog situation is impossible as the dialog manager fails to uniquely integrate the interpretation of the utterance. Hence, it is unable to carry out the current task.

User₁: Ich möchte nachher irgendwas Spannendes sehen. *(I'd like to see something thrilling later on.)*

System₂: Im ZDF kommt um 8 Uhr Derrick. *(There is Derrick on ZDF at 8.)*

User₃: Welche Filme gibt es denn noch? *(Are there other movies on?)*

System₄: Sie können den Actionfilm "Mad Max" via MPEG sehen oder "Wall Street", einen Thriller. *(You can choose between the action film "Mad Max" via MPEG or the thriller "Wall Street".)*

User₅: Worum geht es bei "Mad Max"? *(What's "Mad Max" about?)*

System₆: In einer postapokalyptischen Stadt sitzt Herrscherin Aunty Entity auf der geklauten Ausrüstung von Mad Max. Wenn Mad Max den Master der Energiequelle entmachtet, gibt ihm Entity seine Sachen zurück. *Content description*

User₇: Dann möchte ich den Krimi um acht sehen. *(Well, I want to watch the thriller at 8.)*

System₈: Den Derrick im ZDF oder Wall Street als MPEG stream? *("Derrick" on ZDF or "Wall Street" as MPEG)*

User₉: "Wall Street". *("Wall Street")*

System₁₀: "Wall Street" wird eingeschaltet um 20 Uhr. *(I'll switch to "Wall Street" at 8.)*

However, the dialog situation has been fed by the parser with information about the reasons for the ambiguity and the possible readings. Figure 4 shows an ambiguity report and its incorporation in the dialog situation.

Including syntactic information in dialog situations (see also [11]) is motivated by the necessity to keep a dialog coherent if syntactic or semantic ambiguities of new utterances cannot be resolved. Coherence is accomplished by focusing on the failed preconditions for a unique integration of the utterance. The importance of representing information about micro-conversational events becomes clear when considering the options of a dialog system for a clarification dialog that is not using any ambiguity report: If the user doesn't know in which way his utterance has been ambiguous he might not be able to help disambiguating. We see the ambiguity report as a prerequisite for generating system utterances that are plausible to the user, thereby giving him a chance to really clarify an unclear situation.

Before asking the user, the dialog manager tries to resolve ambiguities on its own. The lexical ambiguity of the word *Filme* (it can refer to several different genres) in utterance **User₃** is resolved by taking user preferences and dialog context into account: the proposals are selected by reasoning on knowledge about the user's `FavoriteAvEvents` and the information entailed in **User₁** *("something thrilling")*.

In **User₇**, the dialog manager knows from the DRS that there are two chunks involved in the ambiguity: C_1 and C_2. In order to ground the utterance, it computes the critical parts of the readings r_1 and r_2 (see figure 5).Then, the dialog manager

r_1, r_2, u, v, w, x, x_0, x_1, y
attachment-ambiguity(x)
has-variant(x,x_0)
ambiguity-variant(x_0)
affects-reading(x_0, r_1)
has-content(x_0, y)
AvEvent(y)
has-genre(y, "Krimi")
Genre("Krimi")
has-variant(x,x_1)
ambiguity-variant(x_1)
affects-reading(x_1, r_2)
has-content(x_1, w)
Record(w)
has-pp(x, v)
TimeInterval(v)
has-starttime(v, u)
clocktime(u) has-hour(u, 8)

r_1, r_2, u, v, w, x, x_0, x_1, y, s_0, U_1
attachment-ambiguity(x)
has-variant(x,x_0)   ambiguity-variant(x_0)
affects-reading(x_0, r_1)   has-content(x_0, y)
AvEvent(y)
has-genre(y, "Krimi")   Genre("Krimi")
has-variant(x,x_1)   ambiguity-variant(x_1)
affects-reading(x_1, r_2)   has-content(x_1, w)
Record(w)
has-pp(x, v) TimeInterval(v)
has-starttime(v, u)
clocktime(u)   has-hour(u, 8)
situation(s_0)
has-event(s_0,U_1)   request(U_1)
has-reading(U_1,r_1) has-ambiguity(r_1,x)
has-reading(U_1,r_2) has-ambiguity(r_1,x)
r_1: ...
r_2: ...

Fig. 4. Report for an Attachment Ambiguity and the Corresponding Dialog Situation

tries to relate the head of each DRS (y or w, respectively) to some already existing discourse referent, where the conditions in the DRS determine whether it actually refers to the assumed antecedent. If this analysis does not result in a disambiguation, the dialog manager verifies whether the content of both DRSs is satisfiable in the current application situation. **System$_8$** shows that the dialog manager failed to disambiguate the attachment ambiguity as well as the referential ambiguity of the noun phrase *den Krimi* as there were two thrillers mentioned already in the dialog context. In this case, a clarification dialog is needed to achieve the currently focused joint purpose.

We think that this approach resembles better the way in which two humans perform clarifications.

6 Conclusion

The paper shows an approach to computing information about micro-conversational events during parsing word lattices. This information reports on ambiguities found by lexical, syntactic and semantic analysis in a two stage parsing process. In this way, the

u, v, y
AvEvent(y)
has-genre(y,"Krimi")   Genre("Krimi")
has-timeinterval(y, v)   TimeInterval(v)
has-starttime(v,u)
clocktime(u)   has-hour(u,8)

u, v, w
Play(w)
has-timeinterval(w,v)
TimeInterval(v)
has-starttime(v,u)
clocktime(u)   has-hour(u,8)

Fig. 5. Readings resulting from the attachment ambiguity

parser is able to "explain" to the dialog manager why it produced several readings for an utterance. The dialog manager benefits from this additional input as appropriate system turns can make the user aware of the system's reception problems. The presented parser and dialog manager have been implemented. Experiments with "naive" users have been conducted and are currently being evaluated. If possible, we want to go even further and rethink the interface and cooperation between parsers and speech recognizers.

Recognition errors often concern morphological information that in turn is important for building and combining chunks. To overcome this problem we plan to test two possible solutions: First, we want to use weak unification to make sure that no possible reading is dismissed in any parsing phase. In the first phase, this means that semantically compatible constituents can form chunks even if their morphological features do not agree; in the second phase, we would allow slot-filling despite of feature clashes. Second, since our main goal is to give pragmatic constraints a higher priority, we will change the order of checking correctness: So far, when combining chunks based on case frames we start with syntactic constraints, i.e. a chunk has to have a certain syntactic function to be a possible slot-filler. If the syntactic constraints are not met, the chunk combination is ruled out, despite the fact that semantic or pragmatic constraints would give different results. By changing the order of constraint application we overcome problems caused by recognition errors and we make sure that at least one interpretation is given to the user's utterance. Whichever way (or a combination of both) turns out to be the most efficient and robust one will be the preferred one for any application.

References

1. Steven Abney, 'Parsing by chunks', in *Principle-based Parsing*, eds., R. Berwick, S. Abney, and C. Tenny, Kluwer, Dordrecht, (1991).
2. Jens Allwood, 'Obligations and options in dialog', *Think*, **3**, 9–18, (May 1994).
3. Jens Allwood, 'Dialog as collective thinking', in *Brain, Mind, and Physics*, eds., P. Pylkko P. Pylkkanen and H. Hautamaki, volume 33 of *Frontiers in Artificial Intelligence and Applications*, Amsterdam, (1997). IOS Press.
4. Maria Aretoulaki and Bernd Ludwig, 'Automaton-descriptions and theorem-proving: A marriage made in heaven?', *Linköping Electronic Articles in Computer and Information Science*, **4**(22), http://www.ep.liu.se/ea/cis/1999/022/, (1999).
5. Nicholas Asher and Alex Lascarides, 'Intentions and information in discourse', in *Proceedings of the 32nd Annual Meeting of the Association of Computational Linguistics*, pp. 34–41, Las Cruces, USA, (June 1994).
6. J. Bos, 'Predicate logic unplugged', in *Proceedings of the 10th Amsterdam Colloquium*, eds., P. Dekker and M. Stokhof, pp. 133–143. ILLC, University of Amsterdam, (1995).
7. Sandra Carberry and L. Lambert, 'A process model for recognizing communicative acts and modeling negotiation subdialogs', *Computational Linguistics*, **25**(1), 1–53, (1999).
8. P. Cohen and H. Levesque, *Intentions in Communication*, chapter Rational Interaction as the basis for Communication, MIT Press, Cambridge, Massachusetts, USA, 1990.
9. Hans Kamp and Uwe Reyle, *From Discourse to Logic*, Kluwer, Dordrecht, 1993.
10. Manfred Pinkal, 'On semantic underspecification', in *Computing Meaning*, eds., H. Bunt and R. Muskens, 33–55, Kluwer Academic Press, (1999).
11. Massimo Poesio and David Traum, 'Conversational actions and discourse situations', *Computational Intelligence*, **13**(3), 309–347, (1997).

A Natural Language Dialogue Manager for Accessing Databases

Salvador Abreu[2], Paulo Quaresma[2], Luis Quintano[1], and Irene Rodrigues[2]

[1] Departamento de Informática, Universidade de Évora, Portugal
spa|pq|ipr@di.uevora.pt
[2] Serviço de Computação, Universidade de Évora, Portugal
ljcq@sc.uevora.pt

Abstract. A logic programming based dialogue system with the capability of inferring user attitudes and accessing heterogeneous external relational databases while doing syntactic and semantic sentence parsing is presented.

The system was built using a logic programming language – Prolog –, a development tool – ISCO [2] – and a language for representing actions – LUPS[4].

An application of the developed system to the Universidade de Évora's Integrated Information System (SIIUE) was developed and some examples of typical dialogues are presented.

1 Introduction

Over the last couple of years Universidade de Évora has committed itself to the development of an Integrated Information System (SIIUE) [3].

The information stored in SIIUE has been in growing demand by many university services and external entities. As more data was gathered, SIIUE has become the main source of information for Universidade de Évora faculty, students and staff. As a consequence, the development of a natural language dialogue system allowing users to interact with SIIUE directly in Portuguese was considered a major requirement.

The dialogue system needs to analyze the sentences (syntactically, semantically, and pragmatically) and to interact with the SIIUE knowledge bases in order to obtain the required information. The different modules were developed in Prolog and the interaction with the knowledge bases was done using ISCO [3, 2], a new logic-based programming framework which is able to handle relational database integration and web-based development.

The pragmatic module was built using a language for describing actions, LUPS[4], which allows the system to make inferences about the user intentions and beliefs and to be able to have cooperative dialogues with the users.

The remainder of this article is structured as follows: in section 2, the ISCO language is described. In section 3, the LUPS language is briefly described. In section 4 the overall structure of the system is presented; section 5 deal with the semantic/ pragmatic interpretation. In section 6 a more extensive example

E.M. Ranchhod and N.J. Mamede (Eds.): PorTAL 2002, LNAI 2389, pp. 161–170, 2002.

is presented and, finally, in section 7 we discuss some current limitations of the
system and lay out possible lines of future work.

2   ISCO

ISCO is a new Logic-Based development language implemented over GNU Prolog [5] that gives the developer several distinct possibilities, useful for the development of applications such as SIIUE:

- Gives a simple database structure description language that can help in
  database schema analysis. Tools are available to create an ISCO database
  description from an existing relational database schema and also the oppo-
  site action, i.e. to create a relational database schema from a ISCO class
  description.
- View relational databases as a part of a declarative/deductive object-oriented
  (with inheritance) database. Among other things, the system maps relational
  tables to classes – which may be used as Prolog predicates.
- Gives simple access to relational data through ODBC using a GNU Prolog interface with unixODBC, which has been developed within the SIIUE
  project.
- Creates ISCO/Prolog executables ready for use from PHP scripts [1] in web-
  based interfaces. The PHP extensions have also been developed specifically
  for use with ISCO.

The dialogue modules use ISCO's capability to establish connections from
Prolog to the relational databases in an efficient way. Moreover, ISCO was directly used to access a relational database containing a fairly complete Portuguese dictionary (Polaris) [8], which is used by the syntactical and semantical
analyzer module.

3   Dynamic LP and LUPS

Knowledge evolves from one knowledge state to another as a result of knowledge
updates.

In [4] it was introduced a declarative, high-level language for knowledge updates called *LUPS* ("Language of UPdateS") that describes transitions between
consecutive knowledge states.

It consists of update commands, which specify what updates should be applied to any given knowledge state in order to obtain the next knowledge state.

Below, a brief description of LUPS that does not include all of the available
update commands and omits some details is presented.

The simplest update command consists of adding a rule to the current knowledge state and has the form: *assert* $(L \leftarrow L_1, \ldots, L_k)$. In general, the addition
of a rule to a knowledge state may depend upon some preconditions being true

in the current state. To allow for that, the assert command in LUPS has a more general form:

$$assert \ (L \leftarrow L_1, \ldots, L_k) \ when \ (L_{k+1}, \ldots, L_m) \qquad (1)$$

The meaning of this assert command is that if the preconditions $L_{k+1}, \ldots, L_m$ are true in the current knowledge state, then the rule $L \leftarrow L_1, \ldots, L_k$ should hold true in the successor knowledge state. The added rules are *inertial*, i.e., they remain in force from then on by inertia, until possibly defeated by some future update or until retracted.

However, in some cases the persistence of rules by inertia should not be assumed. Take, for instance, a user utterance. This is a *one-time event* that should not persist by inertia after the successor state. Accordingly, the assert command allows for the keyword *event*, indicating that the added *rule* is *non-inertial*.

$$assert \ event \ (L \leftarrow L_1, \ldots, L_k) \ when \ (L_{k+1}, \ldots, L_m) \qquad (2)$$

Update commands themselves (rather than the rules they assert) may either be one-time, non-persistent update commands or they may remain in force until canceled. In order to specify such *persistent update commands* (which we call *update laws*) there is the syntax:

$$always \ [event] \ (L \leftarrow L_1, \ldots, L_k) \ when \ (L_{k+1}, \ldots, L_m) \qquad (3)$$

4   Natural Language Dialogue System

As was already stated the main goal of this work was to build a system that could get a Portuguese natural language sentence sent by a user through a web interface and respond accordingly.

To answer the question/sentence the system has to pass it from a web-based interface to a GNU Prolog/ISCO active process (A), the process must analyze the sentence accessing the relational database(s) when needed to get or check any information (B) and finally when acquiring all needed information, it has to build a comprehensive answer and pass it to the web-based interface (C).

The parse that is made to the sentence is split in three different parts: Syntax, Semantics, Pragmatics

The user sends the question about the information that exists in the SIIUE. For that he/she uses a web-based interface using the scripting language PHP[1] and the tools available by the php module of ISCO.

The question is then sent to an active Prolog process that already knows all the relational database structure to be used. ISCO manages the conversion of that structure to Prolog predicates that can access the relational databases through SQL primitives as selects, inserts, updates or deletes. In our case, as we're facing a querying system we only need to use selects.

Besides all database structures, this Prolog process does all syntactic, semantic and pragmatic analysis. For that it previously had to do some pre-processing

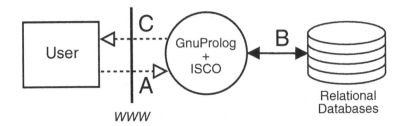

Fig. 1. Simplified SIIUE-NL system architecture

with the relational database structure to generate semantic/pragmatic database driven rules.

After analyzing the sentence received, the process has to generate an adequate answer, which will be shown to the user through the web interface.

Syntax Analysis The question reaches the syntax analysis module in form of a list to be parsed. This syntactic interpreter will identify the correct syntactic structure of the sentence.

This syntactic interpreter was built using *Chart Parsers*[6]. This is one of many techniques to build syntactic interpreters. The decision of developing the interpreter using this technique was mainly because chart parsers can parse incomplete sentences.

The user can place complete or incomplete questions and the system must be able to answer them accordingly, so the need to parse incomplete sentences is essential.

The chart parser uses a set of syntactic rules that identify the Portuguese sentence structures and tries to match these rules with the input sentence(s).

The interpreter also uses a lexicon to identify the syntactic properties of the words in the sentences. For that the interpreter is connected with a relational database (Polaris) which has syntactic (and semantic) information about Portuguese words. This integration is possible through ISCO because this tool already knows the Polaris database structure and can access it through ODBC.

This module will produce an output that consists in a list with all possible syntactic representations of the sentence placed by the user.

As an example, if the user placed the following sentence as input to the system:

"Paulo lecciona Arquitectura?"

("Does Paulo teaches Architecture?")

With this question the user intends to know if Paulo is the responsible for the Architecture course.

The syntax module will return a list with the sentences' syntactic parse

```
phrase([np([n('Paulo',s+m+_)]), vp(v('teach',1+s+_)),
       args_v([np([name('Architecture',s+m+_)])])]).
```

Semantic Interpretation The syntactic parsing output will be sent to the semantic module. This module will get the syntactic structure and rewrite it in a First-Order Logic.

The technique used for this parsing is based on DRS's (Discourse Representation Structures)[7].

This technique identifies triggering syntactic configurations on the global sentence structure, which activates some rewriting rules:

Proper Nouns - When a proper noun syntactic structure is found, a new discourse referent is added replacing the proper noun syntactic configuration.

Pronouns - When a pronoun syntactic structure is found, a new discourse referent (A) is added as a condition A=B in which (B) is a suitable discourse referent that already exists. The syntactic configuration is replaced by the new referent.

Verbs - When a verb (verb) is found with its arguments already rewritten (A and B), the condition verb(A,B) is created and replaces the syntactic configuration that activated this rule.

This module returns two lists, one with the new sentence rewritten and the other with information about the referents that were created in this analysis.

For instance, if this module receives the syntax module output presented in the previous sections it will return the semantic representation of the sentence:

```
name(A, 'Paulo'), name(B, 'Architecture'), teaches(A,B)
```

and a list with information about the discourse referents:

```
[ref(A,s+m+_),ref(B,s+f+_)]
```

5   Pragmatics Interpretation

The pragmatics module receives the sentence rewritten (into a First Order Logic form) and tries to interpret it in the context of the dialogue and in the context of the user model.

In order to achieve this behavior it is necessary to recognize the speech act associated with the sentence (in this domain it can be an *inform*, a *request*, or a *askif* speech act), to model the user attitudes (intentions and beliefs), and to represent and to make inferences over the dialogue domain.

After having interpreted the sentence, the pragmatic module establishes the connection with the databases to fetch data which will be used to give a coherent answer to the user.

As a first step, it was necessary to represent the knowledge conveyed by the database schemas as logic programming rules. Using the ability that ISCO has to describe external relational databases, it was possible to generate these rules according to the existent relations (classes) and its attributes.

This process was described in detail in [11] and, in this paper, we will present only one example:

```
teaches(A,B) <-                                         (4)
  all_ids(si_teacher,A),
  all_ids(si_course,B),
  abduct(si_teaches(course = B, lecturer = A)).
```

The verb `teaches` receives a teacher (`A`) and a course (`B`). It checks both of them against the database information and abducts all possible relations between teachers and courses lectured.

The `all_ids` returns variable `A` and `B` restricted to all known teachers and courses identifiers. This is implemented using FD constraints.

After having defined these domain representation rules it is necessary to pragmatically interpret the sentence. In order to achieve this goal the system needs to model the speech acts, the user attitudes (intentions and beliefs) and the connection between attitudes and actions.

This task is also achieved through the use of logic programming framework rules and the LUPS language (see [10, 9] for a more detailed description of these rules).

For instance, the rules which describe the effect of an inform, a request, and a ask-if speech act from the point of view of the receptor are:

> *always* bel(A,bel(B,P)) *when* inform(B,A,P)
> *always* bel(A,int(B,Action)) *when* request(B,A,Action)
> *always* bel(A,int(B,inform-if(A,B,P))) *when* ask-if(B,A,P)

In order to represent collaborative behavior it is necessary to model how information is transferred between the different agents:

> *always* bel(A,P) *when* bel(A,bel(B,P))
> *always* int(A,Action) *when* bel(A,int(B,Action))

These two rules allow beliefs and intentions to be transferred between agents if they are not inconsistent with their previous mental state.

There is also the need for rules that link the system intentions and the accesses to the databases:

> *always* yes(P) ← query(P), one-sol(P) *when* int(A, inform-if(A, B, P))
> *always* no(P) ← query(P), no-sol(P) *when* int(A, inform-if(A, B, P))
> *always* clarif(P) ← query(P), n-sol(P) *when* int(A, inform-if(A, B, P))

These three rules update the system's mental state with the result of accessing the databases: yes, if there is only one solution; no, if there are no solutions; and clarification, if there are many solutions (the predicates that determine the cardinality of the solution are not presented here due to space problems, but there implementation is quite simple).

After accessing the databases, the system should answer the user:

> *always* confirm(A,B,P) *when* yes, int(A, inform-if(A, B, P))
> *always* not int(A, inform-if(A,B,P)) *when* yes, int(A, inform-if(A, B, P))
> *always* reject(A,B,P) *when* no, int(A, inform-if(A, B, P))
> *always* not int(A, inform-if(A,B,P)) *when* yes, int(A, inform-if(A, B, P))
> *always* ask-select(A,B,C) ← cluster(P,C) *when* clarif(P), int(A, inform-if(A, B, P))

The first two rules define that, after a unique solution query, the system confirms the answer and terminates the intention to answer the user. The next two rules define that, after a no solution query, the system rejects the question and terminates the intention to answer the user. The last two rules define that, after a multiple solution query, the system starts a clarification answer, asking the user to select one of the possible solutions. In order to collaborate with the user we have defined a cluster predicate that tries to aggregate the solutions into coherent sets, but its definition is outside the scope of this paper.

6   A Practical Example

For a better comprehension and to give a generic view of the system implementation we will present a complete example starting from the user input:

"Does Paulo teaches Architecture?"

After the syntax and semantic module analyses we will have:

```
name(A, 'Paulo'), name(B, 'Arquitecture'), teaches(A,B)
```

and a list with information about the discourse referents:

```
[ref(A,sin+masc+_),ref(B,sin+masc+_)]
```

The semantic/pragmatic interpretation will give rise to following expression:

```
si_teach(lecturer=A,course=B)
```

with A a variable constrained to values of all the database identifiers that are named Paulo; and B a variable constrained to the values of the identifiers that are courses with the word Architecture in their name.

After having the sentence re-written into its semantic representation form, the speech act is recognized and we'll have:

```
ask-if(user, system, [si_teaches(lecture=A,course=B)]).
```

Using the "ask-if" and the transference of intentions LUPS rules we'll have:

```
int(system,inf-if(system,user,[si_teaches(lecture=A,course=B)])).
```

Now, using the rules presented in the previous section, the system accesses the databases (using the ISCO modules).

Suppose there are two possible solutions (one having Paulo Silva as the lecturer and the other having Paulo Santos as the lecturer).

We'll have:

```
int(system,inf-if(system,user,[si_teaches(lecture=A,course=B)])).
```

```
clarify([si_teaches(lecture=A,course=B)]).
```

with variable A constrained to the values in set $100, 120,$
where

```
name(100, 'Paulo Silva), name(120, 'Paulo Santos').
```

meaning that object 100 has name 'Paulo Silva and object 120 has name 'Paulo Santos'.

The $cluster(P, C)$ rule will obtain two possible selections and the correspondent ask-selection speech act will be performed:

```
ask-select(system,user,[(name(A, 'Paulo Silva) ;
                         name(A, 'Paulo Santos')]).
```

"Is the lecturer Paulo Silva or Paulo Santos?"

Now, suppose the user answers:

"Paulo Silva."

This answer will be represented by the speech act:

```
inform(user, system, [lecturer(A), name(A, 'Paulo Silva)]).
```

Using the inform and the transference rules, the system is able to start a new belief and to add it to the constraints of the current question:

```
bel(system,[name(A,'Paulo Silva)]).
```

```
int(system,inf-if(system,user,[si_teaches(lecture=A,course=B)])).
```

```
A is constraint to the identifier with name Paulo Silva.
```

With this new constraint the query will have only one solution (yes, for instance) and the system will perform a confirm speech act.

7   Conclusions and Future Work

The dialogue system described in this paper is still in an experimental stage, but we intend to make it available to all users using the University's internal web interface, via Universidade de Évora's web page (http://www.uevora.pt/) in a short period of time.

The evaluation of such a system has to be done by using a test group to be inquired on different parameters such as friendless, answers accuracy, etc; we intend to do this in a near future. A performance evaluation can be done now, but since there are many improvements in the modules implementations to be done we are delaying this evaluation. But, since most of system is available via web the delay between submiting a query and obtaining an answer is not critical (from 30 seconds to 3 minutes).

This system can be easily transposed to another domain, we just need to have the ISCO description of the new domain databases. The main problem will be to collect the new domain vocabulary and to build a synonymous database relating nouns, verbs, etc to the database relations and objects names. The transposition of the system into another language such as English can be done by changing the gramatical rules and the lexicon information.

Clearly, and due to its complexity, all modules have aspects that may be improved:

- The syntactical coverage of the Portuguese grammar
- The coverage of the semantic analyzer (plurals, quantifiers, ...)
- The capability of the pragmatic module to take into account previous interactions and the user models

However, we believe that probably the major positive aspect of the described system is its modularity and the integration of several AI techniques under a logic programming paradigm.

References

[1] Php hypertext processor - http://www.php3.org.
[2] Salvador Abreu. Isco: A practical language for heterogeneous information system construction. In *Proceedings of INAP'01*, Tokyo, Japan, October 2001. INAP.
[3] Salvador Pinto Abreu. A Logic-based Information System. In Enrico Pontelli and Vitor Santos-Costa, editors, *2nd International Workshop on Practical Aspects of Declarative Languages (PADL'2000)*, volume 1753 of *Lecture Notes in Computer Science*, pages 141–153, Boston, MA, USA, January 2000. Springer-Verlag.
[4] J. J. Alferes, L. M. Pereira, H. Przymusinska, T. C. Przymusinski, and P. Quaresma. Preliminary exploration on actions as updates. In M. C. Meo and M. Vilares-Ferro, editors, *Procs. of the 1999 Joint Conference on Declarative Programming (AGP'99)*, pages 259–271, L'Aquila, Italy, September 1999.
[5] D. Diaz. http://www.gnu.org/software/prolog, 1999.
[6] Gerald Gazdar and Chris Mellish. *Natural Language Processing in PROLOG*. Addison-Wesley, 1989.

[7] H. Kamp and U. Reyle. *From Discourse to Logic*. Kluwer, Dordrecht, 1993.

[8] J. Lopes, N. Marques, and V. Rocio. Polaris, a portuguese lexicon acquisition and retrieval interactive system, 1994.

[9] P. Quaresma and J. G. Lopes. Unified logic programming approach to the abduction of plans and intentions in information-seeking dialogues. *Journal of Logic Programming*, 54, 1995.

[10] Paulo Quaresma and Irene Rodrigues. Using logic programming to model multi-agent web legal systems – an application report. In *Proceedings of the ICAIL'01 - International Conference on Artificial Intelligence and Law*, St. Louis, USA, May 2001. ACM. 10 pages.

[11] Luis Quintano, Irene Rodrigues, and Salvador Abreu. Relational information retrieval through natural lanaguage analysis. In *Proceedings of INAP'01*, Tokyo, Japan, October 2001. INAP.

Helping the Composition of Help Contents

Milene Silveira[1,2], Maria Carmelita Dias[3], Violeta Quental[3]

[1] Faculdade de Informática, PUCRS, Av. Ipiranga, 6681, Porto Alegre, 90619-900, Brazil
[2] Departamento de Informática, PUC-Rio, R. Marquês de São Vicente, 225, Rio de Janeiro,
22453-900, Brazil
milene@inf.puc-rio.br
[3] Departamento de Letras, PUC-Rio, R. Marquês de São Vicente, 225, Rio de Janeiro,
22453-900, Brazil
{mcdias, violetaq}@let.puc-rio.br

Abstract. Accessing help systems by means of "What's this?" expressions is easily found in commercial WIMP applications. An improvement is to use interaction phrases, such as "Where is X?" and "Why should I do this?", for instance. The work herein presented describes a way to help designers build answers to these and other help questions while developing the application's help system; and it also discusses possibilities of automatic generation of answers.

1 Introduction

When users look for help, in most cases they have a specific problem to solve. In general, what they get is a generic answer that seldom solves their problem. Sometimes they even get the information they are looking for, but they need to spend excessive time in this search and also deal with unfriendly language.

In order to better help the user, the help system has to capture an understanding of what the user is trying to do, and relate it to the application possibilities. These possibilities come from the application design, and are related to the nature of work in the application domain, the advantages of the application use, the tasks that can be carried out in the application environment, and so on.

Capturing this kind of information gives the help designers the knowledge needed to produce a help system that may better solve the user's problems. But only the information, itself, is not enough. The way the information is organized and delivered to the user is also highly important.

This paper addresses a way to compose help systems and user manuals, based on the designers' knowledge about the application and in a different kind of help access, where users are able to present their specific doubts while interacting. Possibilities of automatic generation of help systems are also discussed.

E.M. Ranchhod and N.J. Mamede (Eds.): PorTAL 2002, LNAI 2389, pp. 171–174, 2002.
© Springer-Verlag Berlin Heidelberg 2002

2   Searching for Contextual Information

Generally, help systems tend to offer information about interface elements by means of "What's this?" expressions. Sometimes they also offer information on how to perform a given task (such as "How do I do this?" expression). But usually this information is not adequate or sufficient.

When users ask for help, they want to obtain answers to their most frequent doubts [1;4], such as "What kinds of things can I do?", "What is this?", "What is happening now?", "Why did it happen?", "What should I do now?", and so on.

Taking into consideration these types of questions, it is desirable that users have better ways to indicate what their problem is. One possible way to do this is to use a set of interaction phrases [5] that represents not only their most frequent doubts, but also what their problem is at a specific moment (Table 1).

Table 1. Set of interaction phrases to access help systems.

Where is X?	How do I do this?	What happened?
What now?	Why should I do this?	Why doesn't it?
What's this?	Who does this affect?	Where was I?
Oops!	Whom does this depend on?	Help!
I can't do it!	Is there another way to do this?	

Appropriate and specialized answers will be given according to, or guided by, these expressions. In most traditional help systems answers are somewhat long descriptions. And the information the users really want is embedded somewhere in the text. Using interaction phrases enables users to receive the answer in parts. Texts are short, in a minimalist strategy [2], and they are delivered according to the phrase chosen and to the current status of the application. If desirable or necessary, they ask for more details in that particular context [3,5].

A very simple example can illustrate the difference between the strategies adopted in most help systems and the minimalist strategy herein proposed.

Consider one user who is using a word processor such as Microsoft Word® for the first time. He is asked to "open a file", but he doesn't know how to do it. He may try using the help assistant, which will open a window for him to search for the unknown action. So if he types *Open*, a new window will be presented with a number of options and each option leads to a rather long text with a lot of information.

It is obvious that it is difficult for a novice to start using this word processor by means of the help system, since he has to read so much useless information.

In the strategy described here, since the user sees no word *Open* on the screen, he searches the toolbar for some hint and finally discovers an icon named *Open*. Clicking the right button upon this word, there comes a list with the interaction phrases available for use in the moment. He chooses **What's this?** and get a very simple text that answers only the question involved. He can go on from this question asking another one, for instance, **How do I do this?** (Figure 1a and 1b), and so on.

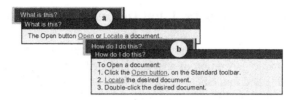

Fig. 1. Looking for help, in the way herein proposed.

3   Composing the Minimalist Answers

In order to elaborate the answers, templates were created related to each interaction phrase listed at Table 1. Table 2 shows how formed sentences are related to the interaction phrase **How do I do this?**.

Table 2. **How do I do this?** templates

To {**desired(action)**|desired
  action | do this} [{[:]|,}]
  {**steps_sequence** |
  alternative_sequence}.
 	
steps_sequence:-
  step, [,|;|.],
  steps_sequence.
steps_sequence.
 	
alternative_sequence:-
  [If **condition(action)**],
  steps_sequence, [,|;|.],
  alternative_sequence.
alternative_sequence.
	step:-
	[**step_number**],
	{select the desired text |
	  [double-] click {the **name(button)**
	  button | **text**} |
	select{[the option] **name(option)**
	  [**location(name(option))**]| **text**} |
	  type the information
	  [**location(name(option))**]}.
	
	location(object) :-
	{on the **name(toolbar)** toolbar|
	  on the **name(menu)** menu|
	  on the dialog box}.

To answer this interaction phrase for the above example, the template used was:

```
To desired(action):          To Open a document:
   steps_sequence.            ┌ 1. Click the Open button, on the Standard toolbar.
                              │ 2. Locate the desired document.
                              └ 3. Double-click the desired document.
```

And, for each step, the template used was:

```
steps_sequence:-
   step,                   ──▶ 1. Click the Open button, on the Standard toolbar.
   [,|;|and|or|.],
   steps_sequence.         ┌ 2. Locate the desired document.
   steps_sequence.         └ 3. Double-click the desired document.
```

Using templates aids to form help messages, guiding the designers' work. In order to help them even further, there are ways to provide automatic generation of this help messages.

4   Generating the Answers: Final Discussion and Future Work

One of the main advantages of the work herein described is that its formalization permits the automatic generation of answers included in help systems. Thus, when a designer is creating and implementing the application, he can generate the help system coupled with it automatically.

As seen in the example above, one expression enables a number of different options used according to specific data to be inserted depending on the template chosen. These data (knowledge about the application domain, the interaction, the tasks, the interface objects, and so on) have to be captured in order to provide the information needed to compose the help answers.

A first approach has been developed, by means of a Help Editor, that support the designer in the capture of these data, throughout the application development process. While designing and developing an application, the designer should answer a series of questions, and this knowledge would be the foundation for the final construction of the application help components.

After the insertion of all necessary data, it is possible to generate a preliminary help text. This text is used both for the writing of the complete help system and for the composing of the messages to be presented to the user during the interaction.

Although answers and help texts can be generated automatically, it is in fact an aid tool, because designer's presence is crucial. Nevertheless, with this kind of tool, the work of the help designers is minimized and improved.

One of the main challenges now is to improve data collecting so that the help generator will be even more useful. The specification of a help-generator – for the interaction phrases approach - is to be completed, based on text templates shown above and on several design models. This generator will be applied to the actual application, so that all these issues can be better studied and improved.

References

1. Baecker, R.M. et. al.: Readings in Human-Computer Interaction: toward the year 2000. Morgan Kaufmann Publishers, Inc., San Francisco (2000)
2. Carroll, J.M. (ed): Minimalism Beyond the Nurnberg Funnel. The MIT Press, Cambridge (1998)
3. Farkas, D.K.: Layering as a Safety Net for Minimalist Documentation. In: Carroll, J.C. (ed.): Minimalism Beyond the Nurnberg Funnel. The MIT Press, Cambridge (1998)
4. Sellen, A.; Nicol, A.: Building User-Centered Online Help. In B. Laurel (ed.): The Art of Human-Computer Interface Design. Addison-Wesley, Reading, MA. (1990)
5. Silveira, M.S.; Barbosa, S.D.J.; Souza, C.S.: Augmenting the Affordance of Online Help Content. In: People and Computers XV – Interaction without Frontiers (Joint Proceedings of HCI 2001 and IHM 2001), BCS Conference Series, Springer-Verlag, London (2001) 279-296

Meteo: A Telephone-Based Portuguese Conversation System in Weather Domain

Pedro Cardoso, Luis Flores, Thibault Langlois, and João Neto

L^{2}F - Spoken Language Systems Laboratory, INESC ID Lisboa / IST
R. Alves Redol, 9, 1000-029 Lisboa, Portugal
http://l2f.inesc-id.pt

Abstract. Dialog systems using speech technology are in expansion all over the world being used for different domains. The main reason for this growing, apart from the motivation on speech and human-machine interaction research, is the potential for mass access to information. In this paper we describe the work done for the development of a conversation system in a weather domain applied to the European Portuguese language.

1 Introduction

Dialog systems are the result of a combination of several technologies, as speech recognition and speech synthesis, accessing databases, natural language processing and dialog management. In the speech processing field, over the past years, several systems for the European Portuguese language have been under development at INESC ID. Speech recognition systems like Audimus [1] and speech synthesis systems like Dixi and Dixi+ [2] . Those systems have been growing in potential and performance every year, being at this point mature enough to be integrated in applications with a generic use.

Meteo, like Jupiter [3] or Mokusei [4], is a weather information system for the European Portuguese language. Through a spoken interface over phone is possible to access meteorological information for the main cities of Portugal for a period of three days starting on the current day. The information includes maximum, minimum and current temperatures, air humidity and sky conditions. This information is collected from different sources on the web updating the internal database.

In the next section we will present the architecture for the implementation of the system and a description of each component. In section 3 we discuss the benefits of such a system and future developments.

2 System Architecture

Our dialog system is based on a dual HUB architecture, with a separation in an Audio subsystem, where are included the speech processing modules, and a dialog subsystem, with the natural language and dialog manager modules. The

E.M. Ranchhod and N.J. Mamede (Eds.): PorTAL 2002, LNAI 2389, pp. 175–178, 2002.
© Springer-Verlag Berlin Heidelberg 2002

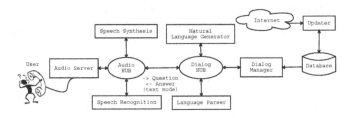

Fig. 1. Global System Architecture.

HUBs communicate on a question-answering mode using a text format protocol for communication. Additionally there is other module called the Updater, responsible for the creation, maintenance and update of the database where the information concerning the application is stored. The architecture of our complete dialog system is presented in figure 1. Below we will give a short description for each of the blocks constituent of the system.

2.1   Updater Module

The Updater runs independently of the main system updating the database and maintaining the integrity of the stored data. Based on a defined schedule the Updater is activated and fetch the information from the web regarding weather conditions. For each information source we have a specialized parser that extract the information from the html pages, and fills the database.

2.2   Audio Subsystem

The main blocks of the Audio subsystem are the Audio Server, the automatic Speech Recognition (ASR) system, the Text-To-Speech (TTS) system and a Log generator module. In our case the ASR is implemented through the Audimus System and the TTS through the DIXI+ system. In figure 2 we present a block diagram of the Audio subsystem followed by a short functional description of each of the blocks.

The **Audio Server** is a phone interface using a Dialogic board, streaming audio between the phone line and the Audio HUB, with the possibility of converting the audio formats when necessary. There is also an inbuilt Endpoint detector based on signal energy, which filter the silence and noise bursts.

The **Automatic Speech Recognition** block is implemented thought the Audimus system, with some new features as multi-session. Different developments were necessary to adapt the specific modules of Audimus to this task. A speech recognition system needs a language model and an acoustic model adapted to the task domain. Since the system is being developed to work over the phone line a specialized acoustic model was created. Audimus is a hybrid System [1] with the acoustic model implemented thought a Multi-Layer Perceptron (MLP). It was necessary to train a new acoustic model for which we used

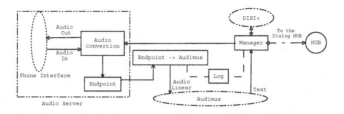

Fig. 2. Detailed architecture for the Audio Hub.

the Portuguese part of the SPEECHDAT database. For the language modelling is usual to extract probabilistic relationships between words from text corpus. In our case we started by defining the vocabulary from some of the Portuguese city names, chosen based on their existence on the information sources, from the different meteorological conditions, and from some specific (like *today, tomorrow, the day after*) and functional sentences. Based on this vocabulary we extracted a 2-gram language model from newspaper texts. Obviously this source of text is not the most appropriate which we expect to overcome when we have enough logs of the use of the system, to generate new language models as was made for other similar systems [3].

In this work we are using a **Text-To-Speech** system developed in our group in the scope of project DIXI+ [2]. This system uses the Festival Speech framework.

The **Log module** stores for every session the audio corresponding to the different questions made by each user, as well as the recognized text and the generated answer. This information will be used to adapt the acoustic and language models of the speech recogniser with the possibility of an extensive evaluation of the behaviour of the system.

2.3   Dialog Subsystem

The Dialog subsystem is based on three different blocks as represented in figure 1. The Language Parser, witch extracts the request from the text generated by the ASR module, the Dialog Manager, where the interface with the database is made, and the Natural Language Generator, which generates the answer to be outputted to the user.

The **Language Parser** is based on a keyword spotting. For a given question we get the city name to which the user refers, the meteorological conditions requested and the time information. With the data gathered, an information structure is created containing the keywords, and sent to the Dialog HUB to be delivered to the Dialog Manager module.

The **Dialog Manager** works on a frame based system. For every question made by the user (frame) a number of information fields need to be filled. Those fields are the city name, the meteorological condition requested, and the time the question refers to. If any of these fields are not present in the Language Parser output, the Dialog Manager tries to use context information fetching the missing fields from previous frames. This contextual information creates a more natural and friendly interaction with the user. If some field is missing, even after using the context, several actions can be adopted according to the kind of information missing. After defining the fields a query to the database is made and a new structure containing the elements and respective information are sent to the Natural Language Generator module.

The **Natural Language Generator** get the information from the Dialog Manager and generates an answer in a human readable way. Presently the work done by the Natural Language Generator is a simple transformation from a keyword-information pair to textual information. This text is sent though the two hubs to the TTS system to be transmitted to the user.

3   Conclusion

Our goal in the development of this system was to show that the necessary technologies are mature enough to be used in new applications where a more natural and friendly interface with the user is possible.

However that naturalness is only possible if the system have mechanisms of readjustment based on the real use of the system. For that reason we built mechanisms of logs in our system that currently is public available. The data resulting from that application is being used to improve the ASR components and the Language Parser.

4   Acknowledgments

This work was started as a Project in the final year of graduation of Pedro Cardoso and Luis Flores supervised by Prof. João Neto and Prof. Thibault Langlois at Instituto Superior Técnico, Technical University of Lisbon. This work was partially funded by FCT project POSI/33846/PLP/2000. INESC-ID Lisboa had support from the POSI Program of the "Quadro Comunitário de Apoio III". The authours would like to thank Prof. Luis Oliveira for his help with the DIXI+ system.

References

1. J. Neto, C. Martins and L. Almeida, "A Large Vocabulary Continuous Speech Recognition Hybrid System for the Portuguese Language", In proceedings ICSLP 98, Sydney, Australia, 1998.
2. M. C. Viana, L. C. Oliveira, and I. Trancoso. "Sistema de síntese a partir de texto – DIXI". In Actas do Encontro Regional da Associação Portuguesa de Linguística, Trás-os-Montes, Maio 1997. (Portuguese text)
3. Zue, Victor et al, "JUPITER: A Telephone-Based Conversational Interface for Weather Information", IEEE Trans. on Speech and Audio Processing, vol 8, No. 1, January 2000, pp. 85-96.
4. Mikio Nakano et al, "Mokusei: A telephone-based Japanese Conversational System in the Weather Domain", In proceedings EUROSPEECH 2001, Denmark, 2001.

Concluding Remarks on Multi-band and Multi-stream Research for Noise-Robust ASR

Astrid Hagen[1,2]

[1] INESC-ID, Rua Alves Redol 9, Lisbon, Portugal
astrid.hagen@l2f.inesc-id.pt
[2] formerly at: IDIAP, Rue du Simplon 4, Martigny, Switzerland

Abstract. This paper summarizes our work carried out over the last four years on multi-band and multi-stream processing as means to achieve robust automatic speech recognition (ASR). Main focused is laid on the "full combination" approach which integrates over all possible positions of reliable data, instead of combining the nominal subbands or streams only. The main combination rules are summarized and the final results from a wide range of experiments are presented.

1 Introduction

Different approaches to increase the robustness of an automatic speech recognizer comprise, among others, more appropriate feature extraction, better acoustic modeling and advanced decoding schemes. In this framework the goal of this work was to investigate and develop new paradigms for noise robust ASR based on multi-band (MB) and multi-stream (MS) processing[1].

After the speech signal has been converted to the spectral domain, in **MB** processing, the entire frequency domain is split into frequency subbands which are processed independently up to a certain point where the information from each band is recombined. In **MS** processing, either the entire frequency domain is considered several times, each time employing different processing strategies, or other modalities, such as visual representations, of speech production are included. The information from each of these streams is correspondingly recombined later in the process.

Both approaches try to better utilize the inherent redundancy in the speech signal either by processing different parts of the signal separately or by different processing of the same signal stream. If the streams are correlated, it can be assumed that combination is best carried out on the feature level so that dependencies between the streams can be modeled. In case when the streams are corrupted by noise, the correlation between the streams is decreased. It can thus be assumed that the streams are better modeled independently, as this is likely to result in independent errors conducted by each stream recognizer due

---

[1] Although the latter is a generic term of the first, we distinguish these two approaches due to historical reasons: MB processing was – as far as our research is concerned – investigated first and its principle was then generalized to multi-stream processing.

E.M. Ranchhod and N.J. Mamede (Eds.): PorTAL 2002, LNAI 2389, pp. 179–188, 2002.

to train/test mismatch. Nothing can be done about these errors when dealing with a single-stream (fullband) recognizer only. However, when combining the outputs of two or more recognizers, independent errors coming from any one of them can be dampened. Thus, the MB and MS systems are expected to provide higher noise robustness to any kind of noise than a single-stream system, without any knowledge of the noise or the necessity of different training databases and noise adaptation phase.

In this framework, we investigated several frame-level **combination approaches**, some of which employ a reliability term for each subband or stream [9]. The MB and MS strategies were developed on clean speech data and their noise robustness was tested and evaluated on noise-corrupted speech with the noise stemming from various additive noise environments. The different MB and MS recognizers were compared amongst each other as well as to the baseline fullband recognizers.

Our research was carried out in the framework of Hidden Markov Model (HMM) based speech recognizers, where HMM emission probabilities were estimated through either Gaussian Mixture Models (GMMs), or Artificial Neural Networks (ANNs). The former outputs likelihoods so that combination of different streams is carried out on these, whereas the latter outputs posteriors which are used for recombination in this case (here on the frame level). After recombination of posteriors, the recombined posteriors are divided by the prior probabilities to obtain (scaled) likelihoods for the regular ("one-dimensional") Viterbi decoder as used here.

2   Multi-band Processing

In *multi-band* processing, the speech signal in the spectral domain is split into several subbands which are processed independently for feature extraction and possibly probability estimation before they are recombined for further processing. In the case when noise only occurs in one frequency subband, it does therefore not mix with the other clean feature coefficients which allow for reliable decoding of the clean part of the speech. Similarly, in *missing data* (MD) [4, 3, 12] processing as applied to robust ASR, it is tried to segregate speech and noise in the input signal, and then to recognize at each time frame the clean speech part only. This includes the necessity for a noise detection algorithm and for the processing of continuously varying combinations of (clean) feature coefficients. Moreover, only one fixed decomposition into clean and noisy data (a so-called "MD mask") is considered at each time frame.

Original subband processing misses important frequency correlation information among subbands and is therefore usually not competitive in real-environmental noise. We developed in this work, an approach to subband processing which provides a solution to the problem of both loss of frequency correlation in MB processing and fixed MD masks through a revised decomposition of the frequency band into an *exhaustive and mutual exclusive set of frequency subbands*. This induces new combination strategies as described below.

Full Combination Processing In MB ASR it was up to now assumed that subbands could be processed independently, with each subband modeled by a distinct recognizer. In the case of noise-corrupted speech in one subband, correct recognition on the remaining clean subbands could then provide enough information to decode the entire input data. In case of clean speech and speech corrupted with wideband noise, however, experiments in ASR have shown that a MB system of this type very often leads to decreased performance as compared to a fullband recognizer, due to missing cross correlation information. To model more closely what is actually going on in humans who integrate information from even dispersed frequency regions, and to obtain higher performance in both clean and (wideband) noise corrupted speech by a MB system, we had to find a revised model which also exploits correlation information between (adjacent and non-adjacent) subbands. This should be done by integrating also dispersed frequency information, when some frequency regions are missing, in order to exploit this correlation and redundancy in the spectrum.

Thus, at each time frame, as much clean correlated information as possible should be modeled. In the MD approach, noise corrupted frequencies in each frame are detected and excluded, while the remaining reliable data is modeled as a single stream. However, accurate noise detection is very difficult. In the "full combination" (FC) approach taken here, data is divided into subbands and recognition is performed on *every possible combination of subbands*, after which the output from these experts is integrated by one of several possible combination strategies.

The FC paradigm for MB ASR For most application areas, the position of the noise is not known and can be in any subband and any number of subbands. We therefore have to find a way in which we can consider all possible subsets of the frequency domain in order to find the clean data set.

For this, let us define the set of all possible combinations of B subbands, which include the streams consisting of no, one, two etc. (adjacent and non-adjacent) subbands up to the combination of all subbands, as C, and the set of events b_i $(i = 1, \ldots, \mathcal{B} = 2^B)$ as follows:

$\mathcal{B}$ denotes the set of events b_i that data in combination i is clean speech data, and data not in combination i is completely uninformative and can therefore be regarded as missing.

On the assumption that each subband is either completely clean or completely uninformative, such a set of events is mutually exclusive and exhaustive, as only one combination of subbands can be the largest clean combination, and one or other must be the true clean combination, because all possible combinations have been considered. Denoting $P(b_i)$ the probability that event b_i occurs, we can write:

$$P(\cup_i b_i) = \sum_{i=1}^{\mathcal{B}} P(b_i) \qquad \text{(mutually exclusive)}$$
$$= 1 \qquad \qquad \text{(exhaustive)}$$

(1)

If some subbands are not corrupted by noise, it is likely that the best stream[2] is the largest combination of clean subbands[3]. However, under wideband noise conditions it can also be the case that some less noisy subset carries more useful information than the empty set.

Let us now consider how this new FC approach to subband processing can be implemented in a speech recognizer. Considering all possible combinations of subbands means that features have to be extracted not only in the nominal subbands but also in each combination of subbands, i.e. in the $\mathcal{B}$ feature streams (note that this includes the empty set). Data within each feature stream can be further processed for decorrelation and/or other transformations, as required. We can then associate with each event b_i an expert i which has at its input the clean data defined by event b_i. In (posterior-based) probability combination, a recognizer has thus to be trained on each of the $\mathcal{B}$ feature sreams, as shown in **Figure 1** for the case of two subbands. Realization of the FC approach in posterior- and likelihood-based systems is discussed below. A further advantage

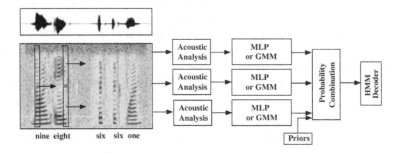

Fig. 1. Illustration of full combination processing with MLP or GMM classifiers for two subbands. Features are extracted from all possible combinations of subbands.

of FC processing over "standard" subband processing is that the question of how many subbands are to be chosen and the exact position of the subbands gets less important as in the FC approach all subbands are considered by themselves *and in combination* and thus correlation between all subbands is considered.

3   Combination Strategies

Different strategies for the recombination of stream probabilities exist, such as the sum or product rule. In each of them, we have to combine likelihoods or

---

[2] Note that, in order to be able to refer to a 'subband ' and 'combination of subbands' in one term, we use the term '(*data*) stream' to account for both.

[3] This is under the assumption that the stream acoustic models are trained on clean speech only.

posteriors according to a function which often depends on weights representing the reliability of each (subband) stream.

In this section, we present the probability combination strategies which were developed in the framework of this work and which are based on the FC approach introduced in the preceding section. Each of the combination strategies is presented for both the posterior-based case and the likelihood-based case. The likelihoods need to be normalized before combination to account for the different range they usually cover.

Despite the fact that the preceding section was concerned with combining subband experts, the expert combination strategies presented here are not specific to subband expert combination, but can be applied to combinations of experts trained on any (preferably complementary) data streams. More specifically, the combination strategies are also an important part of the MS approach.

3.1   FC Sum Rule

FC Posterior Decomposition For posterior decomposition, a separate expert is trained for each of the $\mathcal{B}$ possible combinations. Introducing the hidden variable b_i $(i = 1, \dots, \mathcal{B})$ indicating which band subset is clean, as defined in Section 2, and with the b_i's being mutually exclusive and exhaustive, $P(q_k|x)$ can be expressed as

$$P(q_k|x) = \sum_{i=1}^{\mathcal{B}} P(q_k|x_i)P(b_i|x) \quad \text{by definition of } b_i \tag{2}$$

$P(b_i|x)$ is the *reliability term* for each expert. If b_i is true, then $P(q_k|x_i)$ should be accurately estimated by expert i (which was trained on clean data). Otherwise the estimate will not be reliable.

Approximation to Full Combination (AFC) In the case of posterior-based experts (such as Multi-Layer Perceptrons (MLP)), it is necessary to train 2^B (MLP) experts, and the approach is thus limited to a small number of subbands. We, therefore, proposed an approximation scheme which estimates the probabilities for each *combination* of bands based on the *single* band experts only.

Under the assumption of conditional independence between subbands l in a combination x_i $p(x_i|q_k) \simeq \prod_{l \in x_i} p(x_l|q_k)$, we can derive the posteriors $P(q_k|x_i)$ for each subband-combination from the single-subband posteriors $P(q_k|x_l)$ in this combination (i.e. $l \in x_i$) as follows

$$P(q_k|x_i) = \Theta \, P^{1-|x_i|}(q_k) \prod_{l \in x_i} P(q_k|x_l) \tag{3}$$

where Θ is a normalization constant independent of q_k, such that $\sum_{k=1}^{K} P(q_k|x) = 1$ [8]. These approximated combination posterior probabilities (3) can now be used in any combination strategy where separately trained posteriors are used, such as (2). We see in the following how with FC for likelihoods, under certain conditions the stream likelihoods can be derived from the fullband likelihood without training other than the fullband expert.

FC Likelihood Decomposition Using Marginalization We can convert the
FC SUM rule for posteriors (2) to a FC SUM rule for likelihoods by using Bayes'
rule.

$$\frac{p(x|q_k)}{p(x)} = \sum_{i=1}^{\mathcal{B}} \frac{p(x_i|q_k)}{p(x_i)} P(b_i|x) \tag{4}$$

where $p(x_i) = \sum_{k=1}^{K} p(x_i|q_k)P(q_k)$.

In the FC SUM rule for likelihoods (4), we sum over all possible positions
$(i = 1, \dots, \mathcal{B})$ of reliable subbands. Under the condition that subband combination coefficients are selected from fullband coefficients without further processing (such as orthogonalization within a combination), the parameters for the
marginal probability density functions (pdfs) $p(x_i|q_k)$ can be obtained directly
from the parameters for the fullband pdf by marginalization.

Following the derivation which leads to expression of the marginal pdf for
the data "present" in MD processing [4, 9], we can derive the state likelihoods
$p(x_i|q_k)$ for each stream i by integrating over the unreliable, that is, "missing"
part $x_i' = x - x_i$ of the data, which is disregarded in the respective stream:

$$p(x_i|q_k) = \int_{x_i'} p(x|q_k) \, dx_i' \tag{5}$$

For the mixture pdfs of M mixtures m_j as commonly used for likelihood modeling
it holds:

$$\int_{x_i'} p(x|q_k) \, dx_i' = \sum_{j=1}^{M} P(m_j|q_k) \prod_{l \in s_i} p(x_l|m_j, q_k) \tag{6}$$

where s_i denotes the set of feature coefficients in subband combination i. In the
case where each mixture component pdf $p(x|m_j, q_k)$ is modeled as a diagonal
covariance Gaussian, with mean μ_{jk} and variance vector σ_{jk}^2, the mean and
variance vectors for the marginal pdf $p(x_l|m_j, q_k)$, i.e. μ_{ljk} and σ_{ljk}^2, are simply
obtained by striking out the rows and columns from the mean vector μ_{jk} and
covariance matrix σ_{jk}^2 corresponding to the missing components [4]. Substituting
(6) back into (4) we get the full combination formula using marginalization for
likelihood-based systems.

In the case when each stream only comprises one feature component, the
above implementation of the FC approach can be interpreted in MD terminology
as a *weighted sum over all possible sets of hard MD masks* using marginalization
without bounds.

Preliminary experiments employing marginalization in FC MB ASR revealed
that although this avoids the need to train more than one fullband expert, the
remaining problem of having to evaluate the marginal likelihood for every combination of subbands is still very computationally expensive, and this prevented
us from running further experiments.

3.2 FC Product Rule

Experimental results have often shown that, despite the limitations of the inaccurate independence assumption between the different recognizers working on each combination of subbands, the recombination by a product can be a more effective method of combining the outputs of multiple classifiers than the sum rule [6, 1, 5, 7, 10, 11].

FC Product Rules for Likelihoods Under the inaccurate assumption of independence between the different recognizers, the full likelihood can be decomposed into a product of $\mathcal{B}$ stream likelihoods for each state q_k, according to:

$$p(x|q_k) \simeq \Theta_k \prod_{i=1}^{\mathcal{B}} p^{w_i}(x_i|q_k) \tag{7}$$

with $p(x_i|q_k)$ the state likelihood of expert i, which was trained on part x_i of data x only, and $\Theta_k = \frac{1}{\prod_i \theta_{ik}}$ a normalization constant, where $\theta_{ik} = \int_{x_i} p^{w_i}(x_i|q_k)\, dx_i$ so that $\int p(x|q_k)\, dx = 1$.

FC Product Rules for Posteriors Under the assumption of conditional independence used in (7), we can derive for the posterior-based case the FC PRODUCT rule as follows:

$$P(q_k|x) = \Theta\, P^{1-\mathcal{B}}(q_k) \prod_{i=1}^{\mathcal{B}} P(q_k|x_i) \tag{8}$$

where Θ is a normalization constant, independent of q_k, such that $\sum_k P(q_k|x) = 1$ (for exact derivation see [9, p. 87]).

4 Multi-stream Processing

In *multi-stream* processing, different possibilities exist to incorporate additional knowledge sources. They can stem, among others, from different data recordings (such as audio and visual streams), pre-processing, feature extraction, or from a different choice, structure and training of the classifiers. In this work, we concentrated on the use of different *feature* streams, from either different feature extraction techniques (such as PLP and MFCC features) or the same technique but employing different parameters and/or pre- or post-processing strategies (such as PLP and J-RASTA-PLP features) . Thus, the same (fullband) frequency domain undergoes different processing strategies leading to different feature representations which are used in individual recognizers, the errors of which are hoped to be complementary. The streams are recombined, just as in the MB approach according to FC processing, later in the process to dampen the errors.

5   Experimental Evaluations and Conclusions

The proposed algorithms for combining multiple subband or fullband streams, employing equal weighting, were tested on a continuously spoken digits database (Numbers95) [2] under noise-free (matched) conditions and under noise-corruption by artificial band-limited (stationary and siren) and natural wideband noise (mismatch) [8]. Results are presented for the case when HMM /MLP hybrid systems were used. As our goal was to develop systems which can easily generalize and adapt to unseen data, training was only carried out on clean speech. All tests were run using both PLP and J-RASTA-PLP features. Due to in general higher recognition rates in noisy speech, results are given for J-RASTA-PLP features only.

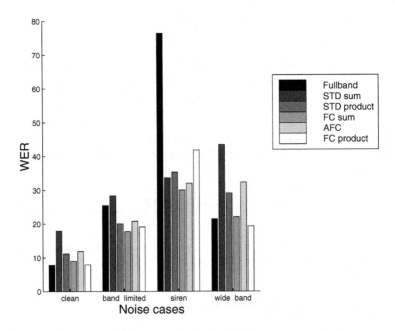

Fig. 2. Multi-band processing (4 subbands) using the "standard" STD (employing 4 trained MLPs) and "full combination" FC (employing 16 trained MLPs) recombination strategies as compared to the fullband approach on clean speech and speech corrupted with various additive noise cases. Features used are the j-rasta features.

It can be seen that the *MB FC* approach (FC Sum and FC Product) is competitive in clean speech (which is not the case for *standard* multi-band processing (STD sum and STD product)) and usually ranges among the best systems for all noise cases (cf. Figure 2). Depending on the noise case, it was observed that the FC Sum rule generally obtains better results in band-limited noise, and the FC Product in wideband noise.

For performance *improvement* in *clean* speech, *MS* processing should be applied (cf. Figure 3), though none of our systems tested gained a significant improvement over the best (i.e. J-RASTA-PLP) baseline.

For MS processing in noise, the results were less conclusive, but again it was observed that the FC SUM rule obtains better results in band-limited noise, whereas in wideband noise it is the FC PRODUCT rule.

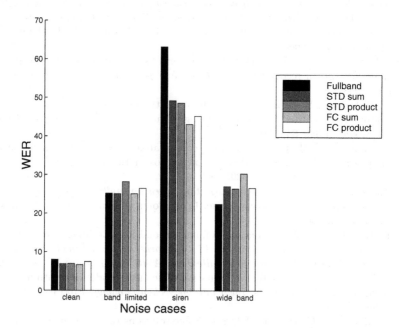

Fig. 3. Multi-stream processing using the "standard" STD (employing 3 trained MLPs) and "full combination" FC (employing 8 trained MLPs) recombination strategies as compared to the fullband (single-stream) approach on clean speech and speech corrupted with various additive noise cases. The streams consist of different features, namely PLP , J-RASTA-PLP and MFCC features. Fullband baseline is again the J-RASTA-PLP based system.

When looking at the performance achieved by PLP versus J-RASTA-PLP features, we observed that PLP features usually gain lower word error rate in clean and non-stationary band-limited noise whereas J-RASTA-PLP features performed better in stationary band-limited noise and wideband noise.

References

[1] H. Christensen, B. Lindberg, and O. Andersen. Employing heterogeneous information in a multi-stream framework. *Proc. Int. Conf. on Acoustics, Speech and Signal Processing*, III:1571–1574, 2000.

[2] R.A. Cole, M. Noel, T. Lander, and T. Durham. New telephone speech corpora at CSLU. *Proc. European Conf. on Speech Communication and Technology*, 1:821–824, 1995.

[3] M. Cooke, P. Green, L. Josifovski, and A. Vizinho. Robust automatic speech recognition with missing and unreliable data. *Speech Communication*, 34(3):267–285, 2001.

[4] M. Cooke, A. Morris, and P. Green. Missing data techniques for robust speech recognition. *Int. Conf. on Spoken Language Processing*, pages 863–866, 1997.

[5] Stéfan Dupont. *Études et Développement de Nouveaux Paradigmes pour la Reconnaissance Robuste de la Parole*. PhD thesis, Laboratoire TCTS, Université de Mons, Belgium, 2000.

[6] A.K. Haberstadt and J.R. Glass. Heterogeneous measurements and multiple classifiers for speech recognition. *Int. Conf. on Spoken Language Processing*, 3:995–998, 1998.

[7] A. Hagen and H. Bourlard. Using multiple-time scales in the framework of full combination multi-stream speech recognition. *Int. Conf. on Spoken Language Processing*, 1:349–352, 2000.

[8] A. Hagen and H. Glotin. Études comparatives des robustesses au bruit de l'approche 'full combination' et de son approximation. *Journée d'Études sur la Parole, Aussois*, pages 317–320, 2000.

[9] Astrid Hagen. *Robust speech recognition based on multi-stream processing*. PhD thesis, Département d'informatique, École Polytechnique Fédérale de Lausanne, Switzerland, 2001.

[10] K. Kirchhoff and J.A. Bilmes. Combination and joint training of acoustic classifiers for speech recognition. *ISCA ITRW Workshop on Automatic Speech Recognition – Challenges for the new millenium (ASRU2000)*, pages 17–23, 2000.

[11] H. Meinedo and J.P. Neto. Combination of acoustic models in continuous speech recognition hybrid systems. *Int. Conf. on Spoken Language Processing*, 2:931–934, 2000.

[12] A. Morris, M. Cooke, and P. Green. Some solutions to the missing features problem in data classification, with application to noise robust ASR. *Proc. Int. Conf. on Acoustics, Speech and Signal Processing*, pages 737–740, 1998.

Groundwork for the Development of the Brazilian Portuguese Wordnet [*]

Bento C. Dias-da-Silva, Mirna F. de Oliveira, and Helio R. de Moraes

Faculdade de Ciências e Letras, Universidade Estadual Paulista
Rodovia Araraquara-Jau Km 1, 14800-901 Araraquara, São Paulo, Brazil
bento@fclar.unesp.br {mirna.oliveira,_hroberto}@uol.com.br

Abstract. Considering the Princeton WordNet built for English as a reference, new Wordnets in other languages are being built, such as the ones for European Portuguese, Galician, Basque, Catalan, and Spanish, just to mention some Iberian languages. In this paper we set the groundwork for the development of the Brazilian Portuguese Wordnet: the compilation of a WordNet-based Brazilian Portuguese Thesaurus, a particular dictionary of synonyms and antonyms stored in a computer for use in word processing. As there were no available machine tractable wide range lexical resources whatsoever for Brazilian Portuguese, and strict manual construction of lexicons from scratch is costly and highly time-consuming, we have focused on the massive acquisition and filtering of lexical knowledge and semantic information from pre-existing structured lexical resources. Accordingly, in this paper we present the methodology we used, the lexical resources we employed, and the computing tools we designed to develop such a thesaurus from conventional dictionaries available for Brazilian Portuguese.

1 Introduction

It is a fact that research in Human Language Technology has proved the need for extensive and complete machine tractable lexical resources for natural language processing [21]. Acquiring such lexical/semantic structures is a hard problem and has been usually approached by reusing, merging, and tuning existing lexical material. While in English the "lexical bottleneck" problem seems to be softened, e.g. WordNet [7, 14, 15], COMLEX [11], there are no similar wide range lexicons available for Brazilian Portuguese. It is also a fact that the English WordNet developed at Princeton University is consolidating as a standard for the representation of semantic (either conceptual or lexical) relations displayed/motivated by natural language word stock [12]: concepts are defined by synonymy sets consisting of English word-forms, the synsets, the building blocks of the whole net.

These two facts set the stage for the work presented in this paper: we present the methodology we used to build a large scale computerized lexical resource within a two-year time span (2000-2001) - the Brazilian Portuguese thesaurus lexical database (henceforth TDb), despite the small team of four linguists and two computer

_____

[*] Work sponsored by CNPq (Brazilian National Research Council), Grant n°552057/01-0.

E.M. Ranchhod and N.J. Mamede (Eds.): PorTAL 2002, LNAI 2389, pp. 189-196, 2002.
© Springer-Verlag Berlin Heidelberg 2002

scientists. As the TDb is a monolingual lexical knowledge base motivated by the Princeton WordNet model, this presentation sets the starting point for the development of the Brazilian Portuguese Wordnet project (henceforth BP-Wordnet), partially sponsored by the Brazilian National Research Council (CNPq), and launched last March by a research team that gathers natural language and computer experts from three public Brazilian universities: São Paulo State University (UNESP), São Paulo University (USP), and Federal University of the State of Santa Catarina (UFSC). The results of the project are intended to be world-wide publicly available.

Having presented the topic in this section, in section 2 we limit the polysemous term *thesaurus*, for it has been used by different specialists to refer to very different objects. Then, we address the conventional lexical resources we selected. Next, we present the computing tools, where we describe both the design of the TDb and the interface which allowed the linguist to consult and modify the TDb. Finally, we conclude the paper by summarizing the TDb statistics and addressing the key development phases of the Brazilian Portuguese Wordnet project.

2 The *Thesaurus* Denotations

In what follows, we present a survey of the denotations of the term *thesaurus* in Brazilian Portuguese, and single out the one we had in mind when we embarked on the compilation of our computerized lexical resource: the Object 6.

The reason for that is the fact that different specialists have used the term *thesaurus* to denote at least six different objets [10, 13, 18, 20]:

1. an inventory of the vocabulary items in use in a particular language;

2. a thematically based dictionary, that is, an onomasiologic dictionary;

3. a dictionary containing a store of synonyms and antonyms;

4. an index to information stored in a computer, consisting of a comprehensive list of subjects concerning which information may be retrieved by using the proper key terms;

5. a file containing a store of synonyms that are displayed to the user during the automatic proofreading process;

6. a dictionary of synonyms and antonyms stored in memory for use in word processing.

As we previously mentioned, the building blocks of the English WordNet developed at Princeton University are the synsets. But, besides the synsets, it also represents other lexical/semantic relations such as antonymy (between nouns, verbs, or adjectives), hyponymy/hyperonym (between nouns), troponymy, entailment, and cause (between verbs), and meronymy (between nouns) [5, 7]. Although the aim of the BR-Wordnet project is the specification of all those semantic relations represented in the Princeton WordNet, the compilation of the TDb focused exclusively on the treatment of synonymy and antonymy, an instance of Object 6.

3 Reference Corpus

Handcrafting lexicons, though the most reliable technique for obtaining structured lexical databases, is a costly and highly time-consuming method. This is the reason why researchers such as Briscoe and Boguraev [4], and the developers of the EuroWordNet themselves, have relied on the massive acquisition of lexical knowledge and semantic information from pre-existing structured lexical resources as automatically as possible. So have we. In fact, we chose a set of seven outstanding Brazilian Portuguese dictionaries to settle our reference corpus. Two are the best, the most updated language dictionaries [9, 23]; three are dictionaries of synonyms and antonyms [2, 8, 17]; one is a Roget-based dictionary [1]; and one is a very specific dictionary of Brazilian Portuguese verbs that contains the categorization frames and semantic roles for over six thousand verbs [3].

In order to guarantee minimum consistency in the compilation process of the synsets, criteria of extracting and filtering the synonyms from the reference corpus were devised [16]. Basically it consisted of taking advantage of the pervasive lexicographers' use of synonymic and antonymic words or expressions to define the headwords of the mentioned dictionaries and confronting the synsets with the NILC corpus (available at the address http://www.portugues.mct.pt/) whenever the semantic lexical information provided by the dictionaries was not clear enough to build or update either the synsets or the antonym links.

4 The Computational Tools

As we have already mentioned, the design of the TDb was motivated by the methodology developed by Miller [14]. Three basic notions were borrowed from him:
1. the differential method, which assumes the activation of concepts by means of a set of lexical forms, systematically arranged in terms of synonymy. Such strategy eliminates the need for specifying a conceptual label, that is, Nirenburg's "onto" [19], to each lexicalized concept in the lexicon;
2. the building block notion of synset, that is, a set of synonyms; and
3. the lexical matrix construct, which guarantees a one-to-one correspondence between a sense and a synset [6].

Such guidelines reduced the work of constructing the TDb to the manual filling in the template, which represents a lexical entry, as shown in Figure 1.

[Entry Word n (Syntactic Category X)

Sense n.1 [Synset; Antonym Synset]

...

Sense n.m [Synset; Antonym Synset]]

Fig. 1. The thesaurus database template.

where n is the entry identification number; X is a noun, verb, adjective, or adverb, and n.1 ... n.m are sense identification numbers of the entry n.

4.1 The TDb Structure

From the logical point of view, the TDb is a database structure made up of two lists: an Entry List (EL), the TDb entries ordered alphabetically, and the Set List (SL), the list of the synsets. Each element of a synset is necessarily an element of the EL. Each EL entry, besides being specified for its graphemic representation, is also specified for a particular Sense Specification (SS). Each SS is indexed by three memory pointers: the "synonymy pointer" points to a particular synset (say synset 1) in the SL; the "antonymy pointer" points to a particular synset in the SL (when there is one) which is the antonym of the synset 1; and the "sense pointer", besides identifying the sense, say sense 1, points to the particular entry in the EL to which both synsets are associated.

Each synset in the SL is represented as "double-faced" list. One side lists specific elements of the EL that are members of the synset and the other side specifies a list SSs to which the synset is part. In other words, let us name the faces: the Entry Face (EF) and the Sense Face (SF). The EF contains pointers to the elements of the EL that are related to one another by means of the synonymy relation. The SF containsn a list of SSs that indicates all SSs to which the synset is linked.

A conventional relational database management system was used. Its main functionalities include: the storage of general information of the TDb and its bookkeeping. The design includes the complete loading of all entries and their related information. The key feature is the automatic entry generation. Once the synset is entered   in the TDb or updated, the system generates the appropriate entries automatically. Just to illustrate with numbers: 3,872 verb synsets generate 10,204 verb entries.

4.2 The TDb Editor

For the manual process of entering the appropriate word-forms into the database, a special editor, so-called Thesaurus-Editor, was developed. Its graphical interface has tools that allow the linguist to perform different actions: create, consult, modify, and save an entry; view the whole TDb; list entries and synsets; view he TDb statistics, such as number of headwords, number of synsets, the ratio headwords/synsets, and the number of synsets generated automatically.

The process of entering word-forms into the TDb can be better understood by an illustrative example. Figure 2 shows the Thesaurus Editor wizard at the moment the linguist is constructing the entry for the adjective "abreviado" (abbreviated). As soon as the editor detects the word-form "abreviado", it checks whether there is an entry for it in the database. In the affirmative case, the fields "Palavra" (Word) ou "Lista de Sinônimos" (Synonym List), and/or "Palavra" (Word) ou "Lista de Antônimos" (Antonym List) are filled in automatically with the appropriate word-forms that were retrieved from the database. In the negative case, empty fields are presented to the linguist. Figure 3 shows the Thesaurus Editor after entering the Sense 1 of the entry "extenso" (extended), one of the antonymic forms of "abreviado".

5   Conclusions

In this paper we described how we constructed what we consider the embryo of the BP-Wordnet, resorting to limited qualified personnel and to no machine tractable lexical resources. Despite those drawbacks, we managed to construct a Brazilian Portuguese lexical database with 10,204 Brazilian Portuguese verb forms (3,872 synsets), 15,073 adjective forms (6,648 synsets), 16,171 noun forms (8,119 synsets), and 1,139 adverbs (566 synsets). For comparison, in EuroWordNet, the developers have been working on four languages (Dutch, Spanish and English), and the size of each of these wordnets, restricted to verbs and nouns, with the exception of the British English wordnet, is expected to be about 30,000 synsets, corresponding to about 50,000 word meanings. German, French, Estonian and Czech wordnets are expected to have 7,500-15,000 synsets.

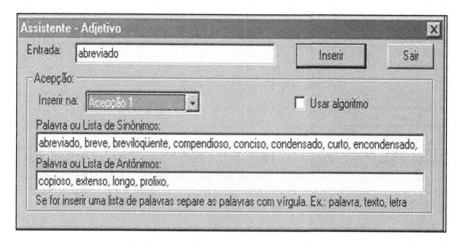

Fig. 2. Screen shot of the Thesaurus Editor wizard.

One particular point should be mentioned concerning the team involved in the project. The main players on the thesaurus development project were four language scientists and two language engineers. Each played a key role in the development of the system. It should be stressed that the language scientists were the ones that had expert knowledge of language, managed to communicate that knowledge, aid in knowledge acquisition, and help define the interface specifications. The language engineers were the ones that had engineering knowledge and programming skills, managed to match the problem to the appropriate software, and aid in the editor development.

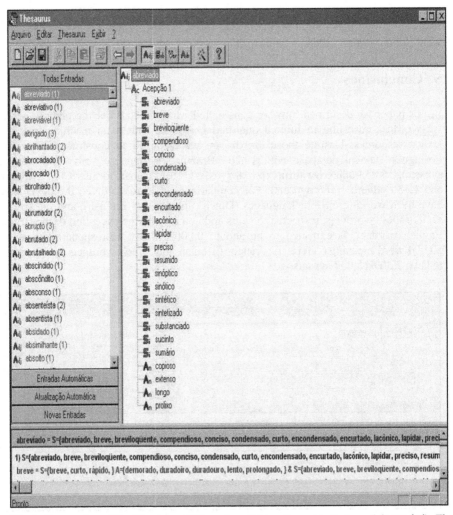

Fig. 3. Screen shot of the Thesaurus Editor after clicking the entry "extenso" (extended). The frame "Entradas Automáticas" (Automatically Generated Entries) displays the entries that were generated automatically.

The next ambitious step is to construct the BP-Wordnet, taking the TDb as the starting point. The following guidelines have already been traced: (i) to filter the synsets for more accurate concept discrimination, by generating concordances from selected corpora; (ii) to contextualize each word-form by means of an appropriate sample sentence extracted from concordance lists; (iii) to implement the BR-Wordnet database editor by means of which the team of linguits are able to encode the remaning relations (hyponymy, meronymy, troponymy, entailment, and cause), and some new cross-categorial relations, such as the ones we get between *chegada/chegar* (arrival/to arrive); *chegada/partir* (arrival/to leave), *entrar/dentro* (enter/inside); *martelar/martelo* (to hammer/hammer), etc.; (iv) to index each synset with the

EuroWordNet Inter-Lingual-Index, i.e., a set of synsets the purpose of which is to inter-link language-specific synsets from different wordnets; (v) to evaluate the results by confronting parts of the BP-Wordnet with other wordnets.

As suggested by the EuroWorNet research teams [22], we have embarked on the construction of the BP-Wordnet by resorting to available existing resources and databases, for this is not only more cost-effective due to the limited time and budget of the project (2002-2003), but its building will be done independentely by using the local tools and databases that are tailored to the specific nature and possibilities of our available resources. Contributions from other wordnet research teams are always welcome.

References

1. Azevedo, F.F.S.: Dicionário Analógico da Língua Portuguesa. Thesaurus, Brasília (1983)
2. Barbosa, O.: Grande Dicionário de Sinônimos e Antônimos. Ediouro, Rio de Janeiro (1999)
3. Borba, F.S. (coord.): Dicionário Gramatical de Verbos do Português Contemporâneo do Brasil. Editora Unesp, São Paulo (1990)
4. Briscoe, E.J.; Boguraev, B. (eds.): Computational Lexicography for Natural Language Processing. Longman, London New York (1989)
5. Cruse, D.A.: Lexical Semantics. Cambridge University Press, New York (1986)
6. Dias-da-Silva, B.C.; Oliveira, M. F.: Estrutura do Léxico: Modelo Lingüístico-Computacional de Representação das Relações Semânticas. Estudos Lingüísticos 30 (2001) 1-6
7. Fellbaum, C. (ed.): WordNet: An Electronic Lexical Database. The MIT Press, Cambridge, Mass (1998)
8. Fernandes, F.: Dicionário de Sinônimos e Antônimos da Língua Portuguesa. Globo, São Paulo (1997)
9. Ferreira, A.B.H.: Dicionário Aurélio Eletrônico Século XXI (Versão 3.0). Lexikon, São Paulo (1999)
10. Flexner, S.B. (ed.): Random House Webster's Unabridged Electronic Dictionary (Version 2.0). Random House Inc, New York (1997)
11. Grishman, R.; Macleod, C. & Meyers, A.: Comlex syntax: building a computational lexicon. In: Proceedings of the 15th Annual Meeting of the Association for Computational Linguistics (Coling'94). Kyoto, Japan (1994) 268-272
12. Levin, B., Pinker, S. (eds.): Lexical and Conceptual Semantics. Cognition 41 (1991) 1-229
13. Lutz, W.D.: The Cambridge Thesaurus of American English. Cambridge University Press, Cambridge (1994)
14. Miller, G. A.: Five Papers on WordNet. In: Special Issue of International Journal of Lexicography: actas (1990)
15. Miller, G. A., Fellbaum, C.: Semantic Networks of English. Cognition 41 (1991) 197-229
16. Moraes, H.R., Dias-da-Silva, B.C.: A Questão da Representação Lingüístico-Computacional da Sinonímia e Antonímia na Compilação de um Thesaurus Eletrônico. Revista de Iniciação Científica da Unesp 2 (2000) 414-423.
17. Nascentes, A.: Dicionário de Sinônimos. Nova Fronteira, São Paulo (1981)
18. Neufeldt, V. (ed.): Webster's New World Dictionary & Thesaurus (Version 1.0). Macmillan, New York (1997)
19. Nirenburg, S.: Machine Translation. Morgan Kaufmann, San Mateo (1992)
20. Roget, P.M.: Thesaurus. Penguin Books, Middlessex (1953) original ed. 1852
21. Saint-Dizier, P., Viegas, E.: Computational Lexical Semantics. Cambridge University Press, Cambridge (1995)

22.Vossen, P.: Introduction to EuroWordNet. Computers and the Humanities 32 (1998) 73-89
23.Weiszflog, W. (ed.): Michaelis Português - Moderno Dicionário da Língua Portuguesa (Versão 1.0). DTS Software, São Paulo (1998)

Linguistic Processing of Biomedical Texts

Caroline Hagège, Ágnes Sándor, Anne Schiller

Xerox Research Centre Europe, 38240 Meylan, France
{Caroline.Hagege, Agnes.Sandor, Anne.Schiller}@xrce.xerox.com

Abstract. In this paper, we describe ongoing work (in the framework of the project BioMiRe) in automatic detection of gene and protein names in biomedical texts. The approach adopted here is one based on robust linguistic analysis of these texts. The first part will show the specific problems encountered in the corpora, from the lexical and syntactic points of view. Then we will describe how the tools we use for linguistic processing perform our task. The problem of evaluation will then be addressed and our first results will be given. Finally, we will sketch how we intend to continue the work.

1   Introduction

With the widespread use of the web there is an ever-growing need for the automatic treatment of big quantities of scientific natural language free texts. The tasks to be carried out automatically include information retrieval (finding documents relevant to a particular domain), information extraction (entity recognition and classification, identification of relationships) and the creation of databases. One of the domains where automatic natural language processing has recently been greatly demanded is that of genetics. The natural language processing community makes considerable efforts to produce tools that could help researchers in this domain to keep up with the literature. Thus, a great number of projects are dedicated to the treatment of genetic texts all over the world, like the GENIA project[1] in Japan that aims at establishing the whole cycle of information extraction from retrieval to database construction, the MedLEE project[2] in the US, an operational system that extracts and structures information from radiology reports or the PIES project[3] in Singapore that detects interactions among proteins. The methods to carry out these tasks are both statistical and rule-based with manually encoded rules.

Most of the projects use tools specifically elaborated for this domain, but some of them like the Highlight system[4] of the University of Cambridge tune tools developed for processing general texts so that they are more efficient for a special corpus. They report to have tuned the FASTUS system[5] in three months to process genetic texts.

---

[1] http://www-tsujii.is.s.u-tokyo.ac.jp/~genia/index.html
[2] http://cat.cpmc.columbia.edu:8080/medleexml
[3] http://sdmc.krdl.org.sg/bic/groups/kleisli
[4] http://www.cam.sri.com/html/highlight_demo.html
[5] http://www.ai.sri.com/~appelt/fastus.html

E.M. Ranchhod and N.J. Mamede (Eds.): PorTAL 2002, LNAI 2389, pp. 197-207, 2002.

The methods used in the different projects are all based on the identification of keywords and key structures that mark the contexts of the entities or relationships that are to be extracted. We esteem that a way of getting better results is refining linguistic analysis by discovering the specificities of this kind of text.

In this paper we would like to show the kinds of linguistic phenomena that need special treatment and adaptation of general linguistic tools to information extraction from texts on genetics. These include the integration of a special vocabulary, solving tokenization problems, guessing unknown words, the recognition of recurring patterns, and characterizing the specificities of the syntax of the genetic literature.

2   Corpus Analysis and Specificities

2.1   Vocabulary Specificities

Working with domain specific texts implies in general working with a special terminology. This may consist in a specialization of common words, either by restricting several meanings to one which is specific to the domain (e.g. "class" is more likely to mean "a principal taxonomic grouping" than "a group of students") or by adding a new meaning (e.g. "library" as "an unordered collection of clones"). More often specialization implies addition of new words to the language. New words in the domain of genetics may be imported from other languages (e.g. Latin "mus musculus") or made up in an arbitrary way ("Ac76E").

A special problem that arises in the automatic treatment of texts on genetics is that the names of genes and proteins are highly ambiguous with one another and also with general language words. Some examples of ambiguous gene names are "A", "if", "so", "pink", "early", "1", "absent", "ago". Whereas adding meanings (as described above) does not always affect the syntactic behaviour of a word, the previous examples show cases of homonyms of common words with completely different functions. Automatic tools such as lexicons, taggers, parsers, have thus to be adapted to cope with these homonyms.

Another aspect of genetic terminology is the complexity of terms. Terms or names are not just simple words ("zebra") or compounds ("nucleic acid"), they may also correspond to any kind of word sequence ("iris yellow spot virus", "Adenylyl cyclase 76E", "4'-mycarosyl isovaleryl-CoA transferase"), or even to phrasal structures, such as fully expressed gene names ("eyes absent", "hHDC for homolog of Drosophila headcase", "infantile convulsions and paroxysmal choreoathetosis").

2.2   Syntactic Specificities

While, as we will see, the deeper syntactic constructions do not present particular difficulties in comparison with other texts of general corpora, we can observe that at the level of nominal chunks [1] there is a special complexity in this kind of texts due to the fact of an unusual number of pre-nominal modifiers.

Examples. Nominal chunks found in the corpus.

The parent-of-origin-determined differential activity of MEA, FIS2 and FIE

Membrane-bound tobamoviral RNA-dependent RNA polymerase activity

The endoplasmic reticulum (ER)-derived structures

A DNA-binding transcriptional regulatory protein

The combination of these complex nominal chunks that are also present in prepositional phrases, make it difficult to analyze NPs, as for example:

A major class of positive strand viruses including agronomically and clinically important viruses of plants and animals

Deep Syntax. Beyond the difficulties linked to the first point, biomedical texts have some syntactic specificities when compared to general texts (like SUZANNE, Brown corpus). Here are some examples:

- **Comment Clauses.** Comment clauses are syntactic constructions of any kind that can appear in many places of a sentence as a kind of remark or parenthesis. By disturbing the canonical syntactical construction of the sentences they make it more difficult to find the correct grammatical relations between words.

   Examples. Some sentences from our biomedical corpus. Comment clauses are in boldface.

   *Here we report the map-based cloning of an Arabidopsis thaliana gene, **TOM1,** which is necessary for the efficient multiplication of tobamoviruses, **positive-strand RNA viruses infecting a wide variety of plants**.*

   *In situ hybridization studies have shown that MEA mRNA occurs, **before fertilization**, in the eight-nuclei embryo sac, in the egg cell, and in the central cell*

   *Lug-16, **a weak lug mutant with the highest fertility among all lug alleles**, allows the direct transformation of homozygous lug-16 plants.*

   *To eliminate the possibility that changes in fluorescence in different cell types and in response to salt treatment were due to differences in glutathione S-transferase activity, **required for conjugation of MCB**, leaves were also labeled with monobromobimane, which does not require glutathione S-transferase activity for labeling.*

- **Incomplete Sentences**. Incomplete sentences appear most of the time as captions in biomedical texts. If the corpus we process in not marked up with (e.g. html or xml) tags that give this information (which is the case in the current version of our work), the fact that the sentences are incomplete can imply disambiguation errors. For example, if we use the criterion that a sentence must contain a finite verb, a token that is ambiguous between noun and verb will erroneously be tagged as a verb.

Examples. Captions or titles from our biomedical corpus.

*Measurement of cytoplasmic GSH **levels** by two-photon laser scanning microscopy.*

*Pedigree of Tangier **disease** kindred.*

*Diagram of the secondary **structure** of the ABC1 transporter.*

3   A Particular Task: The Detection of Biological Entities

3.1   Difficulty in Collecting Reliable Data

The first problem encountered when working on biomedical texts is the unreliability of the resources that are needed to achieve the work.

Several specialized lexicons are accessible through the Web, but they differ considerably with respect to their encoding, the amount and quality of their contents. It is possible to merge different resources to obtain a domain specific dictionary – but with the risk of including incoherent information.

A second point is the difficulty of finding reliably annotated corpora which can be used for training and testing automatic tools. The validity of the corpora annotated by experts is also somewhat doubtful in the light of some experiments (see [7]) that show that the experts fully agreed only in 69.2% of the annotations.

3.2   The Tools

Finite-State Tools. For coding lexical information we use the Xerox Finite-State Tools [5],[6] which allow efficient storage and representation of different resources for lexical analysis (lexicons, unknown word guessers, word form normalizers, etc.) in a uniform way. For the lexical analysis of a text we apply the finite-state run-time tool **NTM** (normalization, tokenization and morphological analysis) which make use of these different resources.

HMM tagger. For POS disambiguation we use a HMM tagger operating on POS tags and ambiguity classes [4]. In the current phase of the project we take a general purpose POS tagger for English without any modification or specialisation for biomedical texts.

XIP. The Xerox incremental parser (XIP) (see [1]) is a robust parser that takes textual input and gives as output the same text enriched with linguistic information. XIP integrates NTM and HMM tagging. It is possible within XIP to carry out the following tasks: Correct the disambiguation, build chunks, create dependencies between the linguistic items. The current version of XIP is used for both encoding local grammar rules for entity detection in genetic texts (see point 3.4) and for carrying out deeper syntactic analysis (see point 3.5).

Syntactic processing with XIP is comparable to Abney's parser (see [2]), but unlike Abney's parser, XIP is not based on finite-state technology.

From the syntactic point of view, XIP carries out two main tasks: The first one is the construction of a chunk tree and the second one the construction of a dependency graph between the linguistic units.

- **Chunking Rules.** Chunking involves two kinds of rules: (1) *Sequence Rules* (very similiar to Context-Free Grammar rules) and (2) *Immediate Dominance Rules* together with a *Linear Precedence* component (very similar to GPSG grammar rules). Neither of the rule type allow recursivity[6].

    The rules are organized in layers. For each layer, rules are applied sequentially, and finally result in a chunk tree. A chunk tree is thus a list of nodes. Each node has a name (part-of-speech for lexical node, or chunk name otherwise) and is attached to a set of features (pairs of attribute names and values).

    Example. The chunk tree below is produced for the analysis of the sentence
    "The chunking rules define and produce a chunk tree"

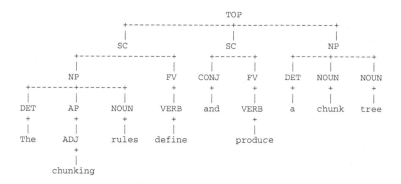

- **Dependency Rules.** In a later stage a set of dependency rules is applied on the chunk tree in order to extract relations between the lexical nodes of the chunk tree.

    The XIP formalism does not stipulate that these relations are binary and does not force to obey the projectivity principle. A dependency rule consists of an optional pattern (a tree regular expression, describing a sequence of nodes in the

---

[6] A limited recursivity however can be simulated by the iteration of rules in the different layers.

chunk tree) and optional conditions (constraints on pre-existing dependencies, linear precedence constraints) and a set of resulting dependencies. If the tree regular expression matches the chunk tree and if the conditions are met, then the dependencies are created.

Dependencies can thus be constructed for a particular syntactic configuration (see the first example below), and/or taking into account general relations that exist between the linguistic units (see the second example below).

Example 1. A dependency rule which creates a dependency SUBJ between a verb and the NP on its left (#1, and #2 are variables that represent respectively the head of the NP and the last lexical element of a FV (finite verb) chunk

| NP{*,#1[last]}, FV{?*,#2[last]} |
   SUBJ(#1,#2)

Example 2. The rule below is more general and indicates that if a dependency SUBJ links a verb to its subject and if this subject is linked to another item by a COORD relation (i.e. this subject is coordinated) then the coordinated element is also the subject of this verb.

If (SUBJ(#1,#2) & COORD(#2,#3))
   SUBJ(#1,#3)

3.3   Specialized Dictionaries

In addition to a general purpose morphological analyzer for English (~350,000 base forms), we use the following specialized lexicons and guessers for word form analysis:
- an *entity lexicon* containing names of entities to be detected (~500,000 forms), i.e. names of genes, proteins and species, including their full names, symbol names and synonyms.
- a *terminology lexicon* with domain specific terminology other than the target entities.
- a *word form guesser* for unknown word forms, based on affixes (e.g. "-ase") or regular patterns for terms (e.g. "22q12.3-q13.1")

As mentioned above, one difficulty in building a domain specific lexicon is to get reliable resources and good coverage. For our task we derived lexicons from various databases with differences in encoding and quality. Due to the large amount of data it is impossible to check and clean up entries manually, and thus the lexicons are very likely to contain incoherent and incomplete entries.

But even with good lexical resources at hand, the problem of non-lexicalised terms or variants remains unsolved. They can partially be covered by finite-state guessers, but in may cases this operation requires additional (contextual) treatment which goes beyond simple word form analysis.

3.4   Disambiguation and Local Grammars

To detect the names of the entities in texts that are not contained in pre-established lexicons of gene names we apply contextual rules. The relevant entities appear in recurrent contexts that are considered as markers of the entity. The markers that we take into account are either lexical, or grammatical. Lexical markers for the detection of gene names are lemmas (canonical forms representing all the inflected forms) of words like "gene", "express", "translation", which occur in the proximity of gene names in different structures. Grammatical markers are the presence or absence of a particular part of speech in the proximity of gene names. For example gene names - like proper nouns - are not preceded by articles in certain contexts where common nouns would be preceded by an article, whereas in some other contexts they are preceded by an article.

The XIP formalism allows us to extract entities easily once their recurrent contexts are identified. Since features can freely be added to lemmas of lexical entries, selections on the features present in the contexts of candidate gene names lead to the assignment of a label to these candidates. Candidate gene names are tokens that satisfy certain conditions: they do not belong to any of the pre-established lexicons, or if they do, they begin with capital letters but do not begin a sentence, etc.

With this method we are able to detect gene names that are in the most frequent lexical or grammatical contexts, but we cannot detect others whose contexts do not determine them so easily. However, the frequency of the recurrent contexts is high enough to yield a fairly big coverage in terms of the detection of entities. On the other hand, we also get erroneous results, since some technical words that are not gene names occur in the relevant contexts.

3.5   Deeper Syntactical Analysis

For deep syntactic analysis the English Xerox parser (XIP, see above) is used. The output of the syntactic analysis is a set of dependencies that link the linguistic units of the sentences.

In a first stage, each sentence is divided in chunks containing one or more words, and in a second stage, each linguistic item present in the chunks is related with other items in the same sentence through labeled and oriented relations. These relations express grammatical functions (like Subject, Object, Determiner ...) between words. It will thus be possible to discover potential gene and protein names when they are involved in certain dependencies with specific lemmas, even when they are not in their immediate context.

Examples. In the following examples we show how some keywords and gene names that are not in their immediate contexts are related with each other through grammatical dependencies.

FIE, on the other hand, **is expressed** *in many sporophytic , as well as gametophytic , tissues...*

SUBJ_PRE(be,FIE)
NUCL_VLINK(be,express)

Unlike other genes known to regulate floral homeotic gene expression, **LUG** *does not* **encode** *any obvious DNA – binding motifs.*

SUBJ_PRE(do,LUG)
NUCL_INSIST_VLINK(do,encode)

Further analysis of **sat5***, which* **encodes** *for the enzyme that provide the carbon skeleton for cysteine biosynthesis....*

NMOD_RELATIV_SENTENCE_POST(sat5,encodes)

4   Evaluation

This section   describes the difficulties of evaluation of the results of the task described in section 2, we establish our criteria and give the first results we obtained.

4.1   Evaluation Method

The basis for evaluation is usually a manually annotated corpus which is independent of any text which is used for lexicon construction or rule definition. We compare the output of automatic processing to this reference text and we provide *recall* and *precision* as evaluation results :
- *recall* := number of correct entities / number of entities in reference corpus
- *precision* := number of correct entities / number of entities in automatic output

Criteria. Whereas the computation of recall and precision is well-defined, the criteria for "correctness" may vary and depend on the goal of the application.
    In the tests described below the minimal matching criterion is that tokens must be *complete* (i.e. multi-word tokens partially recognized are not considered as correct or partially correct hits). Otherwise, a token may count as correct if its analysis corresponds *unambiguously* to the reference entity   (cf. Test 1 below) or only *partially* (cf. Test 2 below), in other words, for ambiguous output we apply different matching criteria.

Reference Corpus. Our reference corpus consists of 323 independent sentences (manually tagged by Violaine Pillet [8]), each of which contains at least 2 gene or protein names. The following table shows the number of the entities annotated that have been taken into account for the evaluation:

	Number of tokens	*Number of types*
Gene	522	190
Protein	150	53
Species	82	18
all	**939**	**377**

4.2 Tests Performed

Lexical Analysis Only. A first test consists in entity mark-up using lexical analysis only. The tool for lexical analysis (NTM) applies longest match (in case of multi-words) and it allows to specify an order for partial lexicons, thus giving priority to preferred readings in some cases of ambiguities. No further disambiguation (e.g. POS disambiguation) or corrections are applied.

Test 1: Count every token which is recognized *unambiguously* as gene or protein or species name, i.e. don't count ambiguous lexical analyses.

Test 2: Count any token recognized as *potential* gene, protein or species name, i.e. including cases of ambiguity with common words, such as "yellow", "if", "as", etc.

	Test 1		Test 2	
	recall	*precision*	*recall*	*precision*
Gene	62.4 %	63.2 %	86.2 %	22.3 %
Protein	0 %	0 %	16.7 %	24.5 %
Species	20.8 %	100 %	87.8 %	40.5 %
All	**45.4 %**	**63.9 %**	**72.5 %**	**23.8 %**

Contextual Disambiguation. The second series of tests is carried out on the same test corpus once disambiguated with an HMM tagger. In this series we are only looking for the recognition of gene names since the contextual rules that have been written up to this point do not apply to any other entities. Three tests have been conducted in this case, and the evaluation criteria are the same as in the previous case:

Test A: Apply full lexical analysis (as above) and POS disambiguation to recognize gene names.

Test B: Apply lexical analysis *without* entity lexicon (i.e. without gene names), POS disambiguation and contextual rules to recognize gene names.

Test C: Apply full lexical analysis, POS-diambiguation and contextual rules

	test A (Dictionary)	test B (Rules)	test C (Dic+Rules)
recall	63.7 %	37.4 %	67.9 %
precision	67.5 %	69.9 %	61.0 %

Syntactic Analysis. It is interesting to see if the results obtained by our English parser differ to a significant extent if we apply it on a general text (SUZANNE Corpus) and on a biomedical text.

With the same grammar we obtained the following results for the SUBJ, OBJ and MOD dependencies which describe respectively the links between a verb and its subject (sentential or not, coordinated or not), its direct object (sentential or not, coordinated or not) and a very general link between either a verb, a noun and an adjective and a (non-sentential, possibly coordinated) complement or adjunct of it. This MOD dependency enables us to check the right attachment of complements/adjuncts to the head they modify

The following table shows the results obtained with the current version of our English parser.

	SUBJ		OBJ		MOD	
	Precision	Recall	Precision	Recall	Precision	Recall
SUZANNE corpus	78,2	85,7	80,1	74	72,7	78,7
BIOMEDICAL text	76	75	61	61	60,7	65,9

The loss in the results are essentially due to errors in the chunking phase that is not tuned to handle the complex NPs of biomedical texts. The consequence of chunking errors is the erroneous determination of NP heads.
A special effort to adapt the chunker to these texts has to be made.

At this stage of the project, we have not yet integrated the local grammar into the syntax, but we have carried out a simulation to see the evolution of the recall when the integration takes place. Theoretically 6% improvement can be expected.

5   Conclusion and Future Directions

We have presented ongoing work on the detection of relevant entities in genetic texts with a special dictionary and context-based rules to find gene names that do not figure in the dictionary. As we have pointed out, this task shows particular difficulties compared to other kinds of entity extraction at every level in our chain of treatments: tokenization, part-of-speech tagging and syntactic analysis. At the present phase of our work we have a first prototype of a system: a dictionary of gene names, protein names and genetic terms as well as a number of contextual rules. The present performance of the system has been given in terms of recall and precision. It is too early to compare our results to other systems that have the same aim. We have made an inventory of the difficulties that we should overcome and we have defined the following steps to take:

- the fine analysis of the internal structure of gene and protein names so that we can improve tokenization
- the extension of the special lexicon of genetic terms
- the extension of contextual rules so that they consider syntactic analysis
- rule-based disambiguation of gene names that are ambiguous with the entries of the lexicons other than that of gene names

The analysis of the errors shows that once these steps are taken, we can expect that both the recall and the precision of the system can be improved.

The preliminary results suggest also that our toolkit is adapted to carry out entity extraction, and its flexibility allows further improvement. We plan in the future to generalize the methods used in this particular task and define a general platform for entity extraction regardless of the special terminology of texts.

References

1. Abney, S.: Parsing by chunks. In: R. Berwick, S. Abney, C. Tenny, eds. Principle-Based Parsing. Dodrecht: Kluwer Academic Publishers. (1991)
2. Abney, S.: Partial Parsing via Finite-State Cascades. In *ESSLI'96 Workshop on Robust Parsing*, Prague, Czech Republic. (1996)
3. Aït-Mokhtar, S., Chanod, J.-P., Roux, C.: Robustness beyond shallowness: incremental deep parsing In: Journal of Natural Language Engineering, Special Issue on Robust Methods in Analysis of Natural Language Data, Afzal Ballim, Vincenzo Pallotta (eds) Cambridge University Press (to appear)
4. Cutting, D., Kupiec J., Pedersen J., Sibun, P.: A practical part-of-speech tagger. In: Proceedings of the 3rd Conference on Applied Natural Language Processing} Trento, Italy. (1992)
5. Karttunen, L., Chanod, J.-P., Grefenstette, G., Schiller, A.: Regular Expressions for language Engineering. In: Journal of Natural Language Engineering vol 2 no 4. Cambridge University Press (1997) 307—330
6. Karttunen, L.: Applications of Finite-State Transducers in Natural Language Processing. In: Proceedings of CIAA-2000. Lecture Notes in Computer Science. Springer Verlag (2000)
7. Krauthammer, M., Rzhetsky, A., Morozov, P., Friedman, C.: Using BLAST for identifying gene and protein names in journal articles. In Gene 259 (2000) pp. 245-252
8. Pillet, V.: Méthodologie d'extraction automatique d'information à partir de la littérature scientifique en vue d'alimenter un nouveau système d'information. Thèse de l'Université de droit, d'économie et des sciences d'Aix-Marseille (2000)
9. Proux, D., Rechenman, F., Juilliard, L.: A pragmatic Information Extraction Strategy for gathering Data on Genetic Interactions In ISMB 2000.
10. Proux, D., Rechenmann, F., Julliard, L., Pillet, V., Jacq, B.: Detecting Gene Symbols and Names in Biological Texts : A First Step toward Pertinent Information Exctraction. In: Genome Informatics 1998 (GIW'98). Miyano S. and Takagi T. editors, Universal Academy Press, Inc, Tokyo, Japan (1998)

DISPARA, a System for Distributing Parallel Corpora on the Web

Diana Santos

SINTEF Telecom & Informatics, Pb 124 Blindern, NO-0314 Oslo, Norway
Diana.Santos@sintef.no,
http://www.portugues.mct.pt/Diana/

Abstract. The main purpose of the present paper is to document the process of creating a parallel corpus available on the Web, thereby illuminating technical and design issues involved in such a project. By this we hope to gather more researchers to help with the building process, as well as boast considerably the number of users of the parallel corpus. We start by noting that resource creation is far from a trivial process, and proceed by providing a brief introduction to COMPARA, the particular parallel corpus in connection with which the present system was developed, although with a view to achieve a general architecture. In the following sections we describe the incremental building process in DISPARA, emphasizing the reuse of software components, and discuss the Web interface. We conclude by discussing remaining work and emphasizing the importance of user feedback.

1 Introduction

Most people outside the corpus linguistics community have absolutely no idea about what is involved in making a corpus available (through the Web). In fact, there are quite a number of misconceptions regarding corpora [14]. Johansson [10] has convincingly argued that creating a corpus is like editing a book; still, many corpus users fail to distinguish between carefully edited corpora and text masses unjudiciously amassed.[1]

Describing thus in detail the process of creating one particular parallel corpus and several issues involved in its creation, distribution and protection can help users making such distinction, as well as teaching them to take a more critical look at what is loosely called "corpora".

By making public the computational work required to build this particular Portuguese-English paralell corpus, we also hope to foster practical collaboration from readers, in order to have a quicker development, as well as enlarge significantly the range of the corpus users.

We will not dwell here into the need and usefulness of parallel corpora, taking it for granted [21] [11] [2].

---

[1] Both can be useful, but for different purposes.

E.M. Ranchhod and N.J. Mamede (Eds.): PorTAL 2002, LNAI 2389, pp. 209–218, 2002.
© Springer-Verlag Berlin Heidelberg 2002

2   A Portuguese-English Parallel Corpus Created from Scratch

COMPARA, the corpus in connection with which the present system was developed, was created as a collaboration between two teams, Ana Frankenberg-Garcia's at ISLA and ours at SINTEF, both with considerable experience in the use of parallel corpora, albeit with different perspectives of use: the first mainly related to language teaching, translation training and error analysis, the second specifically concerned with contrastive linguistics and natural language processing.

This provided a rather broad range of interests for devising a corpus dissemination system. In order to profit from the two backgrounds, design and system issues have been prepared and planned together from the start.

One important motivation for the whole project was the belief that publically available resources for Portuguese linguistics and NLP would greatly benefit all people concerned with Portuguese processing; thus access to COMPARA is freely granted through the Web[2], and the DISPARA system was all along implemented with such a aim, as all other resources built under the framework of the Computatonal Processing of Portuguese project.[3]

3   The Process of Building a Corpus to Be Used in the DISPARA System

The amount of work that goes into the seemingly simple process of creating a corpus may seem surprising for the reader. In this paper we will **only** be concerned with the actual processing, not copyright clearance and/or tracing, which was obviously successfully done beforehand. It is, however, instructive, both for prospective corpus builders (in order to plan realistically their work) and for corpus users to know what lies in a resource now available.

For COMPARA, there was a physical separation between the team concerned with the texts and the team concerned with the programs (henceforth the "text team" and the "programming team"), respectively located at Lisbon and Oslo. While this produced an obvious overhead in e-mail communication, it brought the benefit of structuring very rigorously each team's task.

3.1   Outline of the Creation Process

Phase 1. The first task was to get the texts (English and Portuguese) in electronic form. This was achieved either by using previous electronic editions (e.g. from Projecto Vercial [20], the Gutenberg Project [7], the Biblioteca Virtual do Estudante Brasileiro [3] or the English-Norwegian parallel corpus[9]), or – in the majority of cases – by scanning and proofreading the result.

---

[2] http://www.portugues.mct.pt/COMPARA
[3] http://www.portugues.mct.pt/

The texts were then manually aligned at paragraph level with the help of standard editing facilities of word processor software. Markup concerning titles, foreign words and phrases, and other typographical emphasis was added (see [5] for the algorithm used) whenever subsentential parts of a sentence were highlighted in the original text. Obvious typos were corrected and marked, and translator's footnotes were physically brought to the place to which they refer, and marked up accordingly.

Phase 2. The texts were then sent to the programming team, which separated both texts into sentences (using the tools developed in another project dealing with Portuguese corpora [17]), and aligned them at sentence level using EasyAlign (version 1.0), a tool pertaining to the IMS Corpus Workbench [4].

In order to make the best use of the aligner while not losing any information already manually encoded in the text, two things had to be catered for, previous to invoking it: First, the markup should not be taken into consideration when aligning – this is solved by creating, for each specific pair of texts, intermediary corpora in which markup is encoded as structural attribute. Second, translators' notes have to be physically extracted and saved in an external file in order not to confound the automatic aligner, which employs text length as one decision criterion.

Phase 3. The result of the automatic alignment is then sent to be revised by the text team, in order to make it conform to the 1-to-any policy followed [6] and thereby defining alignment units (**uas**). Information about sentence reordering, sentence addition or dismissal, and type of complex alignment, is inserted in this pass (always in the translation **only**). Examples of reordering, addition and complex sentence splitting are displayed in figures 1 to 3.

```
File EBDL1T2fra.en:
917. <p><s> I shrugged.
918. <p><s> '' I don't know.
```

```
File EBDL1T2fra.po:
917. <p><s2> <reord resp=trans place=1> -- respondi, dando de ombros.
</reord>
918. <p><s2> -- Não sei. <place 1>
```

Fig. 1. Markup inserted in alignment units in case of reordering

Phase 4. The files are then sent back to the programming team, which (automatically) performs the following subtasks: create pairs of texts using the manually revised alignment, insert alignment type and alignment id, put translators' notes in the right place, and create special structural attributes to deal with reordering.

We chose to process automatically the notes, even though it might have been less time-consuming, in the first versions of the corpora at least, to have edited them manually in place after the rest of the processing. Automatic processing

File PBMA3fra.po:
591. <p><s> Mamãe é boa demais; dá-lhe atenção demais.
592. <p><s> Parece até que chorou.
593. <p><s> - José Dias?

File   PBMA3fra.en: 591. <p><s2> Mamma's too good; she pays him too much attention:
592. <p><s1/2+1> there were even tears...   <add>   Who cried? </add>
593. <p><s> José Dias?

Fig. 2. Markup inserted in alignment units in case of addition

File PPMC1fra.po:
648. <p><s> Era um homem simples.
649. <p><s> Limitava-se a cumprir.

File PPMC1fra.en:
648. <p><s2> He was a simple man;
649. <p><s2> he limited himself to complying.

Fig. 3. Markup inserted in alignment units in case of sentence merging (1-1/2)

means that the program has to recover the right position and add the text of the note (preserved during phase 2) inserted as value of an attribute. Due to particularities of the underlying corpus encoding system, the text of the notes itself had to be neutralized for all the "dangerous" characters that might disrupt the normal behaviour of the corpus building tools (tokenization, etc.), and then it had to be restored later so that users had access to the right contents.

The question of reordering, although even rarer (at the date of writing this paper, 5 cases against 97 translation notes, with 14 pairs of texts fully processed), was still more complicated to automate, since it required access to a larger text span than the other cases dealt with. In fact, a reordering of alignment units can only be seen if displaying more than one **ua**, and one of the basic design principles of DISPARA was that it was **ua**-based. The solution found was to create automatically a special structural attribute, called **ur** (unit of reordering) from the original markup (attributes <reord n> and <place n>), encompassing the **uas** containing these two tags. This provided half the solution, namely for the cases when one was looking at translated text (because only in the translation one can talk about reordering). To be able to recover the right size **also** in the source text, one more programming trick had to be used, namely the automatic creation of a program effecting several substitution commands to be run immediately after, in order to insert the corresponding **urs** in the source part(s).

Two reciprocally aligned corpora are finally created, together with automatic documentation (counting tokens, types, and **uas**), namely the (parallel) files Contents.html and Conteudo.html, one in each language.

For each new pair of texts added to the corpus, the Web interface must be accordingly manually updated, to allow the specific selection of that particular text pair.

Phase 5. The text team proceeds, then, already through the Web interface, by testing whether the automatic labelling of the 1-to-many cases conforms to their interpretation of what a sentence in the target language should be. In fact, there are cases far from clear-cut; opinions may differ between the original program writer and the text team; and, most importantly, the programs rely mainly on punctuation clues only, not necessarily present in all cases.[4] Every case where it is considered necessary to change the automatic judgement is written down in a special text file[5], which is sent to the programming team.

Phase 6 (repeatable). The two corpora are then created once more, taking into consideration any `div` files present, and which superseed the alignment type automatically found. Any remaining errors or problems, whenever discovered, provoke changes in the files after the manual revision of the sentence alignment, and subsequent corpus creation is done again, as many times as necessary.

3.2   Some Comments on Reuse

The whole process was designed obeying the following principle: make use of as many automatic tools as were available, minimizing human workload, though still giving the linguist the last word.

Paragraph alignment is done manually because it appeared an extremely simple task – few paragraph changes, and because the linguist would still have to browse through the whole text so that no gross errors appeared, while at the same time inserting the few markup information tags and translation notes in the right place.

Sentence separation inside each paragraph is done automatically reusing the sentence separation programs developed for huge Portuguese corpora in the context of the AC/DC project. Although these programs were developed for Portuguese, they were easily adapted to English literary text (remember, in any case, that there is also manual revision on this subject).

Sentence alignment is automatically performed by an off-the-shelf tool (Easy Align), buffered by a pre-processing stage, implemented in order to remove potential problems to the aligner, and a post-processing phase, added to get the result in a linguist-friendly version for subsequent revision.

Marking up, for each alignment unit, the kind of alignment type was also implemented as automatically as possible, by using (again) the sentence separation module, in all cases where the target part of the alignment unit was not

---

[4] The very same programs have been evaluated in the context of CETEMPúblico, a large newspaper corpus of text from the daily newspaper PÚBLICO [18]; considerable disagreement about the linguistic definition of sentence has also been met with in the Floresta Sintá(c)tica project [1], leading to significant revision [16].

[5] A `div` file, containing the right alignment kind to be used in COMPARA, one per line for each **ua** that requires change, e.g. 156: 1-1.

composed of parts of sentences (which had been previously manually encoded by the text team in phase 3, see figure 3). As mentioned above, this was still subject to scrutiny in phase 6 (and eventual change in following versions of the corpus).

So, the reuse policy is clear: Everything that can be done automatically is automated, but the corpus's creators, with their linguistic sensitivity, have always the last word and may require modifications. These modifications are **not** performed by manual edition, though. They are rather encoded and supported in the building process, in order to prevent having to perform the same modification more than once. This may bring a programming overhead compared to other corpus projects, but we believe it the right way to go.[6]

4   Resulting Web Service

One thing is the process used to create a resource; another thing is the way this resource can be put to use or interrogated (generally described as its user interface). Still another thing are actual patterns of use of a given resource.

In the previous section we described the process of creating the kind of resource the system was designed to build, namely a parallel corpus. The present section is concerned with explaining some of the fundamental options of the service that was implemented on top of the resource: both some that are visible in user options and others which are implicit in the system's behaviour.

An important issue is the clear-cut distinction between a search condition and an output option, even when they are closely related.

Take the interface choices "Search for translation notes" and "Hide/show translation notes". Although, in most cases, one can expect that the user will select one particular combination (if she is looking for notes, then will want to see them), the two options are, from a design point of view, independent. In fact, one may interrogate the corpus looking for alignment units that have translation notes attached, without being interested in the specific content of the translation notes. Or, conversely, one may want to see the translation notes if the search (which may well have obeyed other criteria) happens to find **uas** with them associated.

The same is true about alignment properties, associated with both search and display options: One may want to have a closer look at the alignment kind, by selecting all cases different from 1-1, or in which the translator added or removed whole sentences. Or, one may just want to see the alignment type when looking for non-related questions, such as inquiring whether sentences with perception verbs trigger more sentence restructuring in translation than other constructions (as hinted in [12] for the English-Portuguese pair).

Finally, another obvious example contrasting search and display modes, is either selecting specific parts of the corpus, or looking at the whole corpus, and

---

[6] Note that the reused tools themselves are not static, and may have upgrades that require rebuilding the corpus – it would be an overkill to do manual modifications every time one would want to recreate the corpus.

display the distribution according to source. [7] A little thought should be enough to convince the reader of the different purposes of these two interrogation modes.

Another interesting property of DISPARA is the use of **one** original sentence as definitory of alignment unit. This was motivated by the requirement that DISPARA should handle several translations of the same original, which, in order to be easily compared, had to have the same source side. As far as we know, this is one original feature of our system (one which actually did bring about a lot of extra work since the aligner used – and we believe most aligners – have result categories like 2-1 and 2-3 and 2-2[8]). Note, on this particular, the definition of alignment unit: one has a 1-1 alignment unit even if the target sentence has been moved (reordered) to another place.

DISPARA also provides an original display capability, which we believe very useful for contrastive studies, termed a "quantitative wrapup". Basically, given a parallel search in both languages, i.e., a search specifying conditions on **both** the first and the second language[9], a quantitative wrapup presents the number of hits obeying only the first condition, the number of hits obeying both, and the number of hits conforming to the second restriction. This is meant to give a sketch of the "translation match" between one word, expression or construction in one language and another word, expression or construction in the other. Some examples are shown in Table 1:

Table 1. Examples of quantitative wrapup, in COMPARA's version 1.1

Search	Quantitative Wrapup
(translation from P to E) enquanto - while	46 20 51
(All P to E) enquanto - while	178 92 162
(translation from E to P) while - enquanto	111 73 132
(All E to P) while - enquanto	162 93 178
espert.* - clever	8 2 7
clever - espert.*	7 2 8
home - casa	113 92 284
home.* - casas*	127 98 313
casa - home	284 98 113
casa - home*	284 104 127
thinks* OR thoughts* - pens.+	470 173 277

---

[7] In fact, as soon as we have more texts so that such questions really make sense, we should add the following distribution functions (corresponding to search options already implemented): by date; by date of translation; by variant; by variant of translation; by text type (translated or original).

[8] An interesting question, which we will have to leave to another paper, is how to evaluate different aligners with different output behaviour.

[9] Depending on the search direction, the first may be the source language and the second the target, or vice-versa.

The above data seems to imply that *enquanto* is a pretty good translation for *while*, and vice versa; as far as adjectives are concerned, the mismatch between *clever* and *esperto* is, on the other hand, obvious. We can also appreciate that *casa* is much more general than *home*, while *home* is an almost perfect match for (one of the senses of) *casa*. Finally, we see a rather bad match of the verbs *think* and *pensar* and their corresponding nouns.

DISPARA itself is parallel in both languages – error messages, titles, numbers, etc., appear in the language of the interface used. Since this is done in a modular way, one could actually add further languages for interaction as well, which might come in handy when new corpora in other languages are added.

5   Concluding Remarks

Although we consider the system already useful (see results presented with fewer data in [19]), we are aware that a lot may still remain to be done. This will mostly be discovered through actual use of the system, both directly and by observing others using it.

For example, one of the first and probably most common sources of error by unexperienced users was their attempt to use phrases without conforming to the IMS-CWB syntax. As soon as we discovered this through browsing the logs, we added such information right above the input box, so that users were informed before erring.

Other detected (and now solved) problem was the lack of interaction between the quantitative wrapup facility and the selection of parts of the corpus. In previous versions, only the columns referring to the source text were restricted, not the target (thus yielding uninterpretable numbers).

Other initially too loose definition of the semantics of the interface had to do with variant selection. We assumed, although not stated it, that variant choice concerned exclusively the (language of the) original text. This choice had the unwelcome effect of permitting a user to choose an empty corpus: For example looking at patterns from English to Portuguese, from originals to translations only, if one selected e.g. Brazilian Portuguese. Now, the semantic interpretation of this choice in the interface has been changed: Depending on the search direction, variant is contextually interpreted to refer either to original or to translation.

It is not an easy task to detect mismatches between user expectations and system behaviour. Although we are still in the preliminary stages of a log-based usability study of DISPARA, expecting to uncover somehow the kinds of users the system has nowadays, and the kinds of queries and problems they face, we are aware that an extremely important source of feedback is actual contact with users, which we strongly encourage.

Some things, however, are obviously missing. One is tagging or parsing of both sides. This is not in our short-term plans, though, because there is no free tagger or parser for Portuguese that we could run on the COMPARA texts (and most of them, due to the very narrow copyright terms, cannot even be sent to a third party for parsing purposes).

We are also aware that an ideal display of results has not been achieved yet for the cases of more than one translation of a given original: Ideally, when displaying concordances, the source text would only appear once, with the two (or more) translations on the target side, if the user query concerned simply the source. Likewise, each source text should only count as one in the distribution numbers. On the other hand, if the user specified a pair of conditions (as in the previous examples of quantitative wrapups), then each pair of texts should count as an individual item, and should be counted as such, as well as displayed. (This is the current behaviour of the system as of today, no matter the kind of query.) Such a change in display and counting behaviour based on the form of the query implies, however, rather drastic changes to the whole architecture, and therefore no decision on this issue has been taken yet.

Finally, answering a reviewer's question, we do not envisage an "extension" of DISPARA to multilinguality, due to the lack of any real theoretical or practical basis for such a political concept[15,13]. But we do expect to integrate other bilingual corpora for translations from or to languages different from English, since the whole system design does not hinge on the particular Portuguese-English pair.

Acknowledgements

I am obviously indebted to Ana Frankenberg-Garcia, without whom this project would not have existed, and thank her not only for initiating it but for her truly collaborative spirit, effectiveness and enthusiasm.

I also thank Stefan Evert for invaluable support concerning EasyAlign and the IMS Corpus Workbench as a whole. DISPARA owes a lot to the outstanding capabilities and features of this corpus encoding system.

References

1. Afonso, Susana, Bick, Eckhard, Haber, Renato, Santos, Diana: "Floresta Sintá(c)tica": a treebank for Portuguese. In Proceedings of LREC2002 (to appear)
2. Baker, Mona: Corpora in translation studies: an overview and some suggestions for future research. Target **7** (1995) 223–243
3. Biblioteca Virtual do Estudante Brasileiro. http://www.bibvirt.futuro.usp.br/acervo/literatura/literatura.html
4. Christ, O., Schulze, B., Hofmann, A., Koenig, E.: The IMS Corpus Workbench: Corpus Query Processor (CQP): User's Manual. IMS, University of Stuttgart, March 8, 1999 (CQP V2.2)
5. Frankenberg-Garcia, Ana, Santos, Diana: Introducing COMPARA, the Portuguese-English parallel translation corpus. In S. Bernardini & F. Zanettin (eds.), Corpora in translator training. Manchester: St. Jerome (to appear)
6. Frankenberg-Garcia, Ana, Santos, Diana: Apresentando o COMPARA, um corpus português-inglês na Web. Cadernos de Tradução, Universidade de São Paulo (to appear)

7. Project Gutenberg. http://www.promo.net/pg/
8. Johansson, Stig, Ebeling, Jarle, Hofland, Knut: Coding and aligning the English-Norwegian Parallel Corpus. In Aijmer, K., Altenberg, B., Johansson, M. (eds.), Languages in Contrast: Papers from a Symposium on Text-based Cross-linguistic Studies (Lund, 4-5 March 1994). Lund: Lund University Press, 1996, 87–112
9. Johansson, Stig, Ebeling, Jarle, Oksefjell, Signe: English-Norwegian Parallel Corpus: Manual. Oslo: Department of British and American Studies, University of Oslo, 1999, http://www.hf.uio.no/iba/prosjekt/ENPCmanual.html
10. Johansson, S.: ICAME - Quo Vadis? Reflections on the Use of Computer Corpora in Linguistics. Computers and the Humanities **28** (1995) 243–252
11. Johansson, S., Oksefjell, S. (eds.): Corpora and cross-linguistic research: theory, method, and case studies. Amsterdam: Rodopi, 1998
12. Santos, Diana: Bilingual alignment and tense. Proceedings of the Second Annual Workshop on Very Large Corpora (Kyoto, 4 August 1994), 129–141
13. Santos, Diana: Punctuation and multilinguality: Reflections from a language engineering perspective. In Jo Terje Ydstie & Anne C. Wollebak (eds.), Working Papers in Applied Linguistics **4/98**, Oslo: Department of Linguistics, Faculty of Arts, University of Oslo, 1998 138–160.
14. Santos, Diana: Disponibilização de corpora através da WWW. In Marrafa, P. & Mota, M.A. (eds.), Linguística Computacional: Investigação Fundamental e Aplicações. Lisboa: Colibri, 1999, 323–346
15. Santos, Diana: Toward language-specific applications. Machine Translation **14**, 1999, 83–112.
16. Santos, Diana: Resultado da revisão do primeiro milhão de palavras do CETEMPúblico. 2000.
    http://cgi.portugues.mct.pt/treebank/RevisaoMilhao.html
17. Santos, Diana, Bick, Eckhard: Providing Internet access to Portuguese corpora: the AC/DC project. In Gavriladou et al. (eds.), Proceedings of the Second International Conference on Language Resources and Evaluation, LREC2000, ELRA: 205–210
18. Santos, Diana, Rocha, Paulo: Evaluating CETEMPúblico, a free resource for Portuguese. In Proceedings of the 39th Annual Meeting of the Association for Computational Linguistics (ACL2001). ACL, 2001, 442–449
19. Tsang, Vivian, Stevenson, Suzanne: Automatic Verb Classification Using Multilingual Resources. In Walter Daelemans and Rémi Zajac (eds.), Proceedings of the Fifth Workshop on Computational Language Learning (CoNLL-2001). 2001, 30–37
20. Projecto Vercial. http://www.ipn.pt/opsis/litera/index.html
21. Véronis, Jean (ed.): Parallel Text Processing. Dordrecht: Kluwer Academic Publishers, 2000

Using Morphological, Syntactical, and Statistical Information for Automatic Term Acquisition*

Joana Lúcio Paulo[1], Margarita Correia[2], Nuno J. Mamede[1], and
Caroline Hagège[3]

[1] (L²F - INESC-ID / IST)
joana.paulo@inesc-id.pt, nuno.mamede@inesc-id.pt
[2] (FLUL / ILTEC / SILEX)
margarita-C@netcabo.pt
[3] (Xerox Research Centre Europe)
caroline.hagege@xrce.xerox.com
Rua Alves Redol 9, 1000-029 Lisboa, Portugal

Abstract. Terminologies are useful in all areas that use specialized languages. The development of terminologies is a hard work, when manually done. It can be assisted with tools to ease and improve the achievement of such a work. In this article, we present ATA, an automatic terms extractor using both linguistic and statistical information.

1   Introduction

In the last few years, computational linguists, applied linguists, translators, interpreters, scientific journalists and computer engineers, have been interested in automatically extracting terminology from texts. Different goals have led these professional groups to design software tools to directly extract terminology from texts, basically, all kind of Natural Language Processing (NLP), applications that work with specialized domains and that consequently need special vocabulary.

ATA, is an Automatic Term Acquisition System that processes technical texts and produces a list of noun phrases likely to be terminological units.

This article opens with some background knowledge. Then structural and functional aspects of ATA are presented: the architecture, the input and output data and the main process, responsible for the term's extraction. After this, we describe the evaluation process enumerating the expected results from the use of ATA. Finally we have a brief presentation of the future work and some notes.

2   Background

In this context, a *term* is a linguistic representation of a concept by means of a simple noun or a noun phrase [12]. We consider two term types: simple

---

* This paper has been partially supported by the Fundação Para a Ciência e Tecnologia under project number PLUS/1999/LIN/15150

E.M. Ranchhod and N.J. Mamede (Eds.): PorTAL 2002, LNAI 2389, pp. 219–227, 2002.

and compound. Other phraseological structures characterizing some knowledge domains are not in the scope of ATA.

Simple terms consists of a single lexical unit, a graphical word. The complexity associated with the detection of this kind of terms arises from their unremarkable appearance. This means that there is no way for one to be distinguished from another, unless the system has a morphological structure analyser which can sort term-candidates by the occurrence of specific affixes or roots which is not the case of ATA.

Compound terms consists of more than one lexical unit (graphical form). Thus, they are less prone to ambiguity than simple terms. Nevertheless, they require a previous syntactical study to verify whether a set of words actually defines a term's syntactical structure.

According to several works [16, 13, 3, 12] all lexical units have an associated frequency corresponding to the number of times they appear in a corpus. Using this information we can decide whether a word can eventually be a term: items that are nouns and that appear more than a given number of times can be considered as candidates to be simple terms; words with other categories must be kept in order to complete the processing of compound terms.

Most systems designed for this kind of task take a plain text and extract from it a list of candidate terms. To make the terminologist's task easier, this list is provided with its context and assorted additional information (such as relative frequency for that word and for its root).

The most used techniques for this task are:

- **Statistical based systems:** detect lexical units whose frequency is higher than a given corpus-based threshold definition. The problem with this approach is that it fails to detect low-frequency terms.
- **Systems that use linguistic knowledge:** detect recurrent patterns from complex terminological units such as noun-adjective and noun-preposition-noun. Patterns to be detected are assumed to have been designed by linguists.
- **Hybrid systems:** start detecting some basic linguistic structures, such as noun or prepositional phrases, and then, after the candidate terms have been identified, the relevant statistical information is used to decide whether they correspond to a term. This will be our methodology.

The development of noun phrases extractors is a very delicate task constrained by robustness and accuracy.

Robustness is subject to a strong restriction: it can be used over a wide range of unrestricted texts gathered in large corpora. This means that it has to be domain-independent, that is, it cannot use any a priori semantic or conceptual information. From the point of view of the surface syntactic analysis, the extraction is more difficult, since the system is domain-independent because each domain can have specific restricted surface structures ([8] restricted the extraction to medical terms which have few possible nominal structures).

Accuracy is also an issue because the noun phrases extracted by the system are the candidate terms that will be proposed to the user building a domain's terminology.

The two most frequently used metrics in the evaluation of this type of system are recall and precision [14]. Recall is defined as the relationship between the sum of retrieved terms and the sum of existing terms in the document that is being explored. Precision accounts for the relationship between those extracted terms that are actually terms and the aggregate of candidate terms that are found. These metrics can be seen as the capacity to extract all terms from a document (recall) and the capacity to discriminate between those units detected by the system which are terms and those which are not (precision).

Systems based on linguistic knowledge tend to use noise and silence as a measure of efficiency. Noise attempts to assess the rate between discarded candidates and accepted ones; silence attempts to assess those terms contained in an analysed text that are not detected by the system. Errors in the assignment of morphological categories or syntactic analysis are also shared by these systems.

3   ATA's Structural and Functional Aspects

In this section we describe ATA's structure and functionality. First we take into account the application's structure, that is, the architecture of the system. Then the input and the output data are described. We kept the description of the main process for the next section.

3.1   ATA's Architecture

The used architecture (fig. 1) is similar to the proposed for simple terms in [7]. Taking the system as a whole, it first lemmatizes the text using an external dictionary. The resulting text is then passed to a post-morphological processor that detects and forms special groups according to recomposition and correspondence rules. The system groups the words in phrases (the phrase separators have been previously described in another external file). Before the main process begins, the text is sent to a syntactic analyser that, using a surface grammar groups the phrase constituents. Then the main process extracts the words candidate to terms. After this, a statistical-based process evaluates the candidate lists. The output is finally produced and sent to the system's user.

Lemmatization enriches each word with its morphological characterization. This step needs the dictionary file, which contains not only simple units (corresponding to graphical forms), but also complex units, such as prepositional and adverbial locutions. For this we use SMorph [1] that allows the construction of large dictionaries required for the linguistic analysis of texts. The user declares the dictionary by specifying five types of rules, which are converted into a compact binary file containing a finite state automata. The dictionary is used for generating all inflected forms of a lemma and for segmenting and analyzing a text.

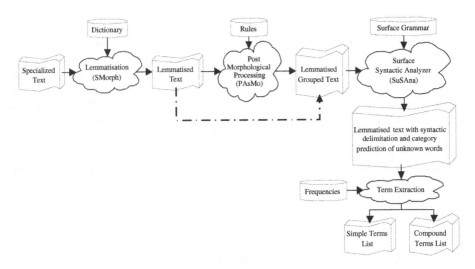

Fig. 1. Main Architecture.

Post-lemmatization Process rewrites the text according to rules based on the morphological features of the words and breaking it into sentences (according to the chosen punctuation). This is done using recomposition and correspondence rules and a list of symbols to be used as breaks in the text. For this we use PAsMo [17]. that can rewrite dates, compound nouns, consecutive unknown words, numbers, and so on. PAsMo may also be used to translate tags, thus facilitating the interface with the syntactic analyzer. At this point we had to rebuilt an old system [9] from scratch in order to improve its efficiency and expressivity this is detailed on 4.

Syntactic Analysis is the stage where we analyse the text grouping the words of each phrase into syntactic chunks. This process is done using surface grammars. For this we use SuSAna [10, 2].

Term Extraction is the main process of the system that will be described latter on 5.

3.2 Input and Output Data

ATA's input data consists of plain text previously analysed both morphologically (in terms of words' categories) and syntactically. If we consider the larger system containing ATA, the input consists of a plain text, a dictionary, a set of rules defining word grouping (recomposition and correspondence rules), a surface grammar, and word's frequencies measured over general corpora.

Recomposition Rules are applied to the morphological analyzer's output and are used to change the segmentation in this input file. The rules are in the form

$A \rightarrow C$, which means that if we find a word (or a sequence of words) with the features declared on the rule's left hand side, A, then we can replace it with the rule's right hand side, C. For instance, a useful rule is one that takes a month, a number, "th" and another number and transforms this sequence into a date, i.e., it takes "December 6th 1978" and tags it is a date. This kind of rule may have variables and special operators that allow recursion on the rule's left side.

Correspondence Rules change the morphological descriptions associated with each word. The idea is the same, if we have something that matches the rule's left side, then it is replaced with what is on the rule's right side.

Surface grammar allows the input text to be segmented into syntactic phrases. Since there is nothing that can decide whether a noun phrase is a good candidate to compound term or not, a simple filter can give us all the candidates to compound terms right after this process without any further process. Later on, if for a specific domain there are some specific better forms the surface grammar can be rewritten in order to reflect that prior knowledge. For now a generic tool is needed so this case is out of our scope.

Frequency of words and noun phrases computed over a general-content corpus [4] allows us to detect terms by comparing frequencies of the entities in the text being analysed and the ones in the corpus of reference.

ATA's output is divided into two sets both of which may be empty. The first set contains simple term candidates identified in the text. The second set contains compound terms candidates detected in the text.

4   PAsMo

PAsMo is a post-morphological analyzer rule-based rewriter whose function is to perform the last processing phase before the syntactic analysis. It is based on the MPS application developed at GRIL. Using recomposition and correspondence rules, it makes some processing based on the morphological characteristics of words rewriting word sequences and changing the tags used. In addition, it splits the text into segments.

PAsMo receives a text where all the words were previously enriched with is morphological features. The old version used Prolog and wasn't efficient enough considering that large corpora had to be analyzed.

Changing the chosen language to C++ and enhancing the algorithm, reduced processing time by a factor of 20 times on the best cases (and even more on worst cases, that is were ambiguity in sequences of words exists); XML input and output is now possible facilitating the communication between modules and data verification; Operators that allows to constrain the minimal number of times a words should appear so the rule can be applied, reduces the number of needed rules.

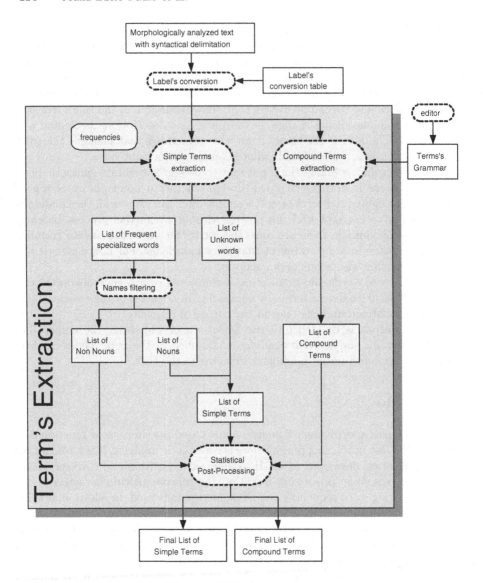

Fig. 2. ATA's Architecture.

5   Term Extraction

This is the process responsible for the terms' detection. As the two types of terms require different processes.

Given the characteristics of simple terms, their processing starts by collecting all input words appearing with frequency higher than the threshold defined by the corpus. From this collection, words classified as nouns may be considered as simple term candidates. Those classified as unknown but considered as nouns due to the syntactic process are also considered as candidates.

Compound terms obey some syntactical and grammar restrictions that make the detection process easier. The structure of the word sequences that are to be considered as compound term candidates are described in an external file merged on the grammar used in the syntactic analysis.

In an hybrid system like this one, high frequency terms will be detected statistically; and low frequency terms (e.g. 1 or 2 utterances) will be detected through the grammar of terms. Then it will be necessary to review both term candidates (those given statistically and those given by the grammar). Yet, we believe that if a term candidate in specialised texts as low frequency that means that maybe they are not terms in the field under scope. In a specialised text of a given domain, terms from that domain will have high chances of being high frequency terms.

In addition, the system must distinguish between high-frequency words occurring within compound terms and isolated occurrences of the same words.

For instance, consider the expression "worldwide computer network". The word "network" will appear at least as much as the expression. So, after the process extracts the candidate terms the system must verify whether the word "network" is also a term, i.e., if the word appears enough times by itself. Yet, the compound has, theoretically, great possibility of being a hyponimic term (with a more restricted reference) and "network" to be it's correspondent generic term, presenting a broader reference [5].

"Computer network" will also be a term candidate (in fact it is a term of a hierarchically higher level). The grammar of terms is designed to give fewer chances to be term candidates to longer nominal phrases (with more components).

On one hand, we think there is no way (for the time being) of letting out sequences like those suggested. Yet, one the other hand, sequences like those presented are predictably low frequency sequences in specialised texts. If they are very frequent it means that we have to reconsider if they are (are not) actual terms of the domain under study, or let that checking for the linguistic using the system.

If one of the criteria when finding terms is the frequency of a word when comparing with general corpora, we need to extract frequencies for each lemma. For that the same architecture will be used enriched with a tool for resolve ambiguity that remains at the end of the process chain. The corpora we are going to use is CETEM-Público [15].

6   Conclusions and Future Directions

In this article a new system for automatic term acquisition has been described. We are especially interested in studying the capability and the implications of building an automatic term acquisition system.

The ATA system will probably be a useful helper in solving the problem of the semi-automatic building of terminological indexes and will be used on different kinds of specialized documents.

We think that knowledge acquisition for knowledge-based systems is also a suitable experimentation ground for such a terminology extraction system, provided that an appropriate tool exists to represent and record information.

Although some of the processes are already implemented, at this time the system is not yet completely functional. That is, the final process, the one responsible for term extraction, has not been implemented yet. Currently, processing stops after syntactic analysis that means that all the relevant linguistic information was gathered and the statistical process can now begin. For now, the architecture and the main algorithm are defined so the implementation process can begin as soon as possible.

The system will be evaluated using the described methods (see 2), hopping to achieve results similar to those of systems for Portuguese [6, 18] and for other foreign languages as English [13] and French [7].

Probably, the price to pay for an automatic acquisition without any intermediary human validation is twofold: the procedure can let relevant information pass through undetected; it can acquire false information. This is the reason why perfecting these procedures requires the adoption of experimental processes, with numerous tests carried on large-scale corpora, that ensure the global empirical validity of the procedures.

Also as a test, we are going to use the system to create automatic subject indexes of specialized books and compare them with the original ones.

Changing language, currently, means having to restart the whole system. This entails considering the new language's dictionary, analysing the morphological behaviour of that language to write new rules, analysing a general corpus and computing word frequency and getting a surface grammar. That work can be done in order to prove that the system is language-independent.

Format information can also be considered by the system. The text format depends on the editor. It is necessary to create an external format description. If the text format has been lost at some point, the initial text has to be considered.

The idea is to give more or less importance to a word according to its format [11]. For instance, if a word appears in a title it must be considered more important that a word that is in the middle of a paragraph. Thus, it is possible to create a hierarchical classification that considers input text format. This classification should consider: Titles of documents, sections, and subsections; Bold, italic, and underline; Type and size of letter; Caps usage; Headers and footers; Footnotes; Quotations; Other styles.

References

[1] Salah Aït-Mokhtar. *L'analyse Présyntaxique en une seule étape*. PhD thesis, Université Blaise Pascal, Feb 1998.
[2] Fernando Batista. Análise sintáctica de superfície e consistência de regras. Master's thesis, Instituto Superior Técnico, UTL, 2002. (work in progress).

[3] D. Bourigault. Surface grammatical analysis for the extraction of terminological noun phrases. *Proceedings of the 15th International Conference on Computational Linguistics, COLING'92*, 1992. p. 977-981.

[4] P.R. Clarkson and R. Rosenfeld. Statistical language modeling using the cmu-cambridge toolkit. *Proceedings ESCA Eurospeech*, 1997.

[5] D. A. Cruse. Lexical semantics, 1986.

[6] J. Ferreira da Silva and G. Pereira Lopes. A local maxima method and a fair dispersion normalization for extracting multi-words units from corpora. *International Conference on Mathematics of Language, Orlando*, July 1999.

[7] B. Daille. Study and implementation of combined techniques for automatic extraction of terminology. *The balancing act combining symbolic and statistical approaches to language*, pages 49–66, 1996.

[8] Rosa Estopà. *Les unitats terminológiques polilexemàtiques en els lèxics especialitzats: dret i medicina*. PhD thesis, Institut Universitari de Lingüística Aplicada, Barcelona, UPF, 1999.

[9] Abbaci Faiza. Développement du module post-smorph. Master's thesis, Mémoire de DEA de linguistique et informatique, GRIL, Université Blaise Pascal, Clermont-Ferrand, 1999.

[10] Caroline Hagège. *Analyse syntaxique automatique du portugais*. Thèse de doctorat, Université Blaise Pascal, GRIL, Clermont-Ferrand, 2000.

[11] C. Jacquemin. Quelques exemples d'application du traitement automatique des langues en accès à l'information. *5emes Journées Internationales d'Analyse de Données Textuelles (JADT)*, 1, 2000.

[12] C. Jacquemin and D. Bourigault. Term extraction and automatic indexin. *R. Mitkov, editor, Handbook of Computational Linguistics*, 2000.

[13] J. S. Justeson and S. M. Katz. Technical terminology: some linguistic properties and an algorithm for identification in text. *Natural Language Engineering, p. 9-27*, 1995.

[14] C. D. Manning and H. Shutze. *Foundations of Statistical Natural Language Processing*. MIT Press, London, 1999.

[15] MCT and Público. Cetempúblico - corpus de extractos de textos electrónicos, 2000.

[16] A. P. Marquez Neto. Terminologia e corpus linguístico. *Revista Internacional de Língua Portuguesa - RILP n. 15, p. 100-108*, 1996.

[17] Joana Lúcio Paulo. Pasmo - pós-análise morfológica. Relatório técnico, Instituto Superior Técnico, Lisboa, 2001.

[18] J. Silva, G. Dias, S. Guilloré, and G. Lopes. Using localmaxs algorithm for the extraction of contiguous and non-contiguous multiword lexical units. *9th Portuguese Conference on Artificial Intelligence*, 1695:113–132, September 1999.

Complex Lexical Units and Automata

Paula Carvalho[1], Cristina Mota[1], and Elisabete Ranchhod[2]

[1] LabEL – CAUTL, Instituto Superior Técnico
Av. Rovisco Pais, 1049-001 Lisboa, Portugal
{paula, cristina}@label.ist.utl.pt
[2] FLUL and LabEL – CAUTL, Instituto Superior Técnico
Av. Rovisco Pais, 1049-001 Lisboa, Portugal
elisabete@label.ist.utl.pt
http://label.ist.utl.pt

Abstract: This paper discusses the problem of disambiguating noun phrases that contain compound words ambiguous with free simple word combinations. Finite-state transducers will be used to both represent the noun phrase ambiguities and to formalize the linguistic constraints that allow the elimination or reduction of the incorrect analyses.

1   Introduction

In Portuguese, sequences of words such as *chávena de chá* and *como o mel* are ambiguous since they can be analyzed *a priori* as complex lexical units, a compound noun and a frozen adverb, respectively, or as free combinations of simple words. Their integration into an adequate syntactic structure clarifies their linguistic status, as it is the case in the examples:

(1) O João partiu uma *chávena de chá* (John broke a teacup)

(2) O João tomou uma *chávena de chá* (John drank a cup of tea)

(3) Ela é doce *como o mel* (She is as sweet as honey)

(4) *Como o mel* é melhor do que o açúcar... (Since honey is better than sugar...)

In sentences (1) and (3), the sequences in italics present combinatorial constraints[1], and they have to be considered as compound lexical units. In a different way, the same sequences behave, in sentences (2) and (4), as free constructions[2].

Using finite-state transducers for representing: (a) the possible analyses of a sequence of lexical units, and (b) the rules that can be applied to disambiguate that

---

[1] For example, in (1), it is not possible to insert a determiner to the left of the noun *chá* (tea): **Ele partiu uma chávena de (esse + o meu) chá* (He broke a cup of (that + my) tea); in (2), we do not find such constraints: *Ele tomou uma chávena de (esse + o meu) chá* (He drunk a cup of (that + my) tea).

[2] Notice that unambiguous compound words - that is, sequences such as the noun *chapéu de chuva* (umbrella), that regardless of the context, can never be analyzed as free combinations of simple lexical units - do not raise any problem of analysis, since they can be immediately coded as non-ambiguous at the lexical level [11].

E.M. Ranchhod and N.J. Mamede (Eds.): PorTAL 2002, LNAI 2389, pp. 229-238, 2002.
© Springer-Verlag Berlin Heidelberg 2002

sequence, we will specify the different behavior that can be observed when the sequence contains compound nouns.

2   Finite-State Transducers

In a general way, the graphical representation of a finite-state transducer (FST) is the one shown in   Fig. 1.

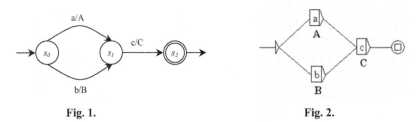

Fig. 1.   **Fig. 2.**

However, in this study, we will adopt the INTEX graphs representation [11], in which (Fig. 2) the states are implicit, the input symbols (words) are inside the nodes and the output symbols (linguistic values) are below the nodes (a transition is simply described by *in/out*).

Henceforth, we will use the terms *finite-state transducer* (or transducer) and *graph*, indistinctly.

3   Disambiguation Using FSTs

The result of applying to a text a set of linguistic resources (electronic dictionaries and grammars) that associate to each recognized lexical unit all available linguistic information is adequately represented by transducers. For instance, the result of applying the linguistic resources[3] to the noun phrase:

(5)   *Uma jovem alegre e dinâmica* (A dynamic and happy young girl)

is represented in the graph of Fig. 3.

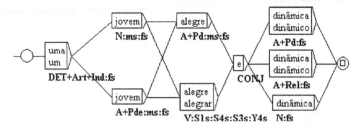

Fig. 3.

---

[3] The electronic dictionaries and grammars used in this study are described in [7], [8].

As the graph shows, with the exception of the conjunction *e* (and), all lexical units are associated with more than one linguistic attribute. Considering that each node corresponds only to one analysis, the noun phrase would have 12 possible analyses. However, a node can represent ambiguous morphological values, introduced by the character ':'. For instance, *jovem* is ambiguous not only at the syntactic level (it can be either a noun or an adjective), but also at the morphological level (it can be both a masculine and a feminine form). Thus, taking into account morphological attributes, the number of analyses associated to the noun phrase is, in fact, 72.

In order to solve or reduce such ambiguities, a set of disambiguation grammars, that describe linguistic constraints, and establish the correct analysis, have to be applied [2]. These grammars are finite-state transducers, like the one in Fig. 4, that contain an input alphabet constituted by lexical units and linguistic attributes, and by an output alphabet only constituted by linguistic information.

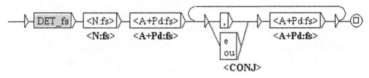

Fig. 4.

The FST formalizes the rules for disambiguating noun phrases similar to the one represented in Fig. 3, containing predicative adjectives in apposition or coordinated by the conjunctions *e* (and) or *ou* (or). In Portuguese, all the NP constituents have to agree in gender and number; the grammar also describes such agreement (:*fs*).

A more detailed description of these disambiguation rules will be given in the following section.

3.1   Disambiguation of Sequences Containing Only Simple Words

The lexical ambiguity of a linguistic sequence $a_1 \, a_2 \, \ldots \, a_k$, constructed only with simple lexical units, is represented by the transducer of Fig. 5, where k is the number of simple words of the sequence, $LA(a_1)^4 = m$, $LA(a_2) = n$ and $LA(a_k) = p$.

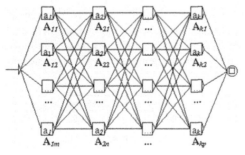

Fig. 5.

---

[4] $LA(a_i)$ is the number of lexical ambiguities of the word a_i.

In order to disambiguate the elements of such a sequence, the disambiguation transducer, in Fig. 6, describes the constraints (represented by the outputs) on the input sequences.

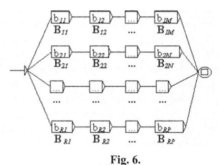

Fig. 6.

This transducer is applied to the sentence transducer in the following way:

i. Identify all paths $b_{r1} b_{r2} \ldots b_{rl}$ $(1<r<R, l \in \{M, N, \ldots, P\})$ that, in part or completely, match a path $a_1/A_{1i} a_2/A_{2j} \ldots a_k/A_{ks}$ $(i<m, j<n$ and $s<p)$. The matching path in the sentence transducer is the sequence: $a_t/A_{ti} a_{(t+1)}/A_{(t+1)j} \ldots a_{(r+l-1)}/A_{(r+l-1)s}$, in which a_t or A_{ti} matches b_{r1}, $a_{(t+1)}$ or $A_{(t+1)j}$ matches b_{r2} and $a_{(t+l-1)}$ or $A_{(t+l-1)s}$ matches b_{rl};

ii. Eliminate all a_x/A_{xy} $(t<x<t+l-1$ and $1<y<LA(a_x))$ that do not match b_{XY} $(1<X<R$ and $1<Y<LU(X)^5)$;

iii. Apply constraints $B_{r1} B_{r2} \ldots B_{rl}$ to $a_t/A_{ti} a_{(t+1)}/A_{(t+1)j} \ldots a_{(r+l-1)}/A_{(r+l-1)s}$ by:

 a. Eliminating all a_x/A_{xy} $(t<x<t+l-1$ and $1<y<LA(a_x))$ which output A_{xy} does not match the constraint B_{XY} $(1<X<R$ and $1<Y<LU(X))$;

 b. Generating an inconsistency[6] if A_{xy} never match B_{XY}.

So, the result of applying this algorithm, a special case of the classical composition algorithm for finite-state transducers, as described in [10], is a transducer that represents only the analyses that respect all the constraints expressed by the disambiguation rules. The optimal result is obtained when the resulting transducer of a sentence contains a unique solution. This means that the construction was completely disambiguated, allowing the tagging of each of its lexical units.

Based on this algorithm, let us return to the disambiguation grammar, represented in Fig. 4, in order to illustrate the different steps throughout its application to the transducer of the text in the Fig. 3. Notice that the text only contains simple words.

According to step (i), only a subset of the disambiguation rules described in Fig. 4 is applicable to the noun phrase being analysed. The selected rules are specified in Fig. 7.

Fig. 7.

---

[5] LU(i) is the number of lexical units analyzed by disambiguation rule i.

[6] An inconsistency means that either the sentence is not grammatical or the grammar is incorrect.

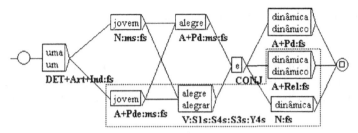

Fig. 8.

After step (ii), the analyses of *jovem* (young) as an adjective, of *alegre* as a form of the verb *alegrar* (to cheer) and of *dinâmica* both as a noun (dynamics) and as a relation adjective (dynamical, as in *dynamical system*) are removed, since they do not match any input of the disambiguation rules.

Finally, the step (iii) eliminates the analyses of *jovem* (young boy) as a masculine noun and of *alegre* (happy) as a masculine adjective, because, in spite of matching the inputs of the disambiguation rules, they do not satisfy the morphological constraints represented in the outputs.

The disambiguation results are represented in the FST of Fig. 9.

Fig. 9.

As the FST in Fig. 9 shows, all the incorrect analyses were removed. This example illustrates a general situation: when the linguistic structures are constituted of simple words, the results of the disambiguation grammars are quite satisfactory[7].

3.2   Disambiguation of Sequences Containing Compound Words

If a sequence $a_1 a_2 \ldots a_k$ contains a complex lexical unit, that can also be analyzed as a free word combination, it means that the lexical ambiguity of such sequence corresponds to the union of two transducers: one representing the lexical ambiguity of $a_1 a_2 \ldots a_k$ as a sequence of simple words, and the other representing the lexical ambiguity of a sequence $a_1 a_2 \ldots a_{k'}$ $(k' < k)$, where one of the a_i $(1 < i < k')$ is a compound word.

In order to disambiguate such a sequence, we will also apply the disambiguation transducer in Figure 6, based on the algorithm described in the previous section. When this disambiguation grammar applies to a sequence that includes one or more ambiguous compound nouns, the analysis results are not always the correct ones.

We will discuss, giving illustrative examples from Portuguese, a few paradigmatic cases that have been observed. As previously mentioned, the disambiguation

---

[7] We obtained a success rate of 93,4% in a *corpus* of 163000 words, when disambiguating the noun phrase structures described by the grammars; 0,7% of the disambiguated words were incorrectly analyzed; 5,9% could not be completely disambiguated.

grammars were built for solving/reducing ambiguity within noun phrases containing adjectives.

Case 1 - Compound nouns are not taken into account. A noun phrase containing a sequence such as *mesa redonda* (round table), which can be either a compound noun or a free noun adjective combination, is represented by the transducer in Fig. 10.

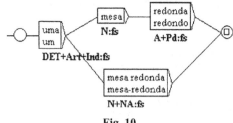

Fig. 10.

The result of applying a disambiguation grammar that includes the rule[8] represented in Fig. 11 to the previous transducer is given in Fig. 12.

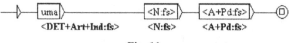

Fig. 11.

As the FST in Fig. 12 shows, the path that included the compound noun was eliminated in favor of the simple word analysis.

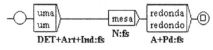

Fig. 12.

Since we are dealing with an operation between transducers, that option is predictable: the sequence containing the compound word, unlike the sequence of simple words, does not match the rule and is hence eliminated.

However, from a linguistic point of view, this result is not satisfactory. The linguistic status of *mesa redonda* depends on the syntactic structure that includes it; if it occurs in the syntactic position of direct object of a verb such as *comprar* (to buy):

(6)   *Ele comprou uma mesa redonda* (He bought a round table)

only the analysis of free noun phrase, given by the grammar, is correct. But if it occurs in the same syntactic position of a verb such as *organizar* (to organize):

(7)   *Ele organizou uma mesa redonda* (He organized a round table)

the analysis is incorrect.

---

[8] This rule describes an elementary noun phrase constituted by a feminine noun in the singular that is specified by a definite article and modified by a subtype of predicative adjective (*Pd*), agreeing in gender and number.

In fact, the establishment of the correct analysis of the numerous compound nouns that behave like *mesa redonda* implies the previous determination of the argument structure of all the verbs of the lexicon.

Case 2 – The simple word analysis is rejected. Let us now consider the transducer in Fig. 13, which represents the construction *uma chávena de chá amarela* (a yellow teacup).

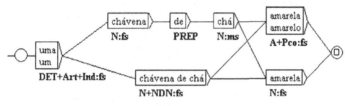

Fig. 13.

As in the previous example, it includes a compound noun, *chávena de chá*, which can also be analyzed as a free word combination: a noun, a preposition and a noun. This ambiguity can be correctly solved by a grammar containing the disambiguation rule represented in Fig. 14.

Fig. 14.

This rule describes a noun phrase constituted by a color adjective (coded in the dictionaries as *A+Pco*) that modifies a noun preceded by an indefinite determiner (*uma*).

In such situation, the analysis of *chávena de chá* as a free combination is eliminated, since the application of the disambiguation rule stops matching when the preposition *de*, which is not specified in the grammar, is reached. On the contrary, the analysis of *chávena de chá* as a compound noun leads to the successful application of the disambiguation rule. Even if the syntactic structure *N Prep N A* was represented in such grammar, as an optional path, the analysis of compound would still be preferred, since there is no agreement between the noun *chá* (:ms) and the adjective *amarela* (:fs).

However, in a linguistic combination such as: *uma chávena de chá verde* (a green teacup/a cup of green tea), the adjective *verde* (green), which does not have morphemes for gender, can be interpreted and analyzed as a modifier of the compound noun *chávena de chá* (teacup) or as a modifier of the last noun of the sequence, *chá* (tea). In the latter analysis (and interpretation) the adjective constitutes with the noun an ambiguous combination of the type described before:

(8)   *Ele tomou uma chávena de chá verde* (He drank a cup of green tea)
(9)   *Ele partiu uma chávena de chá verde* (He broke a green teacup)

In (8), *chá verde* (green tea), in the syntactic position of direct object of a verb such as *tomar* (to drink) has to be analyzed as a compound noun (*chávena* behaves like a determiner of that noun). In (9), *partir* (to break) has a different argument selection: *chávena de chá* (teacup) is a compound noun, and *verde* (green) a free adjectival modifier.

Case 3 – Both compound noun and simple word analyses are kept. The analysis obtained through the application of a disambiguation grammar to the FST that represents an ambiguous construction is not always unique. In fact, in certain cases, ambiguity can only be partially solved. This is the case of the ambiguous noun phrase *um capacete azul escuro* (a navy blue helmet), represented in Fig. 15.

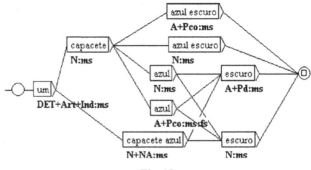

Fig. 15.

As the graph shows, this expression has the particularity of containing overlapped compound analyses: *capacete azul* (blue helmet) can be a compound noun and *azul escuro* (navy blue) can be both a compound noun and a compound adjective. *Capacete* (helmet) can also be analyzed as a simple noun and *azul* (blue) can be analyzed as a simple noun or as a simple adjective.

After applying the disambiguation grammar that contains the disambiguation rules[9] in Fig. 16, the resulting FST, illustrated in Fig. 17, is obtained.

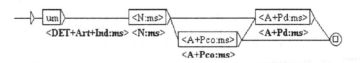

Fig. 16.

Some ambiguities were removed, but two incorrect analysis remain: [*capacete azul*]ₙ *escuro* (navy [blue helmet]), unacceptable for semantic reasons, and [*capacete*]ₙ [*azul*]ₐ [*escuro*]ₐ (blue dark helmet), which corresponds to an unacceptable combination of adjectives.

---

[9] These rules describe that a masculine noun in the singular, specified by a demonstrative determiner, can be modified by a predicative color adjective (coded as *Pco*) or by another predicative adjective (coded as *Pd*), with the same gender and number features; the grammar also establishes that a *Pco* adjective can be modified by a *Pd* adjective.

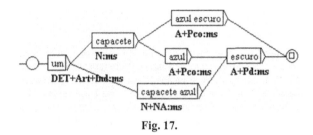

Fig. 17.

The unacceptability of the first structure would not be observed if the adjectival position was filled by an adequate adjective, such as *corajoso* (brave), which modifies "human" nouns:

(10)   *Um capacete azul corajoso* (A brave blue helmet)

Once again, is a predicative relation that has to be previously and adequately analysed and formalized in order to resolve the ambiguity.

4   Conclusion

In this study we discussed some of the issues raised in the analysis of noun phrases that contain compound nouns ambiguous with free word combinations. Our discussion is based on the results of applying a set of grammars, represented by finite-state transducers that were conceived to disambiguate noun phrases containing adjectives.

Those grammars do not explicitly describe constraints that could be applied to constructions in which the noun is a compound word, that is, the disambiguation rules do not make assumptions nor restrict the nature of the noun. When those grammars are applied to sequences containing simple words the disambiguation results are quite satisfactory. On the contrary, when the linguistic structures contain sequences of words that can be analyzed as either free word combinations or compound nouns the disambiguation operations lead to arbitrary analyses of those sequences.

Such inadequacy is related with the algorithm applied: step (ii) compels the elimination of the analyses not expressed in the rules. We believe that this step should be revised, since that no action should be taken when the alternative analyses are not within the scope of the constraints described by the disambiguation grammars. Sometimes, the analysis of a compound noun is rejected not because it violated the constraints imposed by the rules (those constraints were not even applicable to it), but as a consequence of the existence of an alternative analysis as simple words to which the constraints can be observed. In the same way, the compound noun analysis is adopted just because the free word construction is out of the scope of the grammars.

Acknowledgments

This research was partly supported by FCT, Project ENLEX – *Enhancement of Large-scale Lexicons*. Ref. POSI/PLP/34729/99.

References

1. Baptista, J.: Estabelecimento e formalização de classes de nomes compostos, MA Thesis, Faculdade de Letras, Universidade de Lisboa, Portugal (1995)
2. Carvalho, P.: Gramáticas de Resolução de Ambiguidades resultantes da homografia de nomes e adjectivos. MA Thesis, Faculdade de Letras, Universidade de Lisboa (2001)
3. Gross, M.: Methods and Tactics in the Construction of a Lexicon-Grammar. In: Linguistics in the Morning Calm, selected papers from SICOL-86. Seoul: The Linguistic Society of Korea (1988)
4. Joshi, A.: A parser from antiquity: An early application of finite state transducers to natural language parsing. In: Kornai, A. (ed.): Extended Finite State Models of Language. Studies in Natural Language Processing. Cambridge University Press (1999)
5. Laporte, É., Monceaux, A.: Elimination of lexical ambiguities by grammars: The ELAG system. In: Fairon, C. (ed.): Analyse lexicale et syntaxique: Le système INTEX. Lingvisticae Investigationes, XXII (Volume Spécial). Jonh Benjamins, Amsterdam Philadelphia (1998-1999) 341-368
6. Laporte, É.: Resolução de ambiguidades. In: Ranchhod, E. (ed.): Tratamento das Línguas por Computador. Caminho, Lisboa (2001) 49-89
7. Ranchhod, E., Mota, C., Baptista, J.: A Computational Lexicon of Portuguese for Automatic Text Parsing. In Proceedings of SIGLEX' 99: Standardizing Lexical Resources, 37th Annual Meeting of the ACL, Maryland, USA (1999) 74-80
8. Ranchhod, E.: Ressources linguistiques du portugais implémentées sous INTEX. In: Fairon, C. (ed.): Analyse lexicale et syntaxique: Le système INTEX. Lingvisticae Investigationes, XXII (Volume Spécial). Jonh Benjamins, Amsterdam Philadelphia (1998-1999) 263-278
9. Ranchhod, E.: O uso de dicionários e de autómatos finitos na representação lexical das línguas naturais. In: Ranchhod, E. (ed.): Tratamento das Línguas por Computador. Caminho, Lisboa (2001) 13-47
10. Roche, E., Schabes, Y.: Introduction, In: Roche, E., Schabes, Y. (eds.): Finite-State Language Processing. Cambridge, Massachussets London : MIT Press (1997) 1-63
11. Silberztein, M.: Dictionnaires électroniques et analyse automatique de textes: le système INTEX, Masson Ed.: Paris (1993)
12. Tapanainen, P.: Parsing in two frameworks: finite-state and functional dependency grammar, PhD Thesis, University of Helsinki, Finland (1999)

Constructing Empirical Formulas
for Testing Word Similarity
by the Inductive Method of Model Self-Organization*

Pavel Makagonov [1], Mikhail Alexandrov [2]

[1] Moscow Mayor's Directorate, Moscow City Government,
Novi Arbat 36, Moscow, 121205, Russia
makagonov@um.mos.ru

[2] Center for Computing Research, National Polytechnic Institute (IPN),
Av. Juan de Dios Batiz, C.P. 07738, DF, Mexico
dyner@cic.ipn.mx

Abstract. Identification of words with the same base meaning is a necessary procedure for many algorithms of computational linguistics and text processing. We propose to use for this a knowledge-poor approach using an empirical formula based on the number of the coincident letters in the initial parts of the two words and the number of non-coincident letters in the final parts of these two words. To construct such a formula for a given language, we use inductive method of self-organization developed by A. Ivahnenko. This method considers a set of models (formulas) of a given class and selects the best ones using training samples and test samples. We give a detailed example for English. We also show how to apply the formula for creating word frequency list.

1 Introduction

Given a large text (or text corpus), we consider a task of grouping together the words having the same base meaning, e.g., *sad, sadly, sadness, sadden, saddened*, etc.

A possible approach for testing word similarity is a knowledge-rich approach relying on a morphological grammar and a large morphological dictionary. With this, the words are reduced to the standard dictionary form, i.e., singular for nouns, indefinite infinitive for verbs, etc. Another morphology-based method is stemming: the words are truncated to the stem reflecting their invariant meaning. In both cases, after word transformation the word equality is checked. There is a number of morphological analyzers and stemming algorithms; see, for example [Gelbukh, 1992; Gelbukh, 2002, Porter, 1980].

Such knowledge-rich approaches have some technological disadvantages, such as the use of expensive dictionaries [Gelbukh and Sidorov, 2002], the difficulties in their maintenance, poor performance, and low robustness with respect to the changes in the language (new words). In addition, for a given language or subject domain there may not be available any dictionaries providing necessary coverage.

---

* Work done under partial support of CONACyT and CGEPI-IPN, Mexico.

E.M. Ranchhod and N.J. Mamede (Eds.): PorTAL 2002, LNAI 2389, pp. 239–247, 2002.
© Springer-Verlag Berlin Heidelberg 2002

Makagonov [2002] suggested a simple empirical formula for testing similarity of word pairs and showed how to find its parameters on English and Spanish examples. However, this knowledge-poor approach was not properly justified. In this paper, we describe in detail the general method for constructing various empirical formulas based on the number of the coincident letters in the initial parts of the two words and the number of non-coincident letters in the final parts of these two words. As an example, we consider polynomial formulas, though the same approach can be used for constructing other formulas such as exponential ones, etc.

Testing word similarity based on empirical formulas can give erroneous results for infrequent or special words, so an expert should proofread the initial results produced by application of the formula. In case of many mistakes, the parameters of the formula can be adjusted to can fix the problem. To handle texts in a new language, the only thing to be made is a change of these parameters. Such simplicity and flexibility are the main advantages of our empirical knowledge-poor approach.

2   The Problem

2.1 Formulas for Testing Word Similarity

The empirical formulas to be constructed for testing word similarity use the following characteristics of the word pair:

n is the total number of *final* letters differing for the two words,
y is the length of the common *initial* substring ,
s is the total number of letters in the two words.

For example, for the words *sadly* and *sadness*, the maximal common initial substring is *sad-*, thus the differing final parts are *-ly* and *-ness* so that $n = 6$, $y = 3$, and $s = 12$.

We assume a general hypothesis about similarity of two words: Two words are similar if the relative number of their differing final letters is less than some threshold depending on the number of initial coincident letters of the two words:

$$n / s \leq F(y) \qquad (1)$$

where n, s, and y are as defined above. In this paper we will try to find the model function F in a polynomial form:

$$F(y) = a + b_1 y + b_2 y^2 + ... + b_k y^k \qquad (2)$$

The first problem is to determine the best kind of model function (the power of the polynomial), i.e., to find a model of optimal complexity. It is well known that such a problem can be solved only on the basis of some external criteria of model quality.[1] We will use the inductive method of model self-organization described below.

The second problem is to determine the optimal parameters (the coefficients of the polynomial) for the selected kind of model function. Here any internal criteria can be used, for example, the standard least squares method. Both methods require some a priori data about the model to be constructed.

---

[1] A criterion is called *external* if it is defined on the basis of information that is not used for constructing the model itself, otherwise it is called *internal*.

2.2 Limitations of the Approach

The hypothesis about word similarity concerns only the languages where the word's base (the morphologically invariant part) is located at the beginning (and not, say, at the end) of the word. It is the general property of European languages.

The hypothesis of word similarity cannot be applied for irregular words. Indeed, it is impossible to construct a reasonable formula that could detect any similarity between English irregular verbs such as *buy* and *bought*, because these word have only one common letter in the initial part of the string.

Since the empirical formula is constructed on the basis of statistical regularities of a language, it can lead to errors of two kinds, namely, false positive and false negative. The first type means that the formula detects a similarity between two words that in fact have different base meaning. The second one means that the formula does not detects any similarity between two words that in fact are similar. In statistics, such types of errors are called the errors of the first and the second kind, respectively. It is well known that any effort to decrease the number of errors of the first kind increases the number of errors of the second kind, and vice versa. For example, in our case we can take two extreme values $F(y) = -1$ and $F(y) = 1$ and obtain the following two formulas:

$$n / s \leq -1 \quad \text{or} \quad n / s \leq 1.$$

The first inequality gives 0% of errors of the first kind and 100% of errors of the second kind. The second inequality gives 0% of errors of the second kind and 100% of errors of the first kind. Our approach to formula construction gives some intermediate level of both types of errors. The user can obtain an acceptable level of these errors by adjusting the formula's parameters. So the parameters we suggest should be considered only as the initial values for possible future correction.

Some specific errors that can be caused by fuzzy sense of some base meanings. In this paper, we will call such kind of errors the errors of third type. To illustrate this type of errors, let us consider the words *move, moving, moveable*, and *moveability* (the last two words differ from the first two words by the additional meaning 'ability'). When the result of the application of the formula differs from the user's opinion about their similarity, the error of the third kind occurs. It is easy to see that every extended interpretation of base meanings by the user leads to constructing the formula with a high level of the first kind of errors. In the above example it is better to consider similarity between the words *move* and *moving* reflecting the base meaning *movement*, and between *moveable* and *moveability* reflecting the base meaning *ability to movement*. In this case, the formula has significantly lower error level.

3 Inductive Method of Model Self-Organization

3.1 Self-Organization and Regressive Analysis

The inductive method of model self-organization (IMMSO) [Ivahnenko, 1980] allows determining a model of optimal complexity for various processes or phenomena. The method looks from the optimal model in a given class of models using experimental data. It cannot find the optimal model in any continuous class because its work is based on the competition of the models. This approach has been successfully applied to the problems of time series prognosis, dynamic model identification, image recognition, etc. In such problems, considered were polynomial models, finite differential equations, and decision functions.

In order to apply IMMSO to the problem of formula constructing, we consider the extreme cases of the equation (2), i.e., consider examples of word pairs for which the inequalities become equalities. This gives a system of linear equations with respect to unknown parameters a, b_1, b_2, ..., b_k:

$$n_i / s_i = a + b_1 y_i + b_2 y_i^2 + ... + b_k y_i^k, \quad i = 1, ..., m \qquad (3)$$

Here n, s, and y are defined in Section 1.1; i is the number of examples prepared by an expert on the given language. Of course, the number of variables $(k + 1)$ must be less then the number of equations m. The examples forming the system (3) must be prepared by an expert on the given language and can be considered as experimental data. Consider, for example, the pair of word *hoping* and *hopefully*. These two words have a very short common part *hop-* and very long total different part *-ing* and *-efully*. The corresponding equations are:

$$9/15 = a + 3b_1 \qquad \text{for linear model,}$$
$$9/15 = a + 3b_1 + 9b_2 \quad \text{for quadratic model,}$$

etc.

The next steps of the method resemble regressive analyses (RA) procedure:

- For several k starting with $k = 1$, the best solution of (3) for a given criterion is found. For example, the mean square criterion can be considered.
- The criterion values are compared. The minimum value of the criterion defines the number of the model. In our case, this number is the power of polynomial.

Nevertheless, there is a significant difference between the two methods. RA uses all experimental data in the mean square criterion, which is an internal criterion. However, any internal criterion of model comparison leads to a false rule: the more complex model is preferred because it provides the higher precision. So in our case we can expect that the polynomial with the largest number k gives the best results.

External criteria allow avoiding such a paradox. Such criteria consider the data that were not used for calculation of model parameters. For this, the data set is divided into a training set and a test set and the models of various complexity are constructed for every data set separately. The model giving similar results on both data sets is accepted as the model of optimal complexity. It is the external criterion that allows such comparison of the results. The principle of self-organization consists in the fact that some external criteria pass their minimum under step-by-step model complication.

In our case, in order to use external criterion it is necessary to prepare another set of examples. These examples also must reflect the extreme cases when the inequalities (2) become equalities.

3.2 External Criteria

All external criteria consider two or more data sets. Usually IMMSO uses the two following external criteria:

- Criterion of regularity,
- Criterion of unbiasedness.

The criterion of regularity requires a minimum error on a test set for the model constructed on a training set. The criterion of unbiasedness requires closeness between the models constructed on the training set and the test set. There are many forms of representation of the criteria. To represent the criterion used in this paper, we first introduce some notation.

Let L be a vector of constant terms (left part) for a linear system like (3). Consider the vector $L^c = (L_1^c, L_2^c,..., L_m^c)$ of constant terms for the test set used for control, $\| L^c \|$ being Euclidean norm of this vector. Let P be a solution of a system like (3). Consider the solution $P^l = (P^l, P_1^l,..., P_k^l)$ of the system (3) for the training set used for learning and $P^c = (P^c, P_1^c,... P_k^c)$ for the test set used for control. Obviously, P^l and P^c are parameters of the model: $P^l = (a^l, b_1^l,..., b_k^l)$ and $P^c = (a^c, b_1^c,..., b_k^c)$. Using for the test set the model parameters P^l obtained from the training set, we can find a disparity vector $L^{c*} = (L_1^{c*}, L_2^{c*},..., L_m^{c*})$ for the test set.

In our work, we use the following form of the criteria of regularity and unbiasedness:

$$K_r = \frac{\left\| L^c - L^{c*} \right\|}{\left\| L^c \right\|} = \frac{\sqrt{\sum_{i=1}^{m}\left(L_i^c - L_i^{c*}\right)^2}}{\sqrt{\sum_{i=1}^{m}\left(L_i^c\right)^2}} \qquad (4)$$

$$K_u = \sqrt{\sum_{i=1}^{m}\left(\frac{P_i^l - P_i^c}{\max\left(\left|P_i^l\right|,\left|P_i^c\right|\right)}\right)^2} \qquad (5)$$

The best value of both criteria is 0. These values can be used for evaluation of model quality.

Sometimes a model can be better then another one by the first criterion and worse by the second one. In this case, a combined criterion should be used, for example:

$$K = \lambda K_r + (1 - \lambda) K_u,$$

where $0 < \lambda < 1$ is a user-defined coefficient of preference. In our experiments with English and Spanish, we did not use any combined criteria.

4   Constructing Empirical Formula for English

To selecting examples for training and test sets, it is preferable to consider both word pairs with short and long common initial parts. In both cases, the word pairs must have a large number of different letters in their final parts.

4.1 Training Procedure

For training procedure, we considered the following pairs of words having the same base meanings:

N	Short words		N	Long words	
1.	Sad*ly*	Sad*ness*	6.	Suffocat*ed*	Suffocat*ingly*
2.	Eat*ing*	Eat*able*	7.	Scrupulous*ly*	Scrupulous*ness*
3.	Poor*ly*	Poor*ness*	8.	Distribu*tion*	Distribut*able*
4.	Elect*ion*	Elect*able*	9.	Generaliz*ing*	Generaliz*ation*
5.	Sensi*tivity*	Sensi*bility*	10.	Distinguish*ing*	Distinguish*able*

With these examples, we obtained the following systems of linear equations:

N	Linear model	N	Quadratic model
1.	$6/12 = a + 3b_1$	1.	$6/12 = a + 3b_1 + 9b_2$
2.	$7/13 = a + 3b_1$	2.	$7/13 = a + 3b_1 + 9b_2$
3.	$6/14 = a + 4b_1$	3.	$6/14 = a + 4b_1 + 16b_2$
4.	$7/17 = a + 5b_1$	4.	$7/17 = a + 5b_1 + 25b_2$
5.	$12/22 = a + 5b_1$	5.	$12/22 = a + 5b_1 + 25b_2$
6.	$7/23 = a + 8b_1$	6.	$7/23 = a + 8b_1 + 64b_2$
7.	$6/24 = a + 9b_1$	7.	$6/24 = a + 9b_1 + 64b_2$
8.	$7/25 = a + 9b_1$	8.	$7/25 = a + 9b_1 + 64b_2$
9.	$8/26 = a + 9b_1$	9.	$8/26 = a + 9b_1 + 64b_2$
10.	$7/29 = a + 11b_1$	10.	$7/29 = a + 11b_1 + 121b_2$

Similar linear systems were constructed for the cubic fourth order models. For these cases, we took 20 examples. Using the least squares method, we found four sets of model parameters $(a, b_1, ...)$ for each of the mentioned models.

4.2 Testing Procedure

For testing procedure, we considered the following pairs of words having the same base meanings:

N	Short words		N	Long words	
1.	Pay*ing*	Pay*ment*	6.	Justify*ing*	Justifi*cation*
2.	Hop*ing*	Hop*efully*	7.	Classify*ing*	Classifi*cation*
3.	Read*ing*	Read*able*	8.	Distinct*ion*	Distinct*ively*
4.	Child*ren*	Child*hood*	9.	Neighbour*ing*	Neighbour*hood*
5.	Ratify*ing*	Ratifi*cation*	10.	Represent*ing*	Represent*ation*

These examples gave the following systems of linear equations:

N	Linear model	N	Quadratic model
1.	$7/13 = a + 3b_1$	1.	$7/13 = a + 3b_1 + 9b_2$
2.	$9/15 = a + 3b_1$	2.	$9/15 = a + 3b_1 + 9b_2$
3.	$7/15 = a + 4b_1$	3.	$7/15 = a + 4b_1 + 16b_2$
4.	$6/17 = a + 5b_1$	4.	$6/17 = a + 5b_1 + 25b_2$
5.	$10/20 = a + 5b_1$	5.	$10/20 = a + 5b_1 + 25b_2$
6.	$11/23 = a + 6b_1$	6.	$11/23 = a + 6b_1 + 36b_2$
7.	$11/25 = a + 7b_1$	7.	$11/25 = a + 7b_1 + 49b_2$
8.	$6/24 = a + 9b_1$	8.	$6/24 = a + 9b_1 + 81b_2$
9.	$7/25 = a + 9b_1$	9.	$7/25 = a + 9b_1 + 81b_2$
10.	$8/26 = a + 9b_1$	10.	$8/26 = a + 9b_1 + 81b_2$

Similar linear systems were constructed for the cubic and fourth order models. Here we also took 20 examples. Using the least squares method, we found four sets of model parameters $(a, b_1, \ldots)$ for each of the mentioned models. Of course, these models differed from the models constructed on the testing set.

4.3 Results

Using (4) and (5), we found that the linear model proved to be the winner. The results are summarized in the following table:

	Linear model	Quadratic model	Cubic model	4th order model
Criterion K_r	0.13	0.13	0.24	0.78
Criterion K_u	0.14	0.42	1.38	1.73

At the last step, we considered only the linear model. We joined the training set and the test set of examples and obtained the linear system of 20 equations and 2 variables. The solution gave the following formula for testing similarity of English words:

$$n / s \leq 0.655 - 0.040\, y \tag{6}$$

This formula slightly differs from the formula in [Makagonov, 2002], where the model parameters $a = 0.55$ and $b_1 = -0.032$ were obtained. The reason is a limited set of testing examples in the latter case.

Good results for the linear model can be obtained even using a limited set of examples. However, all these examples must reflect the extreme cases, i.e., the words with short and long common initial parts must have a large number of different letters in their final parts. We have checked this conclusion on Russian, Spanish, and English. We believe this holds also for other European languages. Here is an English example:

Examples		Equations
Sad*ly*	Sad*ness*	$6/12 = a + 3b_1$
Eat*ing*	Eat*able*	$7/13 = a + 3b_1$
Justific*atory*	Justific*ation*	$6/24 = a + 10b_1$
Distinguish*ing*	Distinguish*able*	$7/13 = a + 11b_1$

The solution is $a = 0.627$ and $b_i = -0.036$, which is very close to the result (6).

5   Creating Word Frequency List

Consider the task of calculation the frequencies of words in a large text (or text corpus) in the case when by a word, any modification that has the same base meaning is understood, i.e., the strings *sad, sadly, sadness, sadden, saddened* are counted as 5 occurrences of the same word type (meaning) [Manning *et al.*, 1999]. Obviously, this can be done using our (or any other) algorithm for testing word similarity.

5.1 Main Algorithm

Our algorithm consists in the following steps. Initially, the text or a group of texts is transformed into a sequence of words. With every word occurrence (token) in this sequence, a counter is associated and set to the initial value 1. Then the algorithm works as follows:

Step 1. All words are ordered alphabetically. Literally equal strings are joined together and their counts are summed up (e.g., 3 occurrences of the string *ask* with counters 2, 3, and 1 are replaced with one occurrence with the counter 6).

Step 2. The similarity for each pair of adjacent words is tested according to the criterion described above (namely, the first word is compared with the second one, third with the fourth, etc.). If a pair of words is similar then these two words are replaced with one new "word"—their common initial part, with the counter set to the sum of the counters of the two original words. If the list has an odd number of words, then the last word is compared with the immediately preceding one (or with the result of substitution of the last word pair).

Step 3. If no changes were made at the step 2, then the algorithm stops. Otherwise it is repeated from the step 1.

5.2 Example

Consider the following list of English words ordered alphabetically: *transform* (7), *transformed* (5), *transformation* (7), *translating* (6), *translator* (7), *transport* (11), *transported* (2). The numbers in parentheses are the corresponding counters obtained after the first pass of the algorithm. The following table illustrates the work of the algorithm.

After first pass	After second pass	After third pass
transform (7)	transform (12)	transform (19)
transformed(5)	transformation (7)	translat (13)
transformation(7)	translating (6)	transport (13)
translating (6)	translator (7)	
translator (7)	transport (13)	
transport(11)		
transported (2)		

We have tested the suggested algorithm on several domain-oriented texts. For example, we have considered the proceeding of the International Conference CICLing-2000 [Gelbukh, 2000]. With these texts, our algorithm gave approximately 15% of errors of the first and second kinds in total. Of course, for better evaluation of the method it is necessary to carry out more experiments with domain-oriented and general texts.

6   Implementation

The empirical algorithm presented above has been implemented in our system *Dictionary Designer* that belongs to the software family *Document Investigator*.

The system uses as its input either one document or a set of domain-oriented documents and produces as its output the word frequency list. The system allows the expert to change the parameters of the empirical formula and manually correct the obtained word frequency list.

7   Conclusions

We have suggested a knowledge-poor approach for testing word similarity. Our formula does not require any morphological dictionaries of the given language and can be constructed manually or automatically basing on several selected examples.

This formula can be used in an algorithm for creating word frequency lists. The behavior of the algorithm can be easily fine-tuned by adjusting its parameters to give the results of satisfactory accuracy. The suggested technology has been implemented in an end-user-oriented software.

References

1. Gelbukh, A. (1992): Effective implementation of morphology model for an inflectional natural language. *J. Automatic Documentation and Mathematical Linguistics*, Allerton Press, 26, N 1, pp. 22-31.
2. Gelbukh, A. (ed.) (2000): *Computational Linguistics and Intelligent Text Processing*. Proc. of CICLing-2002, IPN, Mexico City, 2002, 430 pp.
3. Gelbukh, A. and G. Sidorov (2002): A Method for Development of Automatic Morphological Analysis Systems for Inflective Languages. In: *Text, Speech and Dialogue*, Proc. of TSD-2002, September 2002, Lecture Notes in Computer Science, Springer Verlag.
4. Gelbukh, A. (2002): A data structure for prefix search under access locality requirements and its application to spelling correction. *J. Computación y Sistemas*.
5. Ivahnenko, A. (1980): *Manual on typical algorithms of modeling*. Tehnika Publ., Kiev (in Russian).
6. Makagonov, P., Alexandrov, M. (2002): Empirical formula for testing word similarity and its application for constructing a word frequency list. In: A. Gelbukh (Ed.), *Computational Linguistics and Intelligent Text Processing*, Proc. of CICLing-2002, Lecture Notes in Computer Science, N 2276, Springer Verlag, pp. 425-432.
7. Manning, D. C., Schutze, H. (1999): *Foundations of statistical natural language processing*. MIT Press.
8. Porter, M. (1980): An algorithm for suffix stripping. *Program*, 14, pp. 130-137.

Multilingual Corpora Annotation for Processing Definite Descriptions

Renata Vieira[1], Susanne Salmon-Alt[2], Emmanuel Schang[2]

[1]Unisinos, Centro de Ciências Exatas e Centro de Ciências da Communicação, Av.
Unisinos, 950, 93022-000 São Leopoldo – RS, Brasil
renata@exatas.unisinos.br
[2]ATILF-Laboratoire d'Analyse et Traitement Informatique de la Langue Française, 44 Av.
de la Libération, 54063 Nancy, France
Susanne.Salmon-Alt@inalf.fr , Emmanuel.Schang@wanadoo.fr

Abstract. This paper presents a multilingual corpora study aimed to verify the applicability of heuristics developed for coreference resolution in English texts to Portuguese and French language.

1. Introduction

The multilingual corpora study presented in this paper brings together two well-known research topics in natural language processing. One topic largely approached in the field of computational semantics is the study of definite descriptions. The other topic, related to the field of information extraction, is the problem of coreference and anaphora resolution in natural language texts. Whereas much work focus on anaphora resolution, mostly for English [3], [5], [7], [9], our work focus on different languages (French, European Portuguese, Brazilian Portuguese) and a different type of referring expression (definite descriptions, defined as noun phrases starting with the definite article, such as *the house, the old house, the house that I bought*). The main motivation for our multilingual corpus study of definite descriptions is the development of a multilingual tool for anaphora and coreference resolution.

It has often been advocated that for the interpretation of definite descriptions[1] one has to find a textual antecedent, which is coreferent[2] with the description - *a house... the house*; or else, to link the description with a non-coreferent discourse entity that is an anchor for the description interpretation - *a house... the door*. In that case, the coreference resolution of definite descriptions would always involve the identification of a textual antecedent. However, other studies of Swedish and English [2], [12], have shown that very often definite descriptions in written discourse do not have a textual antecedent, because the anchor used for interpretation comes from the context, from

---

[1] Considering referential uses of definite descriptions, where interpretation relates to the identification of a previously introduced discourse entity.

[2] Our definition of coreference follows van Deemter & Kibble's [16]: two noun phrases a and b corefer iff Referent(a)=Referent(b).

E.M. Ranchhod and N.J. Mamede (Eds.): PorTAL 2002, LNAI 2389, pp. 249-258, 2002.
© Springer-Verlag Berlin Heidelberg 2002

the speakers' common knowledge, or it is present in the description itself, as a noun phrase complement. Therefore, the multilingual tool we are designing is based on a tool for coreference resolution that also identifies such definite descriptions which are not coreferent or anaphoric to previous text, as proposed by Vieira & Poesio [18]. First, we are investigating if the existing heuristics for English (based on types of definite description uses) are adaptable to other languages such as Portuguese and French. In order to answer the question whether the uses of definition descriptions is cross language consistent, we carried out multilingual corpora studies about definite description uses in written texts through corpora annotation of classes of uses.

2. Previous Work on Classification of Definite Descriptions

In linguistic literature there is a large variety of classifications of definite description uses: they vary from coarse-grained classifications such as Fraurud's first and subsequent mentions [2] to fine-grained classifications such as Strand's taxonomy of linking relations [16]. Here we will refer to Hawkins [4], Fraurud [2], Prince [13], [14] and Poesio & Vieira [12], since they better explain our choice of classes for the corpus study. Table 1 presents examples that illustrate the variety of classifications.

According to Hawkins, the definite article may be used on the basis of a discourse antecedent (anaphoric and associative uses) as well as independently from the previous discourse (situational and unfamiliar with explanatory modifiers). Prince proposes familiarity taxonomy for noun phrases and distinguishes between two kinds of familiarity, hearer and discourse familiarity. A noun phrase may refer to an entity that has been evoked in the current discourse (textually evoked) or an entity that has not been previously mentioned (situationally evoked, unused, inferable, containing inferable, brand new). Fraurud presented a corpus study of definite noun phrases of Swedish texts based on a binary classification scheme, subsequent mention (defined in terms of coreferentiality) and first mention. Regarding the distribution of uses of each class, she found in her corpus analysis that 60% of the definite NPs in the corpus were first mention uses.

Poesio & Vieira's classes for a corpus study of English were: direct anaphora (including descriptions having coreferent antecedents with the same head noun), bridging (including coreferent and non-coreferent textual antecedents with different head nouns) and discourse new (descriptions without textual antecedents). These classes were motivated by the question about the presence of a textual antecedent (coreferent or not) and its type (requiring world knowledge – bridging; or not – direct anaphora). The study presented the average distribution of uses according to three annotators, which was: discourse new = 51.0%; bridging = 16.1%; direct anaphora = 29.8%, doubt = 2.9%. Due to the great number of discourse new descriptions, a system was built to identify these cases, for which computationally expensive world knowledge reasoning was not required [18].

The usual interpretation principle of discourse new definite descriptions is the identification of a unique referent within a given domain based on the lexical content of the head noun (eventually modified). This idea is also presented by Löbner [6]: definite descriptions are said to be "functional concepts" that take explicit (linguistic) or implicit arguments (from situational context).

Following these principles, the heuristics implemented by the system to identify discourse new descriptions considered mainly the use of proper nouns and the syntactic structure of the noun phrase (prepositional phrase, relative clauses, appositive construction), as they provide arguments for the conceptual function. A description of the system is provided in the next subsection.

Table 1. Classifications of definite description uses

Description	Hawkins	Prince	Fraurud	Poesio & Vieira
A book/ the book	Anaphoric	Textually evoked/ Discourse old	Subsequent mention	Direct anaphora
A cat/ the animal	Anaphoric	Textually evoked/ Discourse old	Subsequent mention	Bridging
A book/ the author	Associative	Inferable/ Discourse new	First mention	Bridging
Pass me the salt	Situational	Situationally evoked/ Discourse new	First mention	Discourse new
The Eiffel Tower	Situational	Unused/ Discourse new	First mention	Discourse new
The bottom of the sea	Unfamiliar with expl. modifiers	Containing inferable/ Discourse new	First mention	Discourse new

2.1 A System for Processing Definite Descriptions

Vieira and Poesio's system processes newswire texts from the Penn Treebank, making use of the syntactic information in the parsed version of the texts. The system generates a representation of the discourse that consists of a list of potential antecedents with which definite descriptions may be resolved. The system makes use of this discourse representation and of linguistic knowledge about apposition structures, copular constructions, postmodifying restrictive clauses, etc. to identify discourse new definite descriptions or to resolve them with an antecedent. The system's output consists of a classification of the instances of definite descriptions in the text, and of the identification of co-referential links. The algorithm first resolves direct anaphora (those descriptions that have an antecedent in the text with identical head noun), then recognises discourse new descriptions.

The general structure of the implemented algorithm is summarised as follows. For each NP of the input: the system assigns it an index; NPs that are taken as potential antecedents[3] are made available for description resolution; if the NP is a definite description, the system applies to it the following tests:

The first test passed by the definite (if any) determines its classification, and after that the next NP is processed.

- Examine a list of special predicates in order to identify some of the discourse new uses (*the first..., the best...*).
- Check whether the definite NP occurs in an appositive construction; there is no need to find an antecedent for those either (*Bill Clinton, the president*). They are classified as discourse new.

---

[3] Potential antecedents are noun phrases in the text that antecede each definite description.

- Try to find an antecedent for the definite description by matching head nouns. If the test succeeds the description is classified as direct anaphora and the relation of co-reference between the two NP indexes is asserted.
- Verify if the head of the NP is a proper noun (by checking whether it's capitalised). If so, the description is classified as discourse new (*the Tower Bridge*).
- Check if the definite presents restrictive postmodification. Definites that are not anaphoric and have restrictive postmodifiers are classified as discourse new (*the dream of home ownership*).
- The system verifies if there is a proper noun in premodifier position; if so, it is considered as a restrictive premodification, and the definite description is classified as discourse new (*the Iran-Iraq war*).
- Check if the definite occurs in a copula construction. If so, the description is classified as discourse new (*the president is Bill Clinton*).

The system is not able to classify all occurrences of definite descriptions: when all tests fail the definite description is not classified. Note that before trying to find an antecedent, the system executes a few tests for identifying discourse new descriptions; the strategy adopted is: to eliminate some non-anaphoric cases (first two tests)[4], try to find a same head antecedent (third test), look for an indication that the description is discourse new (following four tests).

3. Multilingual Analysis of Definite Description Use

3.1 The Classification Experiment

In order to investigate the applicability of the heuristics to identify discourse new descriptions developed for English to other languages, we carried out a multilingual corpora study of Brazilian Portuguese newspaper (according to the previous English corpus study), European Portuguese and French written question-answer pairs published in the Official Journal of the European Commission (to investigate also another text genre). Our first goal was to verify whether we could get a similar distribution of types of definite descriptions in the other languages. Our classes are based on Poesio & Vieira [12], with the difference that we divided the *bridging* class into two different classes, separating coreferent and non-coreferent cases. The annotation task then comprised a classification of each definite description *d* into one of the following four classes:

Direct Anaphora: *d* corefers with a previous expression *a*; *d* and *a* have the same nominal head:

(1)   a.   A Comissão tem conhecimento **do livro**...   *the Commission knows **the book***

        d.   a Comissão costata ainda que **o livro** não se   *the Commission remarks that **the book***
             debruça sobre a actividade das várias ...   *ignores the activity of various*

---

[4] Special predicates and apposition are considered as reliable indications of discourse novelty, some errors in anaphora resolution were eliminated by processing them first.

Indirect Anaphora: *d* corefers with a previous expression *a*; *d* and *a* have different nominal heads:

(2)   a.   a circulação **dos cidadões** que dirigem-se (...)   *the flow of **the citizens** heading to*

       d.   do controle **das pessoas** nas fronteiras   *the control of **the people** in the borders*

Bridging: *d* does not corefer with a previous expression *a*, but depends for its interpretation on *a*:

(3)   a.   o **recrutamento** de pessoal científico e técnico...   ***the recruitment** of scientific and technical employees*

       d.   **as condições de acesso à carreira científica**   *the **conditions of employment for scientific jobs***

Discourse New: the interpretation of *d* does not depend on any previous expression:

(4)   d.   o livro não se debruça sobre **a actividade das várias organizações internacionais**...   *the book ignores **the activity of various international organisation**...*

We had four annotators for the Brazilian Portuguese corpus, and two annotators for the European Portuguese and French corpora.[5] The subjects used specific annotation tools for annotating coreference and anaphora in written text. The Brazilian Portuguese corpus has been annotated with ANADESC [15]. The other corpora have been annotated with a recent tool called MMAX [10]. MMAX was suitable for annotating the resources in a format as closed as possible to the MATE recommendations [8], especially concerning the use of XML, the stand-off annotation principle and the compatibility with proposed coreference encoding guidelines [11]. Table 2 gives an overview of the resources we used.

Table 2. Language resources used in the classification experiment

Language	Genre	Size (words)	Number of DD[6]/Annotators	Extraction of DD	Tool
French	Written question-answers of the Official Journal of the EC (MLCC-JOC)	~ 5000	461 / 2	Manually	MMAX
Portuguese		~ 5000	541 / 2	Manually	MMAX
Brazilian Portuguese	Newspaper	~ 5000	880 / 4	Automatically[7]	ANADESC

The numeric results for the classification task are given in Table 3 to Table 5. They show, for each annotator, the distribution of definite descriptions over the four categories (direct anaphora, indirect anaphora, bridging, discourse new) and cases not classified.

---

[5] Different numbers of annotators are relative to resources availability.

[6] DD stands for "definite descriptions".

[7] For the extraction of definite descriptions from Brazilian Portuguese texts, Portuguese parsing tools provided by the VISL-project were used: http://visl.hum.ou.dk/visl/. The parsing was then manually corrected.

Table 3. Classification of DDs (**French/MLCC-JOC**)

Category	Annotator 1	Annotator 2	% Average
Direct anaphora	132	96	**24,7**
Indirect anaphora	23	27	**5,4**
Bridging	63	26	**9,7**
Discourse new	216	241	**49,6**
Not classified	27	71	**10,6**
Total number of DD	461	461	100,0

Table 4. Classification of DDs (**Portuguese/MLCC-JOC**)

Category	Annotator 1	Annotator 2	% Average
Direct anaphora	96	179	**25.4**
Indirect anaphora	51	45	**8,9**
Bridging	46	77	**11,4**
Discourse new	266	198	**42,9**
Not classified	82	42	**11,5**
Total number of DD	541	541	100,0

Table 5. Classification of DDs (**Brazilian Portuguese/Newspaper**)

Category	Annot 1	Annot 2	Annot 3	Annot 4	% Average
Direct anaphora	214	250	263	200	**26,3**
Indirect anaphora	139	82	81	138	**12,5**
Bridging	152	70	67	105	**11,2**
Discourse new	369	478	469	437	**49,8**
Not classified	6	0	0	0	**0,2**
Total number of DD	880	880	880	880	100,0

3.2 Distribution

Regarding the distribution of definite descriptions over the four classes, the most striking point is the great number of descriptions classified as discourse new. Independently on language or genre, this number is over 40% for all corpora. For two of them, we are very closed to the 50% threshold observed in previous annotation experiments [12]. This observation not only confirms the hypothesis that definite descriptions are not primarily anaphoric [2], [12], [18], but brings also new information about a possible cross-language and cross-genre stability of this feature. Another interesting point is the distribution score around 25% for direct anaphora. This score, close to previous results for English (29,8%), also seems to be independent from the languages and text genres we studied. As expected from the previous classification and annotation experiments, the most difficult classes are indirect anaphora and bridging, often confused with discourse new. For those, we have not only fewer cases (between 5% and 18%), but also a wide variation on the distribution. These classes need urgently to be reinvestigated, probably on the basis of a detailed study of the confusions (see section 3.3.), leading then to a more precise definition of what exactly we would like them to cover.

The syntactic structure of discourse new descriptions was analyzed for French and Portuguese. It was found that they were modified (by adjectives, prepositional phrases and relative clauses) in approximately 50% of the cases. These findings and the distribution found indicate that the heuristics developed for English when applied to French or Portuguese texts will deal well with a large number of cases.

3.3 Agreement

In order to evaluate the inter-annotator agreement, we calculated the Kappa[8] [1] for our four classes. For the French/MLCC-JOC corpus and Brazilian Portuguese/Newspaper corpus, we found K = 0.52 and for the European Portuguese /MLCC-JOC corpus K = 0.44. The results of our experiments show worse agreement than the experiments made with English corpus (0.69 for three annotators and three classes) [12]. Our worse agreement is likely to be related to the inclusion of a fourth class (indirect anaphora). The aim of introducing this class was to distinguish coreferent (indirect anaphora) from non-coreferent (bridging) uses. At first we considered that a better specification of the classes could improve the agreement results, but the results lead us to conclude that it is more difficult to the annotators to deal with a greater number of choices.

Table 6 shows that much confusion occurs between discourse new and any of discourse old descriptions (direct anaphora, indirect anaphora and bridging)[9]. For the French part of the corpus, a confusion source involving discourse new descriptions is a relation other than a well-established associative relation such as *a cat... the animal* or *a book... the author*.

Table 6. Confusion between different classes of DD (French – annotators 1 and 2)

direct vs. indirect anap.	direct anap. vs. Bridging	direct anap. vs. disc.new	indirect vs. bridging	indirect vs. disc. new	bridging vs. disc. new
12 (2,6%)	7 (1,5%)	25 (5,4%)	8 (1,7%)	14 (3,0%)	42 (9,1%)

When the interpretation of a description depends in some looser way on a previous mention, there is a low rate of agreement. In (5) for instance, annotator 1 established a bridging link whereas annotator 2 classified it as discourse new. One possibility of making this point clearer could be to restrict the bridging relation to well-defined semantic relations (such as meronymy, hypernymy) in a way that is at the same time convenient for the annotators and suitable from the theoretical point of view.

(5)   a. l'important flux de **réfugiés albanais** en Italie   *the important flow of **Albanian refugees** in Italy*

        d. la Commission s'efforce de venir en aide **aux populations victimes de catastrophes**   *the Commission tries hard to help the populations which are victims of catastrophes*

Regarding the confusions within the discourse old categories only, they are mostly due to the fact that the annotators selected for a same description different antecedents, and therefore a different relation (6). In our experiment, the choice of the

---

[8] Kappa statistics establishes 0.8 as good agreement

[9] For English, worse agreement was between bridging and discourse new.

antecedent was free for the annotator. In order to obtain a better agreement, it would be possible to constrain the selection to the "closest" antecedent, but this could sometimes be conflicting with the one judged as the most salient for the annotator.

(6)   a1. transposition, dans **le droit italien**, de la   *transposition to **the Italian law** of the*
           directive concernant la conservation des oiseaux   *directive   on   wild   bird   species*
           sauvages   *preservation*

       a2. ces oiseaux que **la loi** protège en république   *these birds that **the law** protects in*
           fédérale   d'Allemagne   périssent   lorsqu'ils   *Germany die when flying towards South*
           descendent vers le sud

       d. La Commission estime-t-elle que **la législation**   *Does the Commission estimate that **the***
           italienne sur la chasse soit conforme...   ***Italian legislation on hunting** conforms*

However, even by pointing to same antecedent, we observed same cases of confusion. Example (7) shows confusion between direct anaphora and bridging. Example (8) is a case of confusion between direct and indirect anaphora The distinction between direct or indirect anaphora – *a* and *d* referring to the same entity – and bridging – *a* and *d* referring to different entities – is unclear in case of modified NPs, introducing questions about the extension of referent sets (example 7); second, even the distinction between direct and indirect anaphora – based only on the presence of same nominal head for the antecedent and the anaphor – seems to be difficult to apply for the annotators (example 8).

(7)   a. pour le contrôle des personnes **aux frontières**   *for the control of persons at **the***
           intérieures   ***internal borders***

       d. La Commission a eu l'occasion de le rappeler   *The Commission reminded it in its*
           dans sa récente communication sur la   *recent communication on the*
           suppression des contrôles **aux frontières**   *suppression of the controls at **the***
           borders

(8)   a. dans l'annexe II de **la directive 92/43/CEE**   *in the annex II of **the directive***
           92/43/CEE

       d. en attirant leur attention sur **la directive**   *drawing their attention to **the above-***
           susmentionnée   ***mentioned directive***

4. Conclusion and Future Work

The most important result of our corpus study is the important number of discourse new definite descriptions (over 40%) for texts in other languages than English. This not only confirms previous studies carried out on English texts, but also stresses the need of taking into account the fact that tools for processing definite descriptions should not be based on considering definite descriptions as primarily anaphoric noun phrases.

The fact that 50% of the discourse new descriptions in our multilingual corpus are also complex noun phrases indicates that the heuristics developed to identify them in English (mainly identification of complex noun phrases) are also suitable for French and Portuguese. However, the low agreement between the annotators for four different classes ($K \sim 0.5$) does not allow us to take the resulting annotated corpora as a key for designing and evaluating such heuristics. To decide exactly what a system should do, we plan new annotation experiments, starting with two classes only. In order to avoid previous confusions between these two classes, we have to fix the handling of antecedents located in previous text spans (title, question part) and to refine the definition of bridging, possibly by restricting it first to a few well-defined relations such as part whole or set-subset relations. Depending on the results of this annotation, we will then refine step by step the classification tasks, following thereby the strategy proposed by van Deemter & Kibble [17] for isolating tricky cases in coreference annotation. In order to avoid disagreement likely to be related to the use of the annotation tool, we are specifying improvements needed in the MMAX interface, especially by analyzing the user feedback we collected from the annotators.

Once the agreement on classification is suitable, our work will focus on analyzing the agreement about antecedents for anaphoric definite descriptions, testing the cross-language validity of the heuristics proposed by Vieira & Poesio [18] and developing a similar tool to work on multilingual input. Further interesting investigations could be translation studies (apart from purely grammatical constraints, are definite descriptions translated systematically into definite descriptions?) and, even further, studies on how the notions of *discourse new* vs. *discourse old* are expressed in languages without determiners.

Acknowledgments This work was developed with partial funding of the Brazilian agencies FAPERGS and CNPq (ProTeM-CC) and the French research organizations INRIA and CNRS. We would like to thank Christoph Müller for the help in the use of MMAX.

References

1. Carletta J. Assessing agreement on classification tasks: the kappa statistic. *Computational Linguistics* 22(2) (1996) 249-254.
2. Fraurud, K. Definiteness and the Processing of Noun Phrases in Natural Discourse. *Journal of Semantics* (7) (1990) 395-433.
3. Grosz B.J., Joshi A.K. and Weinstein S. Centering: A framework for modelling the local coherence of discourse. *Computational Linguistics,* 12(2) (1995) 203-225.
4. Hawkins, J. A. Definiteness and Indefiniteness: a study in reference and grammaticality prediction. London: Croom Helm (1978).
5. Lappin S., Leass H. An algorithm for pronominal anaphora resolution. *Computational Linguistics*, 20(4) (1994) 535-561.
6. Löbner, S. Definites. *Journal of Semantics*, 4 (1985) 279-326.
7. McCoy K.F. and Strube M. Taking Time to Structure Discourse : Pronoun Generation Beyond Accessibility. *Proc. of the 21th Annual Conference of the Cognitive Science Society.* Vancouver, Canada, Aug. 19-21 (1999).
8. Mengel, A., Dybkjaer, L., Garrido, J.M., Heid, U., Klein, M., Pirrelli, V., Poesio, M., Quazza, S., Schiffrin, A., and Soria, C. (2000). *MATE Dialogue Annotation Guidelines*, January (2000) (http://www.ims.uni.stuttgart.de/projekte/mate/mdag/).
9. Mitkov, R. Robust pronoun resolution with limited knowledge. *Proceedings of the 18.th Int. Conference on Computational Linguistics COLING'98/ACL'98*, Montreal, Canada (1998).
10. Müller C., Strube M. Annotating anaphoric and bridging relation with MMAX. *Proc. of the 2nd IJCAI Workshop on Knowledge and Reasoning in Pratical Dialogue Systems*. Seattle, 5 Aug. (2001) 45-50.

11. Poesio M. Coreference. *MATE Dialogue Annotation Guidelines-Deliverable D2.1,* January 2000, 126-182. (2000) (http://www.ims.uni-stuttgart.de/projekte/mate/mdag/)
12. Poesio M., Vieira R. A corpus-based investigation of Definite Description Use. *Computational Linguistics,* 24(2) (1998) 183-216.
13. Prince, E.F.   Toward a taxonomy of given-new information. In P. Cole, ed., *Radical Pragmatics.* Academic Press, New York (1981) 223--256.
14. Prince, E.F.   The {ZPG} letter: subjects, definiteness, and information status. In S.Thompson and W.Mann, ed., *Discourse description: diverse analyses of a fund-raising text.* John Benjamins, (1992) 295--325.
15. Rossi D., Pinheiro C., Feier N., Vieira R. Resolução de correferência em textos da língua portuguesa. *REIC.* Novembro 1(2) (2001) (http://www.sbc.org.br/reic).
16. Strand, K. A Taxonomy of linking relations. Manuscript. (1997)
17. van Deemter K., Kibble R. On Coreferring: Coreference in MUC and related annotation schemes. *Computational Linguistics* 26(4), squib (2000).
18. Vieira R., Poesio M. An Empirically-Based System for Processing Definite Descriptions. *Computational Linguistics,* 26(4) (2000) 525-579.

Relational Data Model
in Document Hierarchical Indexing[*]

Alexander Gelbukh, Grigori Sidorov, and Adolfo Guzmán-Arenas

Center for Computing Research, National Polytechnic Institute,
Av. Juan Dios Batiz s/n, Zacatenco 07738, Mexico City, Mexico
{gelbukh, sidorov, aguzman}@cic.ipn.mx

Abstract. One of the problems of the development of document indexing and retrieval applications is the usage of hierarchies. In this paper we describe a method of automatic hierarchical indexing using the traditional relational data model. The main idea is to assign continuous numbers to the words (grammatical forms of the words) that characterize the nodes in the hierarchy (concept tree). One of the advantages of the proposed scheme is its simplicity. The system that implements such indexing scheme is described.

1 Introduction

Traditional document retrieval systems [1] lack the possibility to perform generalized searches (say, for topic or theme). On the other hand, the systems that permit navigation in a hierarchy, for instance, *Yahoo*, have their own shortcuts, for example:

- Document indexing is usually manual, and, thus, imprecise and subjective,
- Searches with various conditions are not allowed, and
- The documents normally are stored only in one place in the hierarchy though they can deal with several topics in the hierarchy.

These problems can be resolved if we apply automatic indexing of documents using a concept dictionary that usually has a form of a hierarchy of concepts (concept tree), see, for example, [4]. Still, in the paper [4] the task of indexing is not mentioned and the data is obtained from re-processing of the texts each time.

There are several linguistic techniques that allow for more exact and effective document processing (for further document retrieval), see, for example, [2], [3], like morphological analysis or synonymy, etc. Morphological analysis permits to reduce several grammatical forms to only one lexeme (e.g., for lexeme *take* the forms *take, took, taken, takes* should be indexed). This may be not of great importance for the languages like English with very few grammatical forms, but it is of great utility for the languages with greater number of grammatical forms for each lexeme as, say, Spanish or Russian.

In this paper we propose the method of the concept tree indexing using the relational data model. The main idea is to give to all grammatical forms that correspond to a lexeme the consecutive numbers, and since the nodes in the tree are

[*] The work was done under partial support of CONACyT, CGEPI-IPN, and SNI, Mexico.

E.M. Ranchhod and N.J. Mamede (Eds.): PorTAL 2002, LNAI 2389, pp. 259–262, 2002.

characterized by a set of lexemes, they also get this numbering. Thus, each grammatical form is represented by the number, while lexemes and nodes are represented by a numeric interval. Usage of the consecutive numbers allows for using of the relational data model that ensures simplicity of the whole method. Namely, it is possible to use any standard database manager available. The corresponding system was developed that implements rather sophisticated query language both for the words and for the nodes of the concept tree.

2 Hierarchical Indexing

The documents about *biology* contain words like *plants*, *animals*, *cellules*, etc. Still, if one is interested more specifically in *zoology*, he/she wants to find the document with the words *crocodiles*, or *mammals*, etc. This specification process finishes with individual words. Still, if the user wants to find documents about biology, this also means that the documents about zoology are acceptable, but not vice versa. The structure of the concept tree resembles this specification process: the terminal nodes have the lists of words that correspond to them; the non-terminal nodes unite several terminal or non-terminal nodes (see example below). Each node has only one parent node except the uppermost node that does not have parent.

The suggested method of indexing establishes correspondence between each node (not necessarily the terminal one) and the words that are below the node in such a way that the words are indexed with continuous numbers and each node in the tree is characterized by a numeric interval. This interval is obtained from the words that are below the node.

We have the concept tree in English, because this tree is the language-independent resource. Still, the lists of words that correspond to terminal nodes are language-dependent. In our case, we used Spanish lists, though the list of words in any language can be used.

Technically, the indexation process is as follows: pass all the terminal nodes in the concept tree starting from the leftmost terminal node and enumerate all the words that correspond to them in an order starting from 0. The words in the lists for the terminal nodes are lexemes, so we generate all their grammatical forms and enumerate these forms (not the lexeme itself). At the same time, the terminal nodes are assigned the corresponding numbers, taking the lower bound of the leftmost lexeme and the upper bound of the rightmost lexeme. In case of terminal nodes their children are lexemes.

The next step is to index all non-terminal nodes. The lower value is taken from the leftmost child; the upper value is taken from the corresponding right-most child. In case of non-terminal nodes their children are terminal or non-terminal nodes.

In case that the word belongs to two or more different terminal nodes it is indexed several times with different numbers (with all its grammatical forms).

Having the concept tree indexed, it is possible to index the documents. If the algorithm finds in the documents the grammatical forms that are not in the tree, they are indexed in the same manner as the words in the tree.

After document indexing we have a database that contains numbers of all grammatical forms that were found in the documents. Now it is possible to search rapidly constructing the query. In the query one can use individual grammatical forms, as well as lexemes, and as well as tree nodes. All of them are substituted by the corresponding intervals of numbers (see Fig. 1 and Fig. 2).

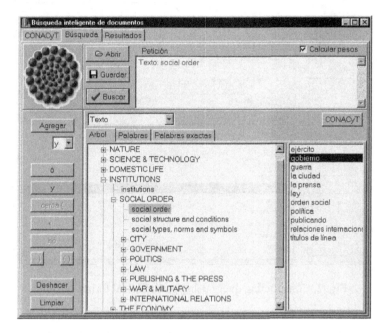

Fig. 1. Constructing a query using the concept hierarchy.

3 Description of the System

We developed the system that implements the method of indexing described above. The system has sophisticated query language with Boolean operations and proximity criteria. The main advantage of the system is the possibility to search combining themes, lemmas, grammatical forms and their logical combinations.

The query is translated automatically into SQL.

Let us have a look at the example query. Say, the word (lexeme) *cobre* (*brass*) is substituted by four numerical intervals (there are several intervals because the word belongs to several terminal nodes).

The first interval belongs to the terminal node "pure metals" and the second to the terminal node "stones, bricks, tiles, glass and metals". Their immediate upper node is "MINERALS, METALS & ROCKS". The third interval belongs to the terminal node "elements" with the upper node "CHEMISTRY". The fourth interval is the terminal node "money, currency and denominations" with the immediate upper node "THE ECONOMY" (the word *cobre* (*brass*) is used in Spanish to denote a small change).

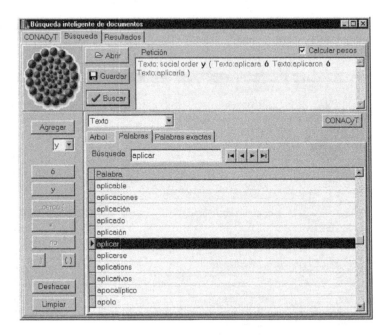

Fig. 2. Constructing query using grammatical forms and lemmas.

The buttons on Fig. 1and Fig. 2 that are on the left side of the window permits to insert Boolean operations (*and, or, no*) and brackets. The proximity button permits to search the elements that are "near" (we use the distance of 10 words).

References

1. Baeza-Yates, R., and B. Ribeiro-Neto. *Modern information retrieval*. Addison-Wesley Longman. 1999.
2. Gelbukh, A. Lazy Query Enrichment: A Simple Method of Indexing Large Specialized Document Bases. Proc. *DEXA-2000*. LNCS 1873, Springer, pp. 526–535.
3. Gelbukh, A. and G. Sidorov. Intelligent system for document retrieval of the Mexican Senate. Proc. *CIC-2000*, IPN, Mexico, pp. 315-321.
4. Gelbukh, A., G. Sidorov, and A. Guzman-Arenas. Use of a weighted topic hierarchy for text retrieval and classification. In *TSD-99*, LNAI 1692, Springer, pp. 130–135.

DMSumm: Review and Assessment[*]

Thiago Alexandre Salgueiro Pardo and Lucia Helena Machado Rino

Departamento de Computação, Centro de Ciências Exatas e de Tecnologia
Universidade Federal de São Carlos
Rodovia Washington Luiz, km 235 – Monjolinho
Caixa Postal 676
13565-905 São Carlos – SP
{taspardo,lucia}@dc.ufscar.br

Abstract. In this paper we review DMSumm, an automatic summary generator based on a discourse model that combines semantic, rhetorical and intentional knowledge. We assess the automatic results in the light of three basic constraints: gist preservation, communicative goal satisfaction and textuality.

1. Introduction

In this paper, we pinpoint some of the main aspects of the DMSumm system, the Discourse Modeling SUMMarizer described in (Pardo and Rino, 2001), predominantly focusing on discourse organization. This addresses a special three-level text planner (Rino, 1996a), bringing together intentional (Grosz and Sidner, 1986), rhetorical (Mann and Thompson, 1987; Hobbs, 1985) and semantic relations. These, in turn, address information content on the basis of the Problem-Solution (P-S) model (Winter, 1977; Jordan, 1980) and resemble Jordan's (1992) clausal relations. We thoroughly show how discourse production is carried out (Section 2), illustrating the DMSumm reasoning (Section 3). Then, we assess the automatically produced summaries (Section 4), in order to discuss the DMSumm potentialities (Section 5).

2. Summary Generation

Summary generation, here, refers solely to the problem of taking an *input message* and recognizing its most relevant information to appear in a summary, organizing it according to communicative goals, and realizing the resulting summary plan into the text itself. This addresses a 3-step pipelined text generator, whose input message is already an internal representation of a source text, as it is shown by the DMSumm architecture in Fig. 1. The input message is a composition of three information units: two single ones – the Central Proposition (CP) and the Communicative Goal (CG) – and a complex, semantically structured one – the so-called Knowledge Base, or KB. In limiting DMSumm to this setting, interpretation is assumed to have been carried out previously, and, actually, it has been so far carried out by hand, by hu-

---

[*] This work has been funded by FAPESP – Fundação de Ampara à Pesquisa do Estado de São Paulo.

E.M. Ranchhod and N.J. Mamede (Eds.): PorTAL 2002, LNAI 2389, pp. 263-273, 2002.

man specialists. Defined in this way, the input indicates that the main components of discourse production are *what brings about the primary discourse motivation* (the CP), *what depicts the intertwining of discourse segments, aiming at building up the discourse* (the CG), and *what allows content to be handled* (the KB). Summary generation proceeds thus under three basic constraints, namely, gist, or CP, preservation (Constraint 1), CG satisfaction (Constraint 2), and textuality warranty[1] (Constraint 3) (Rino, 1996a). In Rino's model, CP is considered to be a single information unit. Conversely, gist is a more general concept, in that it involves not only the CP, but also CG. However, in our automatic summarization (AS) scenario, CP preservation has barely been dealt with on its own, for discourse production is also based upon CG satisfaction. Here, we will see how the referred constraints are handled in DMSumm, by briefly describing its processes, which are introduced in (Pardo and Rino, 2001). Readers should refer to that article for further details on the DMSumm description and its operation.

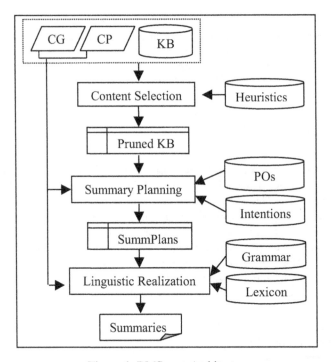

Figure 1: DMSumm Architecture

2.1. Content Selection

This heuristic-based process has been originally proposed by Rino and Scott (1994) and has been refined in DMSumm. The heuristics are based on the semantic structure of the KB, which takes after the P-S paradigm (Winter, 1977; Jordan, 1980). In this way, content selection addresses the P-S well-defined logical sequence of super-components. Additionally, it focuses

---

[1] Textuality, here, is understood as the property of a text being meaningful to the reader. For this reason, it addresses both, the coherence and cohesion of a text.

upon information units that are semantically related through clausal relations (Jordan, 1992). The main underlying assumptions of such heuristics are the following: a) source texts usually address technical issues; b) readers are knowledgeable enough to handle implicit information; c) the P-S paradigm is reasonably common and can be found in a wide variety of texts, no matter their genre or domain (Hoey, 1983; Rino, 1996b; Jordan, 2000); d) by delineating the KB information segments on either the P-S or the clausal account, the heuristics can address KB pruning by considering either of them; and, finally, e) the CP can vary according to the writer's intentions in focalizing information. Assumptions (d) and (e) are of utmost importance in DMSumm, for they provide the means to vary discourse structuring, even when the input message remains invariable. The heuristics are shown bellow, with justifications in brackets:

➢ H1: select only the *problem* and *solution* segments of a KB (provided that gist addresses either problem or solution, these segments are enough in a summary);
➢ H2: select every information but *results* (these should not convey substantial information);
➢ H3: exclude actions pre-conditions (readers can infer them);
➢ H4: exclude instruments and events purposes (readers can infer them);
➢ H5: exclude any proof segment of the KB (one should avoid too much detail);
➢ H6: exclude effect from causal relations (readers can infer them);
➢ H7: exclude objects attributes, details, or examples (these are not essential);
➢ H8: exclude evaluations (in technical and objective communication, personal opinions must be avoided);
➢ H9: exclude events reasons (in certain contexts, these may be superfluous);
➢ H10: exclude *situation* (avoid background information if shared with readers).

Pruning verifies that a) CP, which is a leaf in KB, be also a leaf in the resulting pruned KB (cf. Constraint 1); b) CG lead to intentions that delineate contributing discourse segments (cf. Constraint 2) and c) end up relating CP to other segments (cf. Constraints 1 & 3).

2.2. Summary Planning

This process builds upon the mapping of semantic and intentional relations onto rhetorical ones. Table 1 shows some examples of the constraints to be observed at both, semantic and intentional levels, to rhetorically organize a summary, considering that 1) semantic organization is provided as input in the KB; 2) the intentional account, i.e., the GSDT (Grosz and Sidner Discourse Theory) relations satisfaction-precedes (*sp*), dominates (*dom*), supports (*sup*) and generates (*gen*), and the Rino's relation symmetry (*symm*), is previously defined between every two KB potential information units. In DMSumm, this mapping is carried out by plan operators, or POs (Maybury, 1992; Moore and Paris, 1993), triggered by CGs. The only CGs addressed by Rino (1996a) are *describe, report,* and *discuss*, but they are further refined to observe the contributing GSDT discourse setting. In this way, diverse planning strategies have been devised.

Table 1: Mapping of intentions and semantics onto rhetoric

Semantics	Rhetoric	Intentions
enable(Y,X)	means(X,Y)	X sp Y, Y dom X
cause(X,Y)	nonvolresult(Y,X)	Y sp X, X dom Y, Y gen X

The steps below depict an interpretation of Table 1 in planning a summary, considering that we want to generate a MEANS relation between two discourse segments X and Y (X is the goal to be achieved through Y). Fig. 2 shows a PO that operates on such a mapping to report a concept X. Currently, DMSumm amounts to ca. 89 POs similar to that.

1.   if there is an *enable* relation between information segments X and Y in the KB and
2.   if *sp* and *dom* relations hold between them at the intentional level, then
3.   generate a MEANS relation at the rhetorical level.

Name	report-by-MEANS
Header	report(X)
Effect	know(R,X)
Constraints	not know(R,X), enable(X,Y), sp(X,Y), dom(Y,X)
Nucleus	report(X)
Satellite	know(R,MEANS(X,Y))

Figure 2: Example of PO

2.3. Linguistic Realization

Linguistic realization has been so far simply undertaken by considering a template-based approach. This provides just canned text spans in the final summaries, linked by discourse markers. In linearizing a summary plan (SummPlan), a template choice takes place according to the focused rhetorical relation and this indicates the appropriate discourse markers (see Fig. 3, for the MEANS rhetorical relation). The rhetorically inter-related propositions are, thus, mapped onto the canned text spans and connected at the surface. This process is based on Marcu's work (1997), in that it specifies ordering and clustering constraints to linearize a summary plan. Ordering features pinpoint which text span comes before the other; clustering ones indicate whether text segments will involve a single sentence, adjacent sentences or even different paragraphs. In defining DMSumm templates, canned text spans are entirely and literally extracted from source texts, except when they involve context dependencies. These have been so far hand-resolved, for both clarity and keeping text spans independent from each other. This is particularly convenient for the template-based approach, but should be improved in a more elaborated linearizer.

To assess DMSumm, we have specified two linguistic realization engines by defining two template sets: one for English and another for Brazilian Portuguese (hereafter, referred to just by Portuguese). This process has not been troublesome, since we could reuse most of the English-based counterpart.

MEANS	
Ordering	nucleus before satellite
Clustering	single sentence
Discourse markers	*by means of*

Figure 3: MEANS template

3. DMSumm at Work

In this section, we explore automatic summarizing through the '*Using Computers in Manufacturing*' text (Jordan, 1980, p. 225). Its segmented version is shown below, considering that each text segment corresponds to an information unit, which in turn will be corresponding to a proposition at the discourse level. This segmentation strategy has been formerly undertaken by many other RST human analyzers (e.g., Marcu, 1997).

Using Computers in Manufacturing

1. *Whether you regard computers as a blessing or a curse, the fact is that we are all becoming more and more affected by them.*
2. *Yet, in spite of this, the general level of understanding of the power and weaknesses of computers among manufacturing managers is dangerously low.*
3a. *In order to counteract this lack of knowledge, the Manufacturing Management Activity Group of the IprodE is organizing a two-day seminar on "Computers and manufacturing management"*
3b. *to be held at the Birmingham Metropole Hotel at the National Exhibition Centre from 21-22 March 1979.*
4. *The seminar has been specially designed by the IprodE for managers concerned with manufacturing processes and not for computer experts.*
5. *The idea is that delegates will be able to share the experiences of other computer users and lear of their successes and failures.*
6. *The seminar will consist of plenary sessions followed by syndicates where delegates will be arranged into small discussion groups.*

Fig. 4 illustrates a KB corresponding to such a source text. Nodes in italics represent semantic relations; underlined ones signal P-S super-components, and leaves indicate the basic information units, already annotated by P-S tags. It is important to stress that, although such a structure resembles a rhetorical one, it is purely informative, for it relates content on a domain basis, and not on a discourse basis.

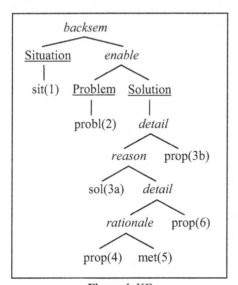

Figure 4: KB

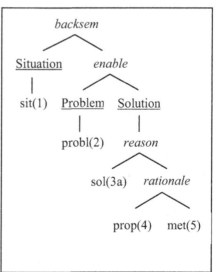

Figure 5: Pruned KB

To illustrate how DMSumm works, we assume that we want to report a problem. So, the DMSumm input message is completely defined by the following three components: the KB, the CP = probl(2), and the CG = report. Fig. 5 shows the pruned KB when we apply, e.g., heuristic H7 during content selection. Along with CP and CG, such a KB amounts to the condensed input message to the summary planner, comprising the very same input CP and CG, but now the pruned KB (refer to Fig. 1). By applying every possible DMSumm planning strategy, we generated 11 summary plans for this example. Two of them are shown in Figs. 6 and 7, along with possible linguistic realizations. They make evident that different degrees of compression are feasible, always preserving the CP at the leftmost nuclei.

MEANS

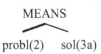

probl(2)   sol(3a)

The general level of understanding of the power and weaknesses of computers among manufacturing managers is dangerously low. In order to counteract the lack of knowledge, the Manufacturing Management Activity Group of the IProdE is organizing a two-day seminar on computers and manufacturing management.

Figure 6: Plan 1

BACKGROUND

MEANS   sit(1)

probl(2)   EXPLAIN

sol(3a)   prop(4)

Whether you regard computers as a blessing or a curse, the fact is that we are all becoming more and more affected by them.

The general level of understanding of the power and weaknesses of computers among manufacturing managers is dangerously low. In order to counteract the lack of knowledge, the Manufacturing Management Activity Group of the IProdE is organizing a two-day seminar on computers and manufacturing management, and, explaining, the seminar has been specially designed by the IProdE for managers concerned with manufacturing processes and not for computer experts.

Figure 7: Plan 2

4. Assessing DMSumm

We followed several approaches (Sparck Jones and Galliers, 1996; White et al., 2000; Mani, 2001) to assess DMSumm in the light of its three posed constraints. We used a test corpus in Portuguese (Feltrim et al., 2001), hereafter named Thesis Corpus, composed of 10 postgraduate introductions (of MSc. monographs and PhD. theses) in Computer Science, for the experiments described here.

4.1. Experiment 1: Identifying CPs

Nine judges, computational linguists and native speakers of Portuguese, were given the Thesis Corpus and asked to select a sentence that best mirrored each source text, assuming that just one, the most voted, sentence would signal that source text CP.

Most judgments (60%) indicated *solution* as the CP; the others related it to *method, problem, result* and *general proposition* (only once, for the remaining source texts). This makes evident that 1) the P-S super-structure played its role in determining texts centrality; 2) since indicative phrases were usually explicit in the pinpointed sentences, they may have been the basis for most judgments, reinforcing previous work on extracting the main topics of a text (e.g., Paice, 1981; Hoey, 1983). We used such results to define our CPs in Experiment 2.

4.2. Experiment 2: Assessing Summaries

Ten judges, also computational linguists and native speakers of Portuguese, were given the very same Thesis Corpus, along with 4 summaries for each source text – 3 automatic and the authentic one. The automatic ones corresponded, in average, to 40% of the source texts length and were completely produced by DMSumm. The judges' task was twofold: to identify the authentic summary (Task 1) and to score each summary according to two decision points: textuality and gist preservation, considered altogether (Task 2). The score range is shown in Table 2. In most cases, the judges readily identified correctly the authentic summaries in Task 1. This can be justified by the fact that such summaries usually convey information that not necessarily appears in the corresponding source texts (due to the author's background knowledge) and/or have a richer syntactic structure than the automatic ones.

Table 2: Scores for assessing summaries

Textuality	Gist	Score
Kept	Preserved	6
Damaged	Preserved	5
Kept	Partially Preserved	4
Damaged	Partially Preserved	3
Kept	Not Preserved	2
Damaged	Not Preserved	1

Chart 1 synthesizes the judges' evaluation in Task 2, showing the average scores for automatic and authentic summaries[2]. Following White et al. (2000), the *means* measure, of the judges' answers, was calculated for such average scores, yielding a baseline score 3 for satisfactory summaries. As we can see, most automatic summaries are acceptable, when we consider textuality and gist preservation. Actually, only two of them are below the baseline. Moreover, they have been judged quite similarly to the authentic ones, in what concerns most of their corresponding scores distances, which show very few quality discrepancies. Promising results are also achieved when we consider the distribution of automatic summaries judgments per score

---

[2] Throughout this paper, solid lines signal automatic summaries and dotted lines, authentic ones.

(84% above the baseline): 25% were given the score 6; 6% the score 5; 31% the score 4; 22% the score 3; 7% the score 2; 9% the score 1[3].

Now, if we consider only textuality as a good indicator of summary quality (Mani, 2001), the majority (67%) of automatic summaries were considered to keep it. However, the corresponding rate cannot be considered satisfactory, when compared to the judgment on the authentic summaries (90% were considered *textual*). Such a low percentage is partly due to the performance of the linguistic realizer, but it may also be the case that assuming CP as conveyed by a unique information unit is a too strong constraint to assess textuality. Actually, most often sparse information is also important in asserting a CP, but this is not considered in our experiment. Such a problem is also evidenced by the gist preservation distribution of the automatic summaries: 61% of the automatic summaries preserved only partially the gist and 31% totally preserved it. In contrast, all the authentic summaries preserved gist, according to the judgments.

Chart 1: Average scores of all the summaries per source text

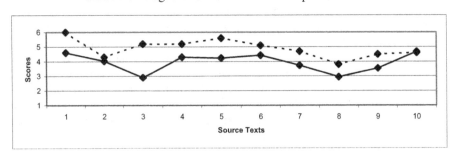

Mani still suggests that a readability score can indicate how close to their authentic summaries and corresponding source texts the automatic ones are. Chart 2 shows the readability scores for the summaries and the source texts (dotted lines with square markers), following the Flesch scores, now adapted to Portuguese (Martins et al., 1996). The bigger the score, the easier it is to read the text (interval 25-50 signals difficult texts; 0-24, very difficult ones).

Experiment 2 also allowed for a comparison between summaries, by measuring their semantic informativeness, i.e., the amount of content information that is conveyed by both the summaries and related source texts (Mani, 2001). The higher the score (maximum=1), the more informative the summary. Chart 3 shows the average scores of our summaries for each source text. The biggest discrepancy, when comparing the scores of the authentic summaries with the corresponding automatic ones occurs only once (source text 3).

A comparison between the automatic and authentic summaries has also been carried out. In this case, our ideal solutions are the information units present in the authentic summaries. DMSumm performance yielded the following rates for precision, recall and f-measure, respectively: 44%, 54%, and 48%. Although authentic summaries can present more information than the source text, this problem was minimally detected in the Thesis Corpus and did not alter significantly the obtained results.

---

[3] However strange it may be to include the baseline in the acceptance level, we stress that we follow White et al.'s approach. This certainly should be reviewed in further work.

Chart 2: Readability scores

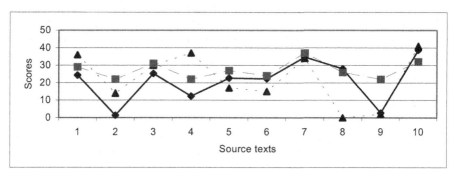

Chart 3: Semantic informativeness scores of all the summaries

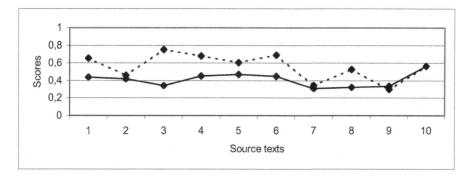

5. On DMSumm Potentialities

It is evident that DMSumm is actually only a text generator that reasons on summarizing constraints. For this reason, we assume that its input message is consistent with the related source texts and proceed in assessing DMSumm as if the automatically produced summaries were corresponding to source texts instead. Our assumption proved harmless by the results shown in the previous section. These make evident that the automatic summaries do not present significant coherence problems and are close to the source texts. Moreover, gist is preserved, in spite of the CP being only partially kept in most cases, since gist is also conveyed by satisfying the CG. It seems to us that CG satisfaction is quite straightforwardly guaranteed due to the technicality of our corpus. However, further exploration is needed for other text genres.

With respect to the AS task, DMSumm is deeply dependent upon the P-S account, adding an extra level of complexity to DMSumm and, actually, consisting of its main bottleneck. Given that DMSumm has so far referred to text generation, such a problem is mostly significant under text planning, which is quite complex due to its strategies based on three different types of discourse knowledge. Actually, both intentions and semantics refer back to the P-S setting. Since semantics is hypothetically addressed at the input, message, level, this should not be the focus of the current DMSumm improvement. Our question is, thus, how to get rid of the P-S dependency with no prejudice of its input. This implies questioning the need for the intentional level. Our first attempt was to suppress such a representation level and run DMSumm again. Although the automatic results showed that there was a substantial performance decrease, the results are still inconclusive and further investigation shall be pursued in the future.

References

Feltrim, V.D.; Nunes, M.G.V.; Aluísio, S.M. (2001). *Um corpus de textos científicos em português para a análise da estrutura esquemática*. Série de Relatórios Técnicos do NILC, NILC-TR-01-4. São Carlos – SP. Brazil.

Grosz, B. and Sidner, C. (1986). Attention, Intentions, and the Structure of Discourse. *Computational Linguistics*, Vol. 12, No. 3.

Hobbs, J.R. (1985). *On the Coherence and Structure of Discourse*. Tech. Rep. CSLI-85-37, Center for Study of Language and Information, Stanford University.

Hoey, M. (1983). *On the Surface of Discourse*. George Allen & Unwin Ltd.

Jordan, M.P. (1980). Short Texts to Explain Problem-Solution Structures – and Vice Versa. *Instructional Science*, Vol. 9, pp. 221-252.

Jordan, M. P. (1992). An Integrated Three-Pronged Análisis of a Fund-Raising Letter. In W. C. Mann and S. A. Thompson (eds.), *Discourse Description: Diverse Linguistic Analyses of a Fund-Raising Text*, pp. 171-226. John Benjamins Publishing Company, Amsterdam.

Jordan, M,P. (2000). A Pragmatic/Structural Approach to Relevance. *Technostyle*, Vol. 16, No. 2, pp. 47-67.

Mani, I. (2001). *Automatic Summarization*. John Benjamins Publishing Co., Amsterdam.

Mann, W.C. and Thompson, S.A. (1987). *Rhetorical Structure Theory: A Theory of Text Organization*. Technical Report ISI/RS-87-190.

Marcu, D. (1997). *The Rhetorical Parsing, Summarization, and Generation of Natural Language Texts*. PhD. Thesis. Department of Computer Science, University of Toronto, Canada.

Martins, T.B.F.; Ghiraldelo, C.M.; Nunes, M.G.V.; Oliveira Jr., O.N. (1996). *Readability Formulas Applied to Textbooks in Brazilian Portuguese*. Notas do ICMSC-USP, Série Computação. São Carlos – SP, Brazil.

Maybury, M.T. (1992). Communicative Acts for Explanation Generation. *Int. Journal of Man-Machine Studies 37*, pp. 135-172.

Moore, J.D. and Paris, C. (1993). Plannig Text for Advisory Dialogues: Capturing Intentional and Rhetorical Information. *Computational Linguistics*, Vol. 19, No. 4, pp. 651-694.

Paice, C. D. (1981). The automatic generation of literature abstracts: an approach based on the identification of self-indicating phrases. *Information Retrieval Research*. Butterworth & Co.

Pardo, T.A.S. and Rino, L.H.M. (2001). A summary planner based on a three-level discourse model. In the *Proc. of the 6th NLPRS – Natural Language Processing Pacific Rim Symposium*, pp. 533-538. National Center of Science, Tokyo, Japan. 27–29 November.

Rino, L.H.M. (1996a). *Modelagem de Discurso para o Tratamento da Concisão e Preservação da Idéia Central na Geração de Textos*. Tese de Doutorado. Universidade de São Paulo, Brasil.

Rino, L.H.M. (1996b). A sumarização automática de textos em português. In *Anais do II Encontro para o Processamento Computacional de Português Escrito e Falado*, pp. 109-119. Curitiba - PR. Outubro.

Rino, L.H.M. and Scott, D. (1994). *Automatic generation of draft summaries: heuristics for content selection*. ITRI Tech. Report ITRI-94-8. University of Brighton, England.

Sparck Jones, K. and Galliers, J. R. (1996). Evaluating Natural Language Processing Systems. *Lecture Notes in Artificial Intelligence*, Vol. 1083.

White, J.; Doyon, J.; Talbott, S. (2000).Task tolerance of MT output in Integrated Text Processes. In the *Proc. of the Embedded MT Systems Workshop*, pp. 9-16 (NAACL-ANLP 2000 Workshop). Seattle, WA.

Winter, E.O. (1977). A Clause-Relational Approach to English Texts: A Study of Some Predictive Lexical Items in Written Discourse. *Instructional Science*, Vol. 6, No. 1, pp. 1-92.

Author Index

Lecture Notes in Artificial Intelligence (LNAI)

Lecture Notes in Computer Science